UNIX System Administration:
A Beginner's Guide

UNIX System Administration:
A Beginner's Guide

Steve Maxwell

McGraw-Hill/Osborne

New York   Chicago   San Francisco
Lisbon   London   Madrid   Mexico City
Milan   New Delhi   San Juan
Seoul   Singapore   Sydney   Toronto

McGraw-Hill/Osborne
2600 Tenth Street
Berkeley, California 94710
U.S.A.

To arrange bulk purchase discounts for sales promotions, premiums, or fund-raisers, please contact **McGraw-Hill/Osborne** at the above address. For information on translations or book distributors outside the U.S.A., please see the International Contact Information page immediately following the index of this book.

UNIX System Administration: A Beginner's Guide

1234567890 FGR FGR 0198765432

ISBN 0-07-219486-3

Publisher Brandon A. Nordin
Vice President & Associate Publisher Scott Rogers
Acquisitions Editor Francis Kelly
Project Editor Lisa Wolters-Broder
Acquisitions Coordinator Emma Acker
Technical Editor John Tiso
Copy Editor Dennis Weaver
Proofreader Brian Galloway
Indexer Valerie Robbins
Computer Designers Carie Abrew, George Toma Charbak, Elizabeth Jang
Illustrators Michael Mueller, Lyssa Wald
Series Design Gary Corrigan
Cover Series Design Sarah F. Hinks

This book was composed with Corel VENTURA™ Publisher.

About the Author

Steve Maxwell has been actively involved with UNIX and computer networking for the last 20 years. He has worked for a number of companies, institutions, and organizations in a variety of capacities that have included network design, software development, and training. Recently, Steve decided that it was time to join another start-up company, and he now works at FineGround Networks, Inc., where he is responsible for ensuring that the company delivers quality software products. Steve welcomes your feedback on any aspect of this book—please send comments, questions, and suggestions to *sjmaxwell@worldnet.att.net*.

About the Technical Reviewers

John Tiso is a senior consultant for NIS, a Boston-based integrator of Sun Microsystems and Cisco Systems. He has a B.S. degree from Adelphi University and is certified in UNIX from HP, Sun, and IBM. John is also a Cisco CCIE (CCIE #5162), MCSE, and MCNE. He has published papers in several leading technical journals, such as *Element K* and *SysAdmin*, and has served as a technical editor for a variety of books. John can be reached at *johnt@jtiso.com*.

Jim Minatel is a freelance writer and editor with more than 13 years of publishing experience in mathematics, statistics, and computing. He has authored and co-authored several books about the Internet and World Wide Web in the early Netscape era, and most recently served as Editor in Chief for two magazines for networking professionals and IT managers. He holds undergraduate degrees in mathematics and physics, and an M.S. in mathematics.

Contents

Acknowledgments

I wish to thank my darling wife, Nita, known also as my better half, corporate buddy, main squeeze, partner in crime, and overall the best companion I have ever known. You truly are a gift from above! To JC for again talking and walking with (and sometimes carrying) me when you were the only one that could help.

I also wish to thank the McGraw-Hill production staff for their outstanding efforts in preparing the manuscript for production. Thanks go to Lisa Wolters-Broder for handing the many details of chapter preparation and to Emma Acker for coordinating the book process. Special thanks to Franny Kelly, my acquistitions editor, for managing the Osborne UNIX series and coordinating the fine art of book publishing. Thanks also to John Tiso for reviewing the manuscript and providing critical feedback. Thanks to Jim Minatel for adding important book elements to the chapters! Finally, special thanks to Sam Yu for reviewing elements of the manuscript.

Introduction

This book addresses the fundamentals of UNIX system administration and focuses on the important elements of maintaining a small, medium, or large network of UNIX systems. It tells you everything you need to know to be a successful system administrator or manager. Even non-networked environments are covered so that you are prepared to address the many different issues and problems that are typically encountered with them.

Enterprise networks (or clusters) of UNIX systems have become the critical link and key component of the information landscape for corporate America. UNIX systems have been deployed within every corporate function and within a broad section of businesses and markets. This widespread acceptance and deployment means that UNIX systems are now more on the critical path than ever before. In many corporations and institutions, a system failure or network outage can have serious implications for the organization's ability to conduct standard business activities or communicate with their customers or key partners. In the financial community as well as other market segments, even a relatively small system failure or outage can result in significant financial impact or have other far-reaching implications.

Many of today's corporate and institutional UNIX sites are characterized by significant growth in the diversity and the total number of systems installed. In these heterogeneous computing environments, it is difficult to effectively manage the many different computer systems and peripherals because much of the system administration tasks are done in an ad-hoc manner, or lack comprehensive tools. Sometimes tasks must even be done manually. A critical system or network failure can significantly impact the use of corporate services and affect the day-to-day operations of an organization. Many systems have also been deployed with very little regard for their manageability or upgrade capabilities. This makes the tasks of the system administrator that much harder due to the added requirements of legacy systems, where key system tools are not available with the basic system.

This book will give you the knowledge of important tools, step-by-step procedures, and the skills necessary to effectively administer UNIX systems. It is meant to be very practical in nature, and focuses on only the more important elements to system administration, not esoteric subjects that have little relevance to the important issues faced by today's UNIX administrator.

Audience

The primary audience for this book is the beginning system administrator or network manager, as the title suggests. If you already know the difference between the `netstat` and `mount` commands, then this book might not be up to your speed. On the other hand, if you have used some of these commands before, but don't really understand the bigger picture, or if you want additional information about the commands or options, then this book will help guide you. The book focuses more on how to use software tools and administration procedures than on lengthy descriptions of operating system design or system architecture. However, where appropriate, some theory of operation and/or design is provided to ensure that you fully understand the mechanics of critical services or functions.

UNIX Versions

All of the tools discussed in this book and the examples provided are from Solaris and Linux, with some tools that are also based on the HP-UX operating system. Because many of the UNIX tools are available across a wide variety of versions of UNIX, you will have little difficulty adapting and using the tools in other environments.

Module 1

Introduction to UNIX

Critical Skills

Before you jump in and type your first UNIX command, you'll benefit from understanding some general background on how computer architecture is organized. When you combine that knowledge with a brief history of UNIX and what features UNIX provides, you'll begin to understand some of the advantages UNIX provides over other operating systems. From there, you are ready to learn what a UNIX system administrator does, and you'll see not all of those duties are technical. So to start at the most basic level, you want to know what UNIX is.

1.1 Uncover the History of the UNIX System

The UNIX system was introduced more than 30 years ago and is still one of the most widely used and popular operating systems to this day. UNIX is used in businesses, universities, institutions, and even individual homes to support a variety of applications and functions. UNIX is quite universal and is used all over the world by many different types of people for a host of different purposes. UNIX is supported on a wide range of computer systems—from a single personal computer to very large, high-end workstations and servers and even mainframe class systems.

Certainly as expected, UNIX has gone through a myriad of changes and modifications, which involved a large number of individuals, institutions, and companies. UNIX has improved in many significant ways and as a result is much more functional and provides a large pool of applications, tools, utilities, and other software. The UNIX operating system has been ported to pretty much every major computing platform and system architecture popular within the computer industry. UNIX is available for just about all general-purpose computer systems.

Typically, UNIX can be found on many common computer platforms and users have direct interaction with the operating system. However, many turnkey systems simply use UNIX to support one or more applications. The users of these specialized systems generally interact with the application, but not UNIX itself. It is very possible that many users of UNIX systems do not actually know they are using UNIX, because their view of the system is restricted to the application running on top of the operating system. UNIX has also found its way and gained popularity in the embedded world, which means, like the turnkey approach, UNIX is hidden from the user community. The embedded world contains a plethora of devices like cameras, controllers, handheld devices, and just about anything else that supports a computer processor, and UNIX can be used to provide a scalable, flexible system that can expand as the device's capabilities improve over time.

UNIX is constantly being improved, refined, and retooled. In other words, it is still going through changes and enhancements. That is the beauty of UNIX; like a fine wine, it gets better with age! As a system administrator, you will be able to grow with UNIX—as it gets better, so will you as you become more familiar with the system and specific tools. UNIX is many things to many people. For the software writer, UNIX is a development platform to build software. For general users of the system, it is using whatever applications they need to accomplish their job. For the administrator, it is a system that changes and must be maintained and improved over time. However, with these changes comes challenges, and as a system administrator you will need to maintain your knowledge of UNIX on a consistent basis in order to be effective.

1.2 Explore the Elements of a Computer System

Every general-purpose computer system, no matter where it was designed or manufactured, can be divided into functional areas or different modules so that it can be explained and understood. Today, there is a large selection of computers on the market. However, despite many different "brands" of systems, many of them are based on a small number of common components and computer architecture types. For example, in the personal computer space, the Intel Pentium processor (and various clones) is one of the most popular throughout the world. Despite this popularity, other computer systems such as the Apple Macintosh and others continue to flourish. Generally speaking, every time a dealer or maker sells a computer, it is shipped with both an operating system and a set of applications. Without such software, the computer system would be virtually useless because the user would have no way to interact with the system.

Figure 1-1 shows a diagram of the typical computer system, which contains the different functional areas or modules within a computer. At the highest level, applications are designed and written to accomplish very specific business functions for users. At the lowest level, we have the physical hardware of the

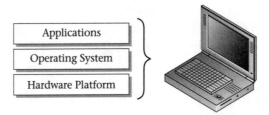

| Applications |
| Operating System |
| Hardware Platform |

Figure 1-1 A diagram of the typical computer system

computer. At this level all of the hardware-related services are available, such as connecting to a network, saving information to secondary storage (that is, hard disk drive), accessing the CPU, and so forth. Typically, these functions are very specific to the type or architecture of the system as well as the different kind of peripheral devices used. For instance, the way memory is allocated for applications can be somewhat different for the different types of computers available on the market today.

An operating system or OS can be generally described as software that provides an interface layer for applications so that they can interact with the hardware components of the computer. Some examples of popular operating systems include the Macintosh OS, Windows 2000, Palm OS, and UNIX. Although each of the operating systems mentioned are different in design and may contain alternative user interfaces, they all provide most of the same basic features. At the middle layer or operating system level, many of the hardware functions are made available for the upper application level. For example, many computers today come with a DVD or CD drive that can be used to view movies or play compact discs (CDs) on the computer. The computer provides the ability to play music though the internals of the system. However, in order to listen to your favorite music CDs, the operating system must provide some user application that permit access and control of the DVD or CD drive. The application must provide the ability to play, stop, skip between tracks, eject the disc, and so forth when necessary. Thus, the software application must control the hardware in order for the user to experience the full use of the hardware. Additional examples of operating system support for hardware include control and access to peripheral devices such as printers, modems, networks, computer monitors, keyboard, pointing devices, etc.

It is important to note that not all hardware functions are always completely supported by the operating system—or even with certain applications. This can be due to several factors such as operating system vendors not wishing to support proprietary hardware designs or even functional defects within the computer hardware itself. However, sometimes, one of the most common reasons is that hardware development improvements are not completely synchronized with operating system releases. In other words, when new computers are sold and provide newer features and functions, the operating system may not completely support these improvements because the software may have been released before the hardware. In this case, the hardware wasn't available while the software was being written. As a result, the operating system vendor might release a "patch" or upgrade, which is a smaller subset of software (also sometimes called a module) that gives the operating system the means to exploit the desired new hardware feature. Patches and/or upgrades are also used to address software defects or other problems within the operating system. The user must install the new software in order for the operating system to support the new hardware. Generally speaking, because operating systems are quite complex, certain patches have been known to cause additional or unanticipated problems. This is where things can get quite interesting, because a specific patch may be needed to support some application, but at the same time it also causes some other problem, which must be addressed as well— possibly by yet another patch or upgrade!

The operating system provides a set of core functions for applications such as memory management, peripheral access, device interfaces, process scheduling, and the like. Figure 1-2 contains a pictorial view of a typical operating system. Each area of the operating system (or module) is responsible for that aspect of the system, but is usually controlled by a single master program or process. Instead of applications talking directly to hardware devices, the operating system layer is defined to make it easier for application designers and writers to produce less complex software. For example, consider an application that must have the capability of producing reports to an output device such as a laser printer. Without an operating system, the application must support the required functionality by printing to these types of devices. Also, given that many different kinds of laser printers are available on the market, it is very difficult to support each of the manufacturers' models within an application. To remedy this situation, the operating system can provide a database of laser printers' description types and applications can simply use one of the predefined templates.

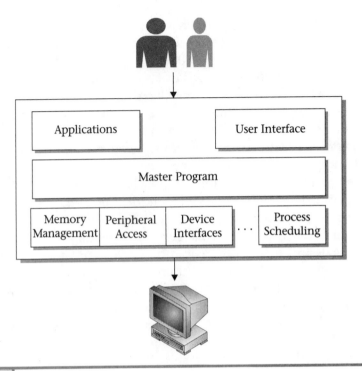

Figure 1-2   Diagram of a typical operating system

As you can see from the figure, many low-level functions are supported within a typical operating system. Also, of equal importance is the user interface that is provided. The user interface usually comes in two different flavors for most operating systems: command line and graphical. The graphical user interface (GUI) also makes the operating system more "user friendly" by insulating the details or automating specific tasks or functions. The GUI is typically used by new users or even by experienced users that choose not to use the command line. The GUI provides a windowing system or some other graphical elements to represent functions and tasks within the operating system. For instance, should the user wish to delete one or more files, a series of file and/or folder icons are displayed and the user simply selects the files they wish to remove and uses the appropriate menu item.

The alternative interface, typically called the "command line", provides a single "prompt" to the system. Generally, the user must know more details about the system in order to use this interface, which is usually used to bypass the

Ask the Expert

Question   Why does the operating system layer make it easier for programmers to write applications to use computer hardware resources?

Answer   Because most personal computers on the market use an open architecture (the hardware specifications are public and many vendors can produce various components) there are thousands of different hard drives, memory modules, video cards, and motherboards and other components that should all work together if you assemble them into a system. Very few programmers or application vendors would have the resources to write code to interact directly with each of these different pieces of hardware. So, the operating system includes the programming so it can interface with any one of thousands of hard drives, but an application programmer can write just one set of code to access any hard drive throughout the operating system.

GUI to accomplish a very specific task. A "power user" sometimes uses this method. Power users are individuals who have mastered the system and can typically use the system without the GUI.

1.3 Show the UNIX Timeline

The UNIX operating system has a long and varied history, which is one of the major reasons why it is alive and well today. The history behind UNIX and the many individuals and organizations that helped mold and shape its past can be quite detailed. As an alternative to providing a rather mundane detailed listing involving all of the historical events surrounding UNIX, a time line and description showing the most significant and key events will be provided instead. Figure 1-3 shows this time line and each of the major events is described below.

AT&T Invents UNIX

AT&T invented UNIX back in the early 1970s to support their internal development efforts and to integrate a scalable operating system within their

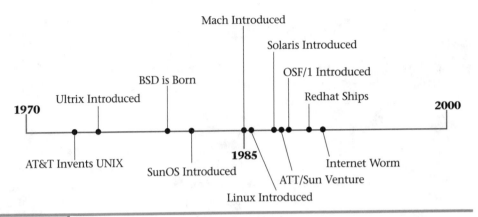

Figure 1-3 The UNIX timeline

communication products. They also released a version of UNIX to corporations and universities, which supported software development, text processing, and other user-level applications. One particularly popular release of UNIX was known as the Programmer Work Bench (PWB). This release provided a wide variety of development and text processing tools, which became very popular in the university community.

BSD Is Born

The University of California at Berkeley was contracted by the government to port AT&T UNIX to the Digital VAX architecture. The subsequent release of this version of UNIX became known as the Berkeley Standard Distribution (BSD) release. The BSD operating system introduced many new features and tools, which played an important role in the future of UNIX. BSD added important networking features such as TCP/IP networking facilities and virtual memory support. Among some of the most popular tools included are the Vi editor, a program called more, the termcap terminal facility and many others. The "r" family of utilities that provides networking capabilities between UNIX systems and users was also introduced with BSD.

The System V Releases

AT&T released several major operating system versions of UNIX, which became known as "System V". Several large computer manufacturers licensed these

1

operating systems and provided ports to their own computer hardware platforms. It was these ports (plus software from BSD) that later would become UNIX products such as AIX, HP-UX, and Solaris.

AT&T/Sun Deal

Due to industry pressures and other important factors, both AT&T and Sun Microsystems formed a partnership where Sun would port the System V release of UNIX onto Sun computer systems. At that time, Sun supported both Motorola- and Sparc-based computer systems. Over time, however, Sun discontinued support for Motorola-based computers and focused quite heavily on their Sparc systems. The porting effort by Sun resulted in the formation of the Solaris operating system that we have today. Prior to the System V port, Sun used the BSD release of UNIX, which was called Sun OS. Over time the Sun OS release was discontinued and Solaris became the dominant operating system. Solaris incorporates AT&T System V, Sun-specific software enhancements, plus BSD packages and tools. Today, Solaris is one of the most popular UNIX operating system in the world.

The Internet Worm

Although the Internet worm of 1988 had much to do with system and network security, it also involved UNIX in a significant way since this security attack demonstrated the vulnerabilities of the UNIX operating system and networking infrastructure of the Internet at that time. The Worm was responsible for infecting many UNIX systems and used the Internet as the connecting medium. It was so virulent that is caused many systems to crash due to the high CPU load that the software consumed when running. Despite the fact that the Worm didn't actually corrupt data files on the systems it penetrated, it did cause major problems since each of the operating systems of the infected systems had to be reinstalled. This was no small task for system administrators. This was certainly a major issue for many since automatic software installation wasn't as good as it is today and many installations were done manually. As a result of the Worm, UNIX and the Internet became more secure.

OSF/1

Due to the activities surrounding the AT&T/Sun partnership, several prominent computer manufactures (HP, Digital Equipment Corporation (DEC), IBM, and others) decided to attempt to even the playing field by forming a new organization called the Open Software Foundation (OSF). The organization was tasked with developing a version of UNIX that would compete with the AT&T/Sun operating system. The product that ultimately was developed was called OSF/1, which was based on the Mach operating system. DEC, among other computer companies, offered the OSF/1 release to their customers. Due to the popularity of the AT&T/Sun operating system, and changes within the UNIX industry, OSF/1 was never widely adopted.

Mach

The Mach operating system, developed at Carnegie Mellon University, was derived from a port of the BSD version of UNIX and introduced in 1985. Mach provided much needed support for multiprocessors and also included other important improvements. Several ports of Mach were made by different computer manufactures, and for a time Mach enjoyed some popularity, but in the long run the operating system wasn't widely adopted.

Linux Is Introduced

Back in 1985, Touvus Linus introduced a version of UNIX for the Intel processor—Linux. Today, Linux (and the variations) stands as a pinnacle of the open source movement and the achievement of many individuals who have contributed to the Linux effort.

Red Hat

Released in 1995, the Red Hat Linux operating system combines several aspects of the Linux system in a popular package. The Red Hat operating system provides a host of important features, contains many third-party tools and utilities, and is one of the most popular Linux variants available today.

Versions of UNIX Today

With most things in life, where there is active competition the best will ultimately survive and triumph. This is the case with several different versions or flavors of UNIX. Although many different versions exist, a common design and/or code base is present in most of them. Also, two major kinds of UNIX operating system software markets exist today. The commercial market is where customers generally have to pay for the operating system software and generally may not get any source code (well, not for free anyway!). The other market is also commercial, but is considered open source. *Open source* means that you get full access to the source code of the system or programs and can make changes or modifications to that source code as long as you maintain the rights of the original software owner.

Today, the UNIX leaders include Solaris, Linux, HP-UX, AIX, and SCO.

Why UNIX Is Popular

Many people ask why UNIX is so popular or why it is used so much, in so many different ways and in so many computing environments. The answer lies with the very nature of UNIX and the model that was used to design, build, and continuously improve the operating system.

Availability of Source Code

One of the most significant points of UNIX is the availability of source code for the system. (For those new to software, source code contains the programming elements that, when passed through a compiler, will produce a binary program—which can be executed.) The binary program contains specific computer instructions, which tells the system "what to do." When the source code is available, it means that the system (or any subcomponent) can be modified without consulting the original author of the program. Access to the source code is a very positive thing and can result in many benefits. For example, if software defects (bugs) are found within the source code, they can be fixed right away—without perhaps waiting for the author to do so.

Another great reason is that new software functions can be integrated into the source code, thereby increasing the usefulness and the overall functionality of the software. Having the ability to extend the software to the user's requirements is a massive gain for the end user and the software industry as a whole. Over time, the software can become much more useful. One downside to having access to the source code is that it can become hard to manage, because it is possible that many different people could have modified the code in unpredictable (and perhaps negative) ways. However, this problem is typically addressed by having a "source code maintainer," which reviews the source code changes before the modifications are incorporated into the original version.

Another downside to source code access is that individuals may use this information with the goal in mind of compromising system or component security. The Internet Worm of 1988 is one such popular example. The author, who was a graduate student at Cornell University at the time, was able to exploit known security problems within the UNIX system to launch a software program that gained unauthorized access to systems and was able to replicate itself to many networked computers. The Worm was so successful in attaching and attacking systems that it caused many of the computers to crash due to the amount of resources needed to replicate. Although the Worm didn't actually cause significant permanent damage to the systems it infected, it opened the eyes of the UNIX community about the dangers of source code access and security on the Internet as a whole.

Flexible Design

UNIX was designed to be modular, which makes it a very flexible architecture. The modularity helps provide a framework that makes it much easier to introduce new operating system tools, applications, and utilities, or to help in the migration of the operating system to new computer platforms or other devices. Although some might argument that UNIX isn't flexible enough for their needs, it is quite adaptable and can handle most requirements. This is evidenced by the fact that UNIX runs on more general computer platforms and devices than any other operating system.

GNU

The GNU project, started in the early 1980s, was intended to act as a counterbalance to the widespread activity of corporate greed and adoption of license agreements for computer software. The "GNU is not UNIX" project was responsible for producing some of the world's most popular UNIX software. This includes the Emacs editor and the gcc compiler. They are the cornerstones of the many tools that a significant number of developers use every day.

Open Software

UNIX is open, which basically means that no single company, institution, or individual owns UNIX—nor can it be controlled by a central authority. However, the UNIX name remains a trademark. Anyone using the Internet may obtain open source software, install it, and modify it, and then redistribute the software without ever having to shell out any money in the process. The open source movement has gained great advances and has clearly demonstrated that quality software can, in fact, be free. Granted, it is quite true that certain versions of UNIX are not open, and you do indeed need to pay to use these operating systems in the form of an end-user licensing agreement. Generally speaking, vendors that charge for UNIX represent only a portion of the total number of UNIX releases available within the UNIX community.

Programming Environment

UNIX provides one of the best development environments available by providing many of the important tools software developers need. Also, there are software tools such as compilers and interpreters for just about every major programming language known in the world. Not only can one write programs in just about any computer language, UNIX also provides additional development tools such as text editors, debuggers, linkers, and related software. UNIX was conceived and developed by programmers for programmers, and it stands to reason that it will continue to be the programmer's development platform of choice now and in the future.

Availability of Many Tools

UNIX comes with a large number of useful applications, utilities, and programs, which many people consider to be one of UNIX's greatest strengths. They are collectively known or commonly referred to as UNIX "tools," and they cover a wide range of functions and purposes. One of the most significant aspects of UNIX is the availability of software to accomplish one or more very specific tasks. You will find throughout this text that the concept of tools is quite universal and is used repeatedly. This book not only discusses the subject of system administration but also provides detailed descriptions of UNIX-based tools. As a system administrator, you will come to depend on certain tools to help you do your job. Just as construction workers rely on the tools they use, so too will the administrator rely on the software that permits them to handle a wide range of functions, tasks, issues, and problems.

There are tools to handle many system administration tasks that you might encounter. Also, there are tools for development, graphics manipulation, text processing, database operations—just about any user- or system-related requirement. If the basic operating system version doesn't provide a particular tool that you need, chances are that someone has already developed the tool and it would be available via the Internet.

Hint

There are several popular Web sites that contain a large collection of public domain and open source tools and applications that are available. These links can be found in an appendix of this book.

System Libraries

A system library is a collection of software that programmers use to augment their applications. UNIX comes with quite a large collection of functions or routines that can be accessed from several different languages to aid the application writer with a variety of tasks. For example, should the need arise to sort data, UNIX provides several different sort functions.

Well Documented

UNIX is well documented with both online manuals and with many reference books and user guides from publishers. Unlike some operating systems, UNIX provides online main page documentation of all tools that ship with the system. Also, it is quite customary that open source tools provide good documentation. Further, the UNIX community provides journals and magazine articles about UNIX, tools, and related topics of interest.

1-Minute Drill

● Why is source code availability a valuable advantage to UNIX users?

● What are some downsides of source code availability?

● Users can modify the code to fit their own needs, such as fixing bugs immediately or implementing new features.
● Tracking and managing multiple versions of code changes can be difficult. Source code availability makes it easier for unscrupulous users to exploit programming errors, particularly relating to security. (However, source code availability means users can patch these bugs quickly, even if the original author or vendor isn't available to patch them.)

Modular UNIX

Like all operating systems, UNIX can be divided into functional areas
(components) where each part is responsible for a given set of services.
This modularity is what gives UNIX its appeal and why it is one of the most
popular operating systems in the world. Figure 1-4 shows the overall picture
of where the individual components of the UNIX system fit together. Each of
the major elements is described in more detail below.

The Kernel

Perhaps the most critical element of the operating system, the kernel is
responsible for many of the operating system tasks and services that applications
and users require. The Kernel is the main program that interfaces with all
hardware components, supports the execution of applications, and provides
an environment for users. Very little can be done on a UNIX system without
accessing some Kernel function or resource. It is the controlling entity of

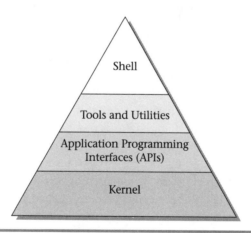

| **Figure 1-4** | UNIX operating system picture |

the system. The kernel itself consists of several parts. From a high-level standpoint, the kernel performs the following services and functions:

- **Interfaces with the computer hardware** Using modules called *device drivers*, the kernel uses these software components to talk directly to hardware-level devices. For example, when an application wants to write data to a secondary storage device such as a hard drive, the kernel "calls" the driver to write the information specific to that device. Thus, for every hardware device, the kernel must have an associated driver. Since every hardware device (such as a disk drive or sound card, for example) is vendor specific, the kernel driver must also be vendor and/or product specific. However, there are times when a common driver will support a family of products or devices. This driver concept is used extensively throughout the system; interfaces to all hardware components use this approach. Some additional examples of drivers include serial port drivers, printer port drivers, keyboard and mouse drivers, video display drivers, sound drivers, and network interface drivers.

- **Provides time-sharing services** The kernel is responsible for providing the resources necessary to handle multiple users, applications, and other processes in what seems like a concurrent, real-time fashion. In other words, UNIX supports a time-share model where users and applications run all at the same time regardless of the underlying hardware characteristics. Computers that support a single processor are said to be *uniprocessor* machines, while *multiprocessor* machines contain more than one processor. Thus, UNIX supports concurrent logins of different users and these users may execute different applications or software all at the same time. However, this reality is an illusion; the kernel makes it appear to the users that everything is happening in a concurrent fashion, but the hardware may not support parallel processing or concurrent processing. The kernel was designed to provide this service regardless of the physical processing characteristics of the machine in question. When the kernel is running on a machine that supports more than one processor, the effects are pretty much the same—multiple users and applications can run in a concurrent fashion.

1

● **Implements security model**   The kernel supports the notion of users and profiles. All users must be defined on the system before they are permitted to access or log in to the system, and each user has a particular profile. User accounts contain information about the user and are used to track the users' activities once they are on the system. The kernel ensures that security between users and between the system and users is always maintained. For example, it is not possible for one user to delete the files of another user if the first user protects his or her files. Similarly, a user will not be able to delete or remove system-related files unless the administrator permits such activity.

Hint

Within UNIX, a special account, called the superuser, is defined. Known as the "root" account, this is the one login that is usually set up by default on most systems to have unrestricted access to every service or file within the system. There isn't any service, file, directory, or information that the superuser can't access. Typically, the system administrator becomes the superuser and uses this account on a regular basis.

APIs

UNIX provides a large number of application programming interfaces (APIs), which help programmers write applications or tools that help to take advantage of the system. Using UNIX APIs makes it easier to write programs and helps software to integrate with the system.

The Shell

UNIX provides a mechanism for a user to log in to the system using what is known as a command-line prompt or shell. The shell is a command interpreter, which takes what the user types in and executes commands, manipulates files, and so forth on behalf of the user. A large number of different shells are available for UNIX, and users have the ability to customize the shell to suit their own personal preferences.

1.4 Discover the Roles of the UNIX System Administrator

The job of the system administrator is one of the best in the entire world! It basically means that you look after the computer systems, and in some cases the network that interconnects those systems as well. The phrase "looking after" actually can mean quite a number of different things. From the system administrator point of view, they are totally responsible for not only the successful operation of the computers themselves—including the hardware, operating system, and applications—but must also ensure that the users of those systems are happy and are using the systems to their full extent. This is a tall order considering the sheer number of users that systems can support and also because users have different requirements and individual needs.

From a technical standpoint, the systems administrator will handle one or more of the following depending on the size, organization structure, and type of company in which they are employed:

- **Manage the computer hardware** This includes dealing with hardware-related problems such as faulty or failed system boards, disk drives, CPUs, printers, and so forth. Also, if the hardware is covered by a vendor maintenance contract, you will need to handle the details of maintaining the coverage and managing the vendor relationship when problems occur. You might need to "watch over" their activity when they are on-site to ensure that they address the real problem or don't cause problems in other areas. For example, they might replace the wrong disk drive when multiple drives are contained within a single system.

- **System backups** You will be responsible for ensuring that regular backups/archiving of the important system and critical data files are done. This is perhaps one of the most important functions of the system administrator and should not be overlooked from a job duty standpoint. It is also one of the most boring parts of being a system administer! Successful administrators typically will automate the backup function so that they might spend more time on more interesting tasks. With the deployment of specialized network backup systems, storage area networks (SANs), and other backup solutions, ensuring correct backup procedures have never been so easy.

1

● **Maintain system capacities** Typically, memory, CPU, and disk storage are the key components that are upgraded when the user base of the systems increases or the system application functions are expanded. The most common is that the disk storage might need to be upgraded more often due to increasing data processing or the addition of users.

Support the Network

With the ever-increasing dependence on computer networking and with the growth of the largest network (the Internet), administrators are continuously faced with handling network-related issues and problems. As a result, administrators not only need to understand their systems but the network and associated components as well. With this in mind, the administrator must "bone up" on the networking protocols, devices, and particular network applications. For example, having a very good understanding of TCP/IP can come in handy when dealing with interaction between applications or general network communication problems related to the Internet or a local network.

You might also need to handle hardware-related problems within the network, such as dealing with failed network components, misconfigured devices, cabling problems, and so forth. This might include dealing with Internet service providers (ISPs) or phone companies, depending on how the network topology and Internet services have been implemented.

Handle Peripherals

In many cases, the administrator will be required to handle the support of associated devices that might be used with the primary systems. These devices might include printers, modems, scanners, and just about anything else that could be used with a UNIX system. Often, systems are purchased with these add-on devices at the same time, but sometimes they are not—in which case, the administrator must integrate or install one or more of the peripheral devices. Printers are one such example, where they might be obtained after the primary UNIX system was installed. With this in mind, the administrator must ensure that the UNIX system is configured to use the printers correctly. If the printer is going to be shared across a number of different systems, the configuration must be replicated to each system supporting the printer. Equally important, the printer devices must be set up and configured to work with the UNIX systems as well. Thus, not only must the administrator understand UNIX, but she or he must also have the ability to learn how other devices function and be able to configure them. Don't be alarmed—no administrator is expected to know every type of device that can be integrated with a UNIX system. Rather, the administrator must be able to learn how to do this when necessary, with the aid of product manuals, technical support, and other resources.

Manage System Upgrades

Due to the nature of computer technology and the need to support more functions and perhaps more users, the administrator might be asked to perform certain (if not all) system upgrades. This will include installing more memory, disk storage, CPUs, updating the computer firmware, and a host of other hardware-related tasks. If the UNIX systems are covered under a vendor maintenance support agreement, the vendor may perform some of the upgrades. For instance, the firmware, which is used to handle lower-level system functions and diagnostics, might be upgraded automatically by the system vendor.

Upgrades are not just made to the hardware components of the system, but also to the operating system, applications, tools, or utilities. Sometimes, dealing with software upgrades can be more difficult than the hardware due to the dependencies on different software components. For example, if the operating system was upgraded to a newer version, it might cause one or more applications to not function correctly. Normally, application vendors do a good job of testing their software on different operating system releases to avoid these types of problems. However, no vendor can guarantee that their product will never crash or experience problems, regardless of which particular operating system release is being used.

Actively Monitor System Security

In certain organizations, the system administrator is responsible for handling all aspects of system security. This includes, for example, ensuring that external attacks (say, from the Internet) as well as internal ones (from local users) are prevented as much as possible. There are many aspects of system security— from running monthly security reports to installing security patches. The most important component of security is being prepared when security-related issues or problems strike. Just as when natural disasters hit a particular city, so too it is very important to be prepared. For example, if it becomes necessary to

1

restore user files due to corruption caused by a malicious program, these files must be restored quickly and accurately. Further, it will be very important to take steps to prevent security problems in the first place. For example, if one or more security vulnerabilities have been found with a software module, application, or utility that is currently being used on the system, that software should be upgraded in order to minimize any potential security risk.

If you demonstrate a positive security model and communicate the need for security, others will follow. The administrator has to set the stage and promote security as a way of life for all users of the system. For example, you might need to teach users not to leave their workstations logged in while they are away for extended periods of time. The users of the system will help to implement and conform to specific security rules, policies, and procedures that you define. In larger companies or organizations, security might rest with a particular security-centric group, which is not typically a part of those that administer the systems. However, the individuals within the security department must work hand in hand with the administrator to ensure that specific policies and security measures are implemented on a system wide-basis.

Maintain System Accounts

As part of general security and administration of UNIX, you will need to maintain a close eye on user accounts, which is the primary way to control access to the system. UNIX uses a system account files to permit users to gain access to the system, and it will be your direct responsibility to ensure that only authorized users are permitted access and that they are set with the correct profiles and access parameters. Also, it will be important that you delete user profiles when employees leave or move to another part of the company, or you might need to adjust user profiles as user access policies change.

Advance Your Knowledge

Believe it or not, you will be asked to learn new technologies, products, applications, and perhaps a host of other interesting subjects related to your job. You will be most valuable to your organization when you know just as much as (or even more than) the vendors that provide your products and systems. You will need to attend professional development classes, vendor-offered training, and other training programs and courses. Also, depending on the company, you might need to seek one or more vendor certification programs, such as from Red Hat or Sun Microsystems. Also, you may need to supplement your understanding and technology knowledge by reading great books (such as from this series!!), trade magazines, journals, and other publications. Further, you might need to attend special conferences and trade shows to gain more insight into a particular technology or product, or to learn more about a vendor.

As you can see, being a system administrator means handling many technical details of the computer systems within your environment. One very interesting aspect of this is that should the computer environment contain different versions of UNIX, in what we call a heterogeneous network, this can complicate the administrator's job to some degree. In general, UNIX is fairly standard, but different vendors provide unique tools just for their platform. As a result, it might be difficult to do certain tasks the same way across different vendors' UNIX machines. However, in most cases this isn't a problem because many of the tools work the same way for most different flavors of UNIX.

The successful administrator not only handles the details of the system but also in certain cases must be a teacher, police officer, politician, parent, and friend, and have good organizational skills and a cheerful disposition. Bear in mind that not all of these skills are absolutely necessary, since many companies define the job of system administrator in different ways. As a result, different skills and tasks may be required.

Teacher

As an administrator, you will find yourself showing the users how to use the system and perhaps giving classes on a wide range of subjects related to the use or operation of a particular application or system capability. For example, new users might not know how to log in and access certain applications in order for them to complete their jobs. You might also need to show experienced users the best way to archive their files or how to use a new system utility or a recently installed application.

Politician

Being an administrator means that you must handle and solve a large number of problems. In certain cases, this might require you to be a politician due to the issues and people involved. Some of these problems can be a conflict between one or more users or can be related to how the system is supported or maintained. The system administrator usually deals with many individuals at all levels of the

1

company. For example, they may deal with administrative assistants, technical staff, managers, and vice presidents, as well as outside customers, suppliers, and vendors. As a result, good negotiation and people skills are necessary.

Parent

Sometimes users can be like children, and they require a strong parent to rein them in. For instance, some users insist that they keep every file they ever used, and as a result the system disks are filled to capacity. This can be unacceptable behavior if every user did this because of the amount of time and trouble caused by having to clean up after these users. Also, since the administrator knows the system, they might need to give advice to users about how best to solve or address some particular issue or problem. For instance, a user might need to obtain a large amount of data for a particular purpose and it must be transferred from one system to another. In this case, you might need to step in and provide assistance.

Police Officer

Sometimes being a politician or parent isn't enough; you might need to become a police officer to enforce some general rules of behavior or exercise critical control of the system. For example, you will need to restrict physical access to the computer system to only those individuals that require it. A curious user attempting to fix a hardware-related problem could spell disaster for the administrator, given the complexity and sensitivity of hardware components. Another good example is system security—should the administrator detect unauthorized access to the system, then the administrator must take immediate action to protect the integrity of the system and users. It might, for example, mean that users are audited to ensure they are not doing bad things on the system.

Hint

Generally, security measures are more successful if they are planned in advance before you need them. For example, user audit trails are most useful when they capture bad behavior when it is happening.

Friend

If the above duties aren't enough, you might actually need to be a friend to your users. For example, one user might be working on a critical project that requires you to help them with a system-related problem (such as the printer not functioning correctly) at an unpopular time—say, during the weekend or in the wee hours of the morning. You might have the option to tell the user to wait until the official workday starts or handle the issue on the spot. In general, users are good-natured and happy individuals, but other times they might be nasty, outrageous, and demanding. It may be in your best interest to help the individual because you want to be helpful, and that is expected. As with most things in life, a simple smile and thick skin (for really difficult users) can go a long way to ensure that a bad situation goes smoothly.

Also, goodwill can flow in both directions. If you help users out of tough situations, they might help you in turn at some point in the future! You may find that having friends on the "inside" can work in your favor. Sometimes, the job of system administrator isn't very popular because you might need to make some decisions that affect users in a negative or unpleasant way. Take, for example, the moment you need to bring the system down for some critical maintenance task. You will need to ask all the users to log off the system, and this can be an unpopular thing to do since users might not want to log off— because, for example, they have their own deadline or other things they must complete, and this downtime can cause them pain. However, having users who understand can help to bolster your position about the system outage and smooth things over for users that might not fully appreciate your need to bring the system down when it is not convenient for them—they may come to realize that in the long run it is in their best interest.

The bottom line is that being a system administrator sometimes requires that one be both technical and have a reasonable knack for dealing with individuals (users) and all levels of management. Certainly this is the ideal situation, but the world is full of situations that are far from perfection. As a result, many successful administrators don't need to deal with the softer side, but more the technical. Conversely, some administrators work within teams where they might not be handling the day-to-day tasks, but rather deal with more of the management aspects of the job. As you can see, your mileage may vary and the exact system administrator requirements will be different depending on the company or the exact job position.

☑ *Mastery Check*

1. Name the three functional areas or layers of any computer system, regardless of brand.

2. Which UNIX component interacts with the system hardware?

    A. Kernel

    B. APIs

    C. Shell

    D. Hardware Administrator

3. Which of the following is not a key reason for UNIX's popularity?

    A. Flexible design

    B. Proprietary software

    C. GNU

    D. Well documented

4. A _____ is a collection of software that programmers use to augment their applications.

5. Which of the following is not a function of the UNIX kernel?

    1. Interfaces with the computer hardware

    2. Provides time-sharing services

    3. Implements security model

    4. Maintains system capacities

6. The UNIX _____ is responsible for regular backups/archiving of important system and critical data files.

Module 2

Basic UNIX Commands

Critical Skills

This module provides an introduction into using the standard shell and some of the basic operating system tools that administrators will need to know to help them maintain UNIX systems. As the system administrator, you will need to learn about a variety of utilities and tools to help accomplish administrative tasks and make your job easier. It will be important that you get familiar with many of the commands within this module and you are encouraged to try running these programs within your own environment just so that you get a feel for the behavior and to begin learning the many program parameters and command-line options.

2.1 Explore the UNIX Shell

The shell is a rather unique component of the UNIX operating system since it is one of the primary ways to interact with the system. It is typically through the shell that users execute other commands or invoke additional functions. The shell is commonly referred to as a command interpreter and is responsible for executing tasks on behalf of the user. Figure 2-1 shows a pictorial view of how the shell fits with the UNIX system. As you can see, the shell operates within the framework just like any other program. It provides an interface between the user, the operating system functions, and ultimately the system Kernel.

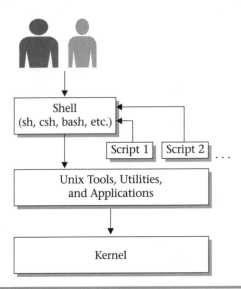

Figure 2-1   The UNIX shell

2

Another powerful feature of the UNIX shell is the ability to support the development and execution of custom shell scripts. The shell contains a mini programming language that provides a lightweight way to develop new tools and utilities without having to be a heavyweight software programmer. A UNIX shell script is a combination of internal shell commands, regular UNIX commands, and some shell programming rules.

UNIX supports a large number of different shells, and also many of the popular ones are freely available on the Internet. Also, many versions of UNIX come with one or more shells and as the system administrator, you can install additional shells when necessary and configure the users of the system to use different shells, depending on specific preferences or requirements. Table 2-1 below lists many of the popular shells and a general description of each.

Once a user has logged into the system, the default shell prompt appears and the shell simply waits for input from the user. Thus, logging into a Solaris system as the `root` user for example, the standard Bourne shell prompt will be

```
#
```

The system echoes this prompt to signal that it is ready to receive input from the keyboard. At this point, this user is free to type in any standard UNIX command, application, or custom script name and the system will attempt to execute or run the command. The shell assumes that the first argument given

Shell Name	General Description
Sh	Standard Bourne shell, which is one of the most popular shells around.
Csh	Standard shell with C like language support.
Bash	GNU Bourne-Again shell that includes elements from the Korn shell and C shell.
Tcsh	Standard C shell with command-line editing and filename completion capabilities.
Ksh	The Korn shell combines the best features of the Bourne and C shells and includes powerful programming tools.
Zsh	Korn shell like, but also provides many more features such as built-in spell correction and programmable command completion.

Table 2-1   Descriptions of Different UNIX Shells

on the command line is a program or a special character sequence that is interpreted by the shell as a command. UNIX supports a large number of commands, which can be classified into several different groupings that include generic user-level commands, superuser-level commands, and built-in shell commands.

User-level commands are those programs that can be run by any user, regardless of their access level or other user account parameters. The date command is one such example; generally speaking, no special permission is required to display the local date and time with the command. UNIX contains a very large number of these types of commands and they are usually contained within standard directories such as /usr/bin or /usr/local/bin.

Hint

Anyone can peruse these directories to obtain a list of the all the available commands contained within the locations. However, the administrator can define restricted users, which can't access common directories or execute a generic program, but this is something the administrator must purposely do.

The superuser commands, which can be found in several different system directories (/usr/bin/usr/sbin, and so forth) are those that require system-level or privileged access to invoke or execute. For instance, the format program is used to format storage media such as disk drives. Typically, this type of administration function is restricted and can't be invoked by typical UNIX users due to the destructive nature of the command; it can completely delete all information from a storage device. Thus, only the superuser can run this command. UNIX provides a special account called the superuser account, or also known as root, which is used to permit system or administrative access. The UNIX administrator will use this account when performing system maintenance and other important administrative tasks. The superuser account is a sacred cow—it provides complete and total access to all aspects of the system, and this account must be guarded at all times; only the administrator will use this account, and it is usually protected by a secret password.

The built-in shell commands are defined as those functions, which are not part of the UNIX command set, but instead are interpreted and supported directly by the shell. They are not stand-alone programs such as date, but are executed within the shell. For example, the set command, which is used to define environment variables, is one such internal command. An environment variable, for example, is one way to pass a program a parameter, which can be

2

used to control the behavior of the software to achieve some desired result. For example, you can use an environment variable to contain the user's default printer, so that any application can use this information to print to the correct output device.

2.2 Investigate Basic UNIX Commands

As you will see in this book, UNIX comes with a large number of commands that fall under each of the categories listed above for both the generic user and the system administrator. It is quite hard to list and explain all of the available UNIX functions and/or commands in a single book. Therefore, a review of some of the more important user-level commands and functions has been provided and subsequent modules provide a more in-depth look at system-level commands. All of the commands discussed below can be run by generic users and of course by the system administrator. However, one or more subfunctions of a command may be available only to the system administrator.

Table 2-2 provides a list of standard commands, which are available across many different versions of UNIX. For example, if we wanted to get a listing of all the users that are currently logged into the system, the who command can be used.

UNIX Command	Meaning
cat	Show the content of file.
date	Show system date and time.
hostname	Display name of system.
find	Search for a specific file.
grep	Search a file for specified pattern.
ls	List files in a directory.
more	Another command to show content of file.
ps	Show status of processes.
strings	Show strings within a file.
uname	Show system-related information.
who	Show current users on the system.

Table 2-2   Basic UNIX Commands

Thus,

```
# who
```

will produce a list of the login names for all users presently on the system, such as

```
bill        pts/1        Sep  9 06:41    (pebbles)
root        pts/10       Sep  9 09:11    (fred)
sjmaxwell   pts/2        Sep  9 08:02    (wilma)
```

You can find this command (and, of course, many others) on Linux, HP-UX, Solaris, AIX, and many other versions of UNIX. However, depending on the version of UNIX, the output might slightly be different. Naturally, this output shouldn't really match what is displayed when you execute this command on one of your systems since the environment and users will be quite different. Despite this, the command displays basically the same information regardless of which UNIX system it is executed on. The who command is very interesting because it shows when the users were logged into the system and from which terminal, and, if networking services is active, the name of the computer system that the user originated the connection from. In the example above, bill is logged in from a system called pebbles, while root and sjmaxwell (yes, that is me!) are from the systems known as fred and wilma, respectively. Knowing and understanding commands like who (and many others) makes it much easier to administer UNIX-based systems. Next to the login name is the terminal associated with that login. In the example, pts followed by a number indicates the terminal device number. When a real terminal or network connection is made to the system, a terminal (real or pseudo if network) is assigned automatically by the system to the user that logged into the system.

Like most UNIX commands, the who utility provides a number of command-line arguments, which control the behavior and output of the program. However, it is not necessary to know all of these arguments to use the basic functions. Having said that, one of the more useful functions of this program is to identify the username of the current shell. In other words, which user account am I logging under? Using the command

```
# who am i
root        pts/8        Dec 27 15:21    (dhcpclient-202)
```

2

will display the login username and other information. This is most useful if you have started to use a terminal or login session and you don't know which user is in fact logged into the system.

Finally, another important function of the who command is to report the system run mode with the use of the −r option. This argument displays the current system run level, which can be multiuser, single user, or some additional level as defined in the /etc/inittab file. See Module 9 for additional information. Thus,

```
# who -r
       .          run-level 3  Dec  8 10:41     3      0  S
```

shows that the system is at run level 3, which is the multiuser mode that the system typically uses during normal everyday operations.

Those new to operating systems find it strange that UNIX doesn't provide positive acknowledgement, with some kind of printed message of successful execution of a command. For example, when the user removes a file using the rm command, the system doesn't respond with a specific message when it is finished, but instead simply removes the file and returns the shell prompt. Thus, when

```
# rm records.dat
#
```

is run, it removes the records.dat file and issues the shell prompt again.

Hint

The command didn't respond by displaying a successful message other than displaying the prompt again. Alternatively, the user could check to see if the command did what it was supposed to do. For instanced by running the following command:

```
# ls  records.dat
records.dat: No such file or directory  ◄──────| Error Message |
#
```

When the ls command is used against a nonexisting file, it produces an error message because the file could not be found. Seasoned UNIX administrators don't typically check that certain commands were in fact executed because should any type of error have occurred during the execution of the `rm` command, it would have issued a message stating that a problem had been encountered. For example, if the `records.dat` couldn't be removed because of a file permission problem, a message would be generated that gives a clue to the problem:

```
# rm records.dat
rm: records.dat not removed: Permission denied
#
```

Generally speaking, most UNIX commands give some kind of error/status message when a problem has been encountered.

cat

The `cat` command will display the content of one or more text-based files. It is considered "more-lite" since it doesn't support fancy scrolling functions like the `more` command. The `cat` program is a fairly simple-minded tool, which supports a small number of command-line options. However, the most useful ones are listed in Table 2-3. Note that the above error message typically wouldn't be displayed if the command was run by the superuser.

Option	Definition
-n	Number each line of output.
-b	Same as −n, but don't number blank lines.
-u	When displaying text, don't use buffering (Solaris and HP-UX only).
-s	Don't display an error when attempting to process nonexisting files (Solaris only).
-v	Display non-printable characters in visual form.
--help	Display list of supported command-line options (Linux only).

Table 2-3   Cat Command-Line Options

To show the contents of a sample `/etc/passwd` file with associated line numbers, issue the following command:

```
              -n option to number        directory and
              output lines               filename to list

              # cat -n /etc/passwd
           →   1   root:x:0:1:Super-User:/:/sbin/sh
               2   smaxwell:x:0:1:Super-User:/:/usr/bin/bash
               3   daemon:x:1:1::/:
               4   bin:x:2:2::/usr/bin:
               5   sys:x:3:3::/:
               6   adm:x:4:4:Admin:/var/adm:
               7   lp:x:71:8:Line Printer Admin:/usr/spool/lp:
               8   uucp:x:5:5:uucp Admin:/usr/lib/uucp:
               9   nuucp:x:9:9:uucp Admin:/var/spool/uucppublic:/usr/lib/uucp/uucico
              10   listen:x:37:4:Network Admin:/usr/net/nls:
              11   nobody:x:60001:60001:Nobody:/:
              12   noaccess:x:60002:60002:No Access User:/:
              13   nobody4:x:65534:65534:SunOS 4.x Nobody:/:
              14   syu:x:100:111::/home/syu:/bin/sh
              15   anonymous:x:101:1::/home/anonymous:/bin/sh
              16   anonymou:x:102:1::/home/anonymou:/bin/sh
              17   samc:x:20001:10:Mr Sam Clinton:/homes/samc:/bin/sh
              18   stevem:x:20003:10:Mr. Steve Maxwell:/homes/stevem:/usr/bin/bash
              19   anitat:x:20004:102:Ms. Anita Tognazzini:/homes/anitat:/bin/sh
              20   samyu:x:20005:10:Mr Samual Yu:/homes/samyu:/bin/sh

       Numbers at beginning of each line are from -n
       option, not part of the /etc/passwd file
```

The `cat` program can be used to display any UNIX file. However, it is not that practical for displaying other types of files such as a software program or binary file. Why? Because programs or other binary data can't be displayed in a meaningful way like text can be. A UNIX tool such as `strings` is more suited for this purpose.

date

The `date` command is used to display the system date and time. Also, sometimes it is necessary to alter the date or time on the system, and the command can be used for this purpose as well. Typing the command

```
# date
```

will show output formatting like the following:

```
Thu Dec 27 16:59:15 PST 2001
```

As with most UNIX commands, the `date` command supports different command-line options and arguments, which can be used to alter what is displayed or to control additional functions. For example, to alter the date and time on the system, and set it to November 5, 2005 at 9:30 AM, the administrator can use the following command:

```
# date 110509302005
Sat Nov  5 09:30:00 PST 2005
```

11	This denotes the month of the year
05	This denotes the date of the month
09	This denotes the hour of the day
30	This denotes the minute of the hour
2005	This denotes the year

When the `date` command is given a correctly formatted date string, it assumes that the system date should be altered and echoes back the new date. Due to security concerns, only the superuser (`root` account) may alter the date and/or time settings.

Ask the Expert

Question Why can only the superuser alter the date or time settings?

Answer Well, the view from many system administrators is that typical users shouldn't be able to alter the date because it could impact the system in negative and unexpected ways. For example, some software license keys are coded to expire on some future date. If someone changes the date and advances the clock, it could invalidate the licenses and stop these software packages from operating. Also, changing the date vicariously can cause problems when files and directories are created or modified, because they pick up time stamp information that is not accurate. It could lead, for example, to files having a future or past date that is in conflict with reality. Also, consider if an order entry system application is running on a system where the date was advanced significantly. This action will negatively impact the ability to handle delivery dates and schedules because of the incorrect date and time information.

hostname

The `hostname` command shows the name of the host when it is typically attached to a network. However, a UNIX system can have a valid hostname without networking services actually configured or when the system is not attached to a network. This name can either be a fully qualified domain name (FQDN) or another name known as a host alias. The FQDN is what has been defined within the Domain Name System (DNS) server for that particular system. An alias is simply another name for the FQDN and can be used interchangeably with the fully qualified name.

To display the hostname of a system, type the following:

```
# hostname
```

If the hostname is defined, a string is displayed as in the following example:

```
pebbles.home.com
```

In this case, the hostname `pebbles.home.com` is the defined system name, and it is this name that should be used when accessing the system over the network. For example, if the administrator wants to determine if the system is reachable from another node on the network, this hostname can be used with the `ping` command. See Module 11 for additional information on this network command. Thus,

```
# ping pebbles.home.com
pebbles.home.com is alive
```

shows that the system is available on the network.

Hint

This name is known as a fully qualified name because it contains both the hostname and the domain name. As previously suggested, the hostname may also be the system alias. Thus, a hostname of `pebbles` would be just as valid or correct.

The `hostname` command can also be used to name the host or rename the host if it already has a defined system name. However, on Solaris and other systems, just running this command doesn't permanently alter the name of the machine across system reboots, nor does it completely change the name of the machine. In other words, using this command on the command line only alters the name of the system until the system is rebooted, and without additional steps would cause the system to not function correctly on the network.

1-Minute Drill

● As a UNIX system administrator, why don't you need to check to see if a command executed after issuing it?

● Why isn't the `cat` command appropriate for listing the contents of program files?

find

The `find` command is used to search the UNIX system for specific files and/or directories. This command is very useful to recursively search a file system when you don't know exactly where a file (or group of files) is located. One very practical use of this command is to clean up file systems by removing unneeded files and thus reclaiming disk space. Additional practical uses include

● Identifying files that contain possible security concerns or problems

● Identifying very large files that consume much disk space

● Identifying files that are owned by specific users

● Identifying files that haven't been accessed in a long time and can be archived off the system

To search for specific files—for example, all files named `core`—use the following command:

```
# find / -name core
```

● You don't need to check to see if a command executed because if it didn't, UNIX will return an error message.
● The `cat` command only displays text characters properly and doesn't handle special characters in program files well.

2

and if one or more `core` files are found, a list of files will be produced as shown in the following example:

```
/home/sjmaxwell/bin/tools/core
/tmp/core1
/usr/local/utils/core
/var/stream/bin/core
```

When attempting to clean up disk space, files with the name of `core` are particularly useful to locate and remove because they tend to be rather larger in size. Generally, `core` files are generated as a result of a binary program that has stopped under some abnormal condition. The file contains program data and other information that is useful for tracking down software problems. Unfortunately, `core` files can hang around within a file system soaking up large amounts of disk space and without some kind of cleaning process can cause a file system to become full and subsequently unusable.

The output of this command shows a series of fully qualified files, each matching the file string arguments shown in the `find` command. In this case, a total of four files have been found. The output of the command is very helpful when additional inspection of the files is necessary. For example, you can further examine the file using the `ls` command with the `-al` options. The `ls` command shows several very useful aspects of a UNIX file as discussed below. Thus, to see the amount of space the file uses, use the following command:

```
                                 filesize
# ls -al /var/stream/bin/core       ↓
-rw-------    1 root    other      678876 Jun 29 16:34
/var/stream/bin/core
```

In our example, we wanted to see the amount of disk space the file consumed. In this case, the file is using approximately 678K (that is 678,000 bytes, or more than half of a megabyte) of disk.

The arguments and syntax of the `find` command include the following:

`find path expression`

The `path` argument tells `find` where to begin searching and will recursively descend the specified path until it reaches the last directory. Many times, the / (root) file system is specified, thus telling `find` to start at the highest level within the system. The `find` command will continue to search each additional mounted file system (because each mounted file system from `/`) in order.

The expression argument includes two components: directives and associated arguments. Directives are action verbs, which tell `find` what to do or modify an action or behavior. Table 2-4 shows these directives and any associated command arguments.

Command	Definition
-atime	Checks to see if the file was accessed by n number of days.
-cpio	Writes the current file on the specified device in the 5120-byte record format known as `cpio` (Solaris only).
-ctime	Checks to see if the file's status was changed n days ago.
-depth	Controls how directories are searched.
-exec	Executes a command once a file is found.
-follow	Causes `find` to follow symbolic links.
-fstype	Search for a file that belongs to a specific file system.
-group	Search for a file that belongs to a specific group ID.
-help	Display appreciated help on command-line arguments (Linux only).
-inum	Search for a file that contains a specific inode number.
-links	Search for a file that has n number of file links.
-local	Searches for a file that is on a local file system (Solaris and HP-UX only).
-ls	Prints current path name and any associated stats.
-mount	Restricts the search to a specific mounted file system.
-mtime	Checks to see if the file's data was changed n days ago.
-name	Search for a file with a specified name.
-newer	Search for a file that has been modified more recently than file argument.
-nogroup	Search for a file with the group name not contained with the `/etc/group` system file.
-nouser	Search for a file with the owner not contained with the `/etc/passwd` system file.
-ok	Prompts the user to input a positive response to continue with the specific `find` command.
-perm	Searches for a file that contains a specific file permission pattern.

Table 2-4 Find Action Commands

Command	Definition
-path	Same as −name, but the full path is used instead of the name string (HP-UX only).
-print	Causes find to print the current path name and is the default option in some versions of UNIX.
-prune	Stops find from entering a directory hierarchy.
-size	Searches for a file that is n blocks long using 512 bytes per block.
-type	Searches a specific type of file such as block special, character special, directory, or plain file.
-user	Search a specific file owned by a given system user.
-xdev	Same as the −mount command.

Table 2-4   Find Action Commands (*continued*)

Sometimes, it is not desirable to search every file system, but instead to scan only a specific one. In this case, use the −mount option to restrict the scan operation to only a single file system tree. For example, the command

```
# find /var -mount -name core -print
/core
```

will search the /var file system for all occurrences of the filename core.

Ask the Expert

Question   Why would you want to search just a specified file system?

Answer   One of the biggest reasons is that you may not want to search file systems that are mounted over the network from other systems such as NFS volumes. Searching on remote file systems can take longer if traffic on the network is high or even if the remote system is overloaded. Even if the remote file system is relatively fast, it just may not make sense to search a file system due to other considerations such as it is a NFS read-only file system or in the case of locally mounted read-only file system contained on a CD-ROM. Searching the contents of a CD-ROM that contains product documentation when you are looking for example, user files is totally a waste of time.

Now that we have a command that searches for core files, let's assume we would like to remove those files when they are found. The following command will accomplish this task:

```
# find / -name core -atime +10 -exec rm {} \;
```

It searches the system looking for core files that haven't been accessed for at least 10 days and once it finds one, it will remove it.

ls

The ls command is used to list files and/or directories within one or more file systems. The basic syntax includes

```
ls [options] [file/directory]
```

Like other UNIX commands, the ls program has a fairly large number of command-line options. However, only the most useful ones are presented in this section. These options are described and summarized in Table 2-5, and some of them are explained below.

Option	Definition
-a	List all files within a directory, including . and ..
-b	Display nonprinting characters in octal format.
-c	Use modification time when displaying files in sort order.
-C	Multicolumn output.
-d	If the file is a directory, list only its name not its subdirectories or subfiles.
-F	Mark each directory with a trailing "/" character, an "*" if file executable, "@" if symbolic link, and "|" if FIFO.
-i	For each file/directory, list its corresponding i-node number.
-l	Give more verbose output, which includes more information about file/directory attributes.

Table 2-5   ls Command-Line Options

2

Option	Definition
-L	If the file is a symbolic link, list the referenced file—not the link itself.
-R	Recursively descend and list each subdirectory.
-t	Sort by time stamp information instead of by filename.
-u	Use last file access time when displaying in sort order.
-1	Display one line for each file shown.

Table 2-5   ls Command-Line Options *(continued)*

Issuing this command in the current directory will list all files and/or directories contained with that directory. Thus, if the administrator was within the /usr directory, issuing the command would yield the following sample output:

```
# ls
4lib          games         local         perl5_readme  snadm
5bin          include       mail          platform      spool
X             java          man           preserve      src
bin           java1.1       net           proc          tmp
ccs           java1.2       news          pub           ucb
demo          kernel        old           sadm          ucbinclude
dict          kvm           openwin       sbin          ucblib
dt            lib           perl5         share         xpg4
```

The output above includes both individual files and directories, but it is difficult to draw a distinction between them because no additional information is provided. To solve this problem, we can use the −1 option, which shows a long listing of file and directory attributes. Thus, running the above command using this option produces the following:

The d at the beginning of this line shows this is a directory

```
# ls -1
total 132
drwxr-xr-x   2 root     bin       1024 Mar 16  2001 4lib
lrwxrwxrwx   1 root     root         5 Mar 16  2001 5bin -> ./bin
lrwxrwxrwx   1 root     root         9 Mar 16  2001 X -> ./openwin
 gdrwxr-xr-x  4 root     bin       8704 Jul 13 15:03 bin
```

```
drwxr-xr-x    4 root     bin          512 Mar 16  2001 ccs
drwxr-xr-x    8 root     bin          512 Mar 16  2001 demo
lrwxrwxrwx    1 root     root          16 Mar 16  2001 dict -> ./share/lib/dict
drwxrwxr-x   10 root     bin          512 Mar 16  2001 dt
drwxr-xr-x    2 root     bin          512 Mar 16  2001 games
drwxr-xr-x   23 root     bin         4096 Mar 19  2001 include
lrwxrwxrwx    1 root     other          9 Mar 16  2001 java -> ./java1.2
drwxrwxr-x    6 root     bin          512 Mar 16  2001 java1.1
drwxr-xr-x    7 root     bin          512 Mar 16  2001 java1.2
drwxr-xr-x    9 root     sys          512 Mar 16  2001 kernel
drwxr-xr-x    2 root     bin          512 Mar 16  2001 kvm
drwxr-xr-x   54 root     bin        12288 Mar 19  2001 lib
drwxr-xr-x    8 root     sys          512 Sep 25 15:24 local
lrwxrwxrwx    1 root     root          11 Mar 16  2001 mail -> ../var/mail
lrwxrwxrwx    1 root     root          11 Mar 16  2001 man -> ./share/man
drwxr-xr-x    4 root     sys          512 Mar 16  2001 net
lrwxrwxrwx    1 root     root          11 Mar 16  2001 news -> ../var/news
drwxr-xr-x    2 root     bin          512 Mar 16  2001 old
drwxr-xr-x    8 root     bin          512 Mar 16  2001 openwin
drwxr-xr-x    5 root     bin          512 Mar 16  2001 perl5
-rw-r--r--    1 root     other        104 Sep 25 18:10 perl5_readme
drwxr-xr-x   15 root     sys         1024 Mar 19  2001 platform
lrwxrwxrwx    1 root     root          15 Mar 16  2001 preserve -> ../var/preserve
drwxr-xr-x    3 root     bin          512 Mar 16  2001 proc
lrwxrwxrwx    1 root     root          15 Mar 16  2001 pub -> ./share/lib/pub
drwxr-xr-x    8 root     bin          512 Mar 16  2001 sadm
drwxr-xr-x    5 root     bin         5120 Mar 19  2001 sbin
drwxr-xr-x    6 root     sys          512 Mar 16  2001 share
drwxr-xr-x    5 root     bin          512 Mar 16  2001 snadm
lrwxrwxrwx    1 root     root          12 Mar 16  2001 spool -> ../var/spool
lrwxrwxrwx    1 root     root          11 Mar 16  2001 src -> ./share/src
lrwxrwxrwx    1 root     root          10 Mar 16  2001 tmp -> ../var/tmp
drwxr-xr-x    4 root     bin         2048 Mar 16  2001 ucb
drwxr-xr-x    4 root     bin          512 Mar 16  2001 ucbinclude
drwxr-xr-x    4 root     bin         1024 Mar 16  2001 ucblib
drwxr-xr-x    5 root     bin          512 Mar 16  2001 xpg4
```

The - at the beginning of this line shows this is a regular file

The l at the beginning of this line and the -> show this is a symbolic link

Although the output above looks quite daunting, each directory and file contains a fixed number of fields, which is illustrated by Figure 2-2.

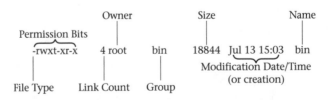

Figure 2-2 Elements of a UNIX file

As you can see, each element within the listing contains a set of file type and permission bits, a link count, ownership fields, size, modification date/time, and name. The first field represents the file type attribute, of which there are two major types. The first is a directory and the second is a regular file. A directory is defined as a special file that contains additional file elements. A directory is noted by a letter "d" in the first field. A regular file contains no flags information and contains a "–" character. The "–" character can be seen by examining the `perl5_readme` file, which is a regular text file.

UNIX supports additional file types, which are shown in Table 2-6. The block special files are used for access to hardware type devices such as disks (floppies, hardware drives, and CD-ROMs). These types of devices typically access information using a certain size, such as 8K worth of information. The character special files are used for devices such as terminals or printers where information may be output in units of a single character. The symbolic link file is simply a pointer to another file, which can span across a different file system. Both socket and pipe files are used for interprocess communication among cooperating programs so that they may share information and data.

The remaining bits of the file permission field represent the fundamental access control mechanism for the file. A total of 9 bits are used to define three levels of access that include the owner, group, and world. The owner level represents the actual username associated with the file, such as `root`. The group is the group name associated with the file, such as `other`, and the world represents everyone else defined on the system.

Within each of these levels, three additional access rights are defined as shown in Table 2-7.

File Flag	Meaning
-	No specific flag; indicates a regular text file
b	Block special file, which is used for hardware-related devices
c	Character special file, which is used for hardware-related devices
d	Directory
l	Symbolic link
s	A socket file
p	A pipe file

Table 2-6 Standard UNIX File Types

Access Bit	Meaning
r	The file is readable.
w	The file is writable.
x	The file can be executed or run as a program. If a directory, it can be searched.

Table 2-7 File Access Bits

Please note that additional access bits are supported on UNIX. These include l for mandatory locking, s for user/group set-ID, and t for sticky bit. The mandatory locking is related to the file's ability to have reading or writing permission locked while a program is accessing the file. The s indicates the file can be executed with the ownership of the file, such as root. This is a way for the administrator to give normal users access to privileged commands in a controlled way. The sticky bit provides the ability to have the file referenced more efficiently.

Each file supports access bits for three security elements for a file or directory. The first group of three denotes the owner, the next three are the group, and the final three are for others. This is shown in Figure 2-3. The administrator can use these permission bits to control access to the file. Also, the owner of the file may control these permission bits.

Each of the bits controls how the file can be accessed. When the r bit is present, the file can be read; when the w bit is present, the file is writable; and when the x bit is present, the file can be executed. In the case of a directory, the x indicates that the directory can be searched. Of course, the execution bit is only meaningful when the file represents a binary program or some type of script.

Table 2-8 contains a few examples of different file permissions that are possible with UNIX files and/or directories.

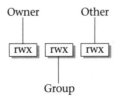

Figure 2-3 File access bits

Permission Mode	Meaning
-rw-r--r--	The file is readable/writable by the owner and only readable by the group and everyone else.
-rw-------	The file is readable/writable only by the owner.
-rw-rw----	The file is both readable/writable only by the owner and group.
-rwxr-xr-x	The file (or directory) is readable, writable, and executable by the owner and both readable/executable by the group and everyone else.
-rwx--x--x	The file (or directory) is readable, writable, and executable by the owner and only executable by the group and everyone else.

Table 2-8   Example File Permission Modes

The next field corresponds to the number of links associated with this file, and in the above example no additional links have been created. This type of link permits the creation of another file from the original, but they share the same contents of the first file. A file link appears to be another copy, but in fact it simply is a pointer to the same file. A modification to one of the files updates the other one as well. This link is known as a hard link and can't be used across different file systems. Symbolic links, as denoted with the "l" character, accomplish the same thing, but can be used across file systems. The other difference with symbolic links is that they are one-directional. The symbolically linked file points to the master file and not vice versa; the master doesn't point to the copy.

Note that several files in the above example are symbolic links and are denoted as such with the "->" string, including ../var/tmp. See Figure 2-2.

Next, the ownership fields represent both the name of the owner and group membership for the file. Both of these names should be defined within the /etc/passwd and /etc/group administrative files. If not, then just the user identification number (UID) and group identification (GID) are shown instead.

The next field shows the actual number of bytes contained within the file, which is the same as saying how much disk space is used to store the contents of the file. Typically, only with regular files does this field have meaning; all other file types (directories, for example) only contain pointers to other files or information—not user data. Administrators will use this field to determine the amount of disk space that is consumed by each file. In fact, monitoring disk space and cleaning up unneeded and/or unused files can occupy a significant amount of time if not completely automated. The next field that follows is the file modification field, and it shows when the file was last updated. The remaining file attribute is the name of the file.

One very powerful argument for the ls command is the –R option. This tells the program to recursively display all lower directories/files within a given path name. For example, consider the directory structure shown in Figure 2-4.

When the ls –R command is issued against this directory, we get

```
# ls -alR local
local:
total 4
drwxr-xr-x    2 root      other           512 Sep 25 19:09 bin
drwxr-xr-x    2 root      other           512 Sep 25 19:09 etc

local/bin:
total 854
-r-xr-xr-x    1 root      other         18844 Sep 25 19:09 ls
-rwx------    1 root      other        409600 Sep 25 19:08 ssh

local/etc:
total 2
-r--r--r--    1 root      other            97 Sep 25 19:09 hosts
```

With this example, we list a top-level directory called local, and within this directory we see two subdirectories called bin and etc. Within the bin directory, two additional files are located, and the etc directory contains a single file. If we didn't use the –R option, the ls command would have only

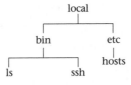

Figure 2-4 Sample directory structure

listed the top-level directory `local`, and not any additional subdirectories underneath:

```
# ls -al local
total 8
drwxr-xr-x   4 root      other        512 Sep 25 19:09 .
drwxr-xr-x   3 root      other        512 Sep 25 19:08 ..
drwxr-xr-x   2 root      other        512 Sep 25 19:09 bin
drwxr-xr-x   2 root      other        512 Sep 25 19:09 etc
```

1-Minute Drill

● Explain what it means that a symbolic link is "one-directional."

● What are the three categories of permissions for a file and what are the three possible permissions for each category?

strings

The `strings` command is used to search for ACSII strings within a software program or binary file. This command is quite helpful when you need to see within a binary file or program or if you are searching for a specific string sequence. Normally, if you were to attempt to display a binary file or program using such UNIX tools as `more` or `cat`, you would have difficulty. For example, imagine that you issue the following command to view the contents of the `ls` program:

```
# more /bin/ls
```

When this command is executed, the following output would be shown:

```
Bl°/usr/lib/ld.so.1SbEM'<]^_3
C*Z[a92/KL
```

● One-directional means that a symbolically linked file points to the master file it is a copy of, but the master file doesn't point to the symbolically linked copy.

● Categories: owner, group, others; permissions: read, write, execute.

Unfortunately, this isn't the desired result since the `more` program has trouble showing binary data to the user's display, and that is why the strange output is presented. Also, depending on the display device (that is, terminal) involved, the characters shown could lock up the terminal, which may result in the user needing to reset the device or log in from another terminal and kill their old session.

However, issuing the following `strings` command would yield the following:

```
# strings /bin/ls
SUNW_OST_OSCMD
RaAdC1xmnlogrtucpFbqisfL
usage: ls -1RaAdCxmnlogrtucpFbqisfL [files]
COLUMNS
total %llu
%llu
%3ld
%-8s
%-8lu
%-8s
%-8lu
%3ld,%3ld
 %b %e  %Y
 %b %e %H:%M
 ->
%s%s
%s%s
%-8lu
%-8lu
%10llu
%llu
%lld
%4lld
%lld
%7lld
%lld
```

Notice that this command displays all strings within the file and doesn't generate strange characters on the display. The command supports a few command line options, as listed in Table 2-9.

Command	Definition
-a	Examine the entire file, not just the initialized data area of an object file.
-n	Use the specific number as the default string length, rather than the value of 4.
-o	Abbreviated option for $-t\ d$.
-t	Display each string with a byte offset in one of the following formats: d for decimal, o for octal, and x for hexadecimal.
-v	Display version information (Linux only).

Table 2-9   Strings Command-Line Options

Ask the Expert

Question   Why display the contents of a program?

Answer   Well, one very good reason is that you might need to search for some specific information within a program that you might not be able to obtain any other way. For example, suppose you wanted to find out which files are used by a given command—say, the more program. The following command would provide that information:

```
# strings /usr/bin/more | grep /
Usage: %s [-cdflrsuw] [-lines] [+linenumber] [+/pattern]
[filename ...].
/usr/lib/locale/%s/LC_MESSAGES/more.help
/usr/lib/more.help
/usr/bin/sh
```

In this example, we search the more binary program and pipe (send the results to) the output to the grep command to search for a particular pattern. In this case, we searched for the "/" character, which is used to denote the start of a file or directory path. As you can see from the sample output, the more program uses three files.

If we are interested in knowing where in the file a specific pattern is located, we can use the −o option, which displays the byte offset from the beginning of the file. For example, the command

```
# strings -o /usr/bin/more | grep /
  25216 Usage: %s [-cdflrsuw] [-lines] [+linenumber] [+/pattern] [filename ...].
  25620 /usr/lib/locale/%s/LC_MESSAGES/more.help
  25672 /usr/lib/more.help
  27260 /usr/bin/sh
```

The numbers at the beginning of these lines show the bytes where the pattern can be found in the file

now displays the bytes where the patterns were found within the file. The −o option is an abbreviation for the −t option. This command-line option takes either d, o, or x arguments, which represent decimal, octal, or hexadecimal display values. To list the byte offset in hexadecimal, use the −t with x parameter:

```
# strings -t x /usr/bin/more | grep /
   6280 Usage: %s [-cdflrsuw] [-lines] [+linenumber] [+/pattern] [filename ...].
   6414 /usr/lib/locale/%s/LC_MESSAGES/more.help
   6448 /usr/lib/more.help
   6a7c /usr/bin/sh
```

The numbers at the beginning of these lines show the bytes (in hexadecimal format) where the pattern /usr/bin/more is found in each file

ps

The process status, or ps, command is used to report on currently executing programs or processes running on the system. System administrators will use this command to monitor the running processes on the system. Sometimes it becomes necessary to stop or kill one or more processes because they may be negatively impacting the system and affecting other processes or the general heath of the system. For example, a particular process may consume too much CPU time because it might have encountered an unexpected condition, and as a result starve other processing on the system. In this case, the administrator might need to stop this rogue process in order to permit other processes to continue or complete.

To obtain a snapshot of all the currently executing processes, use the −e command-line option. Thus,

```
# ps -e
   PID TTY         TIME CMD
     0 ?          0:07 sched
     1 ?          0:00 init
     2 ?          0:00 pageout
     3 ?          0:12 fsflush
   326 ?          0:00 sac
   340 ?          0:00 blender
   175 ?          0:00 automoun
    59 ?          0:00 sysevent
   127 ?          0:00 rpcbind
   333 ?          0:00 ttymon
   206 ?          0:00 nscd
   149 ?          0:00 inetd
   342 ?          0:00 ffssh-ag
   197 ?          0:00 cron
   189 ?          0:00 syslogd
   329 ?          0:00 sendmail
   163 ?          0:00 lockd
   164 ?          0:00 statd
   212 ?          0:00 lpsched
   225 ?          0:00 powerd
   250 ?          0:00 sh
   257 ?          0:00 cimomboo
   235 ?          0:00 utmpd
   253 ?          0:25 smanager
   259 ?          0:00 vold
   327 console    0:00 ttymon
   346 ?          0:00 stamper
   306 ?          0:00 dtlogin
   298 ?          0:00 mountd
   300 ?          0:00 nfsd
   337 ?          0:00 xntpd
   335 ?          0:00 xntpd
   317 ?          0:00 dmispd
   345 ?          0:00 ffsshd
   347 ?          0:00 in.telne
   349 pts/1      0:00 sh
```

```
389 pts/1    0:00 bash
448 pts/1    0:00 ps
```

displays a list of all the known processes in a very simple format. A total of four columns are shown that include PID, TTY, TIME, and CMD. The process identification (PID) is a reference number to help identify the process and it is assigned by the system automatically when a new program is started. The PID is a unique number and can be used to control the process. Specifically, a process may be stopped, started, killed, or sent additional signals, which can modify its behavior in some predetermined fashion. The TTY field shows which terminal device the process started from. When the system first boots, a number of standard processes are started automatically. As a result, no terminal is involved when these processes start and that is why a question mark (?) is assigned in the TTY field for most of the processes listed above. The TIME field shows how much elapsed CPU time the process has consumed. Finally, the CMD field shows the command name or process name. With HP-UX, this field is labeled as COMMAND. Typically, this will be the command name of the program, which might be a binary program or shell script.

This command has a fairly large number of command-line options. However, only the most useful ones are presented in this section. These options are described and summarized in Table 2-10 and some of them are explained below.

Command	Definition
-a	Display a listing of all of the most frequently desired processes currently active on the system (Solaris only).
-A	Display information for all processes known to the system—the same as the –e option.
-C	Select those processes executing a particular command with the name supplied after the argument (HP-UX only).
-e	Display a listing about every process currently known to the system.
-f	Display a full listing for all processes known to the system.
-g	Display only those group leader IDs that correspond to specified IDs.
-G	Display only those processes that correspond to the specified group ID.

Table 2-10   Ps Command-Line Options

2

Command	Definition
--help	Displays help screen (Linux only).
-l	Display long listing of processes that include a large amount of information.
-ps	List only those process IDs that are specified (Solaris only). HP-UX, just use $-p$ option.
-o	Format output according to specific parameters.
-t	Display only those processes that match specified terminal.
-u	Display only those processes that match effective user ID or username.
-U	Display only those processes that match real user ID or username.
-y	When -1 is used, omits the obsolete F and ADDR columns and shows an RSS column that reports the resident set size of the process in kilobytes (Solaris only).
--version	Display version information (Linux only).

Table 2-10   Ps Command-Line Options *(continued)*

The $-e$ option lists every process currently known by the system; by default, without any additional options, just an abbreviated process list is shown. To capture a full list of not only all processes, but a significant number of process attributes, use the $-f$ option. Command-line options for this command may be stacked—that is, they can be grouped together using only a single "-" symbol. So, the commands

```
ps -ef and  ps -e -f
```

are functionally the same and produce identical output, as shown in the sample output below:

```
UID    PID  PPID  C    STIME TTY      TIME CMD
root      0     0  0 06:42:05 ?       0:07 sched
root      1     0  0 06:42:05 ?       0:00 /etc/init -
root      2     0  0 06:42:05 ?       0:00 pageout
root      3     0  0 06:42:05 ?       0:00 fsflush
root    326     1  0 06:44:18 ?       0:00 /usr/lib/saf/sac -t 300
root    329     1  0 06:44:18 ?       0:00 /usr/lib/sendmail -bd -q15m
root    206     1  0 06:43:36 ?       0:00 /usr/sbin/nscd
```

```
   root     59     1  0 06:42:10 ?        0:00 /usr/lib/sysevent/syseventd
   root    212     1  0 06:43:37 ?        0:00 /usr/lib/lpsched
   root    127     1  0 06:42:14 ?        0:00 /usr/sbin/rpcbind
   root    151     1  0 06:42:15 ?        0:00 /usr/sbin/inetd -s
   root    175     1  0 06:43:35 ?        0:00 /usr/lib/autofs/automountd
   root    336   335  0 06:44:19 ?        0:00 /usr/lib/inet/xntpd
   root    197     1  0 06:43:36 ?        0:00 /usr/sbin/cron
   root    189     1  0 06:43:36 ?        0:00 /usr/sbin/syslogd
   root    163     1  0 06:42:15 ?        0:00 /usr/lib/nfs/lockd
 daemon    164     1  0 06:42:15 ?        0:00 /usr/lib/nfs/statd
   root    225     1  0 06:43:37 ?        0:00 /usr/lib/power/powerd
   root    250     1  0 06:43:38 ?        0:00 /bin/sh
   root    257     1  0 06:43:43 ?        0:00 /usr/sadm/lib/wbem/cimomboot start
   root    235     1  0 06:43:37 ?        0:00 /usr/lib/utmpd
   root    259     1  0 06:43:43 ?        0:00 /usr/sbin/vold
   root    335     1  0 06:44:19 ?        0:00 /usr/lib/inet/xntpd
   root    317     1  0 06:43:47 ?        0:00 /usr/lib/dmi/dmispd
   root    298     1  0 06:43:45 ?        0:00 /usr/lib/nfs/mountd
   root    300     1  0 06:43:45 ?        0:00 /usr/lib/nfs/nfsd -a 16
   root    307     1  0 06:43:46 ?        0:00 /usr/dt/bin/dtlogin -daemon
   root    332   326  0 06:44:18 ?        0:00 /usr/lib/saf/ttymon
   root    327     1  0 06:44:18 console  0:00 /usr/lib/saf/ttymon -g -h -p pebb
les.home.com console login:    -T vt100 -d /dev/
   root    347   151  0 06:48:15 ?        0:00 in.telnetd
   root    349   347  0 06:48:20 pts/1    0:00 -sh
   root    371   349  0 06:53:15 pts/1    0:00 ps -e -f
```

Additional columns that are displayed include: UID, PPID, C, and STIME. The UID column represents the user identification or current owner of the process. When a process is started, the user that started that process typically assumes ownership of that process. However, there are instances when a process starts that it assumes the ownership of root regardless of which user started the process.

The PPID column shows the parent process identification for each process. UNIX supports the concept of parent/child relationships within the process structure. As a result, should a process invoke additional subprocesses, they are said to be children of the master or parent process. The PPID field identifies which parent started a given process. Typically, a value of 1 means that the master program known as init started the process, when the system was first initialized or rebooted. Also, if you examine the output more closely, you will see additional processes with the PPID value of 0. These system-related processes were started by the system very early in the boot process and are vital to basic system operations.

The C field indicates an obsolete and unused scheduling flag.

The STIME fields shows when the process was started. If the process was started within a 24-hour period, it shows hours, minutes, and seconds. If the process had begun more than 24 hours before, both the month and day are given instead.

If you are interested in displaying much of the available process information for all processes running on the system, use the −1 option. This option is very useful because it provides a significant amount of detail for each process. For example, the command

```
# ps -efl
```

shows the following output:

F	S	UID	PID	PPID	C	PRI	NI	ADDR	SZ	WCHAN	TTY	TIME	CMD
19	T	0	0	0	0	0	SY	?	0		?	0:07	sched
8	S	0	1	0	0	41	20	?	98	?	?	0:00	init
19	S	0	2	0	0	0	SY	?	0	?	?	0:00	pageout
19	S	0	3	0	0	0	SY	?	0	?	?	0:00	fsflush
8	S	0	326	1	0	41	20	?	219	?	?	0:00	sac
8	S	0	329	1	0	41	20	?	365	?	?	0:00	sendmail
8	S	0	206	1	0	41	20	?	332	?	?	0:00	nscd
8	S	0	59	1	0	88	20	?	164	?	?	0:00	sysevent
8	S	0	212	1	0	59	20	?	382	?	?	0:00	lpsched
8	S	0	127	1	0	41	20	?	278	?	?	0:00	rpcbind
8	S	0	151	1	0	59	20	?	297	?	?	0:00	inetd
8	S	0	175	1	0	41	20	?	367	?	?	0:00	automoun
8	S	0	336	335	0	0	RT	?	268	?	?	0:00	xntpd
8	S	0	197	1	0	49	20	?	238	?	?	0:00	cron
8	S	0	189	1	0	89	20	?	412	?	?	0:00	syslogd
8	S	0	342	253	0	41	20	?	222	?	?	0:00	ffssh-ag
8	S	0	163	1	0	59	20	?	234	?	?	0:00	lockd
8	S	1	164	1	0	50	20	?	336	?	?	0:00	statd
8	S	0	345	253	0	47	20	?	306	?	?	0:00	ffsshd
8	S	0	225	1	0	69	20	?	171	?	?	0:00	powerd
8	S	0	250	1	0	99	20	?	130	?	?	0:00	sh
8	S	0	257	1	0	49	20	?	199	?	?	0:00	cimomboo
8	S	0	235	1	0	40	20	?	127	?	?	0:00	utmpd
8	S	0	253	250	1	41	20	?	1008	?	?	0:29	smanager
8	S	0	259	1	0	51	20	?	326	?	?	0:00	vold
8	S	0	335	1	0	0	RT	?	268	?	?	0:00	xntpd
8	S	0	340	253	0	40	20	?	289	?	?	0:00	blender
8	S	0	317	1	0	57	20	?	381	?	?	0:00	dmispd
8	S	0	298	1	0	69	20	?	334	?	?	0:00	mountd
8	S	0	300	1	0	46	20	?	233	?	?	0:00	nfsd
8	S	0	307	1	0	59	20	?	614	?	?	0:00	dtlogin
8	S	0	346	253	0	67	20	?	231	?	?	0:00	stamper

8	S	0	332	326	0	41	20	?	219	? ?	0:00 ttymon
8	S	0	327	1	0	61	20	?	218	? console	0:00 ttymon
8	S	0	347	151	0	54	20	?	223	? ?	0:00 in.telne
8	R	0	349	347	0	51	20	?	38	pts/1	0:00 sh
8	O	0	412	349	0	41	20	?	235	pts/1	0:00 ps

This command option shows additional columns that include F, S, PRI, NI, ADDR, SZ, and WCHAN. The F field is not used and should be ignored. The S field shows the state of the process and contains one of several different flags, as shown in Table 2-11.

It is interesting to note that during the life of a process, it can bounce between one or more states in a relatively short period of time. Depending on the activities of the system and other factors that impact system load, a process can toggle between the S and O states. Generally speaking, most processes remain in the S state since on a uniprocessor system, a single process is running at any given point in time. A zombie is a process for which the parent is no longer waiting for the process to terminate and as a result, can't be terminated normally. Given the right circumstances, one or more zombie processes can be created that are largely due to software defects with certain applications. When this happens, the process (or application) can't be killed using the kill program. Instead, the system must be rebooted to clear these processes.

State Flag	Meaning
O	The process is running.
S	The process is in sleep state, waiting for an event to complete.
R	The process is in the run queue.
Z	The process has terminated abnormally; the parent is not waiting for this process to finish. This is known as a zombie process.
T	The process has stopped either by a signal (via the kill command or job control) or because the process is being traced.

Table 2-11 Process Status Flags

2

uname

The `uname` command displays more detailed information and characteristics about the system. It can be used to determine basic operating system information, such as

- The O/S version and name

- The name of the system

- Computer hardware type

- Hardware processor type

   When this command is executed without any command-line options, the name of the operating system is displayed. For example, typing

```
# uname
SunOS
```

on a Solaris system will yield the operating system name of SunOS. One of the most popular options, `-a`, is used to display basic information in a concise form. Thus,

```
# uname -a
SunOS pebbles.home.com 5.8 Generic_108528-06 sun4u sparc
SUNW,UltraAX-i2
```

shows a string which contains series of fields. The first field is the name of the operating system, as shown in the previous example. Next, the fully qualified hostname of the system is displayed, which is the same information as shown from the `hostname` command. The third field is the name of the currently installed kernel. The fourth field displays the machine hardware (class) name as defined by the computer system vendor. The fifth field is the type of computer processor. The above example shows that the system is based on Sun's Sparc architecture. If this command were run on a Solaris Intel platform, it would display a processor type of `i686`. The final field shows the hardware platform information, which gives more information about the system architecture or processor type.

The uname command is very useful to the system administrator because each of the fields listed above can be obtained separately from all other fields by using command-line options. Table 2-12 shows the available command-line options for this command.

To display just the hostname of the system, use the −n option:

```
# uname −n
pebbles.home.com
```

If you are interested in just seeing the name of the operating system, use the −s option:

```
# uname −s
SunOS
```

Command	Definition
-a	Displays basic information about the system.
-I	Displays the hardware platform information such as Sparc or i386. For HP-UX, display the system identification number.
-l	Display operating license information (HP-UX only).
-m	Displays the system hardware name or class of machine.
-n	Displays the hostname of the system.
-p	Displays the current processor type (Solaris and Linux only).
-r	Displays the operating system revision number or level.
-s	Displays the name of the operating system such as SunOS, HP-UX, or Linux.
-S	Used to change the hostname of the system.
-v	Displays kernel/system version information.
-X	Displays system information in concise format separated by equal signs (Solaris only).

Table 2-12 uname Command-Line Options

Hint

The -s option on certain releases of Solaris doesn't actually work. This option does change the name of the host, once the system is rebooted, the old name still applies. This is because the uname command doesn't update the /etc/nodename file, which stores the system hostname.

Unlike the other operating systems, Solaris provides one additional option (-X), which can be used to display more concise information about the system in a format that is more suitable for parsing with a shell script. Thus, the command

```
# uname -X
```

would make it very easy to parse the output of uname with a shell script because the information is separated by a command character, which is the = (equals) sign as shown below:

```
System = SunOS
Node = pebbles.home.com
Release = 5.8
KernelID = Generic_108528-06
Machine = sun4u
BusType = <unknown>
Serial = <unknown>
Users = <unknown>
OEM# = 0
Origin# = 1
NumCPU = 1
```

With HP-UX, the -l and -i options are supported. The -i option displays the system identification number, or the node name if the ID can't be determined. The -l argument is used to display software license information. Thus, the command

```
uname -a
```

is a shorthand way of listing the fields from the following arguments: -s, -n, -r, -v, -m, -i, and -l.

This would yield output similar to

```
HP-UX socrates B.11.00 U 9000/800 545770578 unlimited-user license
```

The last two fields correspond to the $-i$ (545770578) and $-l$ (unlimited-user license) fields accordingly.

Project 2-1

This project will familiarize you with the commands from this module and give you firsthand experience with them on your own system.

Step-by-Step

1. At the default shell prompt, type the following command to determine your system's operating system name, hostname, currently installed kernel name, machine hardware (class) name, processor type, and hardware platform information. You'll want to remember this in case your operating system supports special commands or options mentioned in this book.

```
# uname -a
```

2. Use the who command to determine all the users logged onto the system:

```
# who
```

3. Determine what user you are currently logged on as using this command:

```
# who am i
```

4. List the files in the current directory, including file attribute information:

```
# ls -l
```

5. From the list of files, display the smallest normal file onscreen:

```
# cat filename
```

6. Find all the files on your system that belong to the admin group and list them:

```
# find / -group admin
```

7. Display all the currently running processes on your system that belong to you:

```
# ps -u yourusername
```

☑ *Mastery Check*

2

1. Which of the following is not a UNIX shell?

   A. sh

   B. csh

   C. bash

   D. ps

2. What is the command and option syntax to list a text file's contents, numbering each line but not numbering blank lines?

3. What is the command and option to change the system date and time to October 4, 2002 3:30 P.M.?

4. What command do you use just to display a UNIX system's name?

   A. fqdn

   B. ps

   C. hostname

   D. system

5. What command and option syntax would you use to find all the files on your system you haven't accessed in the last year?

6. What kind of file and what permissions does this set of attributes indicate: drwxr-x--x?

7. Which of the following user types' permissions are not defined by the 9-bit permission attributes?

   A. Administrator

   B. Owner

   C. Group

   D. Others

☑ *Mastery Check*

8. What does the ? in the following command output indicate?

```
# ps -ef

   UID   PID  PPID  C    STIME TTY      TIME CMD
   root    0     0  0 06:42:05 ?       0:07 sched
   root    1     0  0 06:42:05 ?       0:00 /etc/init -
```

9. What command do you use to display a system's operating system revision number?

Module 3

Using System Administration Tools

Critical Skills

This section reviews how to perform specific UNIX administration tasks such as adding new users to the system. As such, it is more procedure oriented versus providing complicated details about the underlying structure of configuration files or low-level system function. As the system administrator, it will be very important that you know which tools to use for a given system administration function or task. Also, it would be very good for the tools available to be easy to use in order to help you to be very effective. Sometimes UNIX tools are not easy to use, nor are they documented very well. However, as with most versions of UNIX available today, one or more general-purpose GUI-based administration tools are available—either with the basic operating system or they can be installed after the operating system has been set up. For example, the Solaris system provides the admintool program, which can be used to accomplish a variety of important system administration tasks.

This module reviews the following tools:

```
admintool (Solaris)
control-panel (Linux)
sam (HP-UX)
```

Generally, these utilities provide a large number of functions; however, only the addition and modification of users, accounts will be reviewed.

The tools described in this section share common features: They were designed to be used by administrators with little experience, and they can perform important system administration tasks. These tools are most useful when used against a single system, or in a situation where many systems are networked to use a single set of system files on a single host and the tools are used against that single host—in other words, in a computing environment where the system account files (/etc/passwd, /etc/group, and /etc/shadow) are locally available and maintained. Additional configuration is necessary where Network Information Services (NIS) or some other authentication mechanism is used in conjunction with these local account files. See Module 15 on NIS for more specific information.

Each of the administration tools is a GUI-based program that uses the X-Window system to display a series of windows for each administrative function they support. In order to run this command, you will need an X-Window- compliant workstation, such as a Sun workstation or X-terminal, or a personal computer running some X-Window-compatible software. Note, the HP-UX sam tool also supports basic CRT displays as well; thus, an X-Window system is not required. A very good X-Window-based software package for UNIX and the PC is called VNC. This package is available on the Internet and you can consult Appendix A for additional information. You must also set the DISPLAY environment variable to the workstation you want the application windows to appear.

Hint

Since VNC is a shareware package, it may not be acceptable to use such software in certain corporate environments.

3

3.1 Managing Solaris Using Admintool

To invoke the admintool command, simply type the following on the command line:

```
# admintool&
```

Once this command is run, it will display the base window, as shown in Figure 3-1. This window contains a total of four menu items: File, Edit, Browse, and Help. When the window first appears, it shows a scrollable list of defined users that are contained within the /etc/passwd file.

The Browse menu contains a number of items that correspond to the specific system administration tasks that the application supports. Table 3-1 lists the Browse menu items and their associated functions. Selecting one of the items within this menu causes the application to redisplay the main window with information associated with the menu item.

For example, clicking the Groups item, cause the main window to display a scrollable list of the all the groups defined within the /etc/group file.

Add a New User

To add a new user to the system, use the following procedure:

1. From the Browse Menu, select the Users item.

2. From the Edit Menu, select the Add item. This will cause another window, labeled Admintool: Add User, to appear, as shown in Figure 3-2.

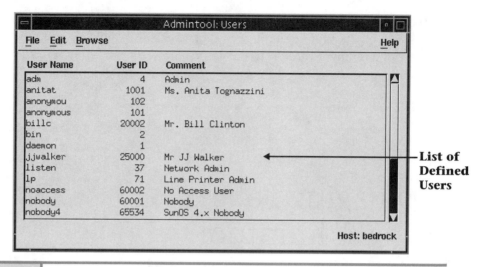

┌───┐
│ ▭   Admintool: Users   □ □ │
├───┤
│ File   Edit   Browse   Help │
│   │
│ User Name   User ID   Comment   │
│ ┌──┐▲ │
│ │adm   4   Admin   │ │
│ │anitat   1001   Ms. Anita Tognazzini   │ │
│ │anonymou   102   │ │
│ │anonymous   101   │ │
│ │billc   20002   Mr. Bill Clinton   │ │
│ │bin   2   │ │
│ │daemon   1   │ │
│ │jjwalker   25000   Mr JJ Walker   ◄──────┼──── List of
│ │listen   37   Network Admin   │   Defined
│ │lp   71   Line Printer Admin   │   Users
│ │noaccess   60002   No Access User   │ │
│ │nobody   60001   Nobody   │ │
│ │nobody4   65534   SunOS 4.x Nobody   │▼ │
│ └──┘ │
│   Host: bedrock │
└───┘

Figure 3-1   Main admintool window

The window that appears is used to add a new user to the system and contains a semiblank form of text box for which the administrator must input information about the new user. This window contains three sections: User Identity, Account Security, and Home Directory. In general, most of the Account Security options are optional, while the other sections are required and must be completed in order to create a valid UNIX user. The user identity section contains the following input fields: User Name, User ID, Primary Group, Secondary Groups, and Comment, which are typical elements for a UNIX account.

Enter the Account Username

The username is the name of the UNIX account, which should represent the name of the user or purpose of the account. Typically, the name may contain

Users	Create/modify system users.
Groups	Create /modify system groups.
Host	Create/modify the entries in the /etc/hosts file.
Printers.	Create/modify system printers.
Serial Ports	Configure serial interfaces.
Software	Administer packages for the system.

Table 3-1   Browser Menu Items

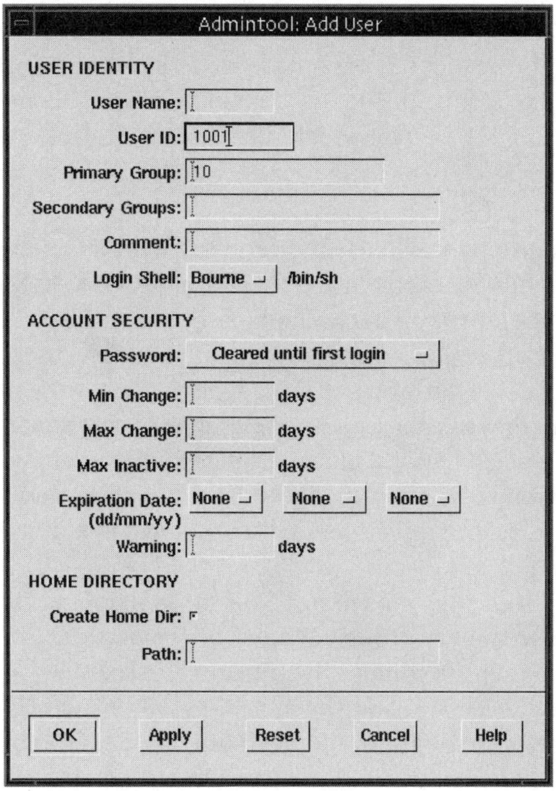

3

┌───┐
│   Admintool: Add User   │
├───┤
│ USER IDENTITY   │
│   │
│   User Name: [   ]   │
│   User ID: [1001]   │
│   Primary Group: [10]   │
│   Secondary Groups: [   ]   │
│   Comment: [   ]   │
│   Login Shell: Bourne ⏷ /bin/sh   │
│   │
│ ACCOUNT SECURITY   │
│   Password: Cleared until first login ⏷   │
│   Min Change: [   ] days   │
│   Max Change: [   ] days   │
│   Max Inactive: [   ] days   │
│   Expiration Date: None ⏷   None ⏷   None ⏷   │
│   (dd/mm/yy)   │
│   Warning: [   ] days   │
│ HOME DIRECTORY   │
│   Create Home Dir: ▢   │
│   Path: [   ]   │
│   │
│ [OK]   [Apply]   [Reset]   [Cancel] [Help] │
└───┘

Figure 3-2 | New User window

letters of the alphabet, plus numbers, and is usually limited to eight characters in length. Many sites use the first initial, middle initial, and last name for the account name if it represents an actual person. Thus, Bill Jefferson Clinton would have the associated UNIX login of bjclinton. If the total number of users on the system is quite small, it is possible to simply use the first name of the user as the account name. Obviously, if a site has more then one person named bill, this approach will be a problem. As an alternative, the first name plus last name initial could be used. So, using our previous example, the new account would be billc. This approach has been used at many sites. If the account doesn't represent a real person—but a group, for example—then names like support, sales, or eng may be acceptable. Bear in mind that group type accounts, where multiple individuals share a single account, are not a very good way to go since you lose the ability to know for certain who is really using the account at any given time.

Enter the User ID

This field represents the identification number associated with the User Name field; the application obtains the next available number. This number is used to track the activity and to associate which files this particular account owns.

Enter the Primary Group ID

Input the primary group for which this account will be a member. Either the group name or ID number can be used. Groups are used to define a class of users that may have something in common. Groups can help control access to both programs and other files on the system. For example, users from the same department or those that perform the same type of job may be members of the same group, where they need access to one or more text or database files. On a new system, only a small handful of standard groups are defined and are usually related to system groups. As a result, you will need to create additional user groups when additional groups are needed. See below for additional information on group creation.

If you have additional groups defined on the system and the user should have one or more secondary groups defined by the account, simply list them in the Secondary Groups text box. The purpose of secondary groups is to further provide user access to additional groups, since each UNIX account may only have one primary group membership. Note that in both the Primary Group and Secondary Group text boxes, an integer is required, not the string name of the group.

Enter a Comment about the Account

Every account can have some associated free text that can be used to explain the purpose of the account or establish the true identity of the account holder. Since this field is simply a string of text, any important information may be included. For example, the field is often used to store the real full name of the account holder, such as `Steve Maxwell's Account` or `The Department's Pager Account`.

Select a Login Shell

The Login Shell field is used to specify which command interpreter should be started when the user logs in to the system. The selection list contains four different choices: Bourne, C, Korn shells, and Other. Using the Other classification permits the inclusion of the path name of an alternative shell. The administrator simply inputs the location of the shell.

3

Select the Desired Password Option

The admintool program permits the administrator to control the access to the account with one of four options as listed and defined in Table 3-2.

Simply choosing the default (thus, no change to the selection field is needed), Cleared Until First Login, means that once the user has logged into the system for the first time, they will be required to change their password before general access to the system is granted. This option is most useful because it permits the administrator to define a standard temporary password for each user—and once the user has accessed the system, they will change their password to their own liking. Note that should the administrator wish to disable a UNIX account, they simply update the Password text field with the Account Is Locked option. This will stop the account from being accessed because it alters the password information. When the user attempts to access this account with this option, they get a permission denied response.

Input the Home Directory Path

The remaining element that needs to be included is the path to the user's home directory. This is the location on a file system where the user will store files and obtain account configuration information. Note that a Create Home Dir check box has been provided if the directory doesn't presently exist.

Selecting the OK Button Will Create This UNIX Account

Any errors will be displayed in a separate dialog box.

Please note: Many administrators copy certain environmental configuration files to the user's home directory as this point. These configuration files may include, for example, a startup file for the shell and other installed utilities. Also, the system recognizes special initialization files, which can be used to

Account Option	Meaning
Cleared Until First Login	No password is assigned to the account until the user first logs in to the system and is prompted automatically for a password.
Account Is Locked	Disables access to the UNIX account.
No Password – Setuid Only	No password is assigned to the account, which is generally not used.
Normal Password	The admintool prompts for a standard password when the account is created.

Table 3-2   Account Security Options

customize the user's environment. Among these files are the `.login` and `.profile` files, for example. The `.login` file is one of the first configuration files executed when the user first logs in to the system. The `.profile` file contains a free format of text that can be used to describe more about the user of the account, such as the projects they are working on and other related information. Using the UNIX `.finger` command will display the contents of the `.profile` file associated with the user.

UNIX Account Example

The following section has been provided to further demonstrate using the "admintool to add a new user to the system. Figure 3-3 shows the Admintool: Add User window with the required text fields filled in.

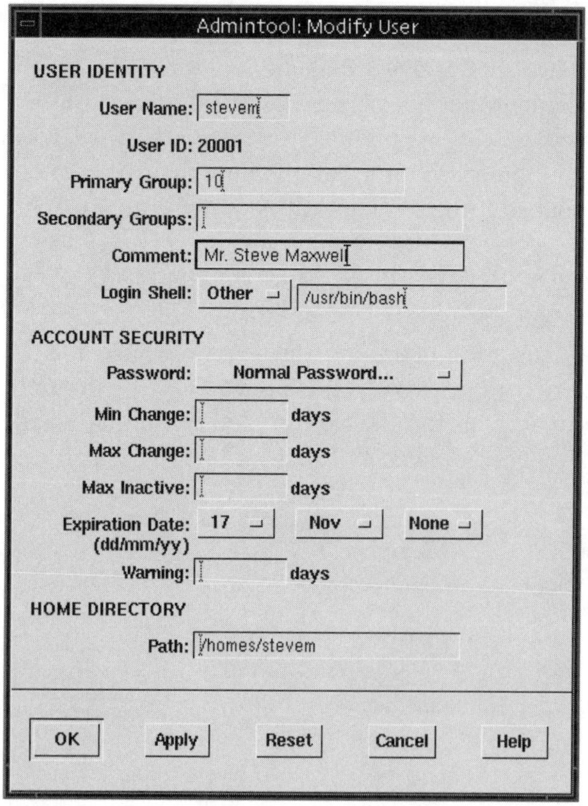

Figure 3-3   Sample UNIX account

As you can see, the account called stevem has input with all the required and associated fields completed. Note the use of the Other category for the login shell. In this case, the user has been set up to use the bash shell instead of the other available shells.

We can verify to make sure that the stevem account has been added to the system as expected. Execute the following command to list the account information:

```
# grep stevem /etc/passwd /etc/group
```

The grep command searches the string stevem in both the /etc/passwd and /etc/group files. If the user account was added successfully, the following output should be displayed and should match the information that was displayed in Figure 3-3.

```
/etc/passwd:stevem:x:20001:101:Steve Maxwell's Account:/homes/stevem:/usr/bin/bash
/etc/group:betagrp::104:stevem
```

Also, you can inspect that the home directory was created as well. Thus, to determine that a directory exists, type the following:

```
# ls -ald /homes/stevem
drwxr-xr-x   2 stevem    dev           512 Oct 22 13:01 /homes/stevem
```

Using the -d option of the ls command, you can show a directory without having to issue the change directory command (cd) or list the contents of it. As you can see, the directory is owned by the stevem, and the group ownership is configured to be dev, which matches our sample account.

Modifying a User

The admintool is also used to make a variety of changes to user accounts that have already been established on the system. To make a modification to an existing account, do the following:

1. Select an account name from the scrollable list and access the Modify… menu item from the Edit Menu.

2. Or, double-click the account name.

Once done, the user account information will be displayed in new window labeled Admintools: Modify User. Just about all account information can be altered using this window. However, the one notable exception is the User ID field. Figure 3-4 shows an example account named `billc`. As you can see, the User ID field is not editable and thus can't be altered using `admintool`.

3. Make the necessary modification(s).

4. Select the OK button to save the changes.

If you want to actually alter the user ID of an existing account, you will have to edit the `/etc/passwd` file directly by hand. However, if the account is new, another approach is that you can delete the user from the system and reenter the account information using the new user ID. This user is considered bad practice if the account was older and contained existing files, and you just randomly changed this account information. Since the ownership of any existing files would remain with the older user ID, the administrator would have to change the ownership of these files to reflect the new user information.

Deleting a User

Deleting an existing user is very easy. However, care should be taken when doing so since the `admintool` has the capability of removing the user's directory. To remove a user, do the following:

1. Select an account name from the scrollable list and access the Delete menu item from the Edit menu.

2. You will be presented a dialog box, as shown in Figure 3-4.

Hint

Exercise extreme caution when removing users; as an important step in account removal, backing up home directories to secondary storage is a requirement. Even if you have a relatively new backup, it is very important that a fresh copy be made to capture any files/directories that have been modified after the last backup was taken.

| **Figure 3-4** | Delete User warning message |

Clicking the Delete button will remove the account entry from the system. Also, if you select the Delete Home Directory check box, the home directory will be removed as well.

3. Once you have determined that, in fact, the account has been backed up and can be removed, select the Delete button.

If you choose to remove an existing account without deleting the home directory, then the home directory and any files underneath will be owned by the user that assumes the previous user's ID or just the user ID number. For example, consider the account name of billc with the user ID of 20002. Before the account is removed, the directory and associated files might look like this:

```
# ls -al /homes/billc
total 1370
drwxr-xr-x   2 billc    exec        512 Oct 22 15:30 .
drwxr-xr-x   4 root     other       512 Oct 22 15:29 ..
-rw-r--r--   1 billc    exec        338 Oct 22 15:30 .login
-rw-r--r--   1 billc    exec        582 Oct 22 15:29 .profile
-rw-r--r--   1 billc    exec     192411 Oct 22 15:29 figure3_1
-rw-r--r--   1 billc    exec     230477 Oct 22 15:29 figure3_2
-rw-r--r--   1 billc    exec     230477 Oct 22 15:29 figure3_3
-rw-r--r--   1 billc    exec        338 Oct 22 15:29 sig
```

However, after the account has been removed (but not the home directory), the files will now look like this:

```
# ls -al /homes/billc
total 1370
drwxr-xr-x   2 20002    exec         512 Oct 22 15:30 .
drwxr-xr-x   4 root     other        512 Oct 22 15:29 ..
-rw-r--r--   1 20002    exec         338 Oct 22 15:30 .login
-rw-r--r--   1 20002    exec         582 Oct 22 15:29 .profile
-rw-r--r--   1 20002    exec      192411 Oct 22 15:29 figure3_1
-rw-r--r--   1 20002    exec      230477 Oct 22 15:29 figure3_2
-rw-r--r--   1 20002    exec      230477 Oct 22 15:29 figure3_3
-rw-r--r--   1 20002    exec         338 Oct 22 15:29 sig
```

billc replaced with 20002

The reason for this is that within UNIX, the ownership of the directories and files use the user identification number—not the name—and in this case, 20002 is the numerical identification for the account billc. UNIX maps the name of the account with the defined user ID within the /etc/passwd file. So, when this mapping is broken—that is, the account name has been removed from the /etc/passwd file—UNIX no longer knows how to map the name and just displays the actual account ID instead. Note also that the group name remains intact. However, should we remove the exec group from the /etc/group file, we would encounter a similar mapping problem where only the group ID number will be displayed.

Adding a New Group

The primary purpose of a group is to associate similar users together to make it easier for those users to share information. Groups are defined with the /etc/group file and contain a mapping between a group name and all members of that particular group. To create a new UNIX group, do the following:

1. Select the Groups menu item from the Browser menu. A list of defined groups will be displayed in a scrollable list, as shown in Figure 3-5.

2. Select the Add menu item from the Edit menu. At this point, a new window appears labeled Admintool: Add Group, as shown in Figure 3-6.

This window contains three text boxes: Group Name, Group ID, and Members List. All of the text fields must be filled in before a new group may

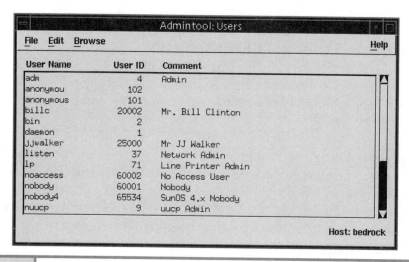

Figure 3-5 Admintool Groups window

be added to the system. Note that the Group ID field has been automatically updated with the next-higher numeric value as derived from the /etc/group file.

Enter the Group Name

The group name is simply the name of the group you wish to define. Like the UNIX account name, the group name is also limited to just eight characters. The group name can be any string that represents a collection of users. For example, the group name of devel can represent the development staff within a particular department. Choose a group name and enter the string within the Group Name text box.

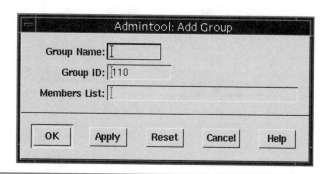

Figure 3-6 List of Groups window

Accept the Default Group ID Number or Alter It to Match Your Requirements

The group ID number can range from 1 to 2137483647. In practice, the number of groups defined on a given system can be quite small—say, fewer than 100. Therefore, it is reasonable to start numbering group IDs after the 100 starting point.

Input the Group Members

The Members List text box is used to input all the existing account names that should be a part of this group. You must use commas to separate each of the account names. Please note that `Admintool` is quite finicky about the use of white spaces when more than one string is supplied. As a result, when inputting more than one account name, don't include spaces between the names. For example, consider the following group member lists:

Wrong:

```
Members List: stevem, anitat, irinav,samyu
```

Correct:

```
Members List: stevem,anitat,irinav,samyu
```

If you use spaces when entering multiple strings, `Admintool` will display an error message similar to that shown in Figure 3-6. Just click the OK button and remove the spaces between each group name.

Figure 3-7   Admintool error regarding white spaces

Modifying a Group

Making changes to a group is similar to making a changes to an established UNIX account name. To make a modification to an existing group, do the following:

1. While the groups are being displayed within the "Admintool main window, select a group name from the scrollable list and access the Modify menu item from the Edit menu.

2. Or, double-click the group name.

3. Modify the group member information.

4. Apply the changes.

Deleting a Group

Deleting an existing user is also similar to deleting an existing UNIX account. As an added safeguard, just like deleting an existing UNIX account, `Admintool` prompts before actually deleting a predefined group.

1-Minute Drill

● Why is the Cleared Until First Login option useful when creating new UNIX user accounts?

● What is the important step to take before deleting a user?

● It is useful because it permits the administrator to define a standard temporary password for each user—and once the user has accessed the system, they will change their password to their own liking.

● Back up all the associated files and directories for the user.

3.2 Manage Linux Accounts with Userconf

Based on the X-Windows system, the `userconf` tool provides a GUI facility for managing both user and group accounts on a Linux system. This tool can be invoked two ways. First, it can be started from the `linuxconf` application. Clicking the Users Account selection tab will start the `userconf` tool. The second way is from the command line. To start this application, issue the following command:

```
userconf&
```

Using either approach, the `userconf` application window will appear. Shown in Figure 3-8, this main window contains four selection tabs and several functional buttons, and is labeled User Account Configurator. The tabs include Normal, Special Accounts, Email Aliases, and Policies. The Normal tab, which is shown by default, provides access to create what are considered normal UNIX users and groups. Also, the `root` account password can be changed.

The Special Accounts tab is used to create application specific or special accounts such as PPP/SLIP, UUCP, and POP accounts for mail. They are special because they are used for a particular purpose to support a system service, unlike general login accounts. The Email Aliases tab is used to set up aliases related to electronic e-mail such as with `sendmail`. The Policies tab provides access to define UNIX account policies such as the default base for home directories and minimum length for passwords.

Add a New User

To add a new user to the system, use the following procedure:

Click the User Accounts Button

This is next to the single penguin. Once this is done, a new window is displayed as shown in Figure 3-9.

3

Figure 3-8   Main userconf window

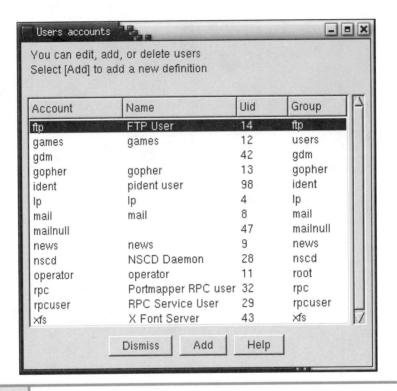

Figure 3-9   Users Accounts window

Click the Add Button on the Users Accounts Window

This is the middle button located at the bottom of the window. When you click it, another window called the User Account Creation window is presented, as shown in Figure 3-10.

> **Hint**
>
> This window contains four selection tabs: Base Info, Params, Mail Settings, and Privileges. The Base Info tab is used to begin the login creation process.

Input the UNIX Login Name

The login name is the name of the UNIX account, which should represent the name of the user or purpose of the account. Typically, the name may contain letters of the alphabet and numbers, and is usually limited to eight characters in length. Many sites use the first initial, middle initial, and last name for the account name if it represents an actual person. Thus, George W. Bush would

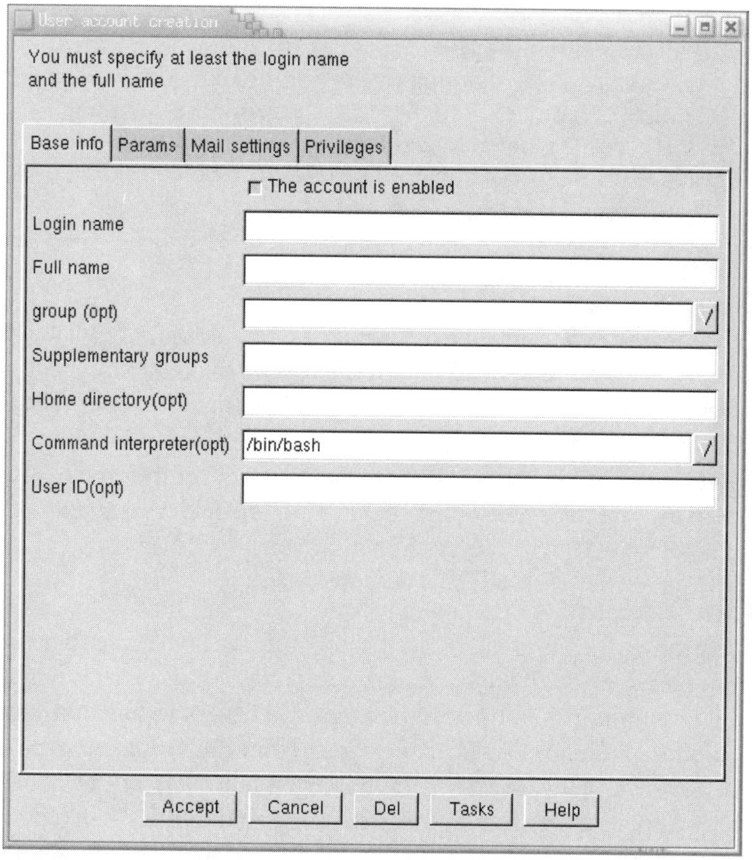

```
┌────────────────────────────────────────────────────────┐
│ ▢ User account creation                        _ □ ✕    │
│  You must specify at least the login name                │
│  and the full name                                       │
│                                                          │
│  Base info │ Params │ Mail settings │ Privileges          │
│ ┌────────────────────────────────────────────────────┐ │
│ │                    ▢ The account is enabled          │ │
│ │  Login name        [                              ]  │ │
│ │  Full name         [                              ]  │ │
│ │  group (opt)       [                            ][▾] │ │
│ │  Supplementary groups [                           ]  │ │
│ │  Home directory(opt)  [                           ]  │ │
│ │  Command interpreter(opt) [/bin/bash            ][▾] │ │
│ │  User ID(opt)      [                              ]  │ │
│ │                                                      │ │
│ └────────────────────────────────────────────────────┘ │
│                                                          │
│   [ Accept ]  [ Cancel ]  [ Del ]  [ Tasks ]  [ Help ]  │
└────────────────────────────────────────────────────────┘
```

Figure 3-10   User Account Creation window

have the associate UNIX login of gwbush. If the total number of users on
the system is quite small, it is possible to simply use the first name of the user
as the account name. Obviously, if a site has more than one person named
george, this approach will be a problem. As an alternative, the first name
plus last name initial could be used. So, using our previous example, the new
account would be georgeb. This approach has been used at many sites. If the
account doesn't represent a real person—but a group, for example—then names
like support, sales, or eng may be acceptable. Bear in mind that group
type accounts, where multiple individuals share a single account, are not a very
good way to go since you lose the ability to know for certain who is really using
the account at any given time.

Hint

Some of the fields within the User Account Creation window are optional, as depicted with the (opt) string next to the text box label. If you leave these fields blank, they will be assigned default or appropriate values. For example, if you leave the Home Directory field empty, the default base directory of /home plus the username will be used instead. The default home directory base can be altered under the Policies tab.

Add the Full Name of the User

The Full Name field represents the actual name of the account holder. This field corresponds to the Comment field within the password file. Every account can have some associated free text that can be used to explain the purpose of the account or establish the true identify of the account holder. Since this field is simply a string of text, any important information may be included. For example, the field is often used to store the real full name of the account holder, such as James Bond's Account or The MIS department's Pager Account.

Select the Account Group

Select the primary group for which this account will be a member using the pop-up menu. Groups are used to define a class of users that may have something in common. Groups can help control access to both programs and other files on the system. For example, users from the same department or those that perform that same type of job may be members of the same group, where they need access to one or more text or database files. On a new system, only a small handful of standard groups are defined and are usually related to system groups. As a result, you will need to create additional user groups when additional groups are needed. See the following section for additional information on group creation.

Add Additional Group Memberships

If you have additional groups defined on the system and the user should have one or more secondary groups defined by the account, simply list them in the Supplementary Groups text box. The purpose of secondary groups is to further provide user access to additional groups since each UNIX account may only have one primary group membership.

Add the Home Directory

This field defines the location of the home directory for the user. This is the location on a file system where the user will store files and obtain account configuration information.

3

Select the Login Shell

The Command Interpreter field is used to specify which command shell should be started when the user logs in to the system. The selection list contains several different choices that include /bin/bash (bash shell), /bin/sh (Bourne shell), and /bin/csh (C shell). If you have an alternative shell, you can simply input the absolute path in the text box.

Input the User ID

This field represents the identification number associated with the login name and the application obtains the next available number. This number is used to track the activity and to associate which files this particular account owns.

Hint

If you want to disable a newly created account, deselect the The Account Is Enabled selection box. This action causes the userconf tool to place a login expiration date within the /etc/shadow file.

Click the Accept Button.

You will then be prompted for the account password when the Changing Password dialog box is displayed, as shown in Figure 3-11.

Enter the Password

Enter the password for this account. If no errors occurred, the new account will be added to the list of accounts within the Users Accounts window.

Figure 3-11   The Changing Password dialog box

Modifying a User

The `userconf` tool can be used to make a variety of changes to user accounts that have already been established on the system. To make a modification to an existing account, do the following:

1. Click on the User Accounts button in the User Account Configurator main window. The User Accounts window that contains a list of the defined users will be displayed, as in Figure 3-12.

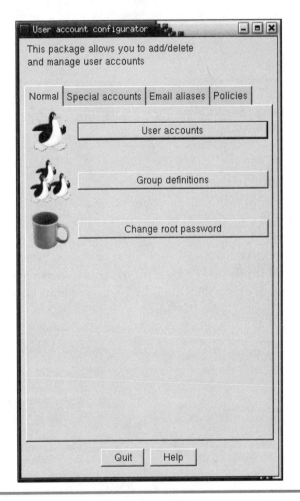

Figure 3-12   User Account Configurator window

2. Select the account you wish to modify by clicking it. A new window displaying the account information is displayed, as shown in Figure 3-13. In this example, the user account `sjmaxwell` has been selected.

3. Make the appropriate account change and then click the Accept button. For instance, change the default login shell to `/bin/csh`.

3

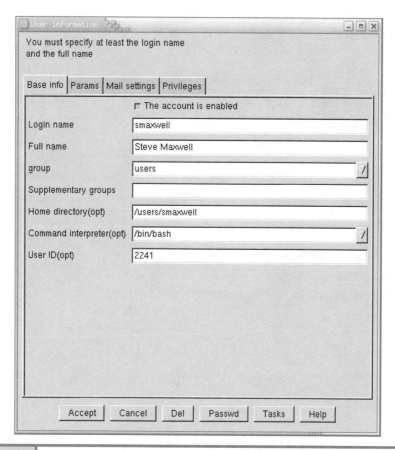

| User information | _ □ ✕ |

You must specify at least the login name
and the full name

| Base info | Params | Mail settings | Privileges |

⬜ The account is enabled

Login name	smaxwell
Full name	Steve Maxwell
group	users ▽
Supplementary groups	
Home directory(opt)	/users/smaxwell
Command interpreter(opt)	/bin/bash ▽
User ID(opt)	2241

| Accept | Cancel | Del | Passwd | Tasks | Help |

Figure 3-13 User information for the sjmaxwell account

Delete an Existing User

To delete an existing user from the system, use the following procedure:

1. Click on the User Accounts button in the User Account Configurator main window.

2. Click the account entry in the User Accounts window that you wish to delete. By way of example, assume we would like to remove the `gwbush` account. Clicking a user account causes the User Information window to appear, as shown in Figure 3-14 for that account.

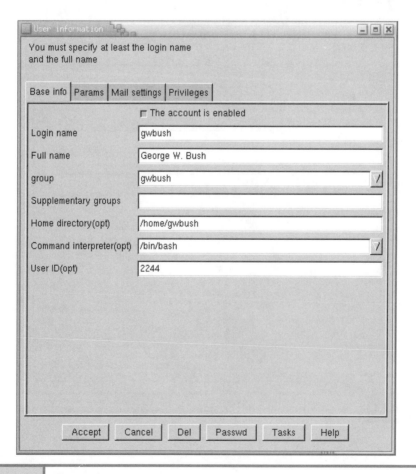

Figure 3-14 User Information window

3. Click the Del button and another window asking for more information about how to delete the account will be displayed, as shown in Figure 3-15. In the example, the account of gwbush will be deleted.

The Delete Account window contains three selection items: Archive the Account's Data, Delete the Account's Data, and Leave the Account's Data in Place. The default, Archive the Account's Data, will make a copy of the files stored in the home directory and the mailbox file of the user and then delete the account. The userconf tool builds a compressed tar archive of the home directory (and contents) and places it in the /home/oldaccounts directory.

The Delete the Account's Data option will delete the home directory and all associated files and then delete the account. The Leave the Account's Data in Place option will not touch the home directory or its contents, but will delete the account from the system.

4. Select the desired account deletion option and then click the Accept button.

| **Figure 3-15** | Delete Account window |

Adding a New Group

The primary purpose of a group is to associate similar users together to make it easier for those users to share information. Groups are defined with the /etc/group file and contain a mapping between a group name and all members of that particular group. To create a new UNIX group, do the following:

1. Click the Group Definitions button located on the User Account Configurator main window. As a result, a list of groups defined on the system will be displayed, as shown in Figure 3-16.

2. Click the Add button and a new window, labeled the Group Specification window, is displayed, as shown in Figure 3-17.

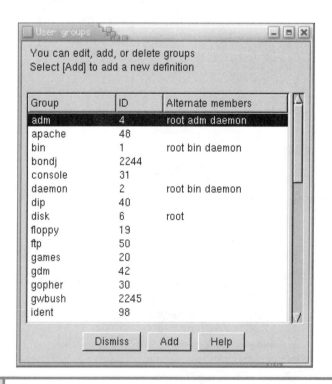

Figure 3-16 User Groups window

3

Figure 3-17   Group Specification window

This window contains three text box fields: Group Name, Group ID, and
Alternate Members. The group name is simply the name of the group you
wish to define. Like the UNIX account name, the group name should be
limited to just eight characters. The group name can be any string that
represents a collection of users. For example, the group name of eng
can represent the development staff within a particular department. The
Alternate Members field is used to contain additional UNIX users that are
members of the group.

3. Type the name of the new group in the Group Name text box.

4. You can accept the default group ID or type a new value. If you input a
new value, make sure that it doesn't conflict with any existing groups.

5. Add additional UNIX account names to the new group using the Alternate
Members field. For instance, in Figure 3-18 the group name devel is
defined with two members: gwbush and smaxwell.

Figure 3-18 The Group devel name is defined.

1-Minute Drill

● By default, what does the Linux userconf tool do with user data when you delete a user account?

● What is the limit for username and group name length?

3.3 Manage HP-UX Using SAM

The sam system management tool provides a one-stop shopping experience for the system administrator. It supports both the standard X-Windows interface and also the regular terminal interface. Thus, it can be used with or without a

---

● The userconf tool makes a copy of the files stored in the user's home directory and mailbox file. It builds a compressed tar archive of the home directory (and contents) and places it in the /home/oldaccounts directory.
● Eight characters.

GUI, which makes this a very powerful application. The software contains a large number of functions that help with a large variety of system administration tasks. However, this section will review both user administration.

To run `sam` in the X-Windows mode and to display the console window on the networked host called `ts-hp6`, issue the following command:

```
sam -display ts-hp6:0.0&
```

3

If you want to run using the standard non-GUI, just issue the following command:

```
sam
```

When this program is run in X-Windows mode, it displays the main `sam` window, as shown in Figure 3-19.

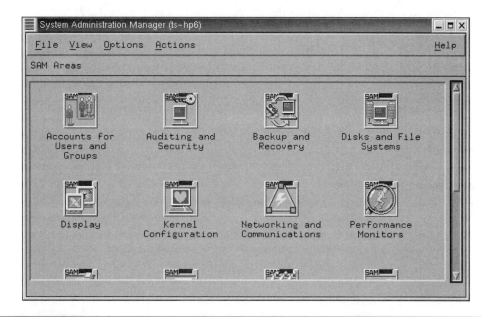

Figure 3-19   Main sam application window

This main `sam` window contains four menu items and a number of icons. The icons represent functional modules or component areas, and double-clicking the icons will access the feature or function. The functions of the menu items are listed in Table 3-3.

Add a New User

To add a new user to the system, use the following procedure:

1. Click the Accounts for Users and Groups button from the main `sam` window. Once this has been done, a new screen is displayed as shown in Figure 3-20.

2. Click on the Users icon and then another new window is displayed as shown in Figure 3-21. This window shows a list of all the defined users on the system.

3. Select the Add... item from the Actions menu. This will cause the Add a User Account window to be displayed, as shown in Figure 3-22. Notice that much of the account information has been filled in on the window using the system defaults.

4. Input the name of the account in the Login Name field. Optionally, you can add additional information about the account such as the real user's name, office location, and so forth. This information is added to the optional fields listed at the bottom of the window.

Menu Item	Meaning
File	Search `sam` for specific string and the `exit` item to close the application.
View	You can change the views of the window by altering the columns. You can also sort and view by name or icon if desired.
Options	Provides access to the `sam` log, controls logging options, and refreshes the display.
Actions	Contains item-specific actions that can be done against selected objects. Also, provides access to application customization functions.

Table 3-3   The sam Main Menus

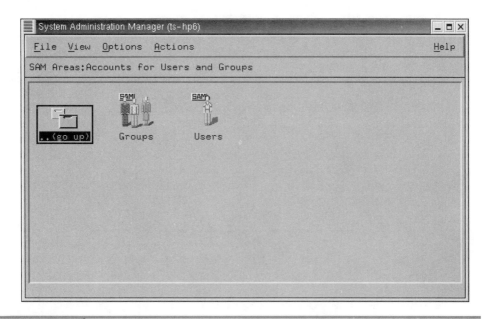

3

Figure 3-20   Group/Users window

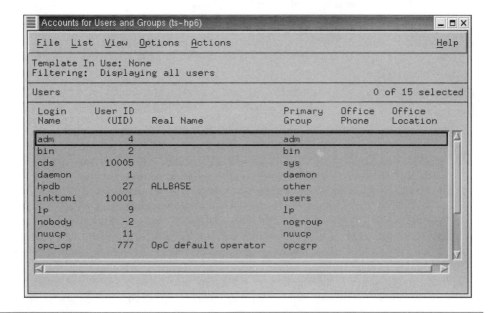

Figure 3-21   List of UNIX accounts

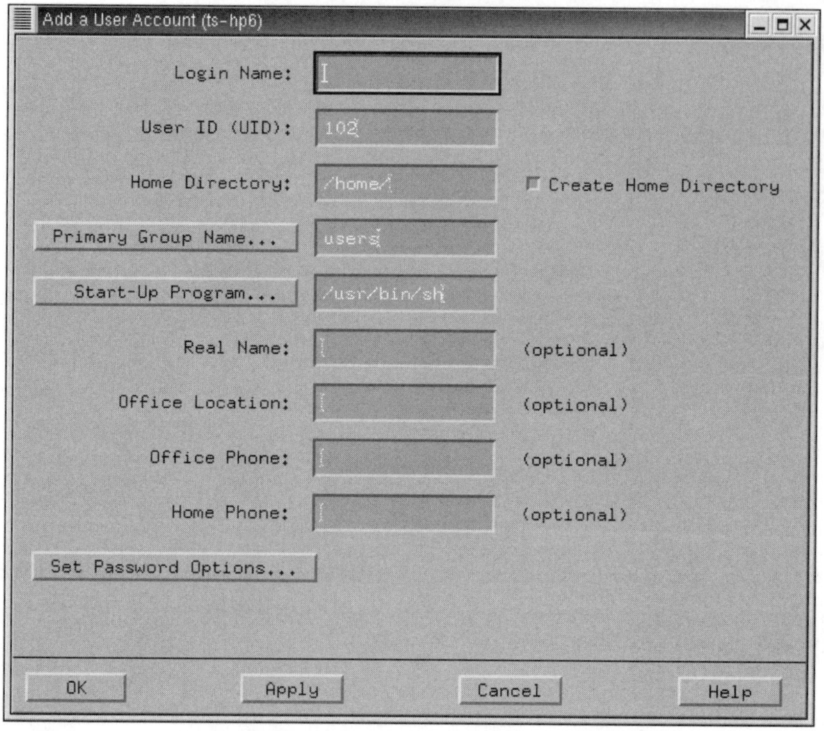

Figure 3-22 New User Account window

5. By default, the home directory is taken from the account name, which is added to the /home entry automatically. Also, the default behavior of sam is to create the home directory for the user.

6. If you want to change the primary group for this user, type in the group name or select the group by clicking the Primary Group Name button and then selecting the appropriate group entry.

7. If you want to change the default login shell, type in the new shell path and name or select the shell by clicking the Start-Up Program button and then selecting the appropriate shell entry.

8. Add a password to the account by clicking on the Set Password Options button. This action will cause a dialog window to be displayed, which is shown in Figure 3-23.

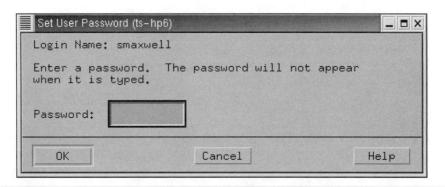

Figure 3-23   Password Dialog window

Type the new password in the Password field. Note the password won't be echoed or displayed on the screen when you are typing. Click the OK button and then you will be prompted to confirm the new password by typing it in again. Click the OK button when you have entered the password for the second time.

Assuming that no errors were encountered when the account was added to the system, sam will display a dialog box showing the confirmation of the new account, as shown in Figure 3-24.

Once the account has been added to the system, the list of UNIX accounts will be updated to include the new account. For instance, when the smaxwell user was added, this name appeared in the account list, as shown in Figure 3-25.

Figure 3-24   New account confirmation

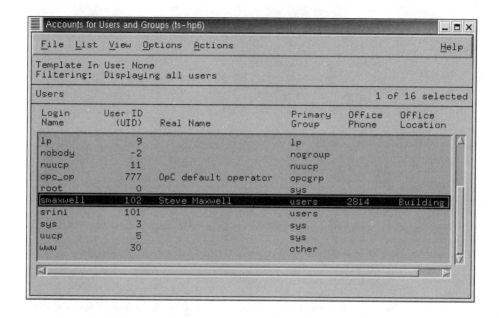

Figure 3-25 The smaxwell account is displayed in the account list.

Modifying a User

The `sam` application can be used to alter an existing UNIX account. To make a change to a user, do the following:

1. Click the Accounts for Users and Groups button from the main `sam` window. When the list of accounts appears, select the account and access the Modify menu item from the Actions menu.

2. A new window is displayed that contains detailed information about the account you selected. Figure 3-26 shows detailed information for the `smaxwell` account.

3. Make the appropriate account changes.

4. Save the changes by clicking the OK button.

3

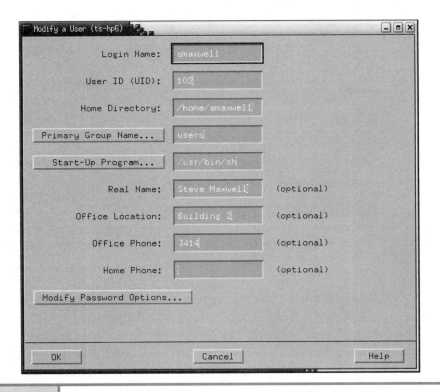

Figure 3-26   Detailed account information

Delete an Existing User

To delete an existing user from the system, use the following procedure:

1. Select the user you want to delete from the list of accounts contained in the Accounts for Users and Groups window (shown in Figure 3-25).

2. From the Action menu, select the Remove menu item. The Remove a User dialog window is shown in Figure 3-27.

Hint

Exercise extreme caution when removing users; as an important step in account removal, backing up home directories to secondary storage is a requirement. Even if you have a relatively new backup, it is very important that a fresh backup be made to capture any files/directories that have been modified since the last backup was taken.

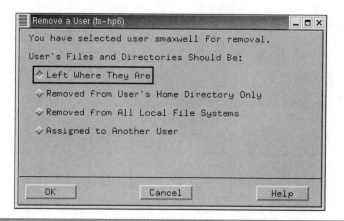

Figure 3-27   Remove a User window

This window permits the system administrator to have more exact control over the user's home directory when the account is removed from the system. The window contains four choices that include leaving the home directory untouched (Left Where They Are), deleting the home contents only (Removed from User's Home Directory Only), removing all user's files within the system (Removed from All Local File Systems), and assigning the files to another user (Assigned to Another User).

If you select the Removed from User's Home Directory Only, then only the files and subdirectories from the home directory will be removed, but not other files contained in other directories or other file systems. Selecting the Removed from All Local File Systems means that all files owned by the user will be deleted from the system, regardless of where the files are located. If the Assigned to Another User item is selected, a new field is added to the window to permit you to add the name of the user that should be assigned the files from the deleted user. This is shown in Figure 3-28 and as you can see, you can input the username or select it from a list of defined users by clicking the New Owner button.

3. Click the OK button and the note, as shown in Figure 3-29, will be displayed, showing that the removal of the account has been done.

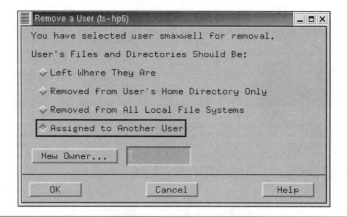

Figure 3-28   Remove a User window

Adding a New Group

To create a new UNIX group, do the following:

1. Click the Accounts for Users and Groups button from the main sam window.

2. Click on the Groups icon and then another new window is displayed, as shown in Figure 3-30. This window shows the list of all the defined groups on the system.

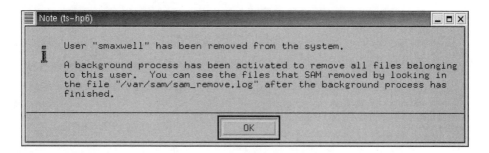

Figure 3-29   Removal Confirmation window

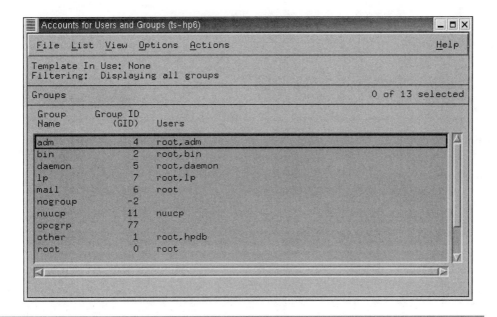

Figure 3-30 Defined Groups window

3. When the list of defined groups appears, select the Add menu item from the Actions menu; a new window is displayed, which is depicted in Figure 3-31.

4. Input the new group name in the Group Name field.

5. Accept the default group identification number, or input a new value. Make sure that the new value added doesn't conflict with any existing groups already defined on the system.

6. As an option, you can add existing users to the new group by selecting users from the list of defined users.

7. Click OK to save the new group.

8. Assuming no errors have occurred, a confirmation window will be displayed, as shown in Figure 3-32, stating that the group was added successfully.

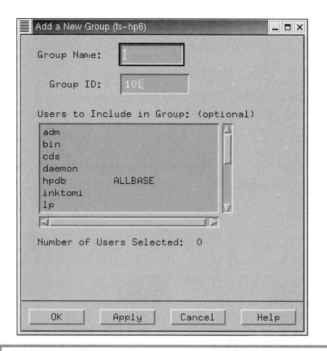

3

Figure 3-31   New Group window

Deleting an Existing Group

To delete an existing group from the system, use the following procedure:

1. Select the group you want to delete from the list of groups contained in the Accounts for Users and Groups window (shown in Figure 3-30).

Figure 3-32   Group Confirmation window

2. From the Action menu, select the Remove menu item. The Remove
Selected Group dialog window is shown in Figure 3-33.

When deleting a group, you must determine the consequences should files
or directories use this group definition. The Remove Selected Group window
contains three options: Leave the files that use the group untouched (Left
Undisturbed), reassign each file with the primary group of the user (Reassigned
to Primary Group of Each File's Owner), and assign the files to a new group
(Reassigned to a Specified Group). If you leave the files untouched and remove
the group, the group's identification number will be used when group
information is displayed.

1. Choose the appropriate action when the group is removed or simply
accept the default, which is the Left Undisturbed item.

2. Click the OK button and then dismiss the Group Confirmation window.

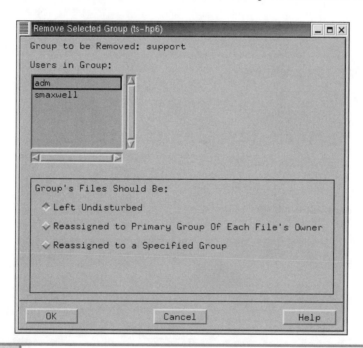

Figure 3-33   Remove the Group support window

3.4 Set Up Better Account Security

In certain situations and computing environments, it may be necessary to have the users change their passwords on a more frequent basis. Often, this may be a part of a larger security regime that involves addressing security on a much larger scale. No doubt, forcing users to change their passwords on some regular basis is important, but one overriding factor is choosing the best frequency to do this. Obviously, changing passwords, say, every week is quite excessive. Equally unreasonable is permitting users to have the same passwords for many years. A balance must be struck between maintaining a reasonable level of security and total chaos. The answer will ultimately depend on the environment, the view of key management, and the system administrator. The best approach to account security is to set up a policy and enforce that policy with specific procedures. For example, assume your policy suggests that every 90 days all individual account passwords must be changed. As a result, you would use the `admintool`, `sserconf`, or `sam` to configure accounts accordingly.

Each provides flexible control over how the administration of account passwords is handled. In particular, you can control the expiration of passwords for individual user accounts, disable one or more accounts, place boundaries over the use of accounts, and warn the user of pending password changes.

Ask the Expert

Question   Why is forcing the users to change their passwords on a regular basis important?

Answer   If users use the same password a long time without changing it, this increases the chance their password will be compromised either accidentally or through others intentionally trying to gain unauthorized access to their account.

Expiring a Password Using Admintool

To control the expiration of an account password, thus forcing the user to change the password the next time they log into the system, do the following:

1. Select an account name from the scrollable list and access the Modify menu item from the Edit menu.

2. Or, double-click the account name and the Admintool: Modify User window will be displayed.

3. The expiration date for an account can be selected from the Expiration Date option boxes. The format is day, month, and then year. Use the mouse to select each of the items until you have a valid date. Also, you can warn the user ahead of the expiration by adding a positive number in the Warning text box. This will give the user a "heads up" that they will need to change their password in the near future. Figure 3-34 shows the `stevem` account, which has been configured to expire the password on October 22, 2002.

Expiring a Password Using Userconf

To control the expiration of an account password, thus forcing the user to change the password the next time they log into the system, do the following:

1. Select the account from the list of defined UNIX accounts shown in the Users Accounts window you wish to expire, which is from the User Accounts button on the main `userconf` window.

2. Select the Params tab from the User Information window.

3. Input the desired number of days to expire the password in the Must Keep # Days field, as shown in Figure 3-35.

4. De-select the Ignored item.

5. Click the Accept button.

In the example, the number of days entered was `30`. This means that 30 days from the current date, the system will prompt for a new password automatically.

3

| **Figure 3-34** | Modify User window with expiration of password |

Expiring a Password Using SAM

To control the expiration of an account password, thus forcing the user to change the password the next time they log into the system, do the following:

1. Select an account name from the scrollable list, which is found from the Accounts for Users and Groups window, and select the Modify option from the Action menu.

2. Click the Set Password Options button on the User Account window. A new window is displayed, as shown in Figure 3-36.

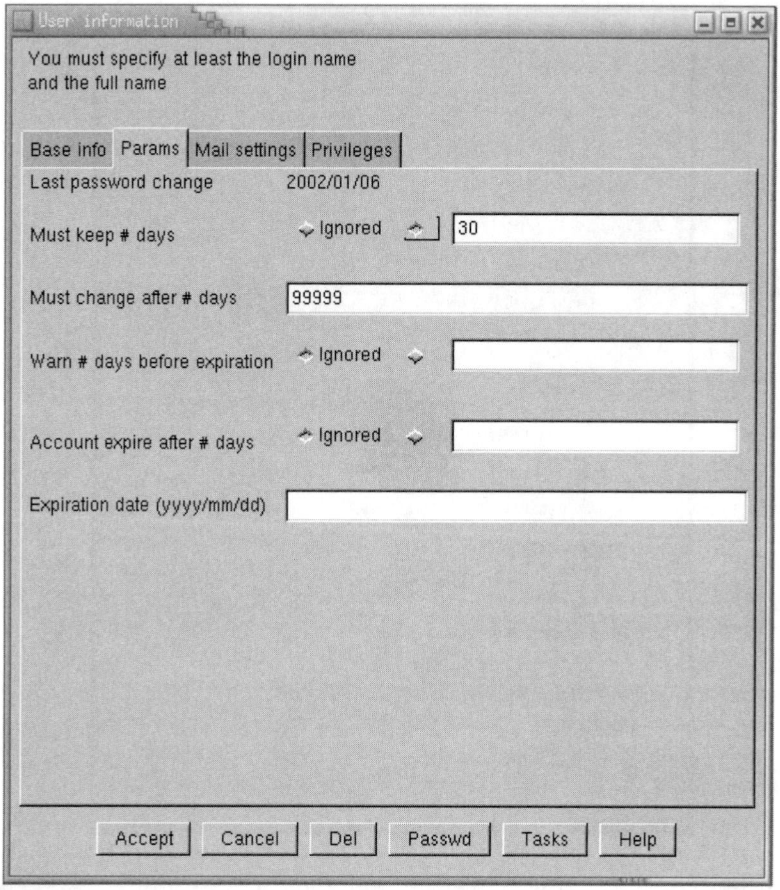

Figure 3-35   Params panel

3. Select Enable Password Aging from the Password Options field if it is not already selected.

4. Enter the expiration time in the Password Expiration Time (1-63 weeks) field that you require for this account. In this example, two weeks was entered.

5. Click the OK button to dismiss this window and accept the change.

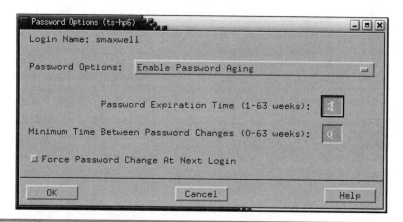

Figure 3-36   Password Options window

Regular Password Changes Using Admintool

To incorporate automatic password aging for user accounts, do the following:

1. Select an account name from the scrollable list and access the Modify menu item from the Edit menu.

2. Or, double-click the account name and the Admintool: Modify User window will be displayed.

3. Enter the number of days that represents the period of time for the password to expire in the Max Change field. For example, assume that you want the password to be changed every 60 days, enter **60** in this field, as shown in Figure 3-37.

4. Enter the number of days to warn the user about the impending password change.

5. Click the OK button to save this change.

```
┌─────────────────────────────────────────────┐
│ ▢ ▬         Admintool: Modify User            │
├───────────────────────────────────────────────┤
│ USER IDENTITY                                   │
│        User Name: │anitat│                      │
│                                                 │
│         User ID: 1001                           │
│     Primary Group: │10                      │   │
│  Secondary Groups: │                        │   │
│         Comment: │Ms. Anita Tognazzini      │   │
│      Login Shell: │Bourne ▬│  /bin/sh           │
│                                                 │
│ ACCOUNT SECURITY                                │
│         Password:   Cleared until first login ▬ │
│       Min Change: │         │  days             │
│       Max Change: │ 60      │  days             │
│      Max Inactive: │        │  days             │
│    Expiration Date: None ▬   None ▬   None ▬    │
│       (dd/mm/yy)                                │
│         Warning: │         │  days              │
│ HOME DIRECTORY                                  │
│           Path: │/home/anita              │     │
│                                                 │
│   │ OK │  │ Apply │  │ Reset │ │ Cancel │ │ Help │ │
└─────────────────────────────────────────────┘
```

| **Figure 3-37** | Modify User window with 60-day expiration |

Regular Password Changes Using Userconf

To set up automatic password aging for user accounts, do the following:

1. Select the account from the list of defined UNIX accounts shown in the Users Accounts window you wish to change, which is from the User Accounts button on the main `userconf` window.

2. Select the Params tab from the User Information window.

3. Input the number of days that the password must be changed in the Must Change After # Days field.

4. Figure 3-38 shows the value of 45 in this field, which indicates that every 45 days the user will be prompted to change the password.

5. Click the Accept button.

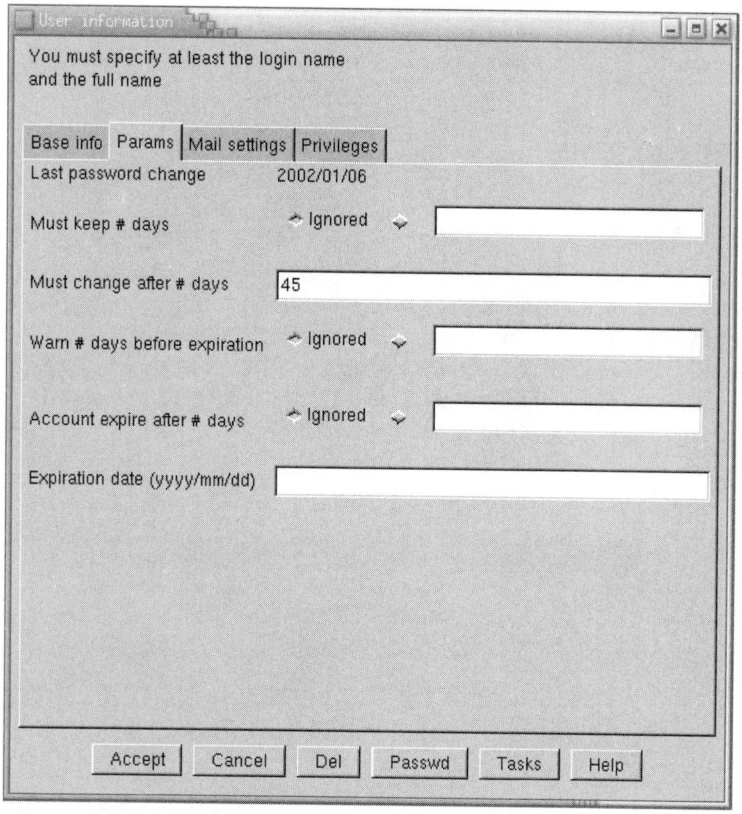

Figure 3-38   Force password change every 45 days

Turning Off an Account Using Admintool

Sometimes it may become necessary to disable one or more accounts so that those users don't have access to the system. This might be due to an employee leaving the company or department, or even because they simply haven't used the system in such a long time that you might need to investigate if they should have an account at all.

To disable an existing account, do the following procedure:

1. Select an account name from the scrollable list and access the Modify menu item from the Edit menu.

2. Or, double-click the account name and the Admintool: Modify User window will be displayed.

3. From the Password Selection box, select the Account Is Locked item, as shown in Figure 3-39. In the example, the account named `billc` has been locked.

4. Select the OK button to save the change.

Hint

When a user attempts to access an account that has been locked, no special message will appear to the user. Instead, they will simple get a Login Incorrect message. This is a generic message, which can mean other things as well—for example, that no account is actually present on the system. It will be up to the user to request additional information as to the actual reason why the account no longer functions.

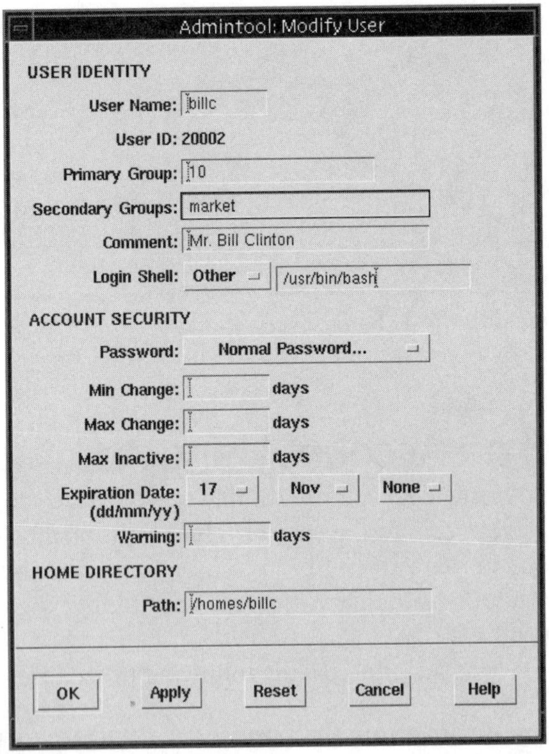

Figure 3-39 Locking the billc UNIX account

Hint

To unlock a locked account select Normal Passwd selection item and input the new password for this account.

Turning Off an Account Using Userconf

To disable an existing account, do the following:

1. Select the account from the list of defined UNIX accounts shown in the Users Accounts window you wish to change, which is from the User Accounts button on the main `userconf` window.

2. Click the The Account Is Enabled selection box located on the top of the User Information window, as shown in Figure 3-40.

3. Click the Accept button.

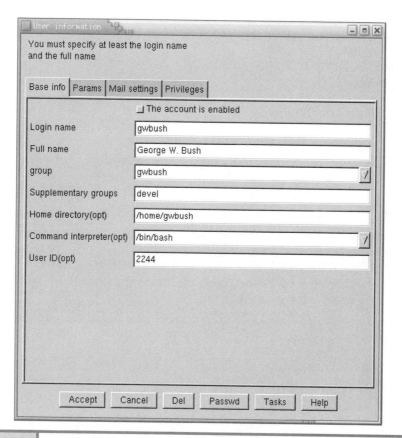

Figure 3-40   Disabling the smaxwell UNIX account

> **Hint**
> To unlock a disabled account, click the The Account Is Enabled selection box.

Automatic Account Expiration Using Userconf

You can automatically expire one or more accounts after some fixed period of time has elapsed. This means that the system administrator can plan to have an account disabled in the future. For instance, the account could be used by a temporary employee that will leave the company after their contract is complete, and you want to ensure that they no longer have access to the system. To set up a future expiration date for a UNIX account, do the following:

1. Select the account from the list of defined UNIX accounts shown in the Users Accounts window you wish to change, which is from the User Accounts button on the main `userconf` window.

2. Select the Params tab from the User Information window.

3. Input the future expiration date in the Expiration Date (yyyy/mm/dd) field.

4. Click the Accept button.

In the example, the expiration date of `September 1, 2002` (`2002/09/01`) has been entered, as shown in Figure 3-41. This means that on this date, the login will not be accessible any longer.

> **Hint**
> Another expiration parameter can be entered that includes the number of days to warn the user before the expiration occurs (Warn # Days Before Expiration). Also, instead of using a fixed date, you can use the number of future days to determine when the account should expire. This information is added to the Account Expire After # Days field.

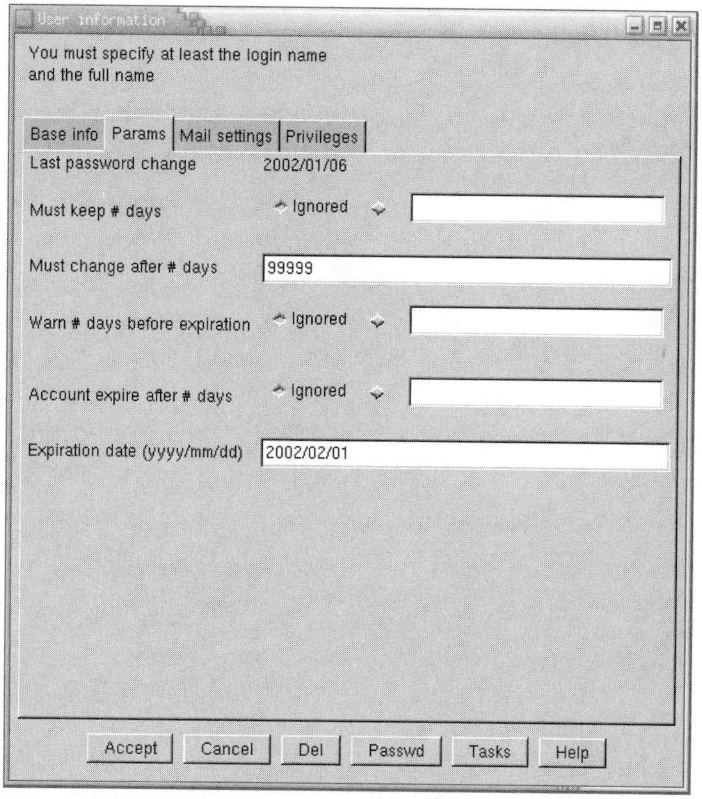

Figure 3-41   Account Expiration From User Information window

☑ Mastery Check

1. True or False: When using admintool to add group members, include a space between each member in the list.

2. When you add a new user account named gwsmith in Linux using the userconf& tool and don't specify a home directory, what directory will userconf& use as the home directory?

3. Which window do you use in admintool to set a password expiration date for a user?

4. In userconf, which tab and window do you use to set up regular password change intervals for a user?

5. In userconf, which button do you click to open the window to create a new group?

6. In HP-UX SAM, what are the menu commands to delete an existing user account?

7. True or False: When using admintool to add new users, admintool automatically selects the next available user ID.

8. In the User Accounts window in userconf, the _____ field is used to specify which command shell should be started when the user logs in to the system.

9. Which of the following is *not* an option for what to do with the users files when deleting a user account in HP-UX with SAM?

   A. Left Where They Are

   B. Archive the Account's Data

   C. Removed from ALL Local File Systems

   D. Assigned to Another User

10. Which UNIX file contains the list of users for the system?

11. Which UNIX file contains the list of groups and the group members for the system?

Module 4

Software Package Management Tools

Critical Skills

This module provides an introduction into using the standard package management tools that are native to the different versions of UNIX. As such, it provides a step-by-step approach for doing actual package management functions that include installing, removing, and verifying installed software.

In the early days of UNIX, many of the third-party tools, public domain software, and commercial applications vendors used to distribute their software using standard package formats such as `tar` or `cpio`. These utilities were great for handling the archiving of a large number of files, but they failed as a general-purpose software management mechanism. Today, many UNIX system vendors use package distribution formats to make it easier to move self-contained software modules from distribution media, such as CD-ROMs to the system instead of using tools such as `tar`. Unfortunately, many of the UNIX vendors support their own particular format and these are typically not compatible with other vendors' package structures. As a result, when you purchase a product, say for HP-UX, you must use the HP-UX installation tools to get the product installed.

Generally speaking, you must use the operating system package utilities to maintain system level software since many software vendors and public domain tools support the native package format. However, many public domain tools generally provide an operating system package and other formats as well. For example, the SSH secure shell software is available in several package formats, including for Solaris, HP-UX, and Linux.

Table 4-1 shows a breakdown of the package management tools that are available for Solaris, HP-UX, and Linux. These individual tools, for each of the operating systems, are described in the following sections.

Operating System	Package Tools		
	Installation	**Removal**	**Informational**
Solaris	`pkgadd`	`pkgrm`	`pkginfo`
HP-UX	`swinstall`	`swremove`	`swlist`
Linux	`rpm --install`	`rpm --erase`	`rpm --query`

Table 4-1   UNIX Software Package Management Tools

4.1 Discover Solaris Package Tools

The Solaris system provides the basic package tools that include

```
pkginfo
pkgadd
pkgrm
```

pkginfo

The package information tool `pkginfo` is used to list all of the installed packages on a system or query information about a package in general, regardless if it has already been installed. This is most useful if you are not sure if a particular package is installed or if you want to obtain a working inventory of packages installed on a series of machines. You must have `root` privileges to execute the Solaris package commands.

To see all the packages on a given system, use the following command:

```
# pkginfo | more
```

Sample output might include

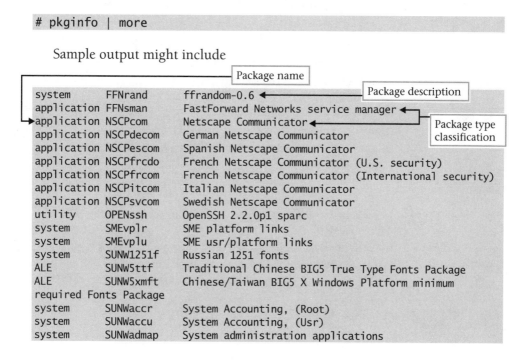

```
system       FFNrand      ffrandom-0.6
application FFNsman      FastForward Networks service manager
application NSCPcom      Netscape Communicator
application NSCPdecom    German Netscape Communicator
application NSCPescom    Spanish Netscape Communicator
application NSCPfrcdo    French Netscape Communicator (U.S. security)
application NSCPfrcom    French Netscape Communicator (International security)
application NSCPitcom    Italian Netscape Communicator
application NSCPsvcom    Swedish Netscape Communicator
utility      OPENssh      OpenSSH 2.2.0p1 sparc
system       SMEvplr      SME platform links
system       SMEvplu      SME usr/platform links
system       SUNW1251f    Russian 1251 fonts
ALE          SUNW5ttf     Traditional Chinese BIG5 True Type Fonts Package
ALE          SUNW5xmft    Chinese/Taiwan BIG5 X Windows Platform minimum
required Fonts Package
system       SUNWaccr     System Accounting, (Root)
system       SUNWaccu     System Accounting, (Usr)
system       SUNWadmap    System administration applications
```

Package name

Package description

Package type classification

4

```
system      SUNWadmc    System administration core libraries
system      SUNWadmfw   System & Network Administration Framework
system      SUNWadmj    Admin/Install Java Extension Libraries
--More--
```

When invoked, it shows all the available Solaris packages installed, sorted by the classification of package types. The output of this command is sent to the `more` command, which permits the user to peruse the output one screen full at a time. Hitting the SPACEBAR on the keyboard displays another screen of text. When packages are created, they contain a primary category parameter, which denotes the classification of application the software represents. The most common categories are `system`, `application`, and `utility`. For example, as you can see from the preceding output, the Netscape package falls under the application package calls, which makes complete sense given that Netscape is a Web browser application. A quick scan of the available packages installed on a generic system reveals that both `system` and `application` are the most widely installed types of software.

The `pkginfo` tool (as well as the other tools) supports several important and common command line options as shown in Table 4-2.

Command	Definition
-a	Display the architecture of the package.
-c	Display all packages that match the specified category.
-d	Defines the device, directory name, or individual package name to query for package information.
-i	Display information on complete installed packages.
-l	Display additional package information in a long format.
-p	Display information on only partially installed packages.
-q	Used by an external program to determine if a package is installed. Doesn't show any output.
-r	Display the installation directory base for any packages that have been relocated.
-R	Defines the directory to be used as the root path for packages.
-v	Display packages with the specified version information.
-x	Display extract listing information from a package.

Table 4-2 pkginfo Command-Line Options

One of the most important is the –d option, which tells the program where to look to determine information about one or more packages. This option is used to specify the hardware device, which contains the packages (that is, CD-ROMs) or other media. However, it can also be used when a single package is specified, or even a directory name. For example, let's assume we would like to examine the contents of the Solaris 8 Companion CD-ROM, which contains useful tools and utilities. In general, we need to specify the directory where the packages are located. The command

```
# pkginfo -d /cdrom/s8_software_companion/components/i386/Package
```

shows all the packages available under the /cdrom/s8_software_companion/ components/i386/Package directory. The following output shows a partial list of the available packages:

4

```
system      SFWaalib      aalib - ASCII Art Library
system      SFWaconf      autoconf - GNU autoconf
system      SFWamake      automake - GNU automake
system      SFWasclk      asclock - the AfterStep clock
system      SFWastep      afterstep - X11 window manager
system      SFWaufl       audiofile - audio library
system      SFWbdb        Berkeley DB - database library
system      SFWbison      GNU bison - a better yacc
system      SFWcdrec      cdrecord - record audio or data Compact Discs
system      SFWcvs        cvs - version control system
system      SFWddd        DDD - GNU Data Display Debugger
system      SFWdiffu      diffutils - GNU diffutils
system      SFWemacs      GNU Emacs - Editor
system      SFWenscr      GNU enscript - convert text files to PostScript
system      SFWesd        esound - The Enlightened Sound Daemon
system      SFWethrl      Ethereal - Interactively browse network traffic
system      SFWexpct      expect - programmed dialogue with programs
system      SFWfile       file - determine file type
system      SFWflex       GNU flex - a lex replacement
system      SFWfnlib      fnlib - X11 font rendering library
system      SFWftype      Freetype - Free TrueType Rendering Engine
system      SFWfvwm       fvwm - X11 virtual window manager
system      SFWgawk       gawk - pattern scanning and processing language
system      SFWgbin       binutils - GNU binary utilities
system      SFWgcal       gcal - the GNU Gregorian calendar program
system      SFWgcc        gcc - GNU Compiler Collection
system      SFWgcmn       gcmn - Common GNU package
```

```
system     SFWgdb           gdb - GNU source-level debugger
system     SFWgfile         fileutils - GNU file management utilities
system     SFWgfind         findutils - GNU find utilities
system     SFWgimp          gimp - GNU Image Manipulation Program
system     SFWglib          GLIB - Library of useful routines for C programming
system     SFWgm4           GNU m4 - macro processor
system     SFWgmake         gmake - GNU make
system     SFWgnome         Gnome - X11 Windowing Environment
system     SFWgplot         gnuplot - The Gnuplot Plotting Utility
system     SFWgrep          grep - GNU grep utilities
system     SFWgroff         GNU groff - document formatting system
system     SFWgs            GNU Ghostscript - postscript interpreter
system     SFWgsfot         GNU Ghostscript Fonts - Other Fonts
system     SFWgsfst         GNU Ghostscript Fonts - Standard Fonts
system     SFWgtar          gtar - GNU tar
```

We can also obtain information on individual packages on the command line. Thus,

```
# pkginfo -d /cdrom/s8_software_companion/components/i386/Packages SFWtop
system     SFWtop           top - display information about processes
```

In this case, we specified the top (SFTop) system-monitoring package, which provides additional information about the package. To learn even more about a particular package, the -l option, which displays a long listing, can be used:

```
# pkginfo -l -d /cdrom/s8_software_companion/components/i386/Packages SFWtop
   PKGINST:  SFWtop
      NAME:  top - display information about processes
  CATEGORY:  system
      ARCH:  i386
   VERSION:  3.5_12,REV=2001.02.19.04.12
   BASEDIR:  /opt ◄─────────────  Directory where package
    VENDOR:  ftp://ftp.groupsys.com/pub/top   will be installed
      DESC:  top - display and update information about the top cpu processes
    PSTAMP:  freeware20010219074803
   HOTLINE:  Please contact the owners of this software
    STATUS:  spooled
     FILES:       10 spooled pathnames
                   4 directories
                   1 executables
                   4 package information files
                  99 blocks used (approx)
                2425 blocks used (approx)
```

The output displayed shows much more information about the package, and includes information about where the package will be installed, the size of the package, and other important details.

1-Minute Drill

● Why is the `more` command useful in conjunction with pkginfo?

pkgadd

4

When it is necessary to install a new package or upgrade an existing one, the `pkgadd` command can be used. This tool uses the same command-line arguments as `pkginfo`. For example, to install a single package that is specified on the command line, we could use the following command:

```
# pkgadd -d /cdrom/s8_software_companion/components/i386/Packages SFWtop
Processing package instance <SFWtop> from </cdrom/s8_software_companion/components/
i386/Packages>
top - display information about processes              Package name to install
(i386) 3.5_12,REV=2001.02.19.04.12
        Top users/processes display for Unix
        Version 3
        This program may be freely redistributed,
        but this entire comment MUST remain intact.
        Copyright (c) 1984, 1989, William LeFebvre, Rice University
        Copyright (c) 1989 - 1994, William LeFebvre, Northwestern University
        Copyright (c) 1994, 1995, William LeFebvre, Argonne National Laboratory
        Copyright (c) 1996, William LeFebvre, Group sys Consulting
        DISCLAIMER
        "top" is distributed free of charge.  It should not be considered an
        official product of Group sys Consulting.  William LeFebvre supports
        "top" in his spare time and as time permits.


        NO WARRANTY:
        BECAUSE "top" IS DISTRIBUTED FREE OF CHARGE, THERE IS ABSOLUTELY NO
        WARRANTY PROVIDED, TO THE EXTENT PERMITTED BY APPLICABLE STATE LAW.
        EXCEPT WHEN OTHERWISE STATED IN WRITING, GROUP SYS CONSULTING, ARGONNE
        NATIONAL LABORATORY, NORTHWESTERN UNIVERSITY, WILLIAM N. LeFEBVRE
        AND/OR OTHER PARTIES PROVIDE "top" "AS IS" WITHOUT WARRANTY OF ANY
        KIND, EITHER EXPRESSED OR IMPLIED, INCLUDING, BUT NOT LIMITED TO, THE
        IMPLIED WARRANTIES OF MERCHANTABILITY AND FITNESS FOR A PARTICULAR
        PURPOSE.  THE ENTIRE RISK AS TO THE QUALITY AND PERFORMANCE OF THE
        PROGRAM IS WITH YOU.  SHOULD THE "top" PROGRAM PROVE DEFECTIVE, YOU
        ASSUME THE COST OF ALL NECESSARY SERVICING, REPAIR OR CORRECTION.
```

● If you have a lot of packages installed on your system, piping the results of `pkginfo` to `more` makes it easier to read them by displaying them one screen at a time.

```
        IN NO EVENT WILL GROUP SYS CONSULTING, ARGONNE NATIONAL LABORATORY,
        NORTHWESTERN UNIVERSITY, WILLIAM N. LeFEBVRE, AND/OR ANY OTHER PARTY
        WHO MAY MODIFY AND REDISTRIBUTE "top", BE LIABLE TO YOU FOR DAMAGES,
        INCLUDING ANY LOST PROFITS, LOST MONIES, OR OTHER SPECIAL, INCIDENTAL
        OR CONSEQUENTIAL DAMAGES ARISING OUT OF THE USE OR INABILITY TO USE
        (INCLUDING BUT NOT LIMITED TO LOSS OF DATA OR DATA BEING RENDERED
        INACCURATE OR LOSSES SUSTAINED BY THIRD PARTIES OR A FAILURE OF THE
        PROGRAM TO OPERATE WITH OTHER PROGRAMS) THE PROGRAM, EVEN IF YOU HAVE
        BEEN ADVISED OF THE POSSIBILITY OF SUCH DAMAGES, OR FOR ANY CLAIM BY
        ANY OTHER PARTY.

So there!
YOU MUST OBSERVE ANY AUTHORS' CONDITIONS WITH RESPECT TO
INDIVIDUAL COMPONENTS PROVIDED WITHIN THIS CODE.   SUPPORT
FOR THE TECHNOLOGIES AND DOCUMENTATION IS NOT PROVIDED
BY SUN MICROSYSTEMS, INC.

THE TECHNOLOGIES AND DOCUMENTATION ARE PROVIDED "AS IS" WITHOUT TECHNICAL
SUPPORT OR WARRANTY OF ANY KIND, EITHER EXPRESS OR IMPLIED, INCLUDING, BUT NOT
LIMITED TO, THE IMPLIED WARRANTIES OF MERCHANTABILITY, FITNESS FOR A
PARTICULAR PURPOSE, OR NON-INFRINGEMENT.
Using </opt> as the package base directory.
## Processing package information.
## Processing system information.
## Verifying package dependencies.
## Verifying disk space requirements.
## Checking for conflicts with packages already installed.
## Checking for setuid/setgid programs.

This package contains scripts which will be executed with super-user
permission during the process of installing this package.
Do you want to continue with the installation of <SFWtop> [y,n,?] y
Installing top - display information about processes as <SFWtop>
## Installing part 1 of 1.
Installation of <SFWtop> was successful.
```

Installer message informing you where the package is being installed.

Installer prompt waiting for your input before continuing.

The above command installs the `top` utility on a Solaris system, and as you can see, a fair amount of output was generated showing all the steps involved with the installation process. Note that the Solaris package tools are sophisticated enough to prompt the user should it be necessary to query for additional information. This is one of the most powerful features of these tools—to install software components in an intelligent manner regardless of the target platform.

pkgrm

In order to remove one or more packages, use the `pkgrm` command. The basic syntax of this command requires the name of the package that should be removed. For example, to remove the FTP client application, `SMCxftp`, issue the following command:

```
# pkgrm SMCxftp
```

The resulting output is shown:

```
The following package is currently installed:
   SMCxftp          xftp
                    (sparc) 2.1

Do you want to remove this package? yes
## Removing installed package instance <SMCxftp>
## Verifying package dependencies.
## Processing package information.
## Removing pathnames in class <none>
/usr/local/man/man1/xftp.1
/usr/local/man/man1 <shared pathname not removed>
/usr/local/man <shared pathname not removed>
/usr/local/lib/XFtp.ad
/usr/local/lib
/usr/local/doc/xftp/README
/usr/local/doc/xftp/NEW_FEATURES
/usr/local/doc/xftp/CHANGES
/usr/local/doc/xftp/BUGS
/usr/local/doc/xftp
/usr/local/doc
/usr/local/bin/xftp
/usr/local/bin <shared pathname not removed>
## Updating system information.

Removal of <SMCxftp> was successful.
```

Prompt asking you to confirm removing package

Your response to prompt

4

As you can see from this output, the pkgrm tool prompts the user to ensure that removal of the specified package is in fact desired. Once done, it also displays all the files that are being removed from the system that are associated with this package. Please note that the pkgrm command must be supplied with the actually package name, not the file that was used to contain the package. For example,

```
# pkgrm xftp
pkgrm: ERROR: no package associated with <xftp>
```

doesn't work and produces an associated error message. If you don't know the actually package name, use the pkginfo command to find out:

```
# pkginfo -d xftp-2.1-sol8-sparc-local
application SMCxftp          xftp
```

Note that once a package has been removed from the system, any associated files and/or programs are permanently removed.

4.2 Discover HP-UX Package Tools

The HP-UX system provides the basic package management tools that include

```
swlist
swinstall
swremove
```

swlist

To display information about the installed product on a HP-UX system, use the swlist package management command. This command has a large number of command line arguments, but the most common ones are listed in Table 4-3. You must have root privileges to execute the HP-UX package commands.

The most basic use of the command is to show the currently installed products on a system. The command that you would use is

```
# swlist
```

Option	Meaning
-a	Display a list of products by attribute.
-d	Display a list of products that are available from a depot, not from the local system.
-I	Invoke the interactive user interface, which can be used on regular terminals.
-l	Display a list of objects that correspond to a specific level. This is how to show the detailed components that make up a particular package.
-r	Display a list of products that are installed on an alternative root file system.
-v	Display more detailed information regarding products.

Table 4-3 Common swlist Command-Line Options

When this command is executed, it displays a list of the currently installed products on the local system. The example output generated includes

```
# Initializing...
# Contacting target "boston-srv"...
# Target:  boston-srv:/
# Bundle(s):
#
  A4929A          B.11.00.11       1000Base-T PCI Gigabit Ethernet Driver
  A5158A          B.11.00.02       HP PCI Tachyon TL Fibre Channel
  B3701AA         C.02.40.000      HP GlancePlus/UX Pak for s800 11.0
  B3901BA         B.11.01.20       HP C/ANSI C Developer's Bundle for HP-UX 11.00 (S800)
  B3913DB         C.03.25          HP aC++ Compiler (S800)
  B3919EA_2A5     B.11.00          Special Edition HP-UX Unlimited-User Lic
  B3929BA         B.11.00          HP OnLineJFS (Advanced VxFS)
  B5456CA         C.01.18.01       HP-UX Development Kit for Java*
  B8342AA         B.11.00.03       Netscape Communicator 4.72
  B8723AA         A.01.02          CIFS/9000 Client Lic. for 9000 Servers
  B8725AA         A.01.02          CIFS/9000 Server Lic. for 9000 Servers
  HPUXEng64RT     B.11.00          English HP-UX 64-bit Runtime Environment
  OnlineDiag      B.11.00.13.16    HPUX 11.0 Support Tools Bundle
  XSWECO226       A.1.0            Patch Replacement bundle
  XSWGR1100       B.11.00.49.3     HP-UX General Release Patches, June 2000
  XSWHWCR1100     B.11.00.49.3     HP-UX Hardware Enablement and Critical Patches, June
2000
#
# Product(s) not contained in a Bundle:
#
  PHCO_21492      1.0              Software Distributor (SD-UX) Cumulative Patch
  PHKL_22209      1.0              fix f_cred, fork DPFs & accept(2) errors
  PHNE_22397      1.0              cumulative ARPA Transport patch
  perl            5.6.0            perl
```

In this example, the system boston-srv was probed with the swlist command, and it shows that a variety of software packages have been installed on the system. The list of packages are broken down into two categories: products contained with a bundle and products that are stand-alone. Products within a bundle simply mean that the package contains a series of files or other objects and the name of the bundle is a container. As you can see from the output, the B8342AA bundle, for instance, corresponds to the Netscape Communicator 4.72 application, while the nonbundle applications include the perl 5.6.0 module.

Specifying a package to `swlist` command, the administrator can drill down and obtain more detailed information about a product or bundle. Thus, the command

```
# swlist A4929A
```

shows the elements of the A4929A package:

```
# Initializing...
# Contacting target " boston-srv "...
#
# Target:  boston-srv:/
#
# A4929A                  B.11.00.11    1000Base-T PCI Gigabit Ethernet Driver
# A4929A.GE-DRV           B.11.00.11    HP PCI/GSC Gigabit Ethernet Driver
  A4929A.GE-DRV.GE-KRN    B.11.00.11    Gigabit Ethernet Kernel Software Distribution
  A4929A.GE-DRV.GE-RUN    B.11.00.11    Gigabit Ethernet Runtime Software Distribution
```

If we desire even more information and details about this package, we can use the -v option, which provides quite a fair amount of information for each element within the package. The command

```
swlist -v A4929A
```

will produce the following output for the network driver:

Hint

The output below was shortened for brevity since several pages were generated by the above command.

```
# Initializing...
# Contacting target "boston-srv"...
#
# swlist    Installed Software Table of Contents
#
# For host:  boston-srv:/
# Date:  Mon Dec 31 00:17:38 2001
#
# A4929A
vendor
tag                 HP
uuid
title               "Hewlett-Packard Company"
description         "Hewlett-Packard Company
"
end
bundle
```

```
tag                     A4929A
software_spec           A4929A,r=B.11.00.11,a=HP-UX_B.11.00_32/64,v=HP
data_model_revision     2.40
instance_id             1
control_directory       A4929A
size                    1370913
revision                B.11.00.11
title                   1000Base-T PCI Gigabit Ethernet Driver
description             "Vendor Name                      Hewlett-Packard Company
This bundle contains the software drivers for the HP 1000Base-SX/T
cards A4924A HSC, A4925A HSC EISA, A4926 PCI and A4929A PCI .
This is for systems running version 11.** of the HP-UX operating system.
The bundle has the Gigabit Ethernet product which contains:
    Subproduct: Runtime
    Filesets  : GE-KRN, GE-RUN"
mod_date                Thu Oct 26 14:31:27 PDT 2000
mod_time                972595887
create_date             Fri Apr 28 16:45:28 PDT 2000
create_time             956965528
install_date            200010261731.27
architecture            HP-UX_B.11.00_32/64
machine_type            *
os_name                 HP-UX
os_release              ?.11.00
os_version              *
install_source          m2403jrw.nsr.hp.com:/var/opt/ignite/depots/Rel_B.11.00/apps_800
is_patch                false
supersedes
category_tag            OrderedApps
vendor_tag              HP
directory               /
qualifier
layout_version          1.0
is_locatable            true
location
copyright
number
contents                GE-DRV,r=B.11.00.11,a=HP-UX_B.11.00_32/64,v=HP
is_protected            false
is_reference            true
associated_bundles
hp_ii                      "factory_integrate=TRUE;
                        title=GELAN;
                        desktop=FALSE"
hp_srdo                    "swtype=I;user=B;bundle_type=C"
```

One extremely useful function of the HP-UX package management tool is that the administrator can query one or more networked remote hosts. It would be great to scan a series of systems from a central system. For example, consider the case where we would like to scan two systems called newyork and chicago. The appropriate swlist command syntax would be

```
swlist  @ newyork chicago
```

As a result, two listings are generated for each of the hosts provided on the command line. Because of this feature, it is very easy to automate the inventory of installed software across a network of systems.

swinstall

The `swinstall` utility is used to install or inspect packages that have been installed on the system. This tool is fairly sophisticated in its approach to package management. For example, when program is started, it automatically scans the system to see if it can find any packages to install.

Project 4-1

Let's imagine that we would like to install a software program called `ethereal`. This tool provides a GUI-based facility to capture a network package. The package name is `ethereal-0.8.20-sd-11.00.depot`.

Step-by-Step

1. Start the `swinstall` program, using the command

```
swinstall -i
```

The `-i` option tells the program to run using the interactive user interface; this interface will function with a regular term or X-term. We could have ran the program without the `-i` option, since the default mode is to use the user interface. When `swinstall` is first executed, it displays the following screen:

```
Starting the terminal version of swinstall...
To move around in swinstall:
- use the "Tab" key to move between screen elements
- use the arrow keys to move within screen elements
- use "Ctrl-F" for context-sensitive help anywhere in swinstall
On screens with a menubar at the top like this:
       ----------------------------------------------------------
        |File View Options Actions                        Help|
        |  ----  ----  -------  -------------------------------  --- |
- use "Tab" to move from the list to the menubar
- use the arrow keys to move around
- use "Return" to pull down a menu or select a menu item
- use "Tab" to move from the menubar to the list without selecting a menu item
- use the spacebar to select an item in the list
On any screen, press "CTRL-K" for more information on how to use the keyboard.
Press "Return" to continue...
```

2. You must hit the ENTER key to continue.

At this point, the `swinstall` utility checks the local CD-ROM device and after a short amount of time you are prompted to specify the source of the package to install. If you have software on the CD-ROM you would like to install, select it or give the location of a directory that contains the software package(s). In this example, we are attempting to install the `ethereal` tool, which is located in the `/tmp` directory.

The screen below shows the window contents that will be displayed when it prompts for the package source:

```
                      Specify Source (boston-srv)

 Specify the source type, then host name, then path on that host.


   Source Depot Type:  [ Local Directory           ->]

 [ Source Host Name... ] boston-srv
 [ Source Depot Path... ]
 [ Software Filter... ] None

 [   OK   ]                      [ Cancel ]                [ Help  ]
```

3. You must navigate to the Source Depot Path... Name item using the TAB key and then enter the full path name and file of the package. Next, TAB to the OK item and then hit ENTER. Once this has been done, the main window is displayed with the ethereal package:

```
                SD Install - Software Selection (boston-srv) (1)
  File View Options Actions                                        Help

                   Press CTRL-K for keyboard help.
 Source: boston-srv:/tmp/ethereal-0.8.20-sd-11.00.depot

 Target:  boston-srv:/


 Only software compatible with the target is available for selection.

 Top (Bundles and Products)                          0 of 1 selected

   Marked?    Name              Revision      Information    Size(Kb)

              ethereal      ->  0.8.20        ethereal         7414
```

4. Next, you must mark the package so that it will be installed, by selecting the package using the TAB key and then accessing the Actions menu and selecting the Mark For Install menu item. Once done, the Marked item on the main window will indicate that the ethereal package has been marked by with YES in the field.

5. Using the TAB key, navigate to the ethereal package and use the SPACEBAR to select it.

6. Then, select the Install (analyze)… menu item from the Actions menu and a new screen will be displayed to confirm the installation.

7. The installation begins and the following screen is displayed with the status of the progress:

```
                    Install Window (boston-srv) (3)

Press 'Products' and/or 'Logfile' for more target information.

Target               :  boston-srv:/
Status               :  Completed
Percent Complete     :  100%
Kbytes Installed     :  902 of 902
Time Left (minutes):  0
Loading Software     :

[ Products... ] [ Logfile... ]

[  Done  ]                                        [ Help ]
```

The Status field will indicate the completion or failure of the installation. If there were errors, inspect the log file for additional details.

Hint

You can view detailed package information by selecting the package with the SPACEBAR and then accessing the Show Description of Software item from the Actions menu. If the ethereal package was selected, the following screen is displayed:

```
Descripton of package..
               Software Description Dialog (boston-srv)


                                        [ Description... ]
Product: ethereal
Revision: 0.8.20
```

```
ethereal                                          [ Dependencies... ]
Size: 7414 Kbytes
Vendor:
                                                  [   Bundles...    ]
Product Number:
Product executes on: HP-UX_B.11.00_700/800
Category:                                         [  Copyright...   ]
Product may not be relocated
Default Directory: /opt/ethereal
Will be installed at: /opt/ethereal              [   Vendor...     ]
Date Copied: Mon Oct 15 07:46:48 2001
Machine: 9000/[678]??
Operating System Name: HP-UX                     [   Readme...     ]
Operating System Release: ?.11.??
[   OK   ]                                                 [ Help ]
```

To exit the `swinstall` application, TAB to the OK item, hit ENTER. Then using the File menu, select EXIT and hit ENTER.

swremove

To remove one or more packages from a HP-UX system, use the `swremove` command.

Project 4-2

Continuing our example from Project 4-1, let's assume we want to remove the ethereal utility that was just installed.

Step-by-Step

1. Execute the `swremove` utility:

```
swremove
```

When this tool is invoked, it shows the same screen information as the `swinstall` program does. Then, it probes the system to determine all the installed packages and displays a list as shown here:

```
                   SD Remove - Software Selection (boston-srv) (1)
File View Options Actions                                            Help
                   Press CTRL-K for keyboard help.
Target:  boston-srv:/


Target Displaying Software: boston-srv:/
```

```
Top (Bundles and Products)                          0 of 21 selected

    Marked?    Name                  Revision        Information

               A4929A         ->     B.11.00.11      1000Base-T PCI Gigabit E
               A5158A         ->     B.11.00.02      HP PCI Tachyon TL Fibre
               B3701AA        ->     C.02.40.000     HP GlancePlus/UX Pak for
               B3901BA        ->     B.11.01.20      HP C/ANSI C Developer's
               B3913DB        ->     C.03.25         HP aC++ Compiler (S800)
               B3919EA_2A5    ->     B.11.00         Special Edition HP-UX Un
               B3929BA        ->     B.11.00         HP OnlineJFS (Advanced V
               B5456CA        ->     C.01.18.01      HP-UX Development Kit fo
               B8342AA        ->     B.11.00.03      Netscape Communicator 4.
               B8723AA        ->     A.01.02         CIFS/9000 Client Lic. Fo
```

2. Navigate to the ethereal package using the DOWN ARROW key and then select
the package using the SPACEBAR. Using the menu shortcut, type the **m** key to
mark the package selection. Alternatively, you could have navigated to the
Actions menu and selected the Mark For Remove menu item. Once done,
the screen should look like the following:

```
                 SD Remove - Software Selection (boston-srv) (1)
File View Options Actions                                              Help
Target:  boston-srv:/


Target Displaying Software: boston-srv:/


Top (Bundles and Products)                          1 of 21 selected

    Marked?    Name                  Revision        Information        x

               HPUXEng64RT    ->     B.11.00         English HP-UX 64-bit Run ^ x
               OnlineDiag     ->     B.11.00.13.16   HPUX 11.0 Support Tools   x
               PHCO_21492     ->     1.0             Software Distributor (SD  x
               PHKL_22209     ->     1.0             fix f_cred, fork DPFs &    x
               PHNE_22397     ->     1.0             cumulative ARPA Transpor  x
               XSWEC0226      ->     A.1.0           Patch Replacement bundle  x
               XSWGR1100      ->     B.11.00.49.3    HP-UX General Release Pa   x
               XSWHWCR1100    ->     B.11.00.49.3    HP-UX Hardware Enablemen   x
               ethereal       ->     0.8.20          ethereal                  x
    YES        perl           ->     5.6.0           perl
```

3. Navigate to the Actions menu and select the Remove (analysis)... menu item.

4. Once done, the Remove Analysis screen is displayed. Once the Status field indicates "Ready," select the OK item.

5. Next, When the confirm screen is displayed, hit the ENTER key.

6. Next, a new screen is displayed which shows the progress of the removal. If the removal was successful, the Status field will show the "Complete" message as shown here. If errors occurred, examine the log file for additional information.

```
              Remove Window (boston-srv) (3)

Press 'Products' and/or 'Logfile' for more target information.

Target             :  boston-srv:/
Status             :  Completed
Percent Complete   :  100%
Kbytes Removed     :  902 of 902
Time Left (minutes):  0
Removing Software  :

 [ Products... ] [ Logfile... ]

 [  Done  ]                                        [ Help ]
```

1-Minute Drill

● Why is the HP-UX package management tool's ability to query remote machines useful?

● Why is the interactive mode useful in swinstall?

● It makes it easy to inventory packages on remote systems without having to physically touch those systems.
● Interactive mode is useful if you want to select the package to install using onscreen menus and prompts rather than specifying all the necessary options on the command line.

4.3 Discover Linux Package Tools

The Linux operating system (and most of the other different versions as well) supports the Red Hat Package Manager (RPM) format. All the system administrator's requirements for package management are contained within a single utility called rpm. This tool has a large number of command-line arguments, but only a few options are necessary to maximize the use of the tool. Therefore, the most common options are listed in Table 4-4. You must have root privileges to execute this command.

To display a list of the currently installed packages, use the -q or --query option. Since the number of packages installed on a given system can be quite large, it is reasonable to filter the query of packages. For example, assume we would like to see all the packages that are related to file transfer. Thus, the command

```
rpm --query -a | grep ftp
```

would show the following output from a standard version of RH7.0:

```
anonftp-3.0-9
ncftp-3.0.1-7
tftp-server-0.17-5
ftp-0.17-6
wu-ftpd-2.6.1-6
gftp-2.0.8-ximian.2
```

Option	Meaning
--help	Display a detailed list of command-line arguments.
--install -I	Install the specified package.
--query -q	Query mode—displays information about packages.
-a	Used with --query option to specify all packages.
--erase -e	Erase or uninstall a package.
-v	Enable verbose output.
--version	Display the software version of rpm.

Table 4-4   Common rpm Command-Line Options

If we didn't filter this command in some manner, we would obtain a rather larger number of packages. For example, let's send the output from the rpm command to the wc command. Thus,

```
[root@socrates /root]# rpm --query -a | wc -l
    375
```

The result from the rpm command is piped to the word count program that will count each line (-l) to give us a total number of installed packages, which is 375. Note too, we used the -a option to indicate the all packages should be displayed; this parameter is required with that --query option.

To install a new rpm, use the -i or --install command option. For example, to install the xchat program, do the following:

```
rpm --install xchat-1.6.3-4.i386.rpm
```

If no errors occurred during the installation, the prompt would be returned to you without displaying any error messages. The name of the rpm contains a few fields to quickly identify the version and supported platform as noted in the xchat example.

To delete a package, use the -e or --erase command-line argument. Thus, to delete the xchat tool from the system, use

```
rpm --erase xchat-1.6.4
```

If no errors occurred during the removal process, the prompt would be returned to you without displaying any error messages.

Project 4-3

This project will help you find all the installed packages on your system.

Step-by-Step

If you are using a Solaris system:

1. Display all the packages on your system.

```
# pkginfo | more
```

2. Choose a package from the step 1 output and display longer information about it:

```
# pkginfo -l packagename
```

3. Choose a CD-ROM and display all the packages on it:

```
# pkginfo -d /cdrom/path | more
```

If you are using a HP-UX system:

1. Display all the packages on your system.

```
# swlist
```

2. Choose a package from the step 1 output and display longer information about it:

```
# swlist -v packagename
```

3. Choose a depot and display all the packages on it:

```
# swlist -d @ pathtodepot
```

If you are using a Linux system:

1. Display all the packages on your system a page at a time.

```
# rpm --query -a | more
```

2. Choose a package from the step 1 output and display longer information about it:

```
# rpm -qv packagename
```

3. Display more information about the rpm command:

```
#rpm --help
```

☑ *Mastery Check*

1. What is the Solaris command to list all the installed packages in the system category?

2. You must have _____ privileges to execute the package information commands discussed in this module.

3. The RPM format and rpm utility are used to (choose all that apply):

   A. Display information about installed packages

   B. Transfer files

   C. Install a new package

   D. Remove an installed package

4. What would this command do: rpm --erase XFree86?

5. In Solaris, the command to install the SFWgimp package from the /cdrom/s8_software_companion/components/i386/Package CDROM path is

   A. # pkgadd -d /cdrom/s8_software_companion/components/i386/ Packages SFWgimp

   B. # swinstall -d /cdrom/s8_software_companion/components/i386/ Packages SFWgimp

   C. # pkginfo -d /cdrom/s8_software_companion/components/i386/ Packages SFWgimp

   D. # pkgadd -a /cdrom/s8_software_companion/components/i386/ Packages SFWgimp

6. In HP-UX, what command do you use to install a package in interactive mode?

   A. swinstall

   B. swinstall -i

   C. swinstall -l

   D. swinfo -i

4

Module 5

Maintaining
UNIX Users

Critical Skills

This module focuses on maintaining UNIX user accounts from a nuts and bolts perspective. As a result, the associated system configuration files, which UNIX uses to maintain users, are fully described. Further, the additional tools that are used to manipulate these files directly are discussed.

UNIX is a multifaceted operating system; it provides more than one way to accomplish a specific task or administrative function. It contains a plethora of tools for solving a wide range of system-related problems and issues. For instance, users can be added to the system using a graphical user interface program, and other tools that operate on the command line can be used as well. Despite the fact that perhaps these tools provide overlapping functionality and are meant to address the same problem, they clearly provide a different approach to solving the particular problem.

Bear in mind also that the administrator isn't restricted in using the specific user accounts tools to maintain system accounts. Rather, since the configuration files are based on normal text, a standard text editor may be used instead—provided the administrator understands the file formats and can use an editor to input the required information.

The relevant UNIX account system configuration files are

- /etc/passwd

- /etc/group

- /etc/shadow

5.1 Discover the /etc/passwd File

The /etc/passwd file is the main configuration file for all UNIX users. It contains an entry for each user defined on the system; a single line within this file represents a single user. To view a single account, simply use the grep command to search the file for a specific account. Thus, to view the user account called stevem, do the following:

```
# grep stevem /etc/passwd
stevem:x:20003:10:Mr. Steve Maxwell:/homes/stevem:/usr/bin/bash
```

The format of the account entry includes seven fields, which are separated by a colon (:) character. Each field within the file represents one element of the UNIX account entry. Table 5-1 shows these fields and associated examples.

Username

The username must be a unique string that can consist of both letters and numbers, and usually can't be longer than eight characters on most systems. The username should represent the actual name of the user as much as possible. For example, Steve Maxwell could be maxwell, smaxwell, stevem, or just steve. This account name will appear when a list of users is displayed using a command such as who or ps. Also, once the user has logged into the system, the name is used to track any account activity. This username will also appear when files

5

Field	Example	Meaning
Username	stevem	This is name of the UNIX account. This is the name that will be shown when the user logs into the system.
Password	X	This is where the password of the account is stored. If the /etc/shadow file is used, then this field contains an "x".
Account UID	20003	This is the user identification number.
Group ID	10	This is the group identification number that indicates the primary group membership for this user.
Comment	Mr. Steve Maxwell	Comments about the account, which typically contains the real name of the account holder.
Home Directory	/homes/stevem	The default directory where the user will store files and will be placed after logging into the system.
Shell	/usr/bin/bash	The program that will be run for the user when logged into the system. Typically, this field contains the desired shell, which acts as the basic command interpreter.

Table 5-1   Fields Within the /etc/passwd File

and directories are displayed using the long format. For instance, we can examine the ownership of the /etc/passwd itself:

```
# ls -al /etc/passwd
-r--r--r--   1 root      sys           861 Oct 22 21:22 /etc/passwd
```

In this case, the /etc/passwd is owned by the root user, as shown by the third field in the preceding sample output.

Hint

When adding new users to the system, it will be important that a scan be done to ensure that no duplicate names are added. To minimize the chance of this happening, use one of the UNIX administrative tools to add the user directly. However, if the account is being added manually, simply use the grep command to ensure that the account doesn't currently exist.

Typically, the username is also the same as the home directory. Thus, in the example above, the username of sjmaxwell would have the home directory of the same name. However, this is just a convention—there is no technical reason for this to be the case. It makes system administration easier if they are the same.

User Password

The Password field holds an encrypted and encoded password string for the account. This password must be supplied when the user logs into the system. Without the password, the user can't log into the system. The exception to this is that the root user can access any UNIX account without knowing the password. Normal users can access the root account by using the su command. This command stands for "substitute user" and running it without any options defaults to accessing the root account, but you must supply the correct password first.

When creating a new user, this field is left blank and the administrator uses another program to add the password for the account file. In the example account, stevem, the Password field contained a single "x" character. This indicates that the password is stored within the /etc/shadow file instead of the /etc/passwd file. Once the UNIX account has been set up, the administrator can add a new password to the account by executing the passwd command. This command is described later in this module.

User Identification

The user ID (UID) is a unique integer number that is used as the primary mechanism to track the user. The UID is contained within every file and directory associated with the user account and is how user account activity is logged by the system. To examine the mapping between the UID and the account name, use the `id` command:

```
# id
UID=0(root) GID=1(other)
```

As you can see from the output example, the UID of 0 maps directly to the `root` user. The maximum value of the UID is 2147483647, while the minimum value is 0. The value of 0 is reserved and indicates the superuser or `root` account. As a result, non-superuser accounts should start above this number.

5

User Comment

This field contains information about the account and contains any general information associated with the login. Typically, this field is used to specify the owner of the account. For example, in the previous example, the string `Mr. Steve Maxwell` represents the real name of the account `stevem`.

Home Directory

This field contains the home directory for the user and is where the users will typically store all their files. Also, once the system has logged the user in, this directory is their starting point within the file system. In other words, when the user executes the `pwd` command right after logging in, it should display their home directory. Thus,

```
# pwd
/homes/stevem
```

shows the home directory of the user `stevem` if he just logged into the system based on the earlier sample `/etc/passwd` entry.

User Login Shell

This field holds the name of the shell that will be executed when the user logs into the system. The shell is responsible for providing a facility to execute additional UNIX commands for the user. The system supports a number of different shells such as bash (Bourne Again shell), csh (C shell), tcsh (newer C shell), and sh (Standard shell). If no shell is supplied within this field, the default shell of sh is used. Sometimes this field may contain a /bin/false entry, which means that user will never obtain a login shell because the value returned is always not true.

Also, in certain cases, no shell is included within this field, but another UNIX program. For example, consider the nuucp UNIX account:

```
nuucp:x:9:9:uucp Admin:/var/spool/uucppublic:/usr/lib/uucp/uucico
```

In this case, the shell field contains a path to the uucico program, instead of a standard shell program that we have seen before. This entry is the file transport program for the UNIX-to-UNIX copy (UUCP) system. This is by no means a standard UNIX account since no user will actually use this account—but it is actually accessed by programs. UUCP provides a facility to transfer files from one system to another using one or more network or serial communication mechanisms. When the nuucp login name is accessed, the uucico program is run to initiate the file transfer, instead of just running a command prompt for a normal UNIX account.

5.2 Discover the /etc/group File

The /etc/group file contains definitions of groups and their corresponding group members. Groups provide a way to establish collections of users that share one or more things in common. For example, the group devel may contain all the users that are responsible in some way for the development of a particular product. If a user must be a member of more than one group, the associated account name can be added to additional groups that are defined within the /etc/group file A sample group, called devel, is shown here:

```
devel::107:samyu,irinav,anitat,stevem
```

Each line within this file represents a single group entry and contains four fields. The required group fields are described in Table 5-2. Like the /etc/passwd entries, the fields within the /etc/group file are also separated by the colon (:) character.

Field	Example	Meaning
Group Name	devel	The name of the group.
Group Password	(blank)	The password for the group is stored in this field.
Group ID	107	The group identification.
Group Members	samyu, irinav, anitat, stevem	A comma-separated list of group members are listed in this field.

Table 5-2   Fields Within the `/etc/group` File

Group Name

The group name is a string that can consist of both letters and numbers, and is typically not more than eight characters wide. This group name will appear within the output of any UNIX program that displays group information. For example, you can use `ls -l` command to obtain additional file information on `/etc/group` file:

```
# ls -al /etc/group
-rw-r--r--   1 root      sys          504 Oct 28 16:30 /etc/group
```

As you can see, the output shows that the file contains the group ownership of `sys`. The `sys` group represents the system group, which is the main group for UNIX programs and configuration files that generally need `root` access to operate correctly or be accessed.

Group Password

This field holds the group password. In practice, a password is not normally defined for groups.

Group Identification

The group ID (GID) is a unique integer number that is used as the primary mechanism to track the group. The GID is contained within every file and directory associated with the user account and is the way group account activity is logged by the system. The maximum value of the GID is 2147483647, while the minimum value is 0. The value of 0 is reserved and indicates the superuser or `root` account. As a result, non-superuser accounts should start above this number.

Group Members

The list of individual members within a group is listed within this field. A comma-separated list of account names can be added to a group entry, thereby adding these accounts to the membership of the group. In the example above, the `devel` group has the following members: `samyu`, `irinav`, `anitat`, and `stevem`.

How Group Membership Work

Consider three users (`fred`, `barney`, and `bambam`), and two groups (`flintstone` and `rubble`). The user fred is a member of the `flintstone` group while both `barney` and `bambam` are members of the `rubble` group. Thus, we would see the following entries within the `/etc/group` file:

```
flintstone::201:fred
rubble::204:barney,bambam
```

Let's also assume that the home directories and file permissions for these users are defined as follows:

```
drwxrwx---  2 barney    rubble       512 Oct  2 16:07  barney
drwxrwx---  2 bambam    rubble       512 Oct 27 18:28 bambam
drwxrwx---  2 fred      flintstone   512 Nov 22 15:27 fred
```

Don't be alarmed; home directories typically will be named the same name as the login account name. That is why, for instance, the `barney` directory is owned by the user `barney`.

Note in this example, all the directories are owned by their respective account names and the directory access permissions are set to `rwxrwx----`. These permission modes indicate that both the owner and group have complete access to search, read, and write files within these directories. In other words, the users barney and bambam have access to not only their own accounts, but to each other's as well. This is made possible because both barney and bambam belong to the rubble group. Also note, the user fred doesn't have any access to either the `barney` or `bambam` directories. The same is also true of both barney and bambam—they can't access any of the files within the `fred` directory either.

If we choose to remove the group restrictions as stated above, the following can be done:

- Add `fred` to the `rubble` group. Thus, the rubble group will look like the following:

```
rubble::204:barney,bambam,fred
```

- Change the access permission of the `barney` and `bambam` directories to include other users. In other words, change the directory ownership to

```
drwxrwxrwx  2 barney    rubble        512 Oct 2 16:07   barney
drwxrwxrwx  2 bambam    rubble        512 Oct 27 18:28 bambam
```

In this case, fred can now have full access to both the `barney` and `bambam` directories. However, bear in mind that this might not be the best solution since this opens access to a larger pool of users, which may not be the desired action. Also, we would need to alter the `fred` directory in order to give both barney and bambam access as well.

Hint

It is entirely reasonable for a UNIX user to be in more than one group at the same time.

5

5.3 Discover the /etc/shadow File

The `/etc/shadow` file is used to store account password information and contains password aging information. In particular, it contains an encrypted password and related parameters that control elements about the password—for example, when the account password should expire. Unlike both the `/etc/passwd` and `/etc/group` files, which can be read by any user, the `/etc/shadow` file is restricted; only the superuser may list the content of the file. This is because of the relatively sensitive nature of the information stored within this file; it is unreasonable to give important account information to just any user. The contents of the `/etc/shadow` includes nine fields separated by colons. Password aging simply means that the password will expire or become invalid at some future date and the user will be forced to input a new password, which will correspond to the password policy that the system administrator has set up.

Ask the Expert

Question Why are there separate `/etc/passwrd` and `/etc/shadow` files?

Answer From a historical perspective, account passwords used to be stored in the `/etc/passwd` file exclusively. Based on additional improvements within the area of UNIX security, user accounts now contain new security features as defined within the `/etc/shadow` file.

A sample password entry for the `/etc/shadow` file is shown here:

```
stevem:JcpRL1Irplkuw:11624:::::11615:
```

This entry is associated with the UNIX account stevem as listed in the previous examples. All of the fields from the `/etc/shadow` file are described in Table 5-3.

Field	Example	Meaning
Account Name	stevem	The name of the associated UNIX account as defined within the /etc/passwd file.
Password	JcpRL1Irplkuw	This field contains the encrypted password.
Last Changed	11624	When the entry was last modified.
Min Days	(blank)	The minimum number of days for the password to be changed.
Max Days	(blank)	The maximum number of days that the password will retain value.
Warn Days	(blank)	The number of days to warn the user of a pending password expiration.
Inactive Days	(blank)	The number of days for the account to be inactive before the account will expire.
Expire Date	11615	The date when the account will no longer be accessible by the user.
Flag	(blank)	Reserved for future use and is currently not used.

Table 5-3 Fields Within the `/etc/shadow` File

Account Name
This is the name of a valid UNIX account as found within the /etc/passwd file. It is important that the order of account names match those within the /etc/shadow file. In other words, both entries should be in the same place within each file. If you use automated account generation tools such as admintool or useradd, name ordering shouldn't be a problem However, if you edit the account files manually, you will need to specifically watch for account name ordering.

Password
This field contains a 13-character encrypted password associated with the account name. The account is locked when the string *LK* is listed within this field. The passwd command is used to add or modify passwords within this field. The password string as shown in the example above bears no resemblance to the actual password string that was used to generate this encrypted form.

Last Changed
This field shows the number of days since this entry was changed. The number of days is measured from 1/1/1970. Thus, in the example above, a total of 11,624 days have elapses since the 1/1/1970 date.

Min Days
This field dictates the minimum number of days between account password changes. This is a handy way to control, on a regular basis, when users should change their passwords.

Max Days
This controls the maximum number of days that a password can remain valid.

Warn Days
This field denotes the number of days that the user will be warned pending an expired password.

Inactive Days
This is the number of days the account can be inactive before the password will expire. This metric is reset if the account is accessed before the actual inactivity timer has expired.

Expire Date

This field denotes the absolute date when the account can't be used any more. This type of configuration may be useful for temporary accounts used by vendors or contractors that are involved with a project where the start and stop points are known in advance. This number is also in the same format as the Last Changed field.

1-Minute Drill

● Why can only the superuser display the /etc/shadow file contents?

● Why does reading the password field in the /etc/shadow file not tell you what the password is?

5.4 Explore UNIX Account Tools

UNIX provides a number of command-line tools to help with account maintenance. These particular tools are for the "power user" or the advanced administrator, because they assume a certain level of knowledge and understanding. However, with the explanations and information presented here, you can effectively use these tools.

The following tools will be discussed in this section:

● passwd

● pwck

● grpck

● useradd

● userdel

● usermod

● groupadd

● The /etc/shadow file contains sensitive password information about all users that shouldn't be read by anyone other than the superuser.

● The original password is encrypted, and only the encrypted form is saved in the /etc/shadow file.

- groupdel

- groupmod

- logins (Solaris only)

- vipw

Hint

These tools operate on the local system and they modify or update the files listed above on the system that these tools are executed on. If you are using NIS, you must specify alterative files that these tools will operate against the NIS-related files. See Module 15 for information about using NIS.

5

passwd

The most common account tool is the `passwd` command. This utility is used to change the password of an established account and can be invoked by generic system users as well as the system administrator. For instance, to change a password, which is the default behavior, the following procedure would be followed:

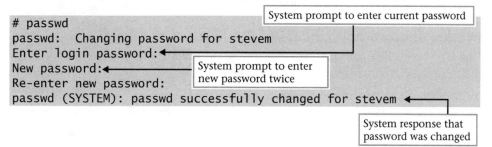

```
# passwd
passwd:  Changing password for stevem
Enter login password:◄──────────  System prompt to enter current password
New password:◄──────────  System prompt to enter
Re-enter new password:      new password twice
passwd (SYSTEM): passwd successfully changed for stevem ◄──── System response that
                                                               password was changed
```

Hint

This example should show what the system will display when the `stevem` user changes his password.

The user `stevem` is asked for the old login password, plus the new password twice. If the password change is complete, a message is displayed indicating success.

When selecting a new password, the following can be used as a general set of guidelines:

- Each user account password must be a minimum number of characters long. This minimum is defined within the `/etc/default/passwd` file. The `PASSLENGTH` variable defined within this file is set to 6 on Solaris systems. However, the system administrator can change it. Making this value smaller means that passwords won't be as tough to forge, while making it larger means that users will have a harder time remembering their passwords. This option is system wide; there is currently no way to alter this variable for individual users.

- A password must have at least one number or special character, plus at least two alphabetic characters. These characters may include both uppercase and lowercase.

- A password must be different from the login name or any standard deviation from the login name. This includes using uppercase letters as well.

- New account passwords must be sufficiently different from the old ones.

Hint

If an account password is changed by root, the old password is not requested.

The `passwd` program supports a number of powerful command-line options. These can be divided into three categories: those that permit the user to alter some information within the account configuration files, those that control the login account system in some way, and those that report account information.

Modification to Account Fields

The command-line options, which control modification to the account configuration files, are listed in Table 5-4.

One of the other really interesting uses of the `passwd` program is to alter specific account text fields within either the `/etc/passwd` or `/etc/shadow`

Option	Meaning
-e	Change the login shell of the user.
-F	Use an alternative password file (HP-UX only).
-g	Change the comment field of the user.
-h	Change the home directory of the user.
-r	Specify which repository the change should be made in (HP-UX only). The supported locations include files, nis, and nisplus.

Table 5-4 `passwd` Account Modification Options

files. For example, to change the comment field of a particular user, use the −g option. Thus, given the sample account

```
stevem:x:20003:10:Mr Stevee Maxwell:/homes/stevem:/usr/bin/bash
```

we notice that the user's name is misspelled. To fix this situation, we can use the passwd command with the option that permits updates to the Comment field:

```
# passwd -g stevem
Default values are printed inside of '[]'.
To accept the default, type <return>.
To have a blank entry, type the word 'none'.

Name [Mr Stevee Maxwell]: Mr. Steve Maxwell
```

As shown above, we type in the fully corrected string. To check to ensure that the change was made, we can do the following:

```
# grep stevem /etc/passwd
stevem:x:20003:10:Mr. Steve Maxwell:/homes/stevem:/usr/bin/bash
```

Displaying of Account Information

The command-line options, which show specific information from the account files, are listed in Table 5-5.

To show the password attributes for all the /etc/passwd account entries, use the −a and −s options. Thus,

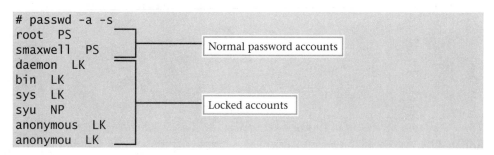

Option	Meaning
-a	Show password attributes for all entries within the /etc/passwd file.
-s	Show password attributes for the specified login name.

Table 5-5 passwd Account Display Options

The attributes listed from the output include LK for locked account, PS for normal password, and NP for no password. Also, the −s option can be used to list a specific login account name, which must be given on the command line.

Controlling Account Access

The command-line options, which can be used to provide a finer grain of control over user accounts, are listed in Table 5-6.

To lock out a particular user from the system, you can use the −l option followed by the user name. Thus,

```
# passwd -l stevem
```

locks the stevem account. We can examine the account to see if the lockout actually occurred:

```
# grep stevem /etc/shadow
stevem:*LK*:11624::::::11644:
```

As you can see, the string *LK* has been replaced within the Password field, which indicates the account has been locked.

pwck

The pwck utility performs a consistence check on the UNIX /etc/passwd administrative file to ensure that it remains free from syntax errors or doesn't contain invalid information. This utility can be used to detect the following:

- Syntax errors

- Invalid fields information

- Incorrect number of fields

Typically, this program would be executed after the /etc/passwd file was updated. However, if the administrator uses standard tools to manipulate the password file, then no consistency check is really need. With many of the system-supplied tools—for example, admintool—it would be very difficult to introduce a syntax error since these programs were written to catch and resolve such problems. The only time it would be needed is when /etc/passwd file

Option	Meaning
-d	Delete the password from the specified user account (Solaris only).
-f	This option forces the user to change their password the next time they log in to the system.
-l	Locks the specified user account immediately.
-n	Sets the minimum number of days between password changes.
-w	Sets the numbers of days to warn the user of a pending password change.
-x	Sets the maximum number of days for the password to be valid.

Table 5-6   `passwd` Account Controlling Options

5

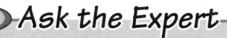

Ask the Expert

Question   Why are so many guidelines necessary for password selection?

Answer   All of these guidelines are intended to make it more difficult for another user to guess your password and gain access to your account. Specifically, mixing numbers, special characters, and alphabetic characters makes it more difficult to match your password by using a dictionary or list of common words. Keeping your password very different from your login name makes it difficult to guess your password by using a list of variations on your login. And making your new password different from any old one makes it difficult to guess your current password should one of your old passwords ever be compromised.

Question   Why is it important for a UNIX system administrator to set password expiration limits for all system users?

Answer   The longer a user uses the same password without changing it, the more chance they will accidentally divulge the password to someone else (for example, writing it on a sticky note that someone else finds) or the more chance someone intentionally trying to break into the system will have enough time to systematically guess until they find a user's password, if the user isn't periodically changing it on their own.

is updated manually. In this case, because the human element is involved, it would be possible to add an invalid character, which could make the file unusable. It would also be possible to overlook an important field or have too much information. If you manually manipulate the /etc/passwd file, it is recommended that you invoke the pwck utility as the last step in the process.

To perform a scan of the local passwd file, issue the following command:

```
pwck
```

Depending on if any problems have been encountered with the file, one or more messages will be displayed. For example, if a particular entry contains too many fields, the following message will be shown:

```
billc:x:20002:10:Mr. Bill Clinton:/homes/billc:::/usr/bin/bash
        Too many/few fields
```

To remedy this problem, edit the passwd file and delete the extra field separators.

If a UNIX account doesn't contain a valid home directory, the following message will be displayed:

```
stevem:x:20001:10:Mr. Steve Maxwell:/homes/stevem:/usr/bin/bash
        Login directory not found
```

To solve this problem, simply create the necessary directory—or, if the account is no longer used, delete it.

If you are using a password file that resides in another directory, simply include the path as an argument to the pwck command:

```
pwck /var/etc/passwd
```

The Linux version of pwck is more sophisticated than the UNIX password file checker; it has the capabilities to delete invalid entries on the fly as they are encountered. For example, given the invalid UNIX /etc/passwd entry of jsmith:x:550:100:Joe Smith, which is missing part of the login account information, the following error output is displayed:

```
invalid password file entry
delete line ` jsmith:x:550:100:Joe Smith'?
```

As shown in the output above, the program prompts for the deletion of the incorrect line, and answering the question with a y will delete the line, while any other input will cause the tool to exit without performing any other actions.

With HP-UX, the -s option is supported, which tells pwck to check the Protected Password database—this provides another level of protection over and above the /etc/passwd database.

grpck

The grpck utility performs a consistence check on the UNIX /etc/group administrative file and operates in the same manner as the pwck tool. It performs similar syntax and field checks on the group file. The syntax is the same as pwck—simply execute the grpck tool on the command line and it will scan and report any problems it finds. The Linux version of this tool also prompts for removal of incorrect or invalid entries.

1-Minute Drill

● Why are the pwck and grpck utilities nice to have available but generally not needed?

● Why is w1Lma not a good password for an account named wilma?

useradd

The useradd tool provides the ability to add a new UNIX user to the system from the command line. Each of the required Account fields are specified on the command line with designated options. This tool has a large number of command-line arguments, and the most common ones are listed in Table 5-7. This tool is very useful if you must add a user to the system but don't have access to a workstation that can display a GUI tool. Also, if you have the need to automate the adding of users, this tool can be used as the basis of such automation.

● pwck and grpck are nice to have to perform consistency checks on /etc/passwd and /etc/group in case you edit these files manually or use scripts to add and modify users and groups. However, you'll usually use standard tools to make these changes, and the tools will make the modifications correctly without requiring a consistency check.
● w1Lma is easily derived from wilma.

Option	Meaning
-c	Specifies the account comment
-d	Specifies the account home directory
-e	Specifies account expiration
-f	Specifies the interval for account deactivation
-g	Specifies the group of the account
-G	Specifies additional account groups
-k	Specifies the directory that contains the skeleton information that will be copied to a new user's account
-m	Instructs to create the user's home directory if it doesn't already exist
-s	Specifies the full pathname of the login shell
-u	Specifies the UID for the user

Table 5-7   Common `useradd` Command-Line Options

To illustrate the function of the `useradd` tool, consider that the following user must be added to the system:

- Login name: `tjones`

- Comment: `Tom Jones`

- Shell: `/usr/bin/bash`

The syntax of the `useradd` command is as follows:

```
useradd -u 345 -g 10 -d /home/tjones -s /bin/bash -c "Tom's
Account" tjones
```

In this case, this command specified both the user ID (345) and the group ID (10) for the user `tjones`. However, you can have the system select these values if necessary. On Solaris, the user ID is defined as the next-highest value currently within the `/etc/passwd` file used. For the group ID, the default value of 1 is used. For instance, assume that the highest user ID value already contained within the `/etc/passwd` file is 25000. If the above command was executed without the -u and -g options, such as

```
useradd -d /home/tjones -s /bin/bash -c "Tom's Account" tjones
```

then the UNIX account for `tjones` would be defined as follows:

```
tjones:x:25001:1:Tom's Account:/home/tjones:/usr/bin/bash
```

With Linux, when the −g option is not specified, it takes the group ID from the user ID instead. So, the entry would look like this:

```
tjones:x:25001:25001:Tom's Account:/home/tjones:/bin/bash
```

Note that the bash shell on Linux is located in the /bin directory, whereas on Solaris and HP-UX it is located in the /usr/bin directory. The above example includes the use of the bash from the correct location.

userdel

The userdel tool provides the ability to remove a UNIX user from the system using the command line. The command supports a single command-line option— r—which will force the program to remove the home directory of the user.

Hint

The removal of users shouldn't be done lightly, and all user accounts should not only be backed up on a continued basis. However, when deleting one or more accounts, these should be backed up just before they are removed.

To remove the `tjones` account in the previous example, issue the following command:

```
userdel tjones
```

In this case, the home directory for the tjones account (/home/tjones) was not removed. To remove it when deleting the account use the −r option:

```
userdel −r tjones
```

When the above command is run, it will delete the account and remove the home directory without any prompts. Again, back up the accounts before removal, unless no user-defined files are there or the user simply doesn't want the files anymore. (However, be on the safe side and make a copy just in case.)

usermod

The usermod tool is used to make changes to already-defined UNIX accounts. It uses many of the same command-line arguments as the useradd command and also supports a few new ones. As a result, only those parameters not listed in the previous table have been included in Table 5-8.

The usermod tool can be used to alter any of the UNIX account fields. All account changes should be made when the account is inactive—that is, when the user is currently not logged into the system. Also, if you are going to change the user ID of an account, make sure that that user isn't running any programs since changing the ID will affect any running processes.

To change the Comment field of the user account named stevex, issue the following command:

```
usermod -c "Mr Steve's Account"  stevex
```

To disable the account tjones on a Linux system, do the following:

```
usermod -L tjones
```

Next, examine the results with the following command:

```
# grep tjones /etc/shadow
tjones:!$1$K98bVe3s$1NnaEYqFw8XRF6r25S/A:11690:0:99999:7:::
```

As you can see, a bang (!) character has been placed in the password file at the beginning of the Password field entry. This effectively disables the account

Option	Meaning
-l	Change the existing user name to a new name.
-L	Lock the user account (Linux only).
-m	Move the user's mode directory.
-U	Unlock the user account (Linux only).
-u	Modify the UID.

Table 5-8 The usermod Command-Line Arguments

because the password supplied by the user will never match the one with the new character. To enable the account, use the –U option:

```
usermod -U tjones
```

and then examine the account again:

```
# grep tjones /etc/shadow
tjones:$1$K98bVe3s$1NnaEYqFw8XRF6r25S/A:11690:0:99999:7:::
```

The bang character is now gone.

> **Hint**
>
> Using the –U option on a Red Hat Linux 7.0 system with a new account didn't completely remove the bang characters the first time. Instead, the command needed to be repeated a second time before they were removed. This is because two bang characters are used when no password has been assigned to a new account.

groupadd

The `groupadd` command provides the ability to add a new group to the system using the command line. The command-line options include the –g and –o arguments. The –g option permits the specification of the group ID number instead of using the next-highest number defined by the system. The –o option permits the inclusion of a duplicate group ID number. To add a new group called support to the system, issue the following command:

```
groupadd support
```

To verify the new group, do the following:

```
bash-2.03# grep support /etc/group
support::1001:
```

groupdel

The groupdel command provides the inverse of the groupadd command; it removes an existing UNIX account group. For instance, to remove the support group that was created above, execute the following command:

```
groupdel support
```

To verify the new group was in fact deleted:

```
# grep support /etc/group
```

groupmod

The groupmod tool is used to alter the name of an existing group. For example, if you wanted to change the name of an existing group, you could issue the following command:

```
groupmod -n devel support
```

This would rename the support group to the devel group while keeping the group membership (that is, the list of account names) intact. The -n option is used to indicate the name of the new group. This command also supports the -g and -o options, and they have the same meaning as those options from the groupadd command.

logins

The Solaris system supports a tool call logins that displays a list of all the defined users on the system. The tool supports a few command-line options, and the most useful ones are listed in Table 5-9.

Issuing the logins command without any command-line arguments displays a list of all the defined accounts on the system sorted by the user ID. Thus, the command

```
logins
```

will show

root	0		1	Super-User
smaxwell	0		1	Super-User
daemon	1		1	
bin	2	bin	2	
sys	3	sys	3	
adm	4	adm	4	Admin
uucp	5	uucp	5	uucp Admin
nuucp	9	nuucp	9	uucp Admin
listen	37	adm	4	Network Admin
lp	71	lp	8	Line Printer Admin
syu	100		111	
anonymous	101		1	
anonymou	102		1	
stevex	345	staff	10	Steve's Account
anitat	1001	staff	10	Ms. Anita
Tognazzini				
stevem	20001	staff	10	Mr. Steve Maxwell
billc	20002	staff	10	Mr. Bill Clinton
samc	20110	staff	10	Mr Sam Clinton
jjwalker	25000		1	Mr JJ Walker
nobody	60001	nobody	60001	Nobody
noaccess	60002	noaccess	60002	No Access User
nobody4	65534	nogroup	65534	SunOS 4.x Nobody

Option	Meaning
-a	Displays two additional password expiration fields to the output
-d	Displays only logins with duplicate IDs
-g	Displays all accounts matching the specified group name
-l	Displays the specified user
-m	Shows multiple group members information
-o	Displays the information using colon-separated fields with one entry per line
-p	Displays logins that contain no passwords
-s	Displays only system logins
-t	Displays entries sorted by login and not the user ID
-x	Displays additional information about each user

Table 5-9   The `logins` Command-Line Options

The output includes the username of the account in the first field, and the second is the user identification. The third field is the primary group, the fourth field is the group ID, and the fifth is the Comment field.

If we wanted to tighten the output from above, we can use the −o option. We could also use it if we only wanted to display generic user accounts (that is, no system accounts). We could use the following command:

```
logins -o -u
```

This command would show

```
syu:100::111:
anonymous:101::1:
anonymou:102::1:
stevex:345:staff:10:Steve's Account
anitat:1001:staff:10:Ms. Anita Tognazzini
stevem:20001:staff:10:Mr. Steve Maxwell
billc:20002:staff:10:Mr. Bill Clinton
samc:20110:staff:10:Mr Sam Clinton
jjwalker:25000::1:Mr JJ Walker
nobody:60001:nobody:60001:Nobody
noaccess:60002:noaccess:60002:No Access User
nobody4:65534:nogroup:65534:SunOS 4.x Nobody
```

Thus, the output has been reduced and only the generic user accounts have been displayed. A user account is one that contains a user ID above 99.

vipw

The vipw command provides a quick way to edit the password file. Running the command starts the vi editor with the /etc/passwd file so that you can edit the contents. Thus, you will need to know how to use the vi editor to make changes to this file. The Linux system also provides the vigr command, which provides the same service but with the /etc/group file.

Project 5-1

In this project you learn about your own permissions and group memberships on your system, and how to manage them and make changes.

Step-by-Step

1. Display your user account from the `/etc/passwd` file:

```
# grep yourusername /etc/passwd
```

2. Find and display all the groups you belong to:

```
# grep yourusername /etc/group
```

3. Create a new group name flintstones:

```
#groupadd flintstones
```

4. Display the group information about the flintstones group:

```
# grep flintstones /etc/group
```

5. Create a new user, wilma, with the comment Wilma Flintstone, and make the home directory for the user `/homes/wilma`. Let the system specify the user ID. Make wilma part of the flintstones group you created in the previous steps.

```
useradd -g flintstones -d /home/wilma -m -c "Wilma Flintstone" wilma
```

6. Change the wilma user account name to wilmaf:

```
usermod -l wilmaf wilma
```

7. Display the group information about the flintstones group to see if wilmaf is a member:

```
# grep flintstones /etc/group
```

8. Delete the wilmaf account and her home directory:

```
userdel -r wilmaf
```

9. Delete the flintstones group:

```
groupdel flintstones
```

5

☑ *Mastery Check*

1. What account has the user ID value 0?

    A. Yours

    B. Root

    C. Admin

    D. Shell

2. What shell will be used by default if no shell is specified for a given user account in the `/etc/passwd` file?

    A. `bash`

    B. csh

    C. tcsh

    D. sh

3. _____ provide a way to establish collections of users that share one or more things in common.

4. In this example from an `/etc/shadow` file, barney:LtyH4YUn3swer: 11764:30:45:5::11800:, how many days warning will the user get before the password expires?

    A. 30

    B. 45

    C. 5

    D. 0

5. What command would you use to force user wilma to change her password the next time she logs in?

☑ *Mastery Check*

6. Which file stores information defining the minimum character length for a password?

   A. /etc/default/passwd

   B. /etc/passwd

   C. /etc/shadow

   D. /etc/group

7. In Linux, what command would you use to lock the wilma user account?

8. What is the command to display password attributes for your account?

9. Which of the following is the best new password for the barney account based on the password criteria in this module if his current password is po82Yq?

   A. ruBBle

   B. po38Yq

   C. KpF4j7

   D. bARn3y

5

Module 6

File Systems, Disks, and Tools

Critical Skills

Perhaps one of the most important and somewhat complicated aspects of a UNIX system administrator involves file systems, peripheral disks, and the tools used to maintain these file systems, which are placed on storage devices. As the system administrator, you will be required to handle file system related problems – such as repairing a corrupt or creating a new file system. Further, you will need to know how to add additional storage devices to the system and be able to configure them correctly. The bottom line is that you must be ready to handle issues, and problems quickly and this module prepares you to address some of the more common problems and situation that may occur during day-to-day system operations.

This section covers the software aspect of adding and configuring new storage to the system; due to the scope of this book, no physical hardware details will be covered. If you have hardware related questions, you should consult the documentation materials that were provided by the hardware manufacturer of the system or peripheral device you are using. Also, as a general rule, when attempting to determine the source of a problem on UNIX, it becomes paramount that as the system administrator, you determine if the problem is hardware based or software. For example, if for some reason one or more particular UNIX files are not available on the system, several different issues could cause this problem. Some of the issues could, in fact, be hardware related. Thus, determining faulty hardware quickly can save valuable time up front instead of assuming the problem must be related to the configuration or some system software issue.

6.1 Explore a UNIX File System

A file system is simply a collection of objects (files or directories, for example) that are organized to include the following elements: optimal data access, ensures data integrity, provides manageable, and can be scalability to support many objects. UNIX file systems provide these elements and more; they are the foundation and capstone for all file access on the system, and without a file system, the UNIX system wouldn't be that useful.

A file system supports objects or containers such as files, directories, and hidden data structure elements. A high level view of a file system is shown in Figure 6-1. Files are defined as individual containers that are used to access text or data. The text of a file can simply be a collection of strings. As we have already seen, we have accessed standard text files on UNIX already. For example, the /etc/passwd file contains a list of users in the form text strings. Files can also

Disk Drive

Figure 6-1   File system view

be used to store data. Data within a file can represent almost anything; a UNIX program, for example, can be considered a data file. In addition, data can take other forms as well; a database may contain lists of names and addresses or statistical information.

As the figure above shows, the definition of a file resides within the context of a directory, which in turn is defined within a file system, and the file system is stored on a disk drive.

A directory is a container of files and with many operating systems, directories may contain additional sub-directories. Thus, a directory permits the file system to become hierarchical. That is to say, directories and sub-directories can be formed in such a manner as to build a reverse tree-like like structure as shown in Figure 6-2. As you can see, the root (base) of the tree is at the top and

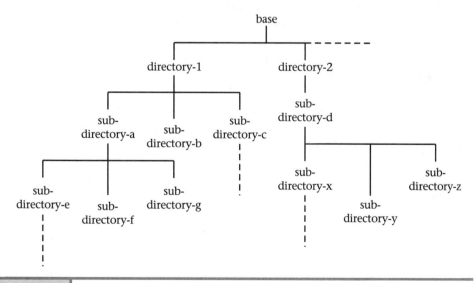

Figure 6-2   Tree structure of a file system

as additional directories are added, the tree becomes larger by expanding the branches or leaves at the bottom of the tree.

The remaining file system elements consist of specific data structures that are used to support and maintain the file system or provide for "housekeeping" tasks and routines. One of the common data structures that you will hear about is the i-node table and super block. The i-node table is used to keep track of all the files within the file system. The i-node contains many of the attributes of the file (such as the size of the file) and pointers to where the actual data of the file is located. When you issue the `ls` command, many of the items contained within the file's i-node are displayed.

The super block is an area on the disk which contains important file system information, such as the state of the file system, the number of i-nodes used, and when the system was last error-checked. Since the super block is important, it is automatically replicated to other areas on the disk to ensure that the information will be available should the disk driver encounter some hardware-related problems and the file system require repair.

All operating systems support some type of file system organization or structure. Thus, all operating systems share this element. Since different file systems exist, in many instances they are incompatible because the structure and format differ. For example, the file system layout of an IBM mainframe system contains a different operating system from what is supported on HP-UX. However, in practice, some of these incompatibilities are minimized by the use of specialized tools and software. File conversion utilities can be used in some cases. Also, due to the extreme popularity of networks, many disparate systems are interconnected and file system objects can be transported from one system to another without the explicit conversion from different file systems. This aspect of networking will be covered in detail with modules on FTP and NFS.

You can view all the currently available file systems on the system by issuing the `df -k` command. A sample is shown below:

Filesystem	kbytes	used	avail	capacity	Mounted on
/dev/dsk/c0d0s0	480815	38088	394646	9%	/
/dev/dsk/c0d0s6	1587078	628757	910709	41%	/usr
/dev/dsk/c0d0p0:boot	10484	1668	8816	16%	/boot
/dev/dsk/c0d0s1	384847	22020	324343	7%	/var

File system name

```
swap                      1007100       384 1006716     1%    /tmp
/dev/dsk/c0d0s5            480815       7016  425718     2%    /opt
/dev/dsk/c0d0s7           4225774        268 4183249     1%    /export/home
/vol/dev/dsk/c1t0d0/s8_software_companion
                          622422      622422       0   100%
/cdrom/s8_software_companion
#
```

The –k option changes the default output of the df command to be more useful. The output includes the file system name, the size, bytes used, bytes available, current capacity used, and the mount point. The Filesystem name presents the actual partition name defined for the disk that file system resides on. With the first entry, the file system name is /dev/dsk/c0d0s0. With UNIX, many hardware elements of the system are represented and accessed with special files. These files don't contain text or user data. Instead, they are access points into the drivers that control the hardware components. In the case of a file system, the special file determines which partition on the disk should be used when accessing the file system.

The Kbytes represents the total size of the file system that can be used to store information, while the used column indicates the amount of space currently used by all files. The avail is the total available space that can be used for new files. The capacity shows the totally used space as a parentage. The Mounted on shows which directory each file system is mounted to.

Depending on UNIX operating system version, the file system name or partition access point can be different. Two major formats are used; for HP-UX and Solaris, the area on the disk is described with the format c0d0s0, while on Linux the standard partition name of /dev/hd is used. The meaning of the first format is shown in Figure 6-3.

The disk controller (c) number corresponds to the interface for which this particular disk is attached. The disk (d) number identifies which disk out of the entire attached disks for that particular controller. The slice (s) number means which particular partition given all the defined partitions on the disk. Thus, c0d0s0 is interpreted as the first partition or slice (s0) on the first disk drive (d0) from the first disk controller (c0).

The Linux output of the df command is quite similar to both HP-UX and Solaris and

6

Hint

The naming convention of file system access points is from the UNIX system V releases; BSD derived release uses a different standard.

regular UNIX
directory

/dev/dsk/c0d0s0

partition name where:
c - disk controller number
d - device number
s - slice number

| **Figure 6-3** | File system access point |

contains basically the same fields. However, the major difference is the name of the file system device files or access points. Thus, when the same `df` command is run on Linux, we see

Partition number

Filesystem	1k-blocks	Used	Available	Use%	Mounted on
/dev/hda6	2071384	1111760	854400	57%	/
/dev/hda1	2071384	497108	1469052	26%	/rh62
/dev/hda5	2071384	391036	1575124	20%	/rh61
/dev/hda7	1035660	20	983032	1%	/ffn
/dev/hda9	521748	79504	415740	17%	/home

Hard drive letter

The `hd` simply means "hard drive" and is followed by a letter to indicate which drive in the system. Next, we see that the partition number is appended to the end of the file system file name. Thus, the root (/) file system is contained within the sixth partition of the first drive known as "a".

6.2 Uncover a Disk Partition

A file system typically is defined within the boundaries of a disk partition. A disk partition is a fixed area defined on a storage medium for the purposes of data access. Figure 6-4 shows the high level view of disk partitions. A partition is also known as the disk layout, partition map, or logical drive. For example, on Linux, / is the root file system. This particular file system resides within a physical partition on one of the disks contained in a system. As you can see from the figure, a disk can have a number of partitions and/or file systems.

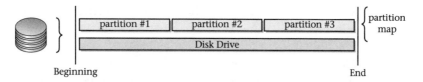

Figure 6-4 View of disk partitions

However, most systems limit the number of partitions that can be configured, and for good reason: attempting to manage a large number of partitions on a single disk can be difficult. Also, in some cases, the upper limit of the number of partitions is controlled by the architecture of system in question.

Typically, disk partitions are defined during system installation and configuration. However, there are times when you need to modify the partition map or to display all the defined partitions on disk. UNIX provides tools for the purpose and depending on which UNIX version, the tool will be different. For example, on the Linux system, the `fdisk` tool can be used to display the partition table for a particular disk, while Solaris uses the format command.

Thus, the command

```
fdisk -l /dev/hda
```

will show on output similar to

```
Disk /dev/hda: 255 heads, 63 sectors, 3737 cylinders
Units = cylinders of 16065 * 512 bytes
                                        ┌─────────────────────────────────┐
                                        │ Bootable partition indicated by * │
                                        └─────────────────────────────────┘
   Device Boot     Start       End    Blocks   Id  System
/dev/hda1    *         1       262   2104483+  83  Linux
/dev/hda2             263      1049   6321577+   f  Win95 Ext'd (LBA)
/dev/hda5             263       524   2104483+  83  Linux
/dev/hda6             525       786   2104483+  83  Linux
/dev/hda7             787       917   1052226   83  Linux
/dev/hda8             918       983    530113+  82  Linux swap
/dev/hda9             984      1049    530113+  83  Linux
```

The output shows each of the partition names (`Device`), the start and stop ranges (`Start` and `End`), the total size of the partition in blocks (`Blocks`), the id for the partition (`Id`), and the type of file system or use for the partition (`System`). The `Boot` field indicates which partition is bootable, with an asterisk, so that when the system is restarted, it boots with the correct partition. In the example, the `/dev/hda1` partition (which is the root file system) is bootable.

Solaris provides the `prtvtoc` command, which displays the geometry or layout of the disk with all the defined partitions. For example, the command

```
# prtvtoc /dev/dsk/c0d0s0
```

provides the following information:

```
* /dev/dsk/c0d0s0 partition map
*
* Dimensions:
*     512 bytes/sector
*      63 sectors/track
*      16 tracks/cylinder
*    1008 sectors/cylinder
*   16654 cylinders
*   16652 accessible cylinders
*
* Flags:
*   1: unmountable
*  10: read-only
*
* Unallocated space:
*       First     Sector     Last
*       Sector     Count    Sector
*     16784208      1008  16785215
*
*                   First     Sector     Last
* Partition  Tag  Flags   Sector     Count    Sector   Mount Directory
        0      2    00       3024   1024128   1027151   /
        1      7    00    1027152    819504   1846655   /var
        2      5    00          0  16785216  16785215
        3      3    01    1846656   2048256   3894911
        5      0    00    3894912   1024128   4919039   /opt
        6      4    00    4919040   3277008   8196047   /usr
        7      8    00    8196048   8588160  16784207
        8      1    01          0      1008      1007
        9      9    01       1008      2016      3023
```

This command provides the same information as the `fdisk` utility, which includes the mapping of each partition defined on the disk. It also includes more information about the size of the disk and related information. The `prtvtoc` command requires a special file (or access point) that represents the disk to probe for the partition information.

1-Minute Drill

- What are some common components of a file system?
- Describe two methods for systems with different operating system file systems to communicate and exchange files

6.3 Determine a Mounted File System

In order to use a file system that has been defined, a connection must be made between the file system itself and the system which will be made available. This is known as mounting and each file system must be mounted onto the system before it can be used. Mounting a file system requires two basic components, the file system and a directory that is used as the access point for the file system. For example, assume that a file system has been created on the `/dev/hda6` partition to store user files, and you would like to make this file system available to users of the system. We need to mount the partition under the root (`/`) file system. Assume also that we would like to associate the home directory with this file system. So, when users access this file system, the UNIX path would begin with: `/home`. Figure 6-5 illustrates the high level view of two mounted file systems.

Figure 6-5 shows two mounted file systems; `hda6` (which is the root file system) and `hda1` (which is for user files). These are combined together, with what appears to be a single file system. In reality they are two separate file systems.

As you recall, the `df` command displays information about the file system and also the mount point. Thus the entry

| /dev/hda9 | 521748 | 79504 | 415740 | 17% | /home |

shows that the `/dev/hda9` file system is mounted on the `/home` directory.

- Files, directories, subdirectories, hidden data file structures
- They could communicate through special file conversion hardware or software tools. Or they could exchange data through a common network facility such as FTP or NFS.

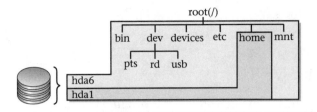

Figure 6-5 Mounting File Systems

Creating a New File System

Setting up a new file system is a straightforward process. However, having said that, care must be taken to ensure that you fully understand what you are doing. Assuming that you already have the partition map defined, do the following high level tasks:

1. Determine which partition will contain the file system.

2. Alter the partition map for the file system.

3. Create the file system.

4. Verify that the file system is functional.

5. Make the file system available by mounting it.

To complete steps 1 and 2, consult the sections "Using the Solaris Format Tool" or "Using the Linux fdisk Tool" depending on the operating system you have. Steps 3 and 4 are described in this section, "Creating a New File System," while the remaining step is covered in "Mounting UNIX File Systems."

As previously discussed, the partition table could be viewed using various UNIX commands. On Solaris and HP-UX, use the `format` command to view partitions for each disk drive. For Linux, use the `fdisk` command.

Using the Solaris Format Tool

The `format` command is used to both modify/define/display a partition table and also format a disk drive. In this example, the command will be used to

Ask the Expert

Question   Why should you make changes to the system when it is
not in use and can be taken "off-line" if at all possible?

Answer   Making disk changes to a live or production system can be
a very dangerous thing to do! A small change could render the system
unusable. However, sometimes you must make modifications to one or
more critical systems even during peak usage. For example, you might
need to create a new file system for additional users in the middle of the
day because you are out of disk space. In cases like these, please make
sure that you double check your work and also ensure that adequate
backups have been done.

6

display and modify the partition table. To run the command, type the following
at the shell prompt as the super user:

```
# format
```

The command displays the following depending on the number of disks
installed on the system:

```
Searching for disks...done
                                            ┌─────────────────────────────┐
                                            │ Two disks available to select│
AVAILABLE DISK SELECTIONS:                  └─────────────────────────────┘
     0. c0t0d0 <SUN9.0G cyl 4924 alt 2 hd 27 sec 133>
        /pci@1f,0/pci@1,1/scsi@2/sd@0,0
     1. c0t1d0 <SUN9.0G cyl 4924 alt 2 hd 27 sec 133>
        /pci@1f,0/pci@1,1/scsi@2/sd@1,0
Specify disk (enter its number):
```

In this case, the system contains two disk drives (c0t0d0) and (c0t1d0)
and one must be selected to continue with executing the format command.
Assume that the second disk (disk number 1) is selected. As a result of
selecting this disk, this command outputs the following:

```
selecting c0t1d0
[disk formatted]
```

```
FORMAT MENU:
        disk      - select a disk
        type      - select (define) a disk type
        partition - select (define) a partition table
        current   - describe the current disk
        format    - format and analyze the disk
        repair    - repair a defective sector
        label     - write label to the disk
        analyze   - surface analysis
        defect    - defect list management
        backup    - search for backup labels
        verify    - read and display labels
        save      - save new disk/partition definitions
        inquiry   - show vendor, product and revision
        volname   - set 8-character volume name
        !<cmd>    - execute <cmd>, then return
        quit
format>
```

Display the Partition Table

To show the partition table, type the `partition` command at the `format>` prompt:

```
format> partition
```

This command can be abbreviated and the "p" character could have been used to save on keystrokes. Once this command is input, another menu is displayed:

```
PARTITION MENU:
        0      - change `0' partition
        1      - change `1' partition
        2      - change `2' partition
        3      - change `3' partition
        4      - change `4' partition
        5      - change `5' partition
        6      - change `6' partition
        7      - change `7' partition
        select - select a predefined table
        modify - modify a predefined partition table
        name   - name the current table
        print  - display the current table
```

```
        label  - write partition map and label to the disk
        !<cmd> - execute <cmd>, then return
        quit
partition>
```

Use the print command to display the current partition table. Thus,

```
partition> print
```

will show the following:

```
                                                    ┌─────────────────────────┐
                                                    │ 8 definable partitions  │
Current partition table (original):                 └─────────────────────────┘
Total disk cylinders available: 4924 + 2 (reserved cylinders)

Part      Tag    Flag     Cylinders        Size            Blocks      ─┐
  0      root     wm      0  -   73      129.75MB     (74/0/0)    265734  │
  1      swap     wu     74  -  147      129.75MB     (74/0/0)    265734  │
  2    backup     wu      0  - 4923        8.43GB   (4924/0/0) 17682084   │
  3 unassigned    wm      0                    0        (0/0/0)         0  │
  4 unassigned    wm      0                    0        (0/0/0)         0  │
  5 unassigned    wm      0                    0        (0/0/0)         0  │
  6       usr     wm    148  - 4923        8.18GB   (4776/0/0) 17150616   │
  7 unassigned    wm      0                    0        (0/0/0)         0 ─┘

partition>
```

The output includes six fields that describe each of the partitions. A total of eight partition slots are available for this disk; and they are numbered 0 through 7 as displayed in the Part column. Thus, the with Solaris operating system, a total of eight partitions can be defined per each disk drive. The Tag field indicates the type of file system or use for the partition. For instance, the first partition (0) is used as the root file system. This file system is used to boot the system. The second partition is used for swap space, etc. The unassigned tag means that the partition is empty or not defined; that is why the remaining fields do not contain any values. The Flag field is used to specify the access permission for each partition. The Cylinders field specifies the range of disk offsets that define the size of the partition. The unit in this case is cylinder groups, which are vertical addresses of the disk drive. The Size field shows the total storage capacity of the partition and the Block field specifies the total number of blocks based on the total size of the partition, which is the rightmost value

6

displayed in the `Blocks` field. The values in parentheses are the absolute block numbers/cylinder group pairs.

Modify Partition Size

To alter the size of an existing partition, type the partition number at the `partition>` prompt. For example, assume that partition 6 will be reduced in size from approximately 8 gigabytes (GB) to 4 gigabytes:

```
partition> 6
Part      Tag   Flag   Cylinders      Size            Blocks
  6       usr   wm     148 - 4923     8.18GB      (4776/0/0) 17150616
```

When the partition number is typed, the `format` program echos the partition definition and then prompts for new information:

```
Enter partition id tag[usr]: Enter
```

Keep hitting the `Enter` key to proceed through the prompts until you are at the `Enter partition size` prompt.

```
Enter partition permission flags[wm]: Enter
Enter new starting cyl[148]: Enter
Enter partition size[17150616b, 4776c, 8374.32mb, 8.18gb]: 4.0gb
```

At this point we have accepted the previous values and the size of the partition can be reduced by inputting the desired size. In this case, `4.0 gb` has been added to make the partition roughly half the size it was before. Use the `p` command to display the partition map and note the change for partition number 6:

```
  6       usr   wm     148 - 2484     4.00GB      (2337/0/0)  8392167 ◄
```
                                                              New partition size

The output shows the expected partition size. Note that the partition size could be expressed in several different values to include the total number of blocks, the number of cylinders, in megabytes, and even gigabytes. You must include one of the unit description characters with the value. For example, to specify megabytes use the `mb` character string. The other description strings are `b` for block, `c` for cylinder, and `gb` for gigabytes.

Create a New Partition

Defining a new partition is a very simple process. For example, assume that another new partition must be defined to contain additional space for system users. With Solaris, the partition maps have been predefined based on the type of disk installed within the system. As a result, when a new partition must be set up for an existing pre-installed disk, the process includes specifying partition parameters and saving the new partition table. For example, based on the disk partition table shown below, partition number 7 is currently unassigned and thus unused.

Total disk size					Two partitions use ~ 260 MB	

```
Current partition table (original):
Total disk cylinders available: 4924 + 2 (reserved cylinders)

Part      Tag    Flag    Cylinders        Size            Blocks
  0       root    wm       0 -   73     129.75MB     (74/0/0)      265734
  1       swap    wu      74 -  147     129.75MB     (74/0/0)      265734
  2     backup    wu       0 - 4923       8.43GB     (4924/0/0) 17682084
  3 unassigned    wm       0                 0       (0/0/0)            0
  4 unassigned    wm       0                 0       (0/0/0)            0
  5 unassigned    wm       0                 0       (0/0/0)            0
  6        usr    wm     148 - 2484        4.00GB     (2337/0/0)  8392167
  7 unassigned    wm       0                 0       (0/0/0)            0
```

Unassigned, unused partition

We would like to define this partition for the purposes of creating a new file system. Also, notice that approximately 4 GB of storage is available for this new partition. This is be determined by examining the total amount of space reported with the `backup` partition (2) and comparing this information with the existing partition's total disk space sizes. The backup partition (or partition c on other older systems) typically is defined to cover the entire disk drive. Based on the total size of this partition, we see the total space is approximately 8.4 GB of storages. The type of disk and the total disk space was also displayed when the format command was first invoked.

Save Partition Changes

The next step is to save any partition changes to the disk and this can be done with the `label` command. Executing this command will update the disk partition that is currently located in a reserved area of the disk, which is usually the first block.

When you run the label command, the format tool prompts for verification:

```
partition> label
Ready to label disk, continue? Y
```

Using the Linux fdisk Tool

The fdisk command is used to make changes to the partition table on the system. Specifying the special disk file, followed by /dev on the command line, tells fdisk which disk should be modified:

```
fdisk /dev/hda
```

When run, this will display the following:

```
Command (m for help):
```

To display a list of the available commands with this tool, use the m command. When this command is run, it will display the following:

```
Command action
   a   toggle a bootable flag
   b   edit bsd disklabel
   c   toggle the dos compatibility flag
   d   delete a partition
   l   list known partition types
   m   print this menu
   n   add a new partition
   o   create a new empty DOS partition table
   p   print the partition table
   q   quit without saving changes
   s   create a new empty Sun disklabel
   t   change a partition's system id
   u   change display/entry units
   v   verify the partition table
   w   write table to disk and exit
   x   extra functionality (experts only)
```

Display the Partition Table

To show the partition table, type the p command at the command prompt:

```
Disk /dev/hda: 255 heads, 63 sectors, 3737 cylinders
Units = cylinders of 16065 * 512 bytes

   Device Boot      Start        End      Blocks   Id  System
/dev/hda1   *           1        262     2104483+  83  Linux
/dev/hda2             263       1049     6321577+   f  Win95 Ext'd (LBA)
/dev/hda5             263        524     2104483+  83  Linux
/dev/hda6             525        786     2104483+  83  Linux
/dev/hda7             787        917     1052226   83  Linux
/dev/hda8             918        983      530113+  82  Linux swap
/dev/hda9             984       1049      530113+  83  Linux

Command (m for help):
```

6.4 Create a New File System

There are at least two ways to create a new file system: the easy way and the hard way. The easy way involves using the newfs command, while the hard way is to use the mkfs command. Both accomplish the same thing, but the mkfs command is much harder to use because it requires the administrator to input the required file system parameters, whereas the newfs requires little input from the system administrator. The easy way will be shown here. The required command line option for the newfs command is the special file that represents the partition the new file system should be created. Assume the new file system will be set up using the special file c0t1d0s6. The command

```
newfs /dev/rdsk/c0t1d0s6
```

will create a new file system, using all the default values. Output of the command will include

```
newfs: construct a new file system /dev/rdsk/c0t1d0s6: (y/n)? y
```

The newfs command will prompt to confirm the procedure and the administrator must input the required response for the command to continue. The output of the command includes

```
Warning: 1 sector(s) in last cylinder unallocated
/dev/rdsk/c0t1d0s6:     8392166 sectors in 2337 cylinders of 27 tracks, 133 sectors
```

```
     4097.7MB in 147 cyl groups (16 c/g, 28.05MB/g, 3392 i/g)
super-block backups (for fsck -F ufs -o b=#) at:
 32, 57632, 115232, 172832, 230432, 288032, 345632, 403232, 460832, 518432,
 576032, 633632, 691232, 748832, 806432, 864032, 921632, 979232, 1036832,
 1094432, 1152032, 1209632, 1267232, 1324832, 1382432, 1440032, 1497632,
 1555232, 1612832, 1670432, 1728032, 1785632, 1838624, 1896224, 1953824,
 2011424, 2069024, 2126624, 2184224, 2241824, 2299424, 2357024, 2414624,
 2472224, 2529824, 2587424, 2645024, 2702624, 2760224, 2817824, 2875424,
 2933024, 2990624, 3048224, 3105824, 3163424, 3221024, 3278624, 3336224,
 3393824, 3451424, 3509024, 3566624, 3624224, 3677216, 3734816, 3792416,
 3850016, 3907616, 3965216, 4022816, 4080416, 4138016, 4195616, 4253216,
 4310816, 4368416, 4426016, 4483616, 4541216, 4598816, 4656416, 4714016,
 4771616, 4829216, 4886816, 4944416, 5002016, 5059616, 5117216, 5174816,
 5232416, 5290016, 5347616, 5405216, 5462816, 5515808, 5573408, 5631008,
 5688608, 5746208, 5803808, 5861408, 5919008, 5976608, 6034208, 6091808,
 6149408, 6207008, 6264608, 6322208, 6379808, 6437408, 6495008, 6552608,
 6610208, 6667808, 6725408, 6783008, 6840608, 6898208, 6955808, 7013408,
 7071008, 7128608, 7186208, 7243808, 7301408, 7354400, 7412000, 7469600,
 7527200, 7584800, 7642400, 7700000, 7757600, 7815200, 7872800, 7930400,
 7988000, 8045600, 8103200, 8160800, 8218400, 8276000, 8333600, 8391200,
```

This command displays the disk configuration information, plus a long series of block numbers. These numbers represent the locations of backup copies of the super block. Recall, the super block is the master record for a file system and contains vital information about the state and configuration of the file system.

In the example, above, the total disk space for this file system is 4GB (4097.7 MBs to be more exact).

Hint

To use one of the backup supers, you must specify the block number (location) when checking the file system with `fsck`. This tool is discussed in the next section.

Checking the New File System

When a new file system has been created, it is wise to check the file system for integrity using the file system consistency check (`fsck`) program. The `fsck` program is necessary because a file system can become corrupt for a variety of reasons and a specialized program is necessary to repair the file system when necessary. The reason a file system can experience problems is that hardware or configuration failures can affect the file system in a negative way. For example, if the physical disk driver media (of which the file system is stored) becomes unstable due to a hardware problem, and can no longer access parts of the disk, the file system will be severely affected. This is an extreme case; one that is more common is that the system crashes before the file system was able to update itself with any changes that were made. This basically means that the version of the information stored on the disk is now out of sync and will cause problems unless the situation is rectified.

Typically, during normal system operations, the `fsck` program is run automatically or when a problem is detected. This is usually when the system is being rebooted. However, in some situations, it will become necessary to run this program manually if the errors encountered are serious enough to warrant this action. This may, for instance, be the case if the root file system is having problems and requires more attention from the system administrator.

The file system scanned by `fsck` should be quiescent, that is to say, the file system shouldn't be used during the `fsck` scan process, which means that no users should be accessing the file system. To ensure that normal system users are not using the file system, the system can be placed in single user mode. It is possible to scan a file system during normal system operations; the administrator must ensure that no users will access the system until the scan is complete.

To examine each of the file systems configured on the system, running the `fsck` command without any command line arguments will scan each file system in turn. However, to scan a single file system, include the special file for that file system on the command line.

```
fsck  /dev/dsk/c0t1d0s6
```

When run, the following is displayed:

```
** /dev/rdsk/c0t1d0s6
** Last Mounted on
** Phase 1 - Check Blocks and Sizes
** Phase 2 - Check Pathnames
** Phase 3 - Check Connectivity
** Phase 4 - Check Reference Counts
** Phase 5 - Check Cyl groups
2 files, 9 used, 4131375 free (15 frags, 516420 blocks,  0.0% fragmentation)
```

The `fsck` program does a 5-point scan against the file system, which involves checking various aspects of the file system for problems. These scanning and checking phases are described in Table 6-1.

The output shows each of the phases, and when no errors are displayed for that phase, it indicates the phase was completed successfully. When the scan is

Phase	Description
1	Determines if the file system i-nodes are consistent
2	Determines if directory entries are correct and file i-nodes are consistent
3	Checks to ensure that all directories are connected to the file system
4	Makes a comparison of link of (files and directories) counts from Phase 2 and 3
5	Checks the free block list and used i-nodes for consistency

Table 6-1 Scanning Phases of fsck Program

complete, the number of files is displayed along with the total free disk space and additional information about the file system.

The fsck program has a number of command line options depending on the operating system. These are listed in Table 6-2 list the most common options for each system.

One of the most useful command line arguments is the y or Y option. When fsck is run and a significant number of problems are encountered, using these arguments will cause all questions prompted by fsck to be answered in the positive. This is very useful when the system administrator must multitask between several important duties and also doesn't want to continue inputting the same response. Of equal value is the n (or N) command line option that does the opposite; it answers negatively to any questions posed by fsck.

Ask the Expert

Question Why should you only use **fsck** to scan unmounted file systems?

Answer Because if the file system is changing during the scan process, it will detect inconsistencies with the file system structures, which will promote more headaches. Since fsck can both detect and fix problems, using it when the file system is active will cause additional severe problems over and above the problems that were first encountered before the scan was started.

Option	Description
-A	Examine the /etc/fstab and attempt to scan each file system listed in this file (Linux only)
-F	Specify the file system type when scanning (Solaris only)
-m	Scan the file system, but don't repair any encountered problems
-n -N	Answer all fsck generated questions with a "no" response (Linux: -N will display what will be done only and doesn't execute any repairs)
-s	Perform the fsck scanning process in a serial fashion (Linux Only)
-t	Specify the file system type when scanning (Linux Only)
-V	Display the command line but not execute the command
-y -Y	Answer all fsck generated questions with a "yes" response
-o	Provide values to specific fsck options
-o b	Supply an alternate location for the super block
-v	Verbose output (Linux only)

Table 6-2   Command Line Options

6

If the super block of a file system gets corrupt (which is not a common occurrence) it will be necessary to supply an alternative location that contains a copy of the original super block. When the newfs command is executed to build a new file system, it makes a series of copies of the super block and places them in various block locations on the partition. Using the -o b option, the administrator can supply the location of one of the copies of the super block.

Hint

Care must be taken when using the positive response with fsck, since you are approving that ALL questions be answered the same way, which in some cases may not be what is needed.

Mounting UNIX File Systems

In order for users to access a file system, it must be explicitly made available on the system for users. The term that is commonly used to describe this step is to "mount the file system." Mounting a file system means an association is created between a specific directory from the root file system and the file system that is to be mounted. To mount a file system or to display the currently available mounted file systems, use the `mount` command. Without any arguments, this command will show all of the existing mounted file systems. The command

```
mount
```

displays all the mounted file systems on a Solaris machine called `bedrock`:

```
/ on /dev/dsk/c0t0d0s0
read/write/setuid/intr/largefiles/onerror=panic/dev=80000
0 on Mon Jan 21 20:10:53 2002
/proc on /proc read/write/setuid/dev=3600000 on Mon Jan 21 20:10:52 2002
/dev/fd on fd read/write/setuid/dev=36c0000 on Mon Jan 21 20:10:54 2002
/tmp on swap read/write/setuid/dev=2 on Mon Jan 21 20:10:57 2002
/export/home on /dev/dsk/c0t0d0s7
read/write/setuid/intr/largefiles/onerror=pani
c/dev=800007 on Mon Jan 21 20:10:57 2002
```

The `mount` command requires two pieces of information when mounting a file system: the special file of the file system and a directory. The directory becomes the "mount point" for the file system. For example, to mount the file system contained with the `/dev/dsk/c0t1d0s6` partition:

```
mount /dev/dsk/c0t1d0s6 /src
```

In this example, this file system is mounted onto the directory called `/src`. Note: the target mount point directory must exist before the `mount` is executed. This is because the mount will not create the directory before you. Thus, you must run the following:

```
mkdir /src
```

before the `mount` command is executed. Otherwise, the mount will fail and an error message similar to "`mount: mount-point /src does not exist.`" will be displayed.

Once the mount is done, the file system can be accessed just like any other file or directory contained on the system. From a user's standpoint, this new file system has been plugged into the root file hierarchy and the integration of the mounted file system appears as an extension to the existing directory branch. In other words, a mounted file system is connected to the system so that it appears like a normal directory. The major exception to this rule is a read-only file system. For example, when a fixed CD-ROM device is mounted on the system, no data can be written onto the devices. Thus, should a user attempt to create, remove, or modify a file, an error message will be generated stating that the file system is "read-only."

The mount command supports the –a option, which indicates that all file systems contained within the /etc/vfstab file will be mounted. On Linux, the file is known as /etc/fstab.

Unmounting a UNIX File System

To do the opposite of mounting a file system, use the umount command. This command will disassociate the mount point from the file system and as a result the file system will no longer be available to the system. Typically, a file system is "un"mounted when the system is halted or when the file system needs some maintenance performed (during the invocation of the fsck command, for example). The umount command accepts either the mount point directory of the special file. For example, assume the following mounted file system:

```
/mnt              (/dev/dsk/c0t1d0s6 ): 8262750 blocks    498620 files
```

Thus, the command

```
Umount /mnt
```

will umount the file system associated with /mnt directory. Also, note that the command below will accomplish the same thing:

```
umount /dev/dsk/c0t1d0s6
```

To unmount all the mounted file systems instead of a single one, use the –a option. Using this option implies that all file systems defined within the /etc/vfstab are unmounted. On the Linux system, the /etc/fstab contains the defined file systems.

Project 6-1

Because making changes to a live file system is not advisable except as absolutely necessary, in this project you'll focus on gathering information about the file systems on your system rather than on making changes. If you are the administrator for this system, you might find it useful to keep the information you gather in a safe place in case you ever need to refer to it for system information to recover from a catastrophic failure or to determine if damage was done during a system intrusion.

Step-by-Step

1. Display all the file systems on your system:

```
df -k
```

2. From these results, determine if any of the file systems are dangerously close to being out of unused space.

3. For each drive, determine how many partitions are in use and how much unused space (if any) isn't allocated to a partition. For Linux do this with the command

```
fdisk -l
```

4. Or if you are using Solaris, perform step 3 with the command

```
# prtvtoc /dev/dsk/c0d0s0
```

repeating it for each drive.

☑ *Mastery Check*

1. A _____ is simply a collection of objects (files or directories, for example) that are organized to include the following elements: optimal data access, ensures data integrity, provides manageable, and can be scalability to support many objects.

2. What keeps track of all the files within the file system?

   A. Super block

   B. Root

   C. i-node table

   D. Partition

3. A _____ is a fixed area defined on a storage medium for the purposes of data access.

4. In this output from the df command on a Linux system, what is the file system's drive letter and partition number?

   ```
   /dev/hda9                  521748      79504     415740   17% /home
   ```

5. In Solaris, which command shows a disk's layout with all of its defined partitions?

6. What is the term for making a connection between a file system and the system which the file system will be made available to?

   A. Mount

   B. Partition

   C. Format

   D. fdisk

6

☑ Mastery Check

7. To create a new file system using default values and not entering additional command line options, which command would you use?

   A. mkfs

   B. newfs

   C. format

   D. fdisk

8. What user mode is best to put the system in when running the fsck command?

9. What command do you use to display all the mounted file systems on your system?

   A. df

   B. format

   C. mount

   D. umount

10. True or false: If the target mount point directory does not exist before you execute the mount command, mount will create the directory for you.

Module 7

System Security

Critical Skills

This module provides an overview and description of key elements to establishing a secure computing environment with the UNIX operating system. It provides procedures, configuration recommendations, and descriptions of tools that will help make the UNIX computing environment more secure.

In general, there are two broad approaches to maintaining and delivering on system security. First, the network that interconnects systems can be made secure by the use of firewalls, proxies, and other mechanisms to ensure that hackers and other malicious users are barred from accessing protected systems. The second approach involves focusing the security on the individual systems, instead of the network. In this case, the system administrator attempts to limit system access and control access to files and directories, along with other related measures. The fact of the matter is that both approaches are necessary when addressing security within the enterprise. Why? Well, the answer is very simple: Security breaches can come from outside the company (over the Internet or via dial-up services), internally from the general user community, or even from business partners.

When the WORM of 1998 struck the Internet, it exposed critical vulnerabilities to a wider audience, which raised the awareness of both network and system security. There are certainly more recent examples of security problems on the Internet, but the WORM was the first of many to follow.

Hint

At that time, many of the UNIX security vulnerabilities were understood and accepted. However, at the same time, the WORM redefined the critical duties of the system administrator because they could no longer ignore operating system security issues. Today, one of the primary roles of the system administrator is to ensure that their systems contain the most up-to-date security and operating system patches available.

As the system administrator, you will be responsible for ensuring security for the systems you control; however, depending on the company's organizational structure and other factors, the system administrator will need to work with others to help with the security efforts. For example, in many corporations security may be handled by a separate security department—or is handled as part of a network design and/or support group. In any event, complete security is a team or group effort, and if security is lacking in one important area (say from a network standpoint), that makes all the attached systems more vulnerable.

The system administrator will need to determine how best to implement security in their computing environment, which certainly may involve using both security methods stated above. With this in mind, here are the high-level steps that are involved with providing robust system security regardless of the specific computing environment or organization:

1. Develop and publish a security policy (and revisit on a periodic basis).

2. Maintain system patches.

3. Continuously harden the systems.

4. Use security tools.

5. Repeat steps 2, 3, and 4.

7.1 Define a Security Policy

A good security policy has a few basic elements. First, it should clearly define what is and what is not acceptable behavior with respect to the use of both network and computing systems. For example, users should not attempt to read files from other users when they have no business need, and users shouldn't leave their workstations unattended when they remain logged into the system.

Ask the Expert

Question How can a security policy help make my systems more secure?

Answer A security policy can't make your systems more secure intrinsically, but it can help you in other ways—which can impact your security approach or determine how successful you will be in implementing some of the steps listed above. For example, having a good policy means it can raise the awareness of senior management of how important security can be, and as a result you may find it easier to acquire the funding to purchase security-monitoring tools or hire extra personnel to help in implementing security tools and procedures.

Second, the policy should clearly state what are guidelines for general-purpose computing. For example, users should not install modems and connect phone lines on their system to provide remote access, but should use the corporate dial-up services—which can be more secure. A how-to of the most common issue or problem should be listed. Finally, the policy should define the roles, responsibilities, and procedures to follow when a security issue or incident has occurred. For instance, when an unauthorized user has gained access to a system, who should be alerted and how? What kind of documentation is necessary to record the security breach? These and related questions should be answered and spelled out in the policy.

The security policy should be published in such a way as to ensure that everyone knows about it and can access it when necessary. Thus, placing it on the company's internal Web site or intranet is the best approach. To ensure that users in fact read the policy, include it as part of the user account setup procedures so that before a user account is set up, the user has both read and understood the policy. Then, they can be granted access to the system.

7.2 Maintain System Patches

One of the most important jobs of the system administrator is to consistently maintain up-to-date patches on the systems. Maintaining software upgrades and maintenance releases has positive benefits that include warding off potential problems, providing a stable computing environment, and simplifying troubleshooting of system problems and issues.

When system patches are applied on a regular basis, certain problems can be avoided. For example, installing a security patch that closes one or more particular security vulnerabilities—say, with the TCP/IP protocol—reduces the overall security exposure of the system.

In general, installing the required system patches should provide for a more stable and secure environment. Typically, the administrator is asked to install the required patches in order for technical support to begin troubleshooting a particular problem. On the other hand, depending on the vendor, installing certain patches can cause system problems if the patch is applied incorrectly or contains one or more software defects. This certainly is the exception and not the rule, but it can happen. For this reason, it is always best to install any patches on a test system to determine any potential impact or problem.

Vendors include in their support policies the provisions about limiting technical support for systems that are not running the latest version of their software or don't contain the correct system-level patches.

7.3 Uncover System Hardening

The concept of system hardening is not new; the military and other organizations have used this phase for quite some time as it relates to fortifying their equipment or armaments and making it less likely that a physical attack will cause serious damage. In the context of computer systems, it basically means the same thing—to reduce the vulnerabilities and also fortify the system against known security issues or attacks.

Limiting any unnecessary system services and also implementing standard operating system configurations accomplish system hardening. Further, substituting a better service for an inferior one is also a part of making sure that systems are secure. For example, the UNIX system supports the Telnet service, which provides basic terminal accessibility from one system to another remote system. This particular service has been around for quite some time and is used by many system administrators. However, the Telnet service has one significant flaw: The communication path between the client and servers is unsecured. As a result, using this service poses a security threat that many consider too risky. To address this problem, Telnet is disabled and the Secure Shell (SSH) is enabled to provide secure access. SSH provides encryption, which makes the communication path secure.

The basic goal of system hardening is to eliminate any unnecessary system services that might pose a security threat, and to configure the system for maximum security without seriously impacting the user community. Thus, two broad categories of hardening exist: elimination of nonessential services and implementing a specific conservative operating profile or configuration. These classifications are described below.

Elimination of Unnecessary Services

One of the best ways to ensure a basic level of security is to remove unused or unneeded services that may represent a potential system security risk. For example, if unrestricted FTP is enabled on a system, but that particular machine doesn't really need file transfer capabilities, then it might be prudent to shut off this particular service. Table 7-1 lists some of the most common services that can be either be disabled or replaced with another more secure package or a newer version of the software, which contain later security features.

Configuration System Profiles

Deploying a set of configuration profiles for how each of the systems will be configured and maintained is an important element to overall security. For instance, many organizations install different kinds of systems for various projects and functions, and as a result, the configuration of those systems will be set up to match specific user requirements. Consider the system and security equipment for a software development group versus a sales team. Since these groups do different things and have different requirements, one or more system configuration profiles may be necessary. A system configuration profile consists of specific configuration parameters (such as permitting the root to access the

Service		Action		New Service
	Disable	**Replace**	**Upgrade**	
inetd		√		Xinetd with tcp wrappers
fingerd	√			
majordomo			√	Upgrade to latest version
NIS		√		NIS+
R family of tools (**rsh,** rcp, and rlogin)		√		SSH
rexd	√			
rpc.statd			√	Upgrade to latest version
telnetd		√		SSH
tftp	√			
uucp	√			

Table 7-1   System Services That Require Hardening

console device over the network or the frequency of password expirations for normal users). Some of the possible configuration profiles are listed below:

Low-Security Profile

This profile represents systems that will have a modest amount of system security because they are isolated from the network or because they are stand-alone or maybe contained behind a firewall. These systems also may fall "under the radar" of corporate security policy, which means that they may not be required to implement all standard security measures or a high-security profile configuration. The security configuration of the low-security profile may include a smaller amount of operating system hardening, no password aging, no security scanning or auditing, and so forth. Clearly, these types of systems can be a nightmare for maintaining a robust corporate security model. However, having said that, there are a small number of instances where using the low-security profile makes sense.

Medium-Security Profile

This profile represents systems that are several layers above the low-security system in terms of system security. System security is a priority for this system profile, but is not the only major issue addressed. For example, systems that are deployed within the customer support or professional services teams may use this profile type. This profile would contain a fairly robust hardening configuration and support many of the security logging/scanning software packages, and use password aging and a variety of other security measures.

High-Security Profile

This profile represents the highest level of security available. The type of system this profile should be applied to is production systems that handle credit cards or other highly sensitive information for customers, suppliers, and vendors. This profile pulls out all the stops in terms of hardening configuration, scanning and reporting tools, robust authentication, and so forth. It is not uncommon for corporations to purchase security products to enhance the basic security supported by the system. For instance, products are available that provide additional password authentication using tokens and other methods that can increase the user-level security model quite significantly.

Certainly, additional security profile types may be defined, and modification to the ones listed above can be set up to closely match your specific environmental requirement. Also, what one site considers medium security may in fact be low security to another, depending on the security goals of the organization. One important point: Whatever profiles you use, apply them consistently to all systems—that way, you will be in a position to better understand where your systems are from a security perspective.

Now that a set of security profiles has been defined, it is quite straightforward to inventory and classify the level of security for each system. In Table 7-2, a small number of systems have been included to show this example. It is recommended that a similar table be developed for the systems that you support.

As noted in the table, each type of system will have different system services and one of the security profiles. With many corporations, it is possible that three security profiles are not enough; additional ones need to be defined to handle special cases or additional types of systems. As a system administrator, you will need to take charge of defining the security attitude and strategy for your area of control, and compiling an inventory of systems is a great place to start.

Host Name	Team	Profile Characteristics			Service(s)
		Low	Medium	High	
station1	Software development		√		C compiler
mailserv	Software development			√	Mail server
bedrock	Software development		√		NFS, NIS, and DNS
barney	Software development			√	CVS source code repository
omega	Marketing			√	Mail server
salessrv1	Sales	√			Web server Sales intranet
salessrv2	Sales			√	Sales support

Table 7-2 Inventory of Systems with Security Profile Types

1-Minute Drill

● How does writing a security policy help you make your systems more secure?

● What are some of the key principles of system hardening?

7.3 Investigate Security Tools

One key component to a successful security model is to deploy security monitoring/scanning tools that can probe the system on a regular basis and provide detailed reports of potential vulnerabilities or other security issues. There are some very powerful monitoring and scanning tools that are available today from both the commercial and public domain sectors. However, a review of specific commercial packages is beyond the scope of this book. On the other hand, some of the more common public domain tools are discussed in the section. Table 7-3 lists the tools that will be covered.

The tools listed in this table are all available for Solaris, HP-UX, and Linux. However, not all of them are shipped with the basic operating system package. As a result, they must be installed separately. In the case of Linux, all of the tools are available on the product CDs. For both Solaris and HP-UX, you will obtain the software from the prospective Internet sites and install them individually. Each of the packages provides detailed installation instructions.

Naturally, a large number of additional security tools are available for UNIX to solve a variety of security-related issues and problems.

Tool	Purpose
nmap	Network port scanner and remote host identification program
SSH	Provides a remote shell and file copy to specified host using secure connection
sudo	Permits regular users to execute privileged commands

Table 7-3   Common Security Tools

● A written security policy helps raise awareness of security issues, it clearly defines what are and aren't allowable system uses so there is no ambiguity or uncertainty among users, and it defines roles and responsibilities for ensuring security and recovering from any potential security breaches.

● System hardening includes establishing a set of standard operating system configurations, eliminating unnecessary system services, and substituting a more secure service for an inferior one.

The NMAP Tool

The nmap tool is a utility that locates and identifies all available TCP and UDP ports on a target host system. Also known as a port scanner, this tool will scan TCP ports from 0 to 1024 (by default) and attempt to determine the service listening on those ports that will accept a connection. This is a very robust security tool because it identifies services running on a system so that you can be alerted about possible security issues or vulnerability.

Hint

The nmap tool is used by those wishing to break into remote computer systems; thus, when you identify security issues on your systems, you are proactively short-circuiting the efforts of those that want to cause destruction to your systems!

This tool was designed to help the system administrator determine security problems on their systems, but if you intend to use this tool on networks, systems, or sites that you do not control, you should seek permission first. Remember, having respect for the privacy of networks and systems that you don't own means that the favor may be returned to you someday.

On occasion, devices that interfere with normal network operations may be added to the network. Also, the origin and configuration of these systems may not be apparent and may represent a potential security risk. It may become necessary to scan the devices to learn more about the services they provide. For instance, let's assume a device is added to the network, but because the device doesn't seem to support services like telnet, it is difficult to identify the device.

Hint

The ping command is fully described in Module 11.

A ping can be an issue against the device, but this doesn't really provide much information about the device itself. The ping command checks to see if basic network services from the device are operational:

```
# ping 216.155.202.110
PING 216.155.202.110 (216.155.202.110) from 216.155.202.163 : 56(84) bytes of data.
Warning: time of day goes back, taking countermeasures.
64 bytes from 216.155.202.110: icmp_seq=0 ttl=255 time=1.035 msec
64 bytes from 216.155.202.110: icmp_seq=1 ttl=255 time=229 usec

--- 216.155.202.110 ping statistics ---
```

```
2 packets transmitted, 2 packets received, 0% packet loss
round-trip min/avg/max/mdev = 0.229/0.632/1.035/0.403 ms
```

As you can see, the device is operational on the network, but we don't really have much additional information about the device. We can now attempt to connect to the device via `telnet` or `ssh`, but the connection never makes it because the device may refuse this type access:

```
# telnet 216.155.202.110
Trying 216.155.202.110...
telnet: connect to address 216.155.202.110: Connection refuse
```

Scanning a Host

When it is necessary to find more information about the device, the `nmap` tool can be used to probe and inventory the services running, which can give a better picture about the device in general. Running the command

```
nmap -O 216.155.202.110
```

7

provides the details we need:

```
Starting nmap V. 2.54BETA22 ( www.insecure.org/nmap/ )
Interesting ports on  (216.155.202.110):
(The 1540 ports scanned but not shown below are in state: closed)
Port        State       Service
139/tcp     open        netbios-ssn ──┐  ┌─ Two services running
6000/tcp    open        X11          ─┘  └────────────────────
Remote OS guesses: Windows Me or Windows 2000 RC1 through final release,◄
Windows Millenium Edition v4.90.3000 ◄
Nmap run completed -- 1 IP address (1 host up) scanned in 28 seconds
```

nmap guess for operating system on the remote device

The `-O` option used here tells `nmap` that we would like it to attempt to identify the target system using what it calls TCP/IP fingerprinting. What this basically means is that several different techniques are used to detect differences within operating systems or the running software contained within the target device. Using the data obtained from probing the TCP/IP protocols and other attributes, `nmap` compares this information with the fingerprints of known devices and systems. Every device that `nmap` attempts to identify is compared to the data stored in a file called `nmap-os-fingerprints`, which is located in the directory `/usr/share/nmap` by default. This file contains a large number of fingerprints for systems and networking devices.

As noted in the output from `nmap`, two network services are running on the system, plus it has identified the type of system as a Windows Me or Windows 2000 workstation. We are now in a position to determine if this system represents a security risk to other systems or the network as a whole. In this case, since the device is configured to support NETBIOS services, which provides file sharing, we should make sure that the system doesn't contain any viruses that may be transmitted within shared documents. Also, `nmap` has detected that X Windows (X server) software is running on the system, which may

Hint

If you encounter a device that doesn't match the entries in the fingerprints file, you may want to consider sending the scan to the nmap author.

not represent a security concern unless the user of this system is accessing sensitive information without using `ssh` or some other security software. This bears some additional investigation with the owner of this system.

Normally, it wouldn't be easy to determine that a device was a Windows workstation, but using `nmap`, most systems can be identified fairly quickly and easily. The `nmap` tool can also examine the networking services running on known systems within the network. This is useful in determining which system services are available to assist with system hardening efforts. For instance, using `nmap` on a Solaris system known as `bedrock` produced the following output:

```
Starting nmap V. 2.54BETA22 ( www.insecure.org/nmap/ )
Interesting ports on bedrock.home.com (216.155.202.100):
(The 1511 ports scanned but not shown below are in state: closed)
Port      State      Service
7/tcp     open       echo
9/tcp     open       discard
13/tcp    open       daytime
19/tcp    open       chargen
21/tcp    open       ftp
23/tcp    open       telnet
25/tcp    open       smtp
37/tcp    open       time
79/tcp    open       finger
111/tcp   open       sunrpc
512/tcp   open       exec
513/tcp   open       login
514/tcp   open       shell
515/tcp   open       printer
```

```
540/tcp    open    uucp
587/tcp    open    submission
898/tcp    open    unknown
2049/tcp   open    nfs
4045/tcp   open    lockd
6000/tcp   open    X11
6112/tcp   open    dtspc
7100/tcp   open    font-service
32774/tcp  open    sometimes-rpc11
32775/tcp  open    sometimes-rpc13
32776/tcp  open    sometimes-rpc15
32777/tcp  open    sometimes-rpc17
32778/tcp  open    sometimes-rpc19
32779/tcp  open    sometimes-rpc21
32780/tcp  open    sometimes-rpc23
32786/tcp  open    sometimes-rpc25
32787/tcp  open    sometimes-rpc27

Nmap run completed -- 1 IP address (1 host up) scanned in 0 seconds
```

As you can see, this system contains a large number of services, some of which can be deactivated.

Scanning Methods

The nmap software supports a number of important functions and a number of command-line options. Also, it provides a large number of system scanning techniques, as shown in Table 7-4. This table also includes the associated command options and a general description of the process involved with each scanning method.

Scanning Method	Command-Line Parameters	Description
FTP proxy	-b	FTP bounce scan; uses proxy feature in FTP services to attempt connection.
ACK scan	-sA	Used to scan firewalls to determine the type.
FIN	-sF	Known as stealth FIN, this scanning option uses FIN TCP packet in an attempt to elicit a response. FIN is used to close a TCP connection.
Reverse indent	-I	Enables TCP reverse ident scanning, which requests that the ident server be running; when enabled, permits the identification of the owner of the process that uses a TCP port.

Table 7-4   Nmap Scanning Techniques

Scanning Method	Command-Line Parameters	Description
Null scan	-sN	Similar to FIN, but turns off all TCP flags.
Ping sweep	-sP	Uses ICMP when scanning probing systems. This is equivalent to issuing a `ping` request.
RPC scan	-sR	Scans to determine Remote Procedure Call services.
TCP SYN (half)	-sS	Scans TCP ports using the *half-open* technique, which means only one side of a TCP connection is open and waiting for acknowledgment.
TCP connect	-sT	Scans available TCP ports in the range of 1 to 1024, plus ports listed within the `nmap-services` file; uses low-level connect system call in attempt to establish connection to target system.
UDP port	-sU	Scans available UDP ports in the range of 1 to 1024, plus ports listed within the `nmap-services` file.
Window scan	-sW	Scans for defects within the window sizing protocol of TCP.
Xmas tree	-sX	Similar to FIN but turns on FIN, URG, and PUSH bits within the TCP packet.

Table 7-4   Nmap Scanning Techniques (*continued*)

The nmap tool was designed to work very efficiently when probing a large number of hosts, even if they are on different networks. Also, it is considered one of the fastest port scanners available within the public domain, and it even rivals some commercial products.

NMAP Command Options

The command-line options are divided into two categories; the first control the scanning technique of nmap, and are listed in Table 7-5. The second category is additional options, which refine or control general behavior of the tool.

Because nmap supports a large number of command-line arguments and options, use the -help option to list a synopsis of the supported command arguments. Thus, the command

```
# nmap -help
```

will display a list of available commands options and associated meanings.

Option	Description
-F	Fast scan mode; `nmap` only scans the ports found in the `nmap-services` file.
-iL	Obtains target information from a specified file as compared to specifying the hosts on the command line.
-o	Logs program results to specified file.
-p	Uses specified port or port range instead of default values.
-v	Enables verbose mode, which provides more detailed information.

Table 7-5   General nmap Command Options

One of the strengths of `nmap` is that it supports many different scanning methodologies. Some scanners only support TCP scanning, which is very useful but has limitations. For instance, some networking devices don't provide generic TCP networking services as traditional UNIX systems do; they may only support a limited set of UDP services. In this instance, using a port scanner that only supports TCP would be useless. Consider the following scan and associated output:

```
# nmap -sT probe.home.com
Starting nmap V. 2.54BETA22 ( www.insecure.org/nmap/ )
Interesting ports on probe.home.com (10.0.2.50):
(Not showing ports in state: filtered)
Port     State        Protocol  Service ◄─────
Nmap run completed -- 1 IP address (1 host up) scanned in 66 seconds ◄───┐
```
                                                                  No services detected

As you can see in this output, `nmap` didn't detect any services on the target system. However, scanning using the -sU option instructs `nmap` to scan a range of UDP ports instead of the default TCP port range. Thus, interestingly enough, the following:

```
# nmap -sU probe.home.com
```

yields the following output when executed:

```
WARNING: -sU is now UDP scan -- for TCP FIN scan use -sF
Starting nmap V. 2.54BETA22 ( www.insecure.org/nmap/ )
Interesting ports on probe.home.com (10.0.2.50):
```

```
Port     State       Protocol  Service  ◄──  SNMP service detecting using UDP scan
161      open        udp       snmp

Nmap run completed -- 1 IP address (1 host up) scanned in 12 seconds
```

The scan reveals an SNMP process listening on the standard 161 port. This tells us that this device only supports SNMP and nothing else. If necessary, the device could be further queried using SNMP-based tools to determine more information about the agent that resides within the device. See Module 13 for additional information about SNMP or related tools.

Scanning TCP and UDP Ports

The default behavior of nmap is to use the TCP port scanning method on the standard TCP ports that have been included within the associated services file. Normally the file nmap-services is located in the /usr/share/nmap directory, and nmap will use these ports plus scan all ports within the range of 1 to 1024. Using just the default values can be very useful. Consider the following command:

```
# nmap rocks
```

It shows a large amount of information on the host known as rocks:

```
Starting nmap V. 2.54BETA22 ( www.insecure.org/nmap/ )
Interesting ports on rocks (216.155.202.117):
(The 1515 ports scanned but not shown below are in state: closed)
Port        State       Service
7/tcp       open        echo
9/tcp       open        discard
13/tcp      open        daytime
19/tcp      open        chargen
21/tcp      open        ftp
22/tcp      open        ssh
23/tcp      open        telnet
25/tcp      open        smtp
37/tcp      open        time
79/tcp      open        finger
111/tcp     open        sunrpc
512/tcp     open        exec
513/tcp     open        login
514/tcp     open        shell
515/tcp     open        printer
540/tcp     open        uucp
```

```
4045/tcp    open        lockd
6112/tcp    open        dtspc
7100/tcp    open        font-service
32771/tcp   open        sometimes-rpc5
32772/tcp   open        sometimes-rpc7
32773/tcp   open        sometimes-rpc9
32774/tcp   open        sometimes-rpc11
32775/tcp   open        sometimes-rpc13
32776/tcp   open        sometimes-rpc15
32777/tcp   open        sometimes-rpc17
32778/tcp   open        sometimes-rpc19
Nmap run completed -- 1 IP address (1 host up) scanned in 0 seconds
```

Unidentified services

The output above was derived from a scan of a Solaris 8 system. As you can see, this scan shows that many of the standard UNIX services are running. Only TCP services are listed because this is the default mode; this is equivalent to using the command-line -sT option. The services running the system include ftp, telnet, smtp, finger, and many others. From a security standpoint, some of the services should be disabled and/or replaced with utilities such as SSH. Also, several ports were not completely identified, and these are marked as sometimes-rpc because they don't support the standard RPC functions.

To scan both UDP and TCP ports at the same time, use the -sU and -sT options together. The command

```
# nmap -sU -sT rocks
```

will yield the following:

```
Starting nmap V. 2.54BETA22 ( www.insecure.org/nmap/ )
Interesting ports on rocks (216.155.202.117):
(The 3076 ports scanned but not shown below are in state: closed)
Port        State       Service
7/tcp       open        echo
7/udp       open        echo
9/tcp       open        discard
9/udp       open        discard
13/tcp      open        daytime
13/udp      open        daytime
19/tcp      open        chargen
19/udp      open        chargen
21/tcp      open        ftp
22/tcp      open        ssh
23/tcp      open        telnet
25/tcp      open        smtp
37/tcp      open        time
```

TCP port

UDP port

7

```
37/udp      open        time
42/udp      open        nameserver
67/udp      open        bootps
79/tcp      open        finger
111/tcp     open        sunrpc
111/udp     open        sunrpc
123/udp     open        ntp
161/udp     open        snmp
177/udp     open        xdmcp
512/tcp     open        exec
512/udp     open        biff
513/tcp     open        login
514/tcp     open        shell
514/udp     open        syslog
515/tcp     open        printer
517/udp     open        talk
540/tcp     open        uucp
6112/tcp    open        dtspc
7100/tcp    open        font-service
32771/tcp   open        sometimes-rpc5
32771/udp   open        sometimes-rpc6
32772/tcp   open        sometimes-rpc7
32772/udp   open        sometimes-rpc8
32773/tcp   open        sometimes-rpc9
32773/udp   open        sometimes-rpc10
32774/tcp   open        sometimes-rpc11
32774/udp   open        sometimes-rpc12
32775/tcp   open        sometimes-rpc13
32775/udp   open        sometimes-rpc14
32776/tcp   open        sometimes-rpc15
32776/udp   open        sometimes-rpc16
32777/tcp   open        sometimes-rpc17
32777/udp   open        sometimes-rpc18
32778/tcp   open        sometimes-rpc19
32778/udp   open        sometimes-rpc20
32779/udp   open        sometimes-rpc22
32786/udp   open        sometimes-rpc26

Nmap run completed -- 1 IP address (1 host up) scanned in 226 seconds
```

Note that now both UDP and TCP ports are displayed, sorted by port number.

Isolating a Specific Service

As with any good port scanner, the ability to scan a particular port is paramount. One good way to determine if all the systems on a network have a standard set of network services or a particular function is to scan the network hosts with a specific port number in mind. For example, assume we would like to determine if all the systems on the 216.155.202.0 network support some sort of SNMP agent. Since SNMP can be a security hole, depending on how it has been configured, the network should be scanned to determine which device supports this protocol. The command

```
# nmap -p 161 -sU -o results 216.155.202/24
```

tells nmap to scan port 161 (the SNMP port) on network 216.155.202.0 using UDP and then save the output information in a file called results. If we display this file, we find the following sample output:

```
# nmap (V. 2.54BETA22) scan initiated Sat Jan 26 17:01:01 2002 as: nmap -p 161 -
sU -o results 216.155.202.0/24
Host   (216.155.202.0) seems to be a subnet broadcast address (returned 2 extra
pings). Skipping host.
Interesting ports on bedrock.home.com (216.155.202.100):
Port        State        Service
161/udp     open         snmp   ←──────────────      The system is found in the
                                                     address range scanned

Interesting ports on dino.home.com (216.155.202.110):
Port        State        Service
161/udp     open         snmp                        161 (SNMP) port found open

The 1 scanned port on didymus.home.com (216.155.202.163) is: closed
The 1 scanned port on  (216.155.202.202) is: closed
The 1 scanned port on  (216.155.202.204) is: closed
Host   (216.155.202.255) seems to be a subnet broadcast address (returned 2 extra
pings). Skipping host.

# Nmap run completed at Sat Jan 26 17:02:21 2002 -- 256 IP addresses (5 hosts up)
scanned in 80 seconds
```

As it turns out, this is a very reasonable mechanism to use to inventory services on a grand scale. Any TCP or UDP service can be queried using this approach.

This example demonstrates another powerful feature of this tool. Namely, we can specify the target systems or networks using a few different notations. First, we can specify an IP address using a list or ranges for each part of the address. Thus we can scan an entire IP class with the "*" character. For instance, 128.197.*.* permits the scanning of the whole B class network. Another way to express this is to use the dash character. Thus 128.197.1-255.1-255 is functionally the same as using the 128.197.*.* syntax. Second, we can use the mask notation as shown in the previous nmap command example. Namely, 128.197.0.0/16 will mask and is equivalent to the two examples using either the "*" or "-" characters. Finally, we can use a numbered sequence combined with the range syntax.

7

Thus 128.197.90.1, 2, 3, 4, 5, 100-105 will scan the following addresses: 128.197.90.1, 128.197.90.2, 128.197.90.3, 128.197.90.4, and 128.197.90.5, as well as addresses 128.197.90.100 through 128.197.90.105. Using these IP formats greatly improves the ease of scanning entire subnets or networks.

When scanning networks, it is sometimes helpful to know exactly what nmap is doing at all times. For this reason, the -v option has been provided. Bear in mind that a fair amount of output may be generated as a result, so it might be important to use this option with caution. In the previous example, we scanned an entire subnet. If we added the -v option when attempting to scan a single host, more detailed information is displayed. For example, the command

```
nmap -v -sU -p 161 bedrock rocks spoons
```

shows the following sample output:

```
Starting nmap V. 2.54BETA22 ( www.insecure.org/nmap/ )
Host bedrock.home.com (216.155.202.100) appears to be up ... good.
Initiating UDP Scan against bedrock.home.com (216.155.202.100)
The UDP Scan took 0 seconds to scan 1 ports.
Interesting ports on bedrock.home.com (216.155.202.100):
Port        State       Service
161/udp     open        snmp

Host  (216.155.202.101) appears to be down, skipping it.
Host  (216.155.202.102) appears to be down, skipping it.

Nmap run completed -- 3 IP addresses (1 host up) scanned in 2 seconds
```

As you can see, more detailed specifics about the port scan are provided. Also, nmap identified a single device that supports SNMP agent and is reachable on the network, as noted by the lines containing the string

```
Host bedrock.home.com (216.155.202.100) appears to be up ... good
```

Both rocks and spoon are down, and nmap can't probe the system for information

Network Ports

The nmap program attempts to probe a standard set of network ports on the target system. Also, it scans the entire range of ports from 0 to 1024 by default. The standard TCP/IP and related protocol ports that nmap scans are listed in Table 7-6 along with the service name and a general description of the network service or function.

Ask the Expert

Question   Why does nmap skip a system if it initially appears to be down?

Answer   nmap is very smart about probing nonexistent or down systems; it doesn't spend much time or resources probing nonresponsive systems. Before nmap attempts to scan a device, it first determines if it is reachable on the network by performing a ping on it. This not only reduces the amount of time required to perform the scan and lessens system resources needed, but it helps to preserve network bandwidth as well. It is important not to underestimate the impact that scanning can have on a network, and nmap does a good job of reducing the network requirements while probing.

Port	Service Name	Description
7	echo	Echoes characters sent to this port; service provided by the inetd or xinetd process; primarily used for testing
8	discard	Discards any data sent to it; acts like /dev/null for networking services and other networking applications; primarily used for testing
13	daytime	Provides time in human-readable format; primarily used for testing
19	chargen	Character generator; produces ASCII character set; primarily used for testing
21	ftp	File Transfer Protocol server
22	ssh	Secure Shell server
23	telnet	Telnet server; provides remote login services
25	smtp	Simple Mail Transfer Protocol; usually sendmail or similar server is listening on this port
37	time	Provides machine-readable time
53	domain	Domain Name Server process
79	finger	Finger server process, which provides more information about a particular user
80	http	Web server process
111	sunrpc	Sun Remote Procedure Calls service
199	smux	SNMP master agent

Table 7-6   Standard NMAP Ports

7

Port	Service Name	Description
382	hp-managed-node	This process provides network management services for HP network manager products.
512	exec	Remote execution server with authentication
513	login	Remote login with authentication
514	shell	Remote shell server with authentication
515	printer	Remote printer server
540	uucp	UUCP server
4045	lockd	Lock daemon (for NFS)
6000	x-windows	X-Windows server

Table 7-6   Standard NMAP Ports (*continued*)

When nmap sees that a port is active and can't identify services running on the port, it specifies the port as "unknown."

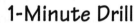

1-Minute Drill

● What are some of the key pieces of information you can obtain with the nmap tool?

● How is nmap useful in helping secure your systems?

Project 7-1

In this project you will create or revise a security policy and you will determine the port and service usage on your system or any systems in your control. You'll then disable any unnecessary ports and services and save the results of a repeat port scan as documentation to compare against future port scans.

● nmap can tell you which systems in a network are up and accepting connections, which ports are open, whether the ports are running TCP or UDP, what services are running on the open ports, and in some cases what operating system the system is running.

● Hackers might use nmap (or other similar tools) to search for open systems and ports to launch attacks. By using it to scan your own networks and systems, you can determine what systems and ports should be open and accepting connections and if there are systems and ports open that shouldn't be, harden them by shutting off those services.

Step-by-Step

1. Find your company's current security policy. (If your company doesn't have a security policy, find example security policies [possible from CERT or other organizations] and create a draft security policy.) Study the policy for any weaknesses, outdated sections, or overlooked areas and submit a revised draft to your IT department manager.

2. Create an inventory of all the current open ports on your system and save this list to a file (such as port*systemname*, where *systemname* is the name of your system).

```
# nmap -sU -sT -o portsystemname
```

3. Study the results of step 2 and look for any ports running services you don't recognize. Be suspicious of any services running on non-standard port numbers (numbers other than the ones listed for them in table 7-6). Look for any obsolete or insecure services you can replace with newer or more secure services.

4. Disable any services that you don't need running after your step 3 investigation.

5. Rerun the command from step 2 and keep the results from this in a secure place so you can refer to them as a "baseline" to compare results of the same command to in the future to see if other services have been added or ports opened without your knowledge.

6. If you are responsible for more than one system, or a group of systems on a network, repeat step 2 and specify the system names for all the systems (if there are just a few) or the IP address range (if there are several systems in the same range). If there are other systems in this IP address range that you are not the administrator for, don't use the IP address range method, as the administrator for those systems probably doesn't want you running the nmap command against those systems. The format for this command would be

```
# nmap -sU -sT -o portsnetwork systemname1 systemname2 ...
```

where *systemname1 systemname2 ...* are the names of the systems to scan, or

```
# nmap -sU -sT -o portsnetwork ipaddressrange
```

where *ipaddressrange* is the range of IP addresses to scan using one of the formats demonstrated earlier.

7. Repeat steps 3 and 4 for each individual system you are responsible for. If you notice patterns of ports that are open or services in use that don't need to be, these may provide you with information to improve your system security profiles in your security policy.

8. Repeat step 5 for each system individually, saving the results in a separate baseline file for each system.

```
# nmap -sU -sT -o portsystemnamex systemnamex
```

The Secure Shell Facility

The secure shell service provides strong security features for remote system access to include file copy and terminal access. It also can be used to provide a secure connection for X-Windows and other services. SSH is the ideal replacement for such tools as rsh, rlogin, rcp, and telnet because it provides the same services, plus it provides a secure connection when passing data so that information between the client and server is private. For example, as shown in Figure 7-1, a workstation can access sensitive information from a server, while the data is traversing the unsecure network, without the worry that a would-be hacker might capture the information flowing between the workstation and server. Assuming that the information was in fact captured by someone in the middle, eavesdropping on the connection, the information captured would be of little value since the information is encrypted and it would require a significant effort to decrypt the information to make it useful. This is a powerful feature and opens up many possibilities for the systems administrator because they can provide secure access regardless of the client location or level of security within the network.

In addition, based on the use of host keys, client and server authentication is greatly enhanced over existing services with the r-commands (rlogin, for instance) or telnet. The SSH model for establishing security requires the user to validate her or his identity on the remote system. SSH uses two broad approaches when authenticating users, which are known as SSH protocol version 1 and 2. These are described in Table 7-7.

The implementation of SSH is meant to be easy; as a result, SSH supports the old style of authentication based on trusted hosts (this is described as Version 1–Option A and B). This was the security model of the r-commands that were introduced in the BSD version of UNIX many years ago—namely,

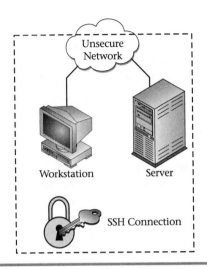

Figure 7-1 SSH secure network

7

SSH Authentication	Description	Files Consulted
Version 1–Option A	If the machine the user is logging from is listed in one of these files on the remote system, and the usernames are the same, the user is granted access.	/etc/hosts.equiv /etc/ssh/shosts.equiv
Version 1–Option B	If the machine the user is logging from is listed in one of the user's files on the remote system, and contains the username, the user is granted access. Note: This may not be true for all implementations of SSH.	$HOME/.rhosts $HOME/.shosts
Version 1–Option C	Uses RSA-based host authentication combined with Version 1–Option A and Version 1–Option B.	/etc/hosts.equiv /etc/ssh/shosts.equiv $HOME/.rhosts $HOME/.shosts $HOME/.ssh/identity.pub

Table 7-7 SSH Authentication Methods

the use of `$HOME/.rhosts` and `/etc/hosts.equiv` files. These files can contain either a username/host (`$HOME/.rhosts`) pair or just a hostname (`/etc/hosts.equiv`), which was compared to the client's username and local hostname. If there is a match, the user is granted access to the remote system. Although SSH supports these older authentication methods, they are inherently insecure and their use is severely discouraged. The security limitations of the r-commands and associated files are widely known (and have been for quite some time), and have been the cause of a large number of security-related problems and issues.

The components of SSH are listed in Table 7-8 and the software package is available for all major operating systems, including Microsoft operating systems. With SSH support for so many operating systems, it is one of the best choices for providing secure client/server connectivity.

ssh

The `ssh` tool provides the capability for logging into a remote machine and for executing arbitrary commands on the remote system. It provides the same remote shell access features as the standard `rsh` or `telnet` connectivity tools and also supports strong security elements so that it is possible to permit sensitive information to flow through an insecure network, such as the Internet. Like `rsh` or `telnet`, when `ssh` is supplied a valid SSH server name on the command line, it attempts to make a connection and provide a shell on the remote machines, if successful. For example, if the remote server called `dino` has to be configured to support an SSH server, the command

```
ssh dino
```

Tool	Purpose
ssh	Provides a remote shell to the specified host using secure connection
scp	Provides remote copy facility using secure connection
ssh-keygen	Generates an SSH key for authentication of the remote system
ssh-agent	Provides a way to preload an SSH key for authentication
ssh-add	Adds a passphrase to a running `ssh-agent`

Table 7-8 SSH Core Elements

would provide a remote shell to the system, once authentication from the client to the server has been established. Thus, before a remote shell was made available, the user would need to authenticate by supplying the remote user's password. The following example shows sample output generated when running the ssh as the root user:

```
root@dino's password: ◄─────────── Password prompt
Last login: Fri Jan 25 13:25:39 2002 from didymus.home.com
Sun Microsystems Inc.    SunOS 5.8       Generic February 2000
No mail.
# dino>
```

As you can see, the user was required to input the root account password for the connection to succeed. If the user didn't know this password, the request would have been denied after the ssh prompted for the password three times:

```
root@dino's password:
Permission denied, please try again.
root@dino's password:
Permission denied, please try again.
root@dino's password:
Permission denied.
```

SSH provides a shortcut for busy system administrators; by placing the client's host key on the remote host, it is possible to prevent SSH from prompting for the remote account password. For example, Figure 7-2 shows a single client and several SSH servers. By placing the user's host key on the other server's system, whenever the user uses SSH to gain access to those servers, the user will need to valid her or his identity further.

scp

The scp command provides remote file copy facilities between a client system and an SSH server. The command provides the same basic features as the rcp command, plus the data is encrypted to ensure privacy.

ssh-keygen

The ssh-keygen command is used to create an SSH host key for the local system. This program does a couple of things. First, it generates both a public

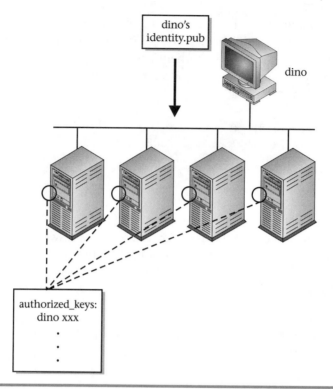

Figure 7-2 SSH host key placement

and private key pair associated with a particular user—the user is responsible for running this command. The private key is stored under the .ssh directory in a file called .identity (note the dot "." at the beginning), which is located within the user's home directory. It stores the public key in the identity.pub file under the same directory. These keys are used as part of the authentication process when the user makes a request to an SSH server.

When a user executes the ssh-keygen program, it asks to specify which file should be used to save the private key. Typically, the default path ($HOME/.ssh) and filename (identity) are suggested. Then, it prompts twice for the SSH passphrase (the second is to confirm the first prompt). Depending on which system this command is invoked on, the output can be somewhat different. On Solaris, for example, ssh-keygen also displays the entire public key string, while other systems don't.

To generate an SSH host key pair, issue the following command

```
# ssh-keygen
```

The example shows the output that was generated from a Solaris system:

```
Initializing random number generator...
Generating p:  ...........++ (distance 190)
Generating q:  .............................................++ (distance 730)
Computing the keys...
Testing the keys...
Key generation complete.
Enter file in which to save the key (//.ssh/identity):
Enter passphrase:
Enter the same passphrase again:
Your identification has been saved in //.ssh/identity.
Your public key is:
1024 33
131002747080850552598435181759036693666098333303044714066279056123049773756023510578
3082576600113762558121351675124104962600689209801039269327397031784881422946150905334
0467209527663138399850223963639073057061948822295225599426944591345678523218150262932
928070176515462990304575837519065722636254119188580761 root@dino
Your public key has been saved in //.ssh/identity.pub
```

When the same command is run from a Linux system, the following sample output is shown:

```
Generating public/private rsa1 key pair.
Enter file in which to save the key (/root/.ssh/identity):
Enter passphrase (empty for no passphrase):
Enter same passphrase again:
Your identification has been saved in /root/.ssh/identity.
Your public key has been saved in /root/.ssh/identity.pub.
The key fingerprint is:
2e:0f:a0:97:6a:62:6b:c8:56:89:00:fa:5c:43:bd:2f root@didymus
```

The major reason for output differences has to do with the versions of SSH. The SSH release running on Solaris is the newer Version 2, while Version 1 is running on the Linux system.

ssh-agent/ssh-add

The `ssh-agent` program is used to hold one or more user authentication keys on the user's behalf. The `ssh-add` command will preload the user's passphrase into a running `ssh-agent`. When `ssh` or `scp` are invoked, these tools check to see if an `ssh-agent` is running and queries to see if a user's host key has been added. If so, it uses the host key that the `ssh-agent` provides; otherwise, the user is prompted for their passphrase. To manually run the `ssh-agent`, do the following:

```
eval `ssh-agent`
```

Then issue the `ssh-add` command to add the user's passphrase:

```
# ssh-add
```

The Sudo Tool

The `sudo` command provides the facility for a generic UNIX user to execute privileged commands that normally can only be run by the `root` user. This security command solves the problem of having different classifications of system accounts; one or more users can be given access to certain privileged commands that they must be able to invoke, but without the assistance of the local system administrator. Figure 7-3 provides a high-level view of how the `sudo` command works. By defining `sudo` users, the administrator can reduce the total number of tasks that he or she must perform by giving other less-important duties to others or meet the requirements of certain power users so that they can perform their jobs satisfactorily. The `sudo` command provides detailed logging capabilities so that all commands executed through `sudo` are recorded for later inspection and review.

The `sudo` command uses a single configuration file (`/etc/sudousers`), which is used to define users and any associated commands they can invoke. For example, to give the users `anitat` and `stevem` permission to do account administration on the system, the following entry can be used:

```
User_Alias    SPECIALUSERS = stevem, anitat
Cmnd_Alias    USERADMIN = /usr/sbin/useradd, /usr/sbin/userdel, /usr/sbin/usermod
SPECIALUSERS  ALL = USERADMIN
```

For the users (`stevem` and `anitat`) to add a new user account to the system (via the `useradd` command) using `sudo`, they would need to execute the command as follows:

```
sudo /usr/sbin/useradd
```

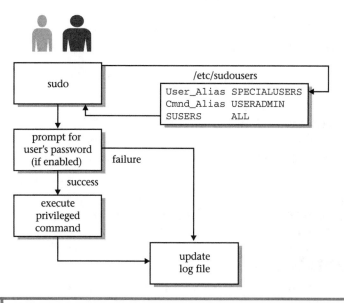

Figure 7-3   High-level function of sudo

7

Thus, to add the user `georgew` to the system, the command

```
sudo /usr/sbin/useradd georgew
```

would need to be executed.

The `sudo` configuration file supports keyword/value directives that control basic operation and functions. These keywords have associated values or parameters and are assigned with the equals (=) character. Keywords can be either aliases or flags. There are four alias types, as listed in Table 7-9. A `sudo` alias is a list of elements separated by a comma (,) and contains a group of strings (such as username). Flags can be variable definitions or options that alter some default behavior, characteristic, or value.

In the example above, two aliases are defined: `User_Alias` and `Cmnd_Alias`. In the first case, the alias `SPECIALUSERS` is defined, which contains the list of users that should be granted privileges. The example includes two UNIX users (`stevem` and `anitat`). Of course, a longer list could have been constructed.

Keyword	Purpose
User_Alias	Defines a list of users that can (or can't) execute a specific command.
Runas_Alias	Defines a username to run a specific command.
Host_Alias	Defines a list of hosts that a user can (or can't) execute a specific command on.
Cmnd_Alias	Defines a list of commands for invocation by sudo users.

Table 7-9   Sudo Keyword Aliases

Hint

When using sudo, it will be important to determine which types of commands should be made available. Also, classifying the users will be important.

Project 7-2

In this project you will lock down your system security by finding and removing any sudo permissions that give users accesses and permissions they don't need.

Step-by-Step

1. Examine the /etc/sudousers file on your system.

2. Look for any users or commands that you don't want other users to have and remove them.

☑ *Mastery Check*

1. Which of these commands lists open ports and associated services on a system?

   A. nmap

   B. find

   C. sudo

   D. ssh

2. What is the command to probe ports with both TCP and UDP scan and direct the results to a file named probeports?

3. What word in the services column of an nmap scan indicates nmap wasn't able to identify the service on this port?

4. Which of the following would be a correct way to TCP scan all systems on a network with addresses beginning 192.168.1., checking all ports from 1–1024 and any additional ports in the `nmap-services` file? (Choose all that apply.)

   A. # nmap -sT 192.168.1.*

   B. # nmap -sU 192.168.1.*

   C. # nmap -sU 192.168.1.1-255

   D. # nmap -sT 192.168.1.1-1024

5. The `sudo` command provides the facility for a generic UNIX user to execute _____ commands that normally can only be run by the `root` user.

6. Which of the following is not one of the general steps for providing robust system security?

   A. Develop and publish a security policy.

   B. Maintain system patches.

   C. Do system backups.

   D. Use security tools.

7

☑ Mastery Check

7. _____ is the ideal replacement for such tools as `rsh`, `rlogin`, `rcp`, and `telnet` because it provides the same services, plus it provides a secure connection when passing data so that information between the client and server is private.

8. What is the correct command to log in securely to the remote system named bedrock as the user named barney?

    A. rlogin bedrock barney

    B. ssh barney

    C. sudo barney

    D. scp bedrock barney

9. What is the Linux command to generate a secure key pair for SSH?

10. A _____ defines what actions groups of users may use their systems for, how to administer security, and how to recover from security breaches.

Module 8

Backup and Restore

Critical Skills

8.1   Define Backup Elements

8.2   Explore Backup Tools

One of the most important (but least enjoyed) duties of the system administrator is performing backups and retrieving (restoring) users' files. Having said that, it is possible to have the entire backup process completely automated to such a degree that these tasks are not that painful to perform. This, of course, requires that you develop your own backup scripts or purchase scripts and/or backup tools that provide these types of services. In fact, many great products are available on the market today that solve many important backup-related problems. However, it is beyond the scope of this book to review third-party commercial tools. Instead, this section reviews some of the standard backup-related tools that are available with the basic operating system.

The funny thing about system backups is that you typically only need them when something goes wrong—a faulty hard drive, a user mistakenly deletes important files, a system crashes and can't be repaired quickly, and so forth. These events are not likely to happen every day or even every week, but we know that eventually the need will arise to retrieve information from backup tapes or other media. Like car insurance, backups protect against future disasters and problems when they strike. We don't know the day or hour when something is going to happen, so that is why it is important to be prepared.

Before attempting to evaluate backup software, develop backup scripts, or learn new backup commands, it is important to determine the exact backup and restore requirements for the computing environment and user community. For example, the requirements for a stand-alone system with a single user will be different versus a large system that supports a critical application with many users. In addition to the user and/or system requirements, there are other important factors that can impact the backup strategy, such as can the corporate and/or individual subnetwork handle the backup traffic or will the network require an upgrade to handle the new load? In most environments, some type of backup solution may already be in place and any new solution might need to provide backward compatibility.

As you can see, the subject of backups can be a complex one. However, information contained within this section can be used to develop a backup approach to address requirements for many different computing environments and organizations.

8.1 Define Backup Elements

This section reviews some of the specific elements when attempting to formulate a backup strategy or approach. Like most things in life, having a plan in place before doing any work is a good thing, since the planning process can identify critical components and issues that may otherwise not be uncovered until the project is well along, which in some situations can be quite disastrous. When formulating a backup plan, the following elements should be examined:

- User perspective

- Density and form factors

- Network bandwidth

- Remote sites

User Perspective

Regardless of the tools used to perform backups, it is extremely important that users understand the backup policies and procedures and any duties that are required of them. For example, given a network of workstations and servers, how are the workstations going to be backed up? What happens when a user reboots her or his system in the middle of the backup process? What should be done in these cases? These types of questions and associated answers should be documented for all users. Should a user need to retrieve one or more files from the backup system, what is the procedure that should be followed? Going further, what is the response time for retrieving the requested information? Certainly, if information is needed for some production service, then the response is related to the importance of the information being retrieved.

In some situations, a user may request that their individual account be backed up so that the information can be made available to another system. How should this be done? If the new system is only available on the network and connectivity can be established between both systems, a simple file transfer might be sufficient. However, suppose the second system is not on the network. Then some other approach to getting the user's information on the system is needed. Thus, the backup plan should include this if users will be making these types of requests.

To address some of the above concerns, it is recommended that a FAQ be developed and made available to the user community. However, this is just documentation—the user requirements must be taken into consideration when determining the backup plan.

Density and Form Factor

Determining the amount of information that will need to be backed up is an important element to the overall backup approach, but this can sometimes be difficult to measure or forecast. Why? Because requirements can change very quickly as the company changes to meet new challenges. However, this is where having some instincts can come in handy. Since it is not possible to know what will happen in the future, it is reasonable to make an educated guess about the backup storage needs given answers to certain questions. For example, how many systems need to be backed up, what is the total amount of storage on each system, and on what basis will backups be done. This is the *who*, *what*, and *when* approach to determining total storage capacity.

The *who* is how many systems will be a part of the backup plan. This should include workstations, PCs, servers, and so forth. Let's assume the following: 20 workstations, 10 PCs, and 4 servers. The *what* relates to the total disk capacity of each system that will be backed up. For example, let's assume that each of the workstation contains a total of 20 gigabytes of storage, each PC contains 5 gigabytes, and each server has 40 gigabytes. Also, it would be helpful to know the amount of available disk space. Use the `df` and `du` commands to determine total disk space, plus what is being used. The *when* is the frequency for when the backup will be performed on some or on all of the target systems. Will the systems be backed up every day or on some other interval? Certainly, in the case of a much-used production system, a very stringent regime will be needed to ensure the best possible coverage for backups. However, this comes with a price, because more backup storage will be needed.

Once the total amount of backup capacity has been determined, you must figure out what kind of backup media to use. Table 8-1 lists some of the common formats that are available today.

Storage Format	Description
Tape	Liner magnetic tape; large densities are available such as 80GB of data with compression. Storage tape comes in all sizes and shapes.
Removable disk	Removable media such as Zip, Jazz, and so forth are quite popular. Storage capacity ranges from 250MB to over 2GB. CD-ROMs and DVDs are another good example of this type of media.
Fixed hard drive	It is becoming more common to back up systems using regular hard drives contained within a special storage unit. These units can be magnetic or optical.

Table 8-1   Different Storage Formats

Network Bandwidth

One factor that is sometimes overlooked when performing backups is the amount of network bandwidth that is required to back up all the required systems. This is particularly important when the backup server is centrally located within the "core" of the network and when most of the systems that are being backed up are on the "edge" of the network. The edge is defined as being closest to the user community but farthest from the core of the network. Edge devices consist of workstations, printers, and so forth, and depending on the network infrastructure, the performance from the edge to the core may not be able to handle backup traffic while other activities are in progress. This is one of the major reasons that many sites do backups at night—because the network is least busy due to the systems not being used.

One very good way to determine the potential bandwidth that might be used during a backup session is to examine the performance of the backup server itself. For example, modern backup systems boast of transferring approximately 20GB per hour onto storage media. This is impressive performance given the capabilities of systems just a few years ago. However, despite this transfer rate, the total overall bandwidth is limited by the network interfaces from the backup server and associated target systems (the systems that need to be backed up). Thus, if the backup system is attached to the network using relatively seasoned equipment, network performance will affect how much time it will take to perform a backup.

Consider a standard 10 MB/s network. You can only get about 1.4 GB per hour of data transfer. Why? Well, for starters, a 10 MB/s network doesn't really deliver that kind of performance. Instead, based on the operating system, network protocols, and other factors, the performance might be in the range of 3–4 MB/s, and this might be on the high side. Next, a consideration must be made for the load on both the server and workstations. This will affect how network requests are handled by each of these systems. On a heavily loaded system, the network traffic may suffer because the system can't keep up with the network traffic. Finally, local area networks (LANs) are shared resources, and typically no single device gets all the available network bandwidth, which means that the backup system will compete with other applications. Of course, if the backups are done during nonpeak times when other applications are not running, this issue is negated.

Luckily, newer LAN technology is available, which significantly increases the network bandwidth and performance that is available for applications such as backups. However, many corporations haven't upgraded to the new technology. Regardless, consideration for the network must be made when determining when and how to perform backups.

8

Remote Sites

If it is necessary to back up systems that are located within one or more remote sites, where network connectivity is limited, then additional planning and examination of the computing environment is necessary. For example, would it be possible to install a backup server at the remote site instead of attempting to back up using a central server located at the corporate site? Another approach is to upgrade the network connection between the remote site and the corporate site to support the backup traffic.

Backup Methods

In general, there are several different kinds of backups that you can perform, and depending on the specific goals you have in mind, you might choose one method over another. However, it is not uncommon for one or more methods to be used for different types of systems. Table 8-2 contains a description of the different backup methods.

Image Backup

These types of backups bypass the file system and access the information using what is known as "raw" mode. This mode simply copies all the data of a file system without knowing any specific details of the components and/or elements, such as files or directories and so forth. Image backups are much faster than other backup types because no interpretation of the information must be done. With UNIX, backup tools access the raw version of the file system by using a special device file.

Backup Type	Description
Image (raw)	Copies the raw bits from the disk without using the file system.
File system – full	Using the file system, copies all files and directories regardless of when the last backup was done.
File system – incremental	Using the file system, copies only the files that have changes since the last time a backup was taken.
File archive	Using the file system, copies all files and directories regardless of previous backups.

Table 8-2 Backup Approaches

File System (Full)

Some backup tools access the file system directly when performing backup activities, which means that they understand the internals of the file system and maintain complete integrity of the information. This is in contrast to other tools, which access the raw version of the file system. Such tools lack the understanding of the specific file system structure and associated elements. Tools that back up the file system directly usually support one more file system types. For example, the `extdump` command supports the EXT file system. Thus, not all tools that perform file system backups are complete compatible.

File System (Incremental)

An incremental backup is one that captures all of the changes made within a file system since the last backup was taken. The purpose of incremental backups is to reduce the amount of time and storage requirements, since only the changes are captured. As compared to full backups, this can significantly reduce the backup resources needed. The only problem with doing incremental backups is that when retrieving files, it can be difficult to find the necessary files, since they can be located on different incremental backups.

File Archive

The file archive method is the simplest backup format, since it just archives individual files and directories onto a regular file or other storage media. UNIX tools that support this backup type are the `tar` and `gnuzip` commands.

8

1-Minute Drill

- Why might you use more than one backup type in your backup plan?
- If you are performing network backups, what factors will limit the amount of data you can back up in one session?

- To conserve backup time but still maximize backup coverage, you might use different backup types. For example, your plan might implement full file system backups once a week on weekends (or another low usage time) and daily incremental backups at night. This minimizes the amount of data to back up each night, ensures a recent backup of all data, and keeps the number of different incremental tapes you'd need to search to just a week's worth when restoring.
- In addition to your backup device's rated speed, the network's overall speed, the operating system's ability to utilize the network, the user and application load on the network during the backup, and competition for bandwidth between other network devices will all limit network backup performance.

8.2 Explore Backup Tools

The UNIX system provides a powerful set of robust backup tools and for the most part the same set of tools are available for most of the UNIX versions currently available on the market today. Some of the most common tools are listed in Table 8-3. The major benefits for common availablity of the tools are consistency and compatibility. For instance, the basic operation of the commands is the same so that if the administrator develops custom scripts, those scripts can be used across a variety of UNIX systems with major operating system changes. Second, if the backed up data is compatible with different UNIX versions, backups can be made on one system and restored on another. This sort of thing isn't something that would be done every day, but administrators might like the option of doing so.

Hint

Both Linux and HP-UX have an official dump command. However, the Solaris system uses the ufsdump command instead, but it provides the same basic services and even supports many of the same command-line arguments. For simplicity, all of these backup tools will be referred to as just dump. In the cases where an important command-line or functional difference exists between the operating system commands, it will be noted.

dump

The dump command provides one of the best ways to perform file system backups. It can be used to provide both full and incremental backups of a number of different file systems. It supports a large number of options to control how backups should be done. Table 8-4 contains the most common options. This tool is used at more sites than any other single backup tool.

Tool	Description
dump	Performs full and incremental backups of file systems (Solaris, ufsdump—for Linux and HP-UX, the command is known as dump).
dd	Can be used to perform image-type backups.
restore	Used to retrieve file and directories from backups taken with the dump command (Solaris uses ufsrestore; restore for the other operating systems).
tar	General-purpose archiving tool.
volcopy	Performs full image backup of a file system for the Solaris platform.

Table 8-3 Backup/Restore Tools

Option	Description
0-9	The backup dump level to use; this controls which files will be saved.
-D	Save the backup to a diskette device. This is somewhat limited since diskettes are quite small and can't store much information.
-S	Determine the total size of a backup, without actually doing the backup.
-a	Specify the archive file to use so that when a restore is performed, it can be searched to determine if a particular file/directory is contained within the backup.
-b	Use the blocking factor when making the backup. The default is 20 and is specific to the storage media used.
-f	Specifies the dump file, which is usually a storage device such as tape or disk. When the "-" character is used, the standard output should be used instead.
-l	Control the backup storage media so that when the dump is complete, dump will pause to give the storage device time to automatically reload a new tape or media.
-n	Inform the operator when dump requests attention, such as mounting a new tape.
-t	Controls the amount of time to wait for the storage device to autoload another tape. Used with the -l option.
-v	Perform a verification on the backup media as the last step in the process.
-w	Issue a warning when dump detects a file system that hasn't been backed up.

Table 8-4   Dump Command-Line Options

Hint

When performing full backups of the system, it is important the system not be used and the file system be unmounted during this time. Failure to unmount the file system during a system backup can lead to problems!

To perform a full backup of the / file system to a local tape unit, use the following command:

```
ufsdump 0f /dev/st0 /
```

When this command is invoked, the following output is generated:

```
DUMP: Writing 32 Kilobyte records
DUMP: Date of this level 0 dump: Wed Jan 30 11:13:41 2002
DUMP: Date of last level 0 dump: the epoch
DUMP: Dumping /dev/rdsk/c0d0s0 (bedrock:/) to /dev/st0.
```

```
DUMP: Mapping (Pass I) [regular files]
DUMP: Mapping (Pass II) [directories]
DUMP: Estimated 78032 blocks (38.10MB).
DUMP: Dumping (Pass III) [directories]
DUMP: Dumping (Pass IV) [regular files]
DUMP: 78014 blocks (38.09MB) on 1 volume at 638 KB/sec
DUMP: DUMP IS DONE
```

dd

The dd command can be used to perform image-level backups. However, this is just one of the many uses for this command. Its primary use is to convert from different file formats (like ASCIII or EBCDIC). Like dump, this command also has a large number of command-line options. The most common ones are described in Table 8-5.

To perform an image-level copy of the root file system to the local tape drive, do the following:

```
dd if=/dev/dsk/c0d0s0 of=/dev/rmt/1
```

When the command has completed, the following will be displayed:

```
1024128+0 records in
1024128+0 records out
```

which shows the amount of data that was both read and written.

restore

The restore command is used to retrieve files and directories that were created using the dump command. One powerful feature of this command is that it has an interface mode, which can help with restoring specific files and/or directories. Like dump, this command also has a large number of command line options. The most common ones are described in Table 8-6.

Option	Description
bs	Determine both the input and output block size.
if	The file (device) to read.
ibs	Specify the input block size.
of	The file (device) to write.
obs	Specify the output block size.

Table 8-5   dd Command-Line Options

Option	Description
-C	Permits the comparison of the files that have been backed up using dump.
-i	Use interactive mode.
-r	Restores a complete backup onto a new file system.
-t	List specific files and/or directories contained on a backup.
-x	Retrieve a specific file or directory.

Table 8-6   Restore Command-Line Options

To restore a complete file system backup onto a brand new file system (assume the new file system is contained within c0d0s5 partition), do the following:

```
newfs /dev/dsk/c0d0s5
fsck /dev/dsk/c0d0s5
mount /dev/dsk/ c0d0s5 /mnt
restore rf /dev/mnt/1
```

tar

The tar command can be used to build an archive of files and directories within a file system. It really isn't the best approach to performing system backups, but it does provide some powerful backup-like features. The most common command-line arguments are described in Table 8-7.

To make an archive of all the files on the system on a local tape, use the following command:

```
# tar -cvf /dev/mnt/1 /
```

Option	Description
-c	Create a new archive file.
-f	Specifies the file (or backup media) to archive the information onto.
-X	Extract files from the archive.
-v	Enable verbose mode.

Table 8-7   Common tar Command-Line Options

In this example, the `tar` command will recursively copy all the files and directories encountered from the root file system. Using the verbose mode option `v`, `tar` produces a list of all the files/directories that have been copied successfully to the tape:

```
a // OK
a //lost+found/ OK
a //usr/ OK
a //usr/lost+found/ OK
a //usr/X symbolic link to ./openwin
a //usr/lib/ OK
a //usr/lib/libICE.so symbolic link to ./libICE.so.6
.
.
```

Because this command produces a significant amount of output, it has been reduced to save on space.

To extract the archive, use the `x` option as shown below:

```
tar -xvf /dev/mnt/1
```

To list the contents of an existing archive, use the `t` option, which shows the contents within the archive:

```
# tar -tvf /dev/mnt/1
```

It will show the following:

```
drwxr-xr-x   0/0        0 Jan 30 11:20 2002 //
drwx------   0/0        0 Nov 11 16:00 2001 //lost+found/
drwxr-xr-x   0/3        0 Nov 11 16:55 2001 //usr/
drwx------   0/0        0 Nov 11 16:01 2001 //usr/lost+found/
lrwxrwxrwx   0/0        9 Nov 11 16:01 2001 //usr/X symbolic link to ./openwin
drwxr-xr-x   0/2        0 Nov 11 16:59 2001 //usr/lib/
lrwxrwxrwx   0/0       13 Nov 11 16:01 2001 //usr/lib/libICE.so symbolic
link to ./libICE.so.6
lrwxrwxrwx   0/0       26 Nov 11 16:01 2001 //usr/lib/libICE.so.6 symbolic link
 to ../openwin/lib/libICE.so.6
```

Project 8-1

This project will familiarize you with the backup and restore commands and give you some practice preparing a backup.

Step-by-Step

1. Determine the amount of data on your system that you need to back up. Display all the file systems on your system and the amount of data used by each:

```
df -k
```

2. Determine if you have a backup device to create a backup on or if you have an unused partition with enough free space for a backup.

3. If so, create a full system backup to the device or partition with the dump command. You'll use level 0 to indicate a complete backup of all files and use the appropriate options to create the backup on your backup device or partition. (Remember, don't do this at a time when the system is in heavy use.)

4. After modifying or adding some files (create or copy some dummy test files) create an incremental backup of just the files created or changed since your level 0 backup in step 1. Do this as a level 1 dump, with the appropriate options for your backup device or location.

5. Use the restore command to restore just the files from your level 1 incremental dump, working in interactive mode and follow the prompts:

```
#restore -i
```

8

☑ Mastery Check

1. What type of backup copies the bits from the disk without using the file system?

   A. Image

   B. File system - full

   C. Dump

   D. File archive

2. A _____ backup is one that captures all of the changes made within a file system since the last backup was taken.

3. Which command is the primary UNIX command most often used for backup tasks?

   A. dump

   B. dd

   C. restore

   D. tar

4. Which command is used to retrieve files backed up with UNIX's primary backup command?

   A. dump

   B. dd

   C. restore

   D. tar

5. Which command is used primarily to convert data between different formats but also performs backups?

   A. dump

   B. dd

   C. restore

   D. tar

☑ Mastery Check

6. In the following set of steps, what action does each of the first 3 steps perform?

```
newfs /dev/dsk/c0d0s5
fsck /dev/dsk/c0d0s5
mount /dev/dsk/ c0d0s5 /mnt
restore rf /dev/mnt/1
```

7. In this command, what device is the file system being backed up to?

```
dump 0f /dev/st0 /
```

8

Module 9

System Operations

Critical Skills

The UNIX system is a complex arrangement of tools, applications, and processes. When the system has booted and is operating normally, certain key processes and services are automatically activated. As the administrator, you will need to control and/or alter how the system boots, as well as monitor and control system processes and services. Sometimes when critical system administration tasks must be performed, the system will need to be brought into maintenance mode. This mode provides an environment where the tasks can be performed while keeping users off the system. When the required administration tasks are complete, the system can be brought back to the normal operating mode. Also, depending on the nature of the administration tasks, it is not always necessary to change the operating mode of the system.

9.1 Determine the Boot Process

When a UNIX system is started, it goes through a series of steps to bring the system to the desired operating mode. This is known as the UNIX boot process and is controlled by automated scripts that can be modified by the system administrator. Typically, the system's boot process doesn't change that much once the system has been set up and configured. However, if new services are added or removed, the system boot configuration can be modified. Also, if the system is having problems, the boot process can be altered on the fly so that the problem can be fixed and system restored to normal operations.

Booting the system basically involves loading and executing the operating system so that the normal system is available to the users. As you might imagine, every operating system contains booting elements that are different. Despite this, all operating systems follow the same generic procedure to start the system. The difference is in the specifics of how the bootstrap process is accomplished for each system. For example, the System V variant operating systems are really different as compared to the BSD-related versions. Luckily for the system administrator, most versions of UNIX have a standard boot process, which is shown in Figure 9-1.

Hint

The standard boot process presented may not include boot services or functions, which can be found in different releases of UNIX today.

The boot process involves several important steps; first, the UNIX Kernel program is started which is the master controlling entity within the system.

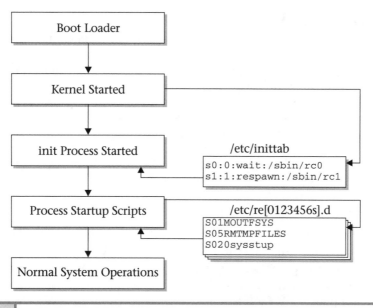

Figure 9-1   UNIX boot process

Under Linux, for example the LILO boot loader can be used to boot the kernel. Next, the Kernel starts the `init` process. This process has the process id of 1 and is known as the father or master system process. The `init` process is responsible for starting all the correct processes by executing specific startup scripts (script files that begin with "S") that reside in the `/etc` directory. Finally, any additional system processes (such as checking the file systems) are done and the system starts normal operations.

9.2 Explore the Shutdown Process

The UNIX shutdown process is not completely the reverse of the boot process; instead, the administrator executes a specific command, which brings the system down in a graceful fashion. There are several ways to bring the system down; it really depends on what you really want to accomplish. Table 9-1 shows some of the most common ways to either reboot or halt the system.

Figure 9-2 shows the generic steps involved with bring a UNIX system shutting down a system. One of the commands listed in the table is executed by the

9

Command	Description
halt	Halts the computer; it kills all processes and brings the system to the boot prompt level.
init	Controls the master system process; given a valid run-level argument, places the system in that run level.
reboot	Restarts the system; brings the system down and then restarts the system, and returns it to default normal operating mode.
shutdown	Brings the system to the single-user mode level. All users are asked to log in off the system.

Table 9-1   Commands to Shut Down the System

system administrator, which causes a chain reaction to bring the system down. First, the shutdown scripts (script files that begin with "K") are invoked in the /etc directory, which basically stops all the system processes. Next the file systems are checked (unless the administrator explicitly doesn't have them checked) and then the system is halted. Typically, the system is brought to the boot prompt or boot loader level. At this point, the power to the computer system can be turned off.

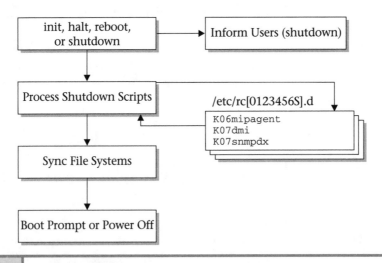

Figure 9-2   UNIX shutdown process

Halting the System

To halt the system basically means to bring the system to lowest boot level.

Hint

This is not the preferred way to bring the system down when users are logged in. For many systems, this means placing the system at the computer firmware level so that the system can be powered down or rebooted in a different manner. Halting the system when users are logged in and are active is not the best way to bring the system down.

For example, boot an upgrade program from CD-ROM so that the system can be updated with newer operating system software. Using this command is typically one of the fastest ways to safely turn off the system without shutting down the power. To bring the system down or to halt the system using the `halt` command, do the following:

```
# /etc/halt
```

When executed on a Solaris Sparc system called `dino`, the following will be displayed:

```
Feb  3 13:50:25 dino halt: halted by root
Feb  3 13:50:25 dino syslogd: going down on signal 15
syncing file systems... done
Program terminated
Ok
```

> Root user executed the halt command

> Important step where system updates file systems

The example shows that the `root` user halted the system, a similar message was logged to the `syslog` logging facility, and the file systems were synced. The most important step here is that the file systems were synced or updated by the system. This means that all information (data) that was contained within system buffers was flushed (or written) to all associated disk files.

When this command is executed on Intel Linux system called `didymus`, the following is displayed:

```
Red Hat Linux release 7.2 (Enigma)
Kernel 2.4.7-10 on an i686
```

```
didymus login: cardmgr[626]: shutting down socket 0
cardmgr[628]: executing: 'modprobe -r 3c5745_cs'
unloading Kernel Card Services
md:recovery thread got woken up…
md:recovery thread finished …
md:recovery(8) flushed signals.
Md: stopping all md devices.
System halted.
```

The `halt` command provides a few command-line arguments that can further refine how the system is brought down. The command options are listed in Table 9-2.

If you need to shut down the system down in the quickest manner possible, use the `-q` option. The `init` command can also be used to halt the system, by issuing the

```
init 0
```

command. The system will be halted in the same manner as when `halt` command is used. The `init` command permits the administrator to control the run-level the system will be operating under. When the above command is run, the following will be displayed:

```
INIT: New run level: 0
The system is coming down.  Please wait.
System services are now being stopped.
Print services stopped.
Feb  3 13:44:50 dino syslogd: going down on signal 15
The system is down.
syncing file systems... done
Program terminated
```

Rebooting the System

The system can be shut down and then restarted using the `reboot` system command.

Hint

The `reboot` command is not the preferred way to bring the system down when users are logged into the system. This command is very handy because the administrator is given a little more control about how the system is restarted.

Option	Description
-d	Instruct the system to perform a system crash dump before the system is restarted (Solaris and HP-UX only).
-f	Don't call the `shutdown` command when bringing the system down (Linux only).
-l	Don't log a message to the system when halting.
-n	Don't run the `sync` command before halting the system.
-q	Don't gracefully shut down the system; just do it fast.
-w	Don't reboot or halt the system; just update the log file (Linux only).

Table 9-2   The `halt` Command-Line Options

When invoked, the `reboot` command displays the same basic information as the `halt` command. The difference between the `reboot` command and the `halt` command is that with `reboot`, it will automatically restart the system

Ask the Expert

Question   Why would you need to shut down the system as quickly as possible with the halt -q command without going through a complete proper shutdown process?

Answer   Only in a rare situation would the administrator need to halt the system without doing a complete and proper shutdown—for instance, when a hardware problem has occurred and must be corrected quickly. Also, if you have physical access to the system, hitting the power off button would also be necessary.

Question   Why would you need to restart the system?

Answer   There are a number of reasons for why the system will need to be shut down and brought back up again. One reason for example, the administrator introduced some configuration changes to the system and wants to ensure that the system will boot with no problems despite these changes.

9

after it is brought down. One very useful feature of `reboot` is that it accepts additional command-line arguments, which control how the system should be started back up. For example, to restart the system and place it in single-user mode, use the following command:

```
reboot -- -s
```

In this case, the `-s` option was preceded by the two dashes (`--`) to instruct this command to pass the `-s` option to the boot process when the system is restarted. The `-s` option tells the boot loader program to bring the system up to single-user(s) mode. Thus, the following output was generated by the command when run on a Solaris Sparc system:

```
Feb  3 15:54:09 dino reboot: rebooted by root
Feb  3 15:54:09 dino syslogd: going down on signal 15
syncing file systems... done
rebooting...                          ┌──────────────────────────┐
Resetting ...                         │ After restarting, the system│
                                      │ executes the -s option for │
                                      │ single user mode           │
Netra t1 (UltraSPARC-IIi 440MHz), No Keyboard
OpenBoot 3.10.25 ME, 512 MB memory installed, Serial #14242136.
Ethernet address 8:0:20:d9:51:58, Host ID: 80d95158.

Executing last command: boot -s ◀────────────────────────┘
Boot device: /pci@1f,0/pci@1,1/scsi@2/disk@0,0:a  File and args: -s
SunOS Release 5.8 Version Generic_108528-03 64-bit
Copyright 1983-2000 Sun Microsystems, Inc.  All rights reserved.
configuring IPv4 interfaces: hme0.
Hostname: dino               ┌──────────────────────────┐
                             │ System notification that  │
                             │ it is in single user mode │
INIT: SINGLE USER MODE ◀─────┘
Type control-d to proceed with normal startup,
(or give root password for system maintenance): ◀──── System Prompt
                                                      for root password
```

When the system is placed in single-user mode, the system prompts for the root password. The output above would be comparable when run on either the Linux or HP-UX systems. However, the Linux `reboot` command doesn't support the `--` option, nor can it pass additional command-line options to the boot loader program.

The `init` command can also be used to reboot the system, using the

```
init 6
```

command. Again, this isn't the preferred way to reboot the system when the system has active users.

Normal System Shutdown

When the system is in multi-user mode, users are logged into the system, and are actively working on the system; the best way to shut the system down is with the shutdown command. This command provides the users with the ability to schedule the shutdown at a fixed point in the future, knowing when the system will become unavailable. Also, a warning message or information about why the system is coming down can be included with the shutdown command. For example, assume the system bedrock must be shut down for some disk maintenance one hour from the current time. On Solaris and HP-UX, use this command:

```
shutdown -g 3600 "###### Down for Disk Maintenance: System back in
two hours ######"
```

The -g option is used to tell the command to wait the supplied number of seconds before proceeding with shutting down the system. In this example, the value 3600 is given to represent one hour.

Hint

In practice, the administrator should give more time than just an hour to the user community when bringing the system down. However, if the maintenance task is very important and must be done right away—say, to fix an important disk failure—giving advance notice to a pending shutdown can't be done.

Each user that is logged into the system will be notified for the pending shutdown. When the shutdown command is first executed, a message like the following will be sent to all users currently on the system:

```
Broadcast Message from root (console) on dino Sun Feb  3 15:23:55...
The system dino will be shut down in 1 hour
###### Down for Disk Maintenance: System back in two hours #####
```

When the time for the system to be brought down approaches, the users are notified on a periodic basis. The format is similar to the message above.

9

Hint

if you want to cancel the `shutdown` command once it has started, simply type a ^C (CTRL-C). If the command was placed in the background when executed, bring it to the foreground or use the `kill` command with the associated process ID.

The `shutdown` command also supports the `-i` option and controls which run level the system will be placed in when it reboots.

On Linux, the `shutdown` command is more functional and supports a number of useful command-line arguments, as listed in Table 9-3.

For instance, to have the system rebooted and not have the file systems checked on startup, use the following:

```
shutdown -r -f     Down for Disk Maintenence: System back in two hours
```

Determining When the System Was Halted

When the system is shut down, a record is kept in the `/var/adm/messages` file. Simply search for the keyword `halt` or other related strings. Thus, the command

```
# grep halt /var/adm/messages
```

will yield similar output if the system has been halted in the past:

```
Oct 30 23:09:31 dino halt: [ID 662345 auth.crit] halted by root
Nov  1 22:51:22 dino halt: [ID 662345 auth.crit] halted by root
Feb  3 13:50:25 dino halt: [ID 662345 auth.crit] halted by root
```

Option	Description
-F	Make sure that the `fsck` is done when the system is rebooted.
-f	Don't perform a `fsck` on the file systems when the system is restarted.
-c	Stop a shutdown that is already in progress.
-k	Don't actually shut down the system. Instead, send a warning message to all users logged into the system.
-r	Reboot the system after it has shut down.

Table 9-3 Shutdown Command-Line Options

1-Minute Drill

- What are the key steps in the startup process?
- When might you need to change the system boot settings?

9.3 Uncover UNIX Operating Levels

The UNIX system is a multi-user, time-sharing system that supports different operating levels or service levels. The system supports a number of different operating or run-level modes. In general, the system is operating in what is known as multi-user mode. More specifically, the multi-user mode maps to run level 2, which is usually the default mode configured when the system boots. This run level is defined as permitting users to access the system, and also critical system processes and resources are available. Table 9-4 lists the available run levels within UNIX.

The UNIX system uses a standard `init` configuration file to control run levels and which services are started (or stopped when the system is brought down) when the system is booted. The `/etc/inittab` is read by the `init`

Run Level	Description
S or s	Place the system in single-user mode. This mode is used for system maintenance.
0	Causes the system to be halted.
1	Places the system in single-user mode (Linux only).
2	Multi-user mode without NFS (Linux). Multi-user mode, but without network services (Solaris and HP-UX).
3	Multi-user mode; typically the default run level with full system services.
5	X11 workstation (Linux only) Shut down the system so that the power can be off (Solaris and HP-UX). This is the default run level for Linux.
6	Causes the system to be rebooted.

Table 9-4   Standard UNIX Operating (Run) Levels

9

- First the UNIX kernel starts, then the kernel starts the init process. The init starts all the correct processes by executing startup scripts, and finally additional system processes are done.
- When you add or change services or if you are having system problems and need to reconfigure to correct the problems.

process during system startup or shutdown. Also, when the system administrator modifies this file, the `init` process can reread this file when necessary. The `/etc/inittab` files for Solaris, HP-UX, and Linux differ not so much in syntax, but in contents. In other words, the services started for their run levels are different, but the basic structure of the files is the same.

On Solaris, the `/etc/inittab` file contains the following entries:

```
    1  ap::sysinit:/sbin/autopush -f /etc/iu.ap
    2  ap::sysinit:/sbin/soconfig -f /etc/sock2path
    3  fs::sysinit:/sbin/rcS sysinit           >/dev/msglog 2<>/dev/msglog
</dev/console
    4  is:3:initdefault:
    5  p3:s1234:powerfail:/usr/sbin/shutdown -y -i5 -g0 >/dev/msglog
2<>/dev/msglog
    6  sS:s:wait:/sbin/rcS                     >/dev/msglog 2<>/dev/msglog
</dev/console
    7  s0:0:wait:/sbin/rc0                     >/dev/msglog 2<>/dev/msglog
</dev/console
    8  s1:1:respawn:/sbin/rc1                  >/dev/msglog 2<>/dev/msglog
</dev/console
    9  s2:23:wait:/sbin/rc2                    >/dev/msglog 2<>/dev/msglog
</dev/console
   10  s3:3:wait:/sbin/rc3                     >/dev/msglog 2<>/dev/msglog
</dev/console
   11  s5:5:wait:/sbin/rc5                     >/dev/msglog 2<>/dev/msglog
</dev/console
   12  s6:6:wait:/sbin/rc6                     >/dev/msglog 2<>/dev/msglog
</dev/console
   13  fw:0:wait:/sbin/uadmin 2 0              >/dev/msglog 2<>/dev/msglog
</dev/console
   14  of:5:wait:/sbin/uadmin 2 6              >/dev/msglog 2<>/dev/msglog
</dev/console
   15  rb:6:wait:/sbin/uadmin 2 1              >/dev/msglog 2<>/dev/msglog
</dev/console
   16  sc:234:respawn:/usr/lib/saf/sac -t 300
co:234:respawn:/usr/lib/saf/ttymon -g -h -p "`uname -n` console login: " -T
sun-color -d /dev/console -l console -m ldterm,ttcompat
```

On Linux, the `/etc/inittab` file contains the following entries:

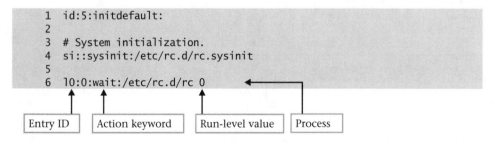

```
    1  id:5:initdefault:
    2
    3  # System initialization.
    4  si::sysinit:/etc/rc.d/rc.sysinit
    5
    6  l0:0:wait:/etc/rc.d/rc 0
```

| Entry ID | Action keyword | Run-level value | Process |

```
 7  l1:1:wait:/etc/rc.d/rc 1
 8  l2:2:wait:/etc/rc.d/rc 2
 9  l3:3:wait:/etc/rc.d/rc 3
10  l4:4:wait:/etc/rc.d/rc 4
11  l5:5:wait:/etc/rc.d/rc 5
12  l6:6:wait:/etc/rc.d/rc 6
13
14  # Things to run in every runlevel.
15  ud::once:/sbin/update
16
17  # Trap CTRL-ALT-DELETE
18  ca::ctrlaltdel:/sbin/shutdown -t3 -r now
19
20  pf::powerfail:/sbin/shutdown -f -h +2 "Power Failure; System Shutting
Down"
21
22  # If power was restored before the shutdown kicked in, cancel it.
23  pr:12345:powerokwait:/sbin/shutdown -c "Power Restored; Shutdown
Cancelled"
24
25  Run gettys in standard runlevels
26  1:2345:respawn:/sbin/mingetty tty1
27  2:2345:respawn:/sbin/mingetty tty2
28  3:2345:respawn:/sbin/mingetty tty3
29  4:2345:respawn:/sbin/mingetty tty4
30  5:2345:respawn:/sbin/mingetty tty5
31  6:2345:respawn:/sbin/mingetty tty6
32
33  # Run xdm in runlevel 5
34  # xdm is now a separate service
x:5:respawn:/etc/X11/prefdm -nodaemon
```

9

Regardless of the operating system version, `/etc/inittab` entries contain a standard set of fields and syntax. Figure 9-3 shows a sample entry and associated field names.

Each `/etc/inittab` entry contains the following:

● **Entry ID** This ID uniquely specifies each entry within the file. Any two characters can be used.

● **Run-level value** The run-level value determines which run level this entry will be invoked. For example, run level 3 indicates multi-user mode.

● **Action keyword** The action keyword denotes the way that `init` will execute the command at the specified run level. The most common action keywords are listed in Table 9-5.

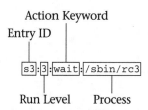

Figure 9-3   The /etc/inittab entry format

● **Process** This field contains the actual program that will be invoked when the run level is entered. Typically, this invokes the startup scripts that are associated with each run level.

1-Minute Drill

● Explain how the /etc/inittab files for Solaris, HP-UX, and Linux are similar and how they are different.

● What's the difference between run levels 2 and 3?

Keyword	Meaning
respawn	Start the process and don't wait for it to terminate. Restart the process when the run level is entered.
wait	Star the process, but wait until it terminates.
once	When the run level is entered, invoke the process and don't wait for the process to finish. If the process terminates, don't restart it.
boot	Process this entry only when the boot phase is started
bootwait	Process this entry when the system enters multi-user mode from single-user mode after the system has booted.
powerfail	Invoke this entry when the process associated with this entry is sent a powerfail signal.
off	If the process of this entry is currently running, shut down. Otherwise, do nothing.
initdefault	Specifies the default run level.

Table 9-5   Common /etc/inittab Action Keywords

● They all use the same general syntax but the services each one starts are different.
● Run level 2 and 3 are both multi-user mode run levels but 2 doesn't include networking services.

The Default Run Level

The default run level is defined within the /etc/inittab file. When the system is rebooted or started when the power is applied to the system, the system is restored to the default run level—which for most systems is multi-user mode (run level 2). If a Linux system is configured to support X11 on the console device, the default run level is 5. It is at this level that X11 support is active and users can access the console using a standard X11 login application. Without X11 support configured, the default run level is 3 and the user receives the standard login prompt. On Solaris and HP-UX, the sample default run-level entry looks like this:

```
is:3:initdefault:
```

While on Linux, the default run-level entry is this:

```
id:5:initdefault
```

To change the default run level, change the 3 or 5 value for the run level. Once the default run level has been changed, use the init command with the q option to reread the /etc/inittab configuration file.

List the Current Run Level

It is important to know which run level the system is at. This is especially true when doing maintenance work at a certain level (such as single-user mode) and the system needs to be reported to the default mode. In this case, the administrator should check to make sure that the system is at the correct level.

To show the current run level on both Solaris and HP-UX, use the who command. Thus,

```
who -r
```

shows

```
         run-level S  Feb  3 20:09      S      2  3
```

In this example, the current run level is (S), which stands for single-user mode.

9

On Linux, use the `runlevel` command:

```
runlevel
3 5
```

This shows the previous and current run levels. In this example, the system was previously at run level 3 (multi-user mode without X11), but now the system is at run level 5 (multi-user mode, with X11).

Single-User Mode

When the system is placed in "s" (S) or single-user mode, regular users are not able to log into the system. Also, no networking facilities or typical operating system services are available. In general, this mode is used to conduct system maintenance tasks such as checking the file systems with `fsck`, adding new services, and a host of other related tasks that must be accomplished when the system is in a quiescent state.

To place the system in this mode when the system has already been booted, issue the following command:

```
init s
```

The following will be displayed when this command is run on a Solaris system:

```
INIT: New run level: S

The system is coming down for administration.  Please wait.
Unmounting remote filesystems: done.
Print services stopped.
Feb  3 20:09:46 dino syslogd: going down on signal 15
Killing user processes: done.

INIT: SINGLE USER MODE

Type control-d to proceed with normal startup,
(or give root password for system maintenance):
```

As the last step in the process, the system prompts for the `root` password. This is a necessary precaution so that unauthorized users can't access the system when placed in this mode. When the correct password has been entered, a shell prompt is displayed. When a Linux system is brought to single-user mode, it doesn't prompt for the root password; instead, it gives a shell prompt. On HP-UX, different messages are displayed when single-user mode is entered.

To bring the system to the default run-level, type a ^d (CTRL-D) or exit the shell. At this point, the system will continue to boot to multi-user mode, which is the default run level for most systems.

Boot to Single-User Mode

If the system must be placed in single-user mode (the system is currently at the boot prompt)—due to some problems or because some maintenance task must be performed—use the −s option that is available with most boot loader programs. Table 9-6 shows the appropriate boot command for each operating system. For example, at the Linux boot prompt, use the `linux -s` command to boot the system in single-user mode.

Project 9-1

This project will familiarize you with the commands from this module and give you firsthand experience with them on your own system.

Step-by-Step

1. Display the current run level for your system. On Solaris or HP-UX:

```
# who -r
```

Or on Linux:

```
runlevel
```

9

O/S	Boot Command
Linux	linux -s
Solaris	boot -s
HP-UX	b -s

Table 9-6   Single-User Boot Commands

2. Display all the processes running on your system and identify the init process and its process ID:

```
# ps -e
```

3. Determine what users are currently logged onto your system:

```
# who
```

4. If you are the only user logged on, shut down your system giving yourself a 1 minute warning before shutdown. (If other users are logged on, perform this step at a later time when the system can be shut down without inconvenience. If this system must remaining running except for emergency maintenance, skip this step):

```
# shutdown -g 60 "##### testing shutdown process in 60 seconds #####"
```

5. Check your system to see when the most recent shutdowns occured:

```
# grep shutdown /var/adm/messages (Linux/var/log/messages)
```

6. Restart the system in default mode

```
# reboot
```

7. After logging back on to the system, display the default run level in the /etc/inittab file for your system:

```
# grep initdefault /etc/inittab
```

8. Display the current run level for your system. (This should be the same as the default run level.)

```
# who -r
```

✓ *Mastery Check*

1. Which system mode is used for system maintenance?

   A. Multi-user mode

   B. Single-user mode

   C. Maintenance mode

   D. Reboot mode

2. The normal or default running mode for most UNIX systems is _____.

3. What process has the process id of 1 and is known as the father or master system process?

   A. Init

   B. Kernel

   C. Boot

   D. Shutdown

4. What keyword do you use in an inittab entry for a process you want to restart whenever it terminates?

   A. Respawn

   B. Init

   C. Reboot

   D. Boot

5. What user mode is your system in if it displays the following output from a `who -r` command?

   ```
   .        run-level 3  Dec  8 10:41      3      0  S
   ```

9

☑ Mastery Check

6. Which command will restart the system after you run the command to bring the system down?

   A. Respawn

   B. Halt

   C. Reboot

   D. Shutdown

7. Which directory contains script files that `init` runs at startup?

   A. /etc/initab

   B. /etc

   C. /etc/script

   D. /etc/startup

8. Which `init` command is equivalent to the `halt` command?

   A. `init 0`

   B. `init 3`

   C. `init 6`

   D. `init s`

Module 10

The TCP/IP Suite

Critical Skills

As a system administrator, you will be required to handle problems that may affect one or more networked UNIX systems or involve network services at a lower level where protocol operation knowledge is necessary. As a result, direct interaction with TCP/IP and related services might be needed. Therefore, you will need a good understanding of TCP/IP, associated protocols, and applications. Today, many corporations, institutions, and other organizations use TCP/IP extensively and universally to address all aspects of network connectivity in a multi-vendor environment. It is the protocol family of choice with networking manufacturers, operating system vendors, and users alike. In fact, the world's largest network, the Internet, uses TCP/IP exclusively. UNIX was the first popular operating system to use TCP/IP, and TCP/IP continues to be the most widely used set of networking protocols for this and other operating systems.

If you have accessed the Web using a browser, transferred files using FTP, accessed a remote NFS file system, or sent email via the Internet, you have indirectly used TCP/IP. Fundamentally, TCP/IP provides a standard way to deliver information from one system to another without concern for operating system differences and network hardware characteristics. TCP/IP is an acronym that stands for two separate protocols: Transmission Control Protocol (TCP) and Internet Protocol (IP). However, TCP/IP generally refers to these protocols, plus a suite of related protocols and services. For example, the File Transfer Protocol (FTP) uses TCP/IP and provides a basic file transfer facility between a pair of systems. If the system supports TCP/IP, it is generally assumed to support FTP and a host of other protocols and services as well.

Today, the TCP/IP suite is supported on every major computer operating system available. For example, it is supported on HP-UX, Solaris, Linux, AIX, and many more. As such, it is considered the most popular networking protocol, and many of the same TCP/IP services are available on different versions of UNIX. This is good news, because many of the core functions of TCP/IP and applications are the same across different versions of UNIX. The operations of TCP/IP are independent of operating system or computer platform. The protocols hide the underlying operating system details and provides a common framework for establishing connectivity among systems. For instance, an FTP client program is normally available across most implementations of TCP/IP, and a result of using this program, which implements the FTP protocol, is that data files may be transferred between dissimilar systems. In other words, a file may be copied from, say, a Windows machine to Solaris (or vice versa) without the need to worry about how the actual data of the file is stored with each operating system. The client and/or server processing the file automatically handles the file structure differences and adjusts accordingly.

The TCP/IP suite is built on industry standards and is documented quite completely in Request for Comments (RFCs) papers. These documents are widely available on the Internet from several Web sites, but the general authoritative source of such information can be obtained from `http://www.ietf.org/rfc.html`. TCP/IP is defined within an open standards organization, which means that the protocols will remain open and common, and no single vendor can own the protocols or develop proprietary extensions.

TCP/IP is independent of any data link protocol and can be used with many different networking technologies, including FDDI, Ethernet, ATM, token ring, Frame Relay, and SMDS. TCP/IP makes it possible to build a truly heterogeneous network consisting of products and network technologies from many different vendors and sources. In fact, the Internet, which is considered the world's largest network, consists of devices from many networking vendors that operate together in a uniform fashion. That's not to say the Internet doesn't have its share of networking issues or problems, but, for the most part, many would agree that interoperability between equipment vendors isn't a major factor for the established core set of TCP/IP, protocols, and applications.

From a system administration point of view, many of the tools used to administer, monitor, and configure TCP/IP on systems are consistent across most UNIX operating system versions. However, one issue that can be a problem is that each UNIX operating system vendor can and does implement nonprotocol details differently. For example, the way IP address and hostname information is stored on each network device or UNIX systems is not covered by any RFC standard, nor should it be, since it is an implementation detail. Thus, for Solaris, the system name is stored in a file called `/etc/hostname.device`, where `device` is the name of the default LAN interface. Other operating systems use different files or other mechanisms. The present TCP/IP suite provides a mechanism to dynamically assign IP addresses to devices, and it also mandates that they be uniquely assigned to each device attached to the network. However, IP addresses are stored on a local system and are not a protocol matter, but rather a network management or system configuration issue, which is traditionally resolved at the operating system level. Each operating system vendor provides its own solutions to how IP address information or other operating system parameters are to be stored. Since operating systems are completely nonstandardized between vendors, the name of the file or its location (or even the presence of a hostname file) varies between different operating systems and releases.

10

10.1 Uncover the General Seven-Layer OSI Network Model

Networking protocols including TCP/IP can be mapped to a general theoretical network model, which is quite common within the network industry. This model defines the relationship and services that each protocol will provide to other associated protocols, services, and applications. The most common standard network model is based on Open Standard Interconnect (OSI). The OSI seven-layer model is represented by a series of layers stacked one upon another, which, when viewed collectively, represent the operation of a single device within a larger framework of a network of systems. Each layer represents a unique view of the nodes that make up the network or individual devices within the network. The layers of the OSI model consist of the following:

- Application
- Presentation
- Session
- Transport
- Network
- Data link
- Physical

Application Layer

The application layer provides services to users that include file transfer, electronic email, remote host access, among others. This layer might also be referred to as the end-user layer since end users typically execute application at this layer.

Presentation Layer

This layer provides a common interface for applications to the lower layers, which implement common services that may include, for example, encryption, reformatting, and compression of data.

Session Layer

The session layer provides the mechanism to establish, maintain, and terminate sessions between cooperating applications. A session can be viewed as a coupling of services between a pair of systems.

Transport Layer

The transport layer ensures reliable transparent data transfer, flow control, error detection, and recovery between two endpoints.

Network Layer

This layer provides upper-layer protocol transparency, because different network communication methodologies may be used. The network layer is responsible for establishing, maintaining, and terminating connections for different networks. This layer is also responsible for address and routing information between networks.

Data Link Layer

The data link layer provides data transfer service on the physical link using frames; it also handles error detection, flow control, and related low-level services. Some common frame types include Ethernet, FDDI, and token ring.

Physical Layer

The physical layer addresses the mechanical connectivity requirements (such as cables and connectors) and provides transmission of a bit stream that involves controlling voltage characteristics to produce the appropriate signals for each of the networking standard. Examples include cabling for Ethernet, Fast Ethernet, FDDI, and Token Ring. Cabling standards such as 100Base-T, 10Base-T, fiber, and coax, for example, are implemented on this layer.

10

1-Minute Drill

- At which OSI layer do the tools most end users interact with most often operate?
- What TCP/IP property makes it possible to build a truly heterogeneous network consisting of products and network technologies from many different vendors and sources?

- Application layer
- This is possible because TCP/IP is independent of any data link protocol.

10.2 Discover the TCP/IP Protocol Architecture

Placing or overlaying the TCP/IP suite on the OSI model helps demonstrate TCP/IP's operation and its relationship to other protocols. Figure 10-1 shows a pictorial view of where TCP/IP fits into the OSI model.

As shown in Figure 10-1, the TCP/IP model consists of four layers. Each layer maps to one or more of the OSI layers, which include

● Process

● Host-to-host

● Internet

● Network access

Except for the network access layer, the other three components are software-based and consist of programmed modules that provide the required functionality. Typically, these components are incorporated into operating systems to provide generalized access so that network applications can invoke basic network services without concern for implementation details.

Process/Application Layer

This layer provides user applications and interfaces with the host-to-host layer. Additional protocols and services are also found on this layer. The process

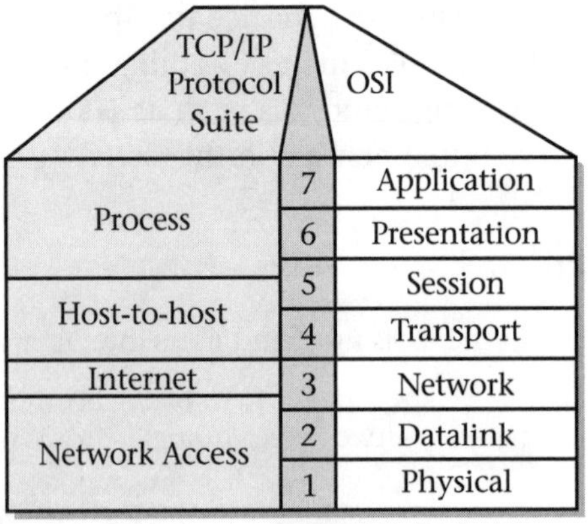

Figure 10-1   TCP/IP and the OSI networking model

layer maps to the presentation and application layers, which are defined within the OSI model. Applications on this layer include Telnet, FTP, sendmail, and many others.

Host-to-Host Layer
This layer is responsible for ensuring that data is reliable and that each higher-level service obtains the correct information from the sending entity. The protocol supported on this layer is TCP. The layer maps to the OSI transport layer. The term used to describe information (units of data) on the host-to-host layer is *segment*.

Internet Layer
This layer provides an unreliable flow of information from one network to another. From an OSI standpoint, this layer is defined as the network layer. The Internet layer (or network) is responsible for routing between different IP networks. The protocol supported on this layer is IP. The term used to describe the information processed on this layer is *packet*.

Network Access Layer
The network access layer involves the physical attachment to a network, which traditionally requires a hardware interface from the network to a computer's internals. This layer includes both physical and data link layers from the OSI model. The network access component defines the network architecture and topology. Some examples include Ethernet, FDDI, and Token Ring. The term used to describe the information on this layer is *frame*. A small driver program, which is provided by the network interface manufacturers, is also needed to connect the hardware to the operating system.

The TCP/IP and associated protocols can also be placed on the OSI seven-layer model, as shown in Figure 10-2. Here, we can see how the protocols and services relate to the model. The next few pages further describe the many additional services provided by the TCP/IP protocol suite.

Process Layer Services
The TCP/IP services on the process layer include end-user tools, additional protocols, and system services. Found on different UNIX platforms, TCP/IP provides a common mechanism to share files, send/receive email, access systems remotely, transfer files between systems, and accomplish other networking tasks. Although the TCP/IP protocol and application suite is large, many UNIX system vendors provide a smaller subset of these services.

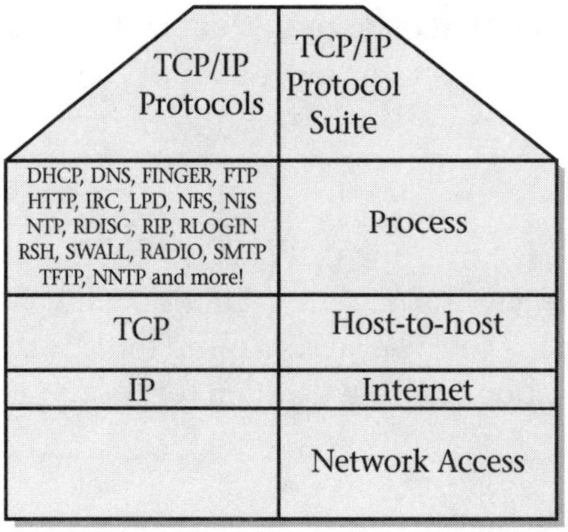

Figure 10-2   TCP/IP suite and model

End-User Tools

The end-user tools, which are common to many UNIX system implementations of TCP/IP, are applications that are generally available to normal system users. As a result, these tools do not require system root privileges for operation. For example, general users without any special consideration from an administration standpoint can invoke the Telnet and FTP commands. Some services within the TCP/IP suite refer to both end-user applications and protocols. Telnet is a good example of this because it represents both a user tool and a communication protocol. In practice, however, this isn't a big problem, because end-user applications on UNIX are lowercase (such as `telnet`) and protocols are generally written in uppercase.

It is interesting to note that certain organizations disable some TCP/IP services as a way of tightening security. One organization in particular did not want its users to have the ability to send or receive email on core development systems and removed the SMTP servers from those systems. Another way that organizations typically disable services is by blocking access to system ports using a firewall device or router.

Additional Protocols

The TCP/IP suite includes additional higher-level protocols that exist above the network layer and provide the necessary details to ensure that applications can communicate. For example, the File Transfer Protocol (FTP) defines how files and associated information are transmitted across the network. The protocol handles all the details related to user authorization, naming, and data representation among heterogeneous systems.

System Services

TCP/IP system services include those facilities that are provided to all users of the system and can only be controlled by the system administrator. System services include specific system processes and special configuration files used by those processes. System network services are usually started automatically when the system is started, but some start in response to requests.

The TCP/IP protocols and services are listed in Table 10-1, and are further described here:

Service	Description
ARP	Address Resolution Protocol
RARP	Reverse Address Resolution Protocol
DHCP	Dynamic Host Configuration Protocol
DNS	Domain Name Service
FINGER	Look up remote/local user
FTP	File Transfer Protocol
HTTP	Hypertext Transfer Protocol
ICMP	Internet Control Message Protocol
LPD	Line Printer Daemon
NFS	Network File System
NIS	Network Information Services
NTP	Network Time Protocol
RDISC	Router Discovery Protocol
REXEC	Remote execution service
RIP	Routing Information Protocol
RLOGIN	Remote login service
RPC	Remote Procedure Call
RSH	Remote Shell Service
RWHO	Remote monitoring of users
RWALL	Remote message broadcast
RADIO	Radio transmitter/receiver
SMTP	Simple Mail Transfer Protocol
SSH	Secure Shell Services

Table 10-1 Associated TCP/IP Protocols and Services

10

Service	Description
TALK	Talk to remote/local user
Telnet	Access to remote system
TFTP	Trivial File Transfer Protocol
WHOIS	Remote Lookup Service

Table 10-1   Associated TCP/IP Protocols and Services (*continued*)

ARP

The Address Resolution Protocol provides mapping between lower-level data link protocols (such as Ethernet and Token Ring) and higher-level protocols such as IP. ARP maps data link (that is, hardware interface) addresses to IP addresses. The Reverse Address Resolution Protocol (RARP) is used to go the other way; it maps IP addresses to data link protocol addresses. ARP and RARP are described fully later in this section. ARP/RARP operates on the network and data link layers.

DHCP

The Dynamic Host Configuration Protocol provides startup (booting) information to client systems. DHCP supports IP address information, operating system configuration information, and other related information. From a network address standpoint, DHCP is an excellent, efficient, and scalable way to manage IP addresses across an enterprise. For example, clients can dynamically obtain IP information while booting, thus removing the burden of having to configure each machine. This protocol operates on the network layer and uses UDP. DHCP takes its origins from the BootP (Boot Protocol) server, which was used to boot diskless workstations over the network.

DNS

The Domain Name System maps between hostnames and IP addresses. The client side provides the ability to resolve names and addresses by making requests to one or more DNS servers only. The server-side component, named, listens for requests and either looks up entries in a local database or contacts another name server for resolution. DNS is an application layer service and can use either TCP or UDP.

Finger

The finger services permit the lookup of user information on either a local or a remote system. The finger service isn't a protocol, just an end-user program that uses TCP for communication with the in.fingerd server. This service operates on the application layer.

FTP

The File Transfer Protocol transfers files between systems. FTP provides basic user authorization that includes using the login name and password on the remote system. The FTP interface is basic, but provides a simple way to transfer single or multiple files. FTP supports transmission of both binary and ASCII data files. FTP is an application-based service and uses TCP.

HTTP

The Hypertext Transfer Protocol transmits Web pages and documents from a Web server to a browser. HTTP uses TCP as its transport facility and operates on the application layer.

ICMP

The Internet Control Message Protocol is a network diagnostic facility that uses the IP protocol. The `ping` tool uses the ICMP echo request/reply protocol to determine node connectivity. ICMP operates on the network layer and uses IP for communication.

LPD

The Line Printer Daemon provides a printing facility for either the network or directly attached printers. This service is an application-based facility and uses TCP.

NFS

The Network File System facility provides file sharing between systems on a local network. NFS uses UDP and resides on several layers, such as application and transport layers.

NIS

The Network Information Service is a directory lookup facility that provides client access to server databases. The types of information typically used within NIS include login, host, file sharing, and other system configuration information. NIS is an application layer service.

NTP

The Network Time Protocol provides an excellent way to ensure that time and date information is synchronized between all networked UNIX systems. NTP is an application layer service and uses either TCP or UDP.

10

RDISC

The ICMP network Router Discovery Protocol finds routers on the local network and builds a table of routes to attached networks. This protocol operates on the network layer and uses IP.

REXEC

The Remote Execution Service provides execution of UNIX commands on remote systems. REXEC uses a specialized authentication procedure that includes reading both the login name and password and comparing this information with the remote system. If the login information matches, the UNIX command is executed. The family of remote commands includes `rsh`, `rwho`, `rlogin`, and others. This service operates on the application layer and uses TCP. Note that the services are considered unsecure.

RIP

The Routing Information Protocol propagates routing information between network system devices such as routers. UNIX systems support RIP as well. On some UNIX systems, if two or more network interfaces are installed, the system will automatically perform routing functions. The routing function is incorporated in the `in.routed` system process that is started when the system is initialized. RIP operates on the application and network layers and uses UDP.

RLOGIN

The Remote Login Service accesses a remote UNIX system. It provides the same basic services as the Telnet program, and operates on the application layer and uses TCP.

RPC

The Remote Procedure Call is a mechanism and protocol that permits the execution of procedures across the network in a vendor fashion. This is an application-layer-based service and uses UDP or TCP.

RSH

The Remote Shell Service provides a shell to the remote system, and operates on the application layer and uses TCP.

RWHO

RWHO provides a list of logged-in users on a remote system. This command is similar to the UNIX `who` command and operates on the application layer and uses TCP.

RWALL

RWALL provides a way to write to users on a remote system. This command is similar to the UNIX `wall` command and operates on the application layer and uses TCP.

RADIO

This is the radio broadcast facility, and operates on the application layer and uses UDP.

SMTP

The Simple Mail Transfer Protocol provides the mail delivery mechanism that is used by many electronic mail packages and is the standard mailing protocol for the Internet. The sendmail system program implements SMTP and is responsible for mail propagation between systems.

SSH

The Secure Shell provides remote access with some level of security for the communication channel. User tools include `ssh`, `scp`, `ssh-keygen`, and the `sshd` server process. This service operates on the application layer and uses TCP.

TALK

Talk is a two-way communication facility that can be used to talk to other system users either on local or remote systems. Talk isn't a protocol, but is just an end-user system utility that uses the UDP protocol and can be accessed by running the `talk` command. This service operates on the application layer and uses TCP.

Telnet

Telnet is the name for a protocol and end-user system utility. The Telnet utility provides a user interface to a remote UNIX system. Users can log into other systems over the network and execute commands as if they were local to that system. Their terminal is connected via the Telnet protocol to the remote system using the `in.telnetd` server process. The Telnet protocol defines a network virtual interface that controls the flow and interpretation of a character stream between systems. This service operates on the application layer and uses TCP.

TFTP

The Trivial File Transfer Protocol provides a more simplistic file transfer facility than FTP. TFTP is considered a light version of FTP because it doesn't support a robust authorization mechanism or command set. TFTP is used mainly to download system configuration information or data. This service operates on the application layer and uses UDP or TCP.

10

WHOIS

WHOIS is a white pages lookup utility. The WHOIS service will search for individual users and other information from standard Internet servers. This service operates on the application layer and uses TCP.

Additional Services

Many public domain TCP/IP services and applications are also available via the Internet. Some of the resources available are improvements over the existing core set of services, while other applications provide new services and features. Table 10-2 lists some of these TCP/IP applications.

AIM

AIM is one of several popular instant messenger services where users are connected to a central server and can exchange text and voice massages.

ARCHIE

ARCHIE supports a database of anonymous FTP sites and their contents. ARCHIE keeps track of the entire contents of a very large number of anonymous FTP sites and allows you to search for files on those sites using various kinds of filename searches.

GOPHER

This is a document retrieval system that is available via a menu-driven interface (for character-based devices) and the World Wide Web (WWW).

IRC

Internet Relay Chat is a way to send either public or private text messages to one or more subscribers in real time.

Service	Description
AIM	AOL Instant Messenger
ARCHIE	FTP search facility
GOPHER	Document retrieval system
IRC	Internet Relay Chat service
NNTP	Network News Transfer Protocol

Table 10-2 Additional TCP/IP Services

NNTP

The Network News Transfer Protocol provides the ability to transfer news files (also known as Usenet) between a client and server.

1-Minute Drill

- Which services in Table 10-1 operate on the network layer?
- Which applications and services from Table 10-1 operate on more than one layer?

Host-to-Host Layer

The host-to-host layer, or OSI network layer, is responsible for providing a robust data delivery mechanism between different network entities. The standard that provides this service is the Transmission Control Protocol (TCP). Within a network, data can be lost or destroyed when transmission errors or network hardware failures occur. Data can also be delivered out of order and with significant delays before reaching the final destination. TCP was designed and developed to address these types of network-related problems. TCP is responsible for ensuring that data arrives in the correct order and is free from errors. It accomplishes these tasks by providing the services described in the following section.

Virtual Connections

TCP provides a virtual connection interface to the network that is analogous to the way phone calls are established in the telephone network. Conceptually, a user calls another machine to request data transfer. After all the details of the connection setup are complete, data transmission can occur between applications. From an application perspective, the TCP connection looks and behaves as if a dedicated hardware link has been established. However, this is only an illusion provided by the TCP streams interface.

10

- ARP, RARP, DHCP, ICMP, RDISC, RIP
- ARP, RARP, NFS, RIP

Sequenced Data

To ensure reliable transfer, TCP keeps track of the data it transmits by assigning a sequence number to each segment. The sequence number uniquely identifies each data segment within a connection and provides a positive acknowledgment to the sending entity. No acknowledgment indicates that the message should be retransmitted. The sequence number is also used to reorder any segments that might have arrived out of order. How can segments arrive out of order? Consider, for example, the network in Figure 10-3.

Because more than one network path to node C exists, it is possible that some TCP segments might travel via router R2 instead of router R1. Should the path between node C and R1 become temporarily heavily loaded, for example, segments may be routed via the alternate path. As a result, segments using the R2 path could arrive at the destination sooner than segments using the R1 path. Also, if a packet becomes corrupted during transmission, the sequence number can be used to request that the packet be resent.

Stream Abstraction Interface

From the application layer standpoint, TCP provides a buffered byte-oriented interface between two applications or processes. The data transmitted from the source entity is exactly the same information that the destination receives. For example, if the sending entity transmitted the message "Hello World", the destination would receive "Hello World". As it turns out, this is a very useful and convenient feature for developing networking applications and services. Also, the TCP stream is buffered, which means that applications have more flexibility when it comes to processing the data from the network.

Ports, Sockets, and Connections

TCP ports are addresses that specify a network resource and are used to uniquely identify an individual application or service on the system. There are quite a few well-known address ports in use today, and many of them can be found in the /etc/services file on UNIX systems. Table 10-3 contains a partial list of some of the most commonly used TCP ports.

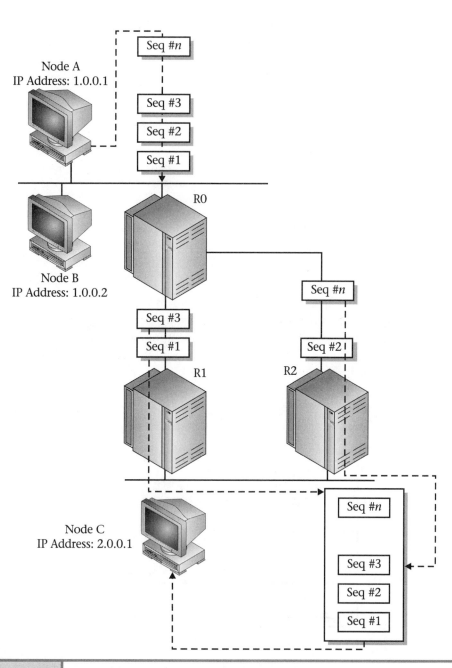

Figure 10-3 TCP sequence numbers in action

Port	Application/Service
20	FTP data
21	FTP
22	SSH
23	Telnet
25	SMTP
53	DNS
119	NNTP
161	SNMP
80	HTTP

Table 10-3   Common TCP Ports and Associated Services

To further understand the function of these ports, consider the services of the UNIX `inetd` process or `xinetd` (for Linux). This process is known as the super Internet server because it is responsible for connecting service requests from the network to the actual server program with the operating system. The superserver knows which process to invoke because it can determine relationships between ports and services. By processing the `/etc/services`, `/etc/inetd.conf`, or `/etc/xinetd.d` directory for Linux, these files (`inetd` or `xinetd`) can make the network request to the appropriate service as needed. Figure 10-4 shows the operation of the superserver when a remote user requests a Telnet session.

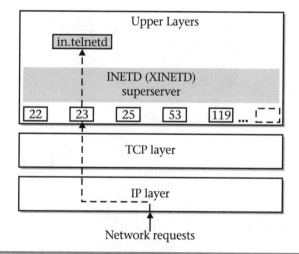

Figure 10-4   `inetd` operation with a Telnet request

It is important to understand that TCP uses a connection-oriented model whereby one network entity may call another to establish either a half- or full-duplex session. In the full-duplex mode, two independent channels are established between systems, and data can flow between the systems. In the half-duplex mode, only a single channel is established. A network entity may first establish a full-duplex session and then shut down one channel if necessary. On the other hand, a service may initially establish a single half-duplex session for control purposes and then start another channel to carry out some specific action or task. This application behavior might seem a little strange, but the FTP service, for example, operates in this fashion.

When an FTP session begins, it establishes a single session to the destination system first. This session is used for user authentication and the command interface. When the user specifies a file transfer or executes a remote command, another session is established to service the transfer request. After the transfer is complete, the newly created session is closed. This process is repeated for each separate transaction or transfer of files.

Sockets are ports that the system allocates on the user's behalf when executing network applications or other services. Because the operating system generates a unique socket number, no two simultaneously running applications on the same system will have the same socket number. On some UNIX systems, the allocation of sockets begins above 1024.

In the context of a connection, TCP uses a total of four elements to uniquely identify one session from another: source IP address, source port, destination IP address, and destination port. This is important to remember because many sessions to the same application or service can be established, even from the same host. For example, two different users can `telnet` to the same destination host without any conflicts among the ports. This is accomplished by the fact that TCP uses all four addressing elements to distinguish a unique session. Figure 10-5 shows the relationship of the TCP elements in different sessions.

10

Positive Acknowledgment

TCP provides reliability by ensuring that every message transmitted is confirmed by the receiving entity. The confirmation of TCP messages is known as positive acknowledgment and is used to ensure that the receiving entity has obtained all the segments that have been sent. When a TCP message is sent, the sending entity starts a timer. If no acknowledgment is received before the time expires, TCP assumes the message was lost or damaged in some way, preventing its delivery. As a result, TCP sends another message to replace the first and starts the timer process over again. This process continues until all segments have been acknowledged or until an internal error threshold is reached. If the sender

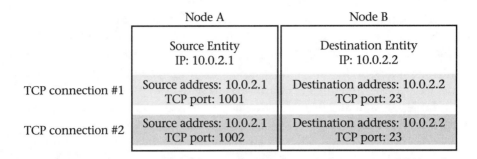

Node A   Node B

	Source Entity IP: 10.0.2.1	Destination Entity IP: 10.0.2.2
TCP connection #1	Source address: 10.0.2.1 TCP port: 1001	Destination address: 10.0.2.2 TCP port: 23
TCP connection #2	Source address: 10.0.2.1 TCP port: 1002	Destination address: 10.0.2.2 TCP port: 23

Figure 10-5   Two TCP sessions from the same source/destination

receives no acknowledgment for outstanding segments after the internal error
count has been reached, the connection will be terminated.

Establishing and Closing a TCP Connection

As previously discussed, TCP uses connections that provide a reliable and robust
data transfer facility. The procedure for establishing or shutting down a connection
is not a magical process. Instead, each TCP entity follows the same set of rules
when creating a session or terminating one. To establish a connection, TCP uses
a three-way handshake protocol, outlined in Figure 10-6.

First, the source transmits a SYN message segment. The SYN (pronounced
"sin") or synchronization is a request to start a TCP session and the SYN bit
set in the code field. Next, the destination responds with an ACK segment that
has both the SYN bit and ACK bits set in the code field, indicating that it has
accepted the request and is continuing the handshake protocol. Finally, the
source sends an ACK segment, which informs the destination that both entities
agree that a connection has been established and that segments can now be
transmitted and received.

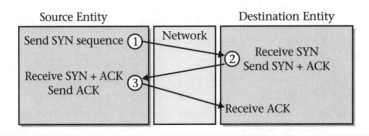

Figure 10-6   Opening a TCP connection using the three-way handshake

To close an established session, TCP uses a modified three-way handshake, shown in Figure 10-7. First, the source transmits a FIN or finish segment (the FIN bit is set in the code field) as a result of the application wishing to close its side of the connection. Recall that TCP views these connections as full duplex; therefore, either party may terminate their side of the connection. Once the application on the destination closes the connection, TCP emits a FIN segment to the source. Next, the source receives the FIN sequence and sends an acknowledgment. Also, in special cases, the remote end may emit an RST (reset) packet that automatically causes the connection to be closed.

Closing a TCP Connection

Please note that it takes three segments to create a TCP connection, and four additional segments to shut it down. A total of seven messages are required to operate a TCP connection, not including any data transfer segments.

State Machine

The operation of TCP is best described using a state machine model, which controls the basic operation of the protocol. Figure 10-8 shows a representative picture of the TCP state machine, where each TCP connection goes through a series of defined phases. Movement from one state to another is the result of an event or transition. The label on each transition shows what TCP receives to cause the change between states. For instance, we discussed that TCP must open a connection before data can be transferred. Normally, each TCP side of the connection starts in the CLOSED state. When a connection is desired, a transition from the CLOSED to SYN SENT state is made. At this point, the client side sends a SYN packet. If the SYN packet is accepted, the remote side emits an

10

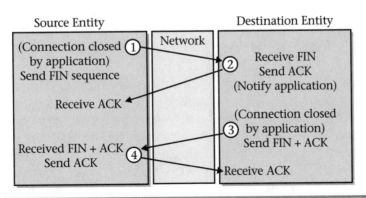

Figure 10-7 | Closing a TCP connection

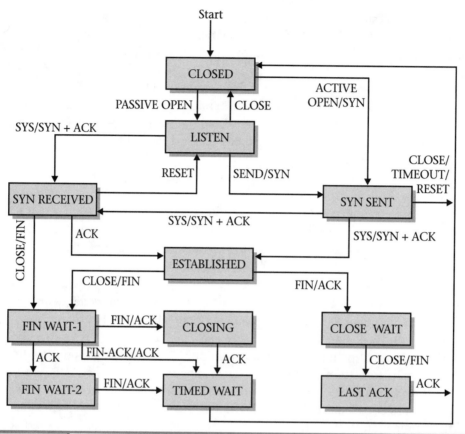

Start

Figure 10-8 TCP state machine diagram

ACK, which causes a transition from the SYN SENT to the SYN RECIEVED
state. Once the final ACK has been received, the ESTABLISHED state is reached
and data transfer may begin. When a TCP connection has been made, it will
remain in the ESTABLISHED state until either side wishes to terminate the
connection.

When a TCP connection is terminated (either by the source or destination),
the connection moves to either the CLOSED WAIT or FIN WAIT-1 state. If the
source sends a FIN segment, TCP transitions to the CLOSE WAIT state, which
eventually terminates the connection. When the destination wants to close the
connection, a change is made to the FIN WAIT-1 state. TCP has an elaborate
mechanism to ensure that segments from previous connections do not interfere
with existing ones. TCP maintains a timer, known as the maximum segment

lifetime (MSL), which contains the maximum time an old segment may remain alive within the network. As a result, TCP moves to the `TIMED WAIT` state after closing the connection. It remains within this state for twice the MSL. After this, if any segments arrive for the connection, they are rejected. Why do we care about these details? Well, it sometimes is helpful in tracking down connectivity problems. The `netstat` command, for example, provides TCP port state information to assist with this type of activity.

TCP Sequence Format

TCP defines a sequence format that includes all the necessary information to ensure that segments get to the correct destination, and also contains additional control information. Figure 10-9 shows the TCP segment format.

The TCP segment fields include the following:

- **Source Port**   The protocol (or service) that sent this segment.

- **Destination Port**   The protocol (or service) that will receive this segment.

- **Sequence Number**   The position in the byte stream of the sender.

- **Acknowledgment Number**   The number of the bytes that the source expects to receive in the next segment.

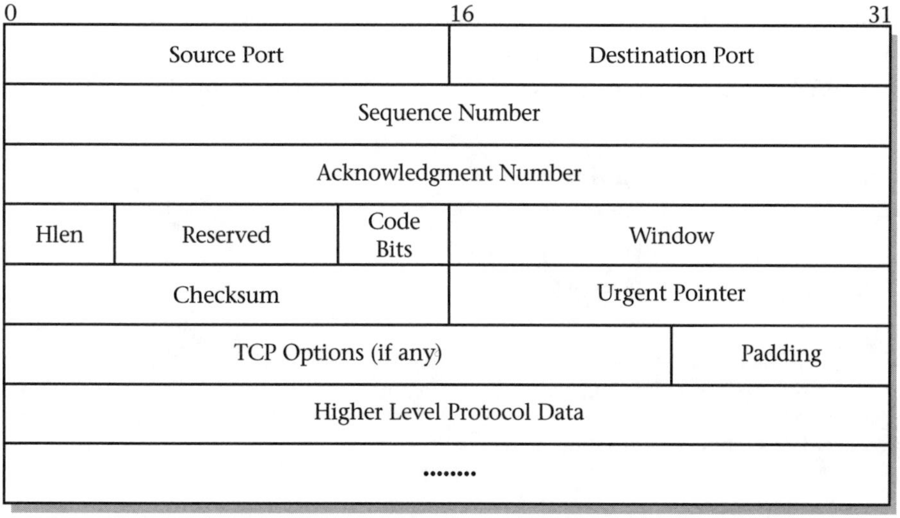

10

Figure 10-9   TCP segment format

- **Hlen**   Integer that specifies the length of the segment header.

- **Code Bits (C Bits)**   Details on the purpose and content of the segment.

- **Window**   Specification of how much data TCP is willing to accept.

- **Checksum**   Integer used to verify the TCP header and data integrity.

- **Urgent Pointer**   Field for indicating that this segment should be processed right away.

- **Options**   Details for negotiating the maximum segment size.

- **Data**   High-level protocols or application-specific information.

Code Bits

These bits indicate the type of TCP segment and how it should be processed. Table 10-4 shows established codes and their associated meanings. These codes are analogous to the type field in the Ethernet frame, which means that TCP segments are self-identifying.

Window

TCP has an elaborate mechanism to handle data buffering, flow control, and retransmission of unacknowledged segments. The window field helps TCP determine how much data it is willing to accept in the next segment. The data size of a transaction can significantly impact overall network and application performance. To understand why, assume for the moment that a TCP connection has been established between two nodes named socrates

Codes	Meaning
URG	Urgent pointer
ACK	Acknowledgment
PSH	Request a push
RST	Reset
SYN	Synchronize sequence numbers and start connection
FIN	Reached end of byte stream

Table 10-4   TCP Segment Code Types

and `durer`. During previous transactions, `socrates` has specified to `durer` a TCP window of 1024 (which is the default). Now, `durer` begins to experience high usage and begins to run low on available resources such as memory. Many reasons can cause this situation. At this time, `socrates` is still sending TCP messages to `durer`, but `durer` is having trouble acknowledging (or perhaps even processing) segments from `socrates` due to the number of the messages. Because `durer` is having resource problems, the next segment sent to `socrates` contains a smaller window size, which informs `socrates` that it must adjust the amount of data contained in subsequent TCP messages. This mechanism is known as the "back-off" algorithm. After `socrates` receives the new window size, it begins sending `durer` smaller amounts of data.

After the resource limitation has been resolved on `durer`—either by explicit action on the part of the system administrator or by the completion of the tasks that caused the resource problem in the first place—`durer` sends `socrates` a larger window size and resumes processing as before. Without the ability for TCP to dynamically adjust the size of segments, in the example `durer` would begin to drop the messages it couldn't process. This, in turn, would cause `socrates` to retransmit them—not only wasting processing cycles on `socrates`, but also wasting networking bandwidth due to the retransmitted messages.

Urgent Pointer

Because TCP provides a streamed interface, it is sometimes important that an application has a way to send an out-of-band or an urgent message to the other end of the connection without having to wait for the previous messages to be processed. An example of why out-of-band is important is when a user wishes to terminate a remote login session using Telnet. Often terminals provide interrupts or control signals, which can be used to inform applications that they should terminate. In this case, TCP uses the URG bit to indicate that this is an out-of-band segment and sets the urgent pointer to specify the position in the segment where the urgent data ends.

TCP Options

This field indicates the negotiation of the TCP segment size, which is useful in a situation when it is possible to establish either a higher or lower maximum transfer unit (MTU). MTU values can be different on different physical networks. For example, ATM has a higher MTU than Ethernet.

10

1-Minute Drill

- Describe the important function of the Transmission Control Protocol (TCP).
- Why is window size an important property in TCP?

Internet Layer

The Internet (or network layer of the OSI model) layer provides a delivery service that is unreliable and based on a connectionless transfer protocol. As previously indicated, the Internet Protocol (IP) operates on this layer, providing a best-effort transfer service, and is responsible for routing packets among different IP networks. IP packets may be lost, delayed, duplicated, and delivered out of order.

Two versions of the protocol have been defined. The most widely implemented version is 4 (known as IPv4), and due to protocol deficiencies and resource limitations of this version, enhancements were made that resulted in a new version known as IPv6. IPv6 contains a much wider address space (128 bit address) and provides quality of service facilities. However, version 6 hasn't been widely implemented within the networking industry.

The major characteristics and services of IP (version 4) include the following:

- Unreliable delivery
- Connectionless protocol
- Packet travel over different paths
- Address format
- Subnetting
- Routing

Unreliable Delivery

The term *unreliable* indicates that IP makes no attempt at guaranteeing the delivery of a packet to its destination. This is in sharp contrast to the behavior and services of Transmission Control Protocol, which provides a reliable transfer facility that ensures message delivery. IP, on the other hand, provides

---

- TCP is responsible for ensuring that data arrives in the correct order and is free from errors.
- Changing the window size allows a host to alter the amount of data it accepts per segment (making the window and data per segment smaller when the host is experiencing heavy loads, for example), thus minimizing the number of segments it receives that it can't process (and would subsequently need to be resent) and maximizing the amount of data it can reliably receive per segment (by not making the window any smaller than necessary).

a best-effort delivery facility and does not ensure packet transfer—but it doesn't capriciously discard them, either. Despite the fact that IP is not reliable, it doesn't mean that data carried with IP isn't delivered correctly. IP simply uses an upper-level protocol like TCP to ensure guaranteed data delivery.

Connectionless Protocol
IP is said to be connectionless because it does not establish a connection through which to transfer packets, which is contrary to the behavior of reliable transfer protocols. Packet delivery is based on IP address information contained within the packet itself. Each IP packet is self-contained, independent of any other packet, and not part of a preestablished agreement between network entities. Because no connection information is maintained within IP, packet delivery is simplified and efficient.

Packets over Different Paths
With IP, packets may travel different paths to reach their final destination, even though each packet might carry a smaller portion of a much larger message. This behavior is observed when IP packets travel within an Internet. Also, packets might arrive out of order.

IP Addressing
IP defines the format of addresses and requires that each network entity have its own unique address. Addresses contain both a network and a node identification pair, which are expressed as a single number. With IPv4, 32 bits are used to represent an IP address and are expressed in dotted notation. Each address is written as four decimal integers separated by decimal points. Five different classes have been defined within IPv4. However, in practice, only the first three primary classes are used to define a network/node pair, as shown in Figure 10-10.

Each class specifies the format used to interpret how much of the address is used to represent the network and how much of the address is used to represent the node. The interpretations of addresses include the following:

- **Class A**   The first byte is the network identification, and the remaining bytes specify the node. The network address range (first byte) is 1–127.

- **Class B**   The first two bytes are the network identification, and the remaining bytes are the node. The network address range is 128–191.

- **Class C**   The first three bytes are the network identification, and the remaining byte is the node. The network address range is 192–223.

Bytes in Address

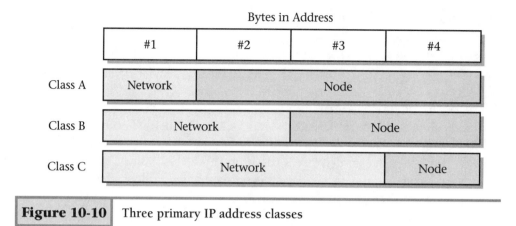

Figure 10-10 Three primary IP address classes

Two additional (D and E) classes are defined, but they are reserved and can't be used for normal network addresses. Class D addresses are used for multicast support, and Class E addresses are reserved for future use. One way to distinguish the different classes is to use the first byte rule. With this rule, the first byte determines to which class the address belongs. For example, using the IP address of 10.1.3.2, 10 is the first byte of this address. The number 10 falls in the range of 1–127, so this IP address is a Class A type and the network portion is 10, while the node portion is 1.3.2.

IP also defines some reserved addresses that include loopback and broadcast addresses. The loopback network is defined as address 127 and is used as a private network for internal diagnostics and support with an IP device. This network address is reserved and is not supposed to be used as a genuine network address. In fact, the IP protocol specifications don't recommend its use on a live network. The loopback address can be observed by issuing the UNIX ifconfig -a command. The broadcast address defined as 255 is also considered special, because it denotes a shorthand way to address all hosts within a given range. For example, given the network of 134.110.0.0, which is a B Class network, the broadcast address of 134.110.255.255 addresses all devices within the entire 134.110 network. Because of the special meaning associated with 255, it should not be used as a node address.

Assignment of IP addresses is accomplished through a central agency known as the Network Information Center (NIC)—www.nic.org. The NIC is responsible for assigning unique IP network addresses to any organization wishing to connect to the Internet. In many instances, a local Internet service provider (ISP) will request an IP address on your behalf or provide one of its own.

Subnetting

Subnetting is a mechanism used to divide a network into smaller subnetworks or subnets. One major motivation for implementing subnets is to distribute administration control of IP address allocation. Subnets also permit more effective use of existing addresses. With subnets, the node portion of the IP address is divided into two sections: the subnet address and node address, as shown in Figure 10-11.

To implement subnetting, the following requirements must be met. First, a subnet mask must be created for use on each of the devices that will participate within the subnet. This subnet mask is a special 32-bit address, which is expressed like a normal IP address using dotted decimal notation. As with a regular IP address, each of the octets within the subnet is in the range of 1 to 255. But unlike IP addresses, the octets represent a set of masked bits that are combined with the device's IP address to yield the subnet network. In particular, determining the subnet involves combining the subnet mask and host IP address with the Boolean AND operator.

Second, each device that will participate in a subnet must use the same subnet mask address. In particular, for each interface defined on the local system, the subnet mask should be defined along with other interface parameters. For instance, under UNIX, the `ifconfig` command is invoked on every system interface installed in the system. The subnet mask information must be included when this system command is executed.

To further illustrate the implementation of a subnet, consider the sample network shown in Figure 10-12. In this figure, we have four devices attached to

10

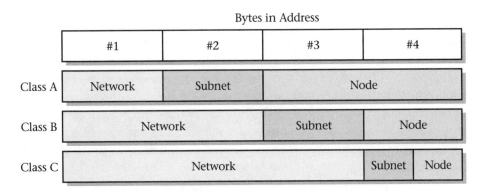

Figure 10-11 | IP network classes with subnets addressing

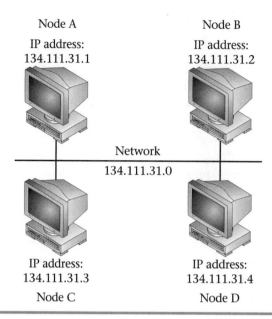

Node A
IP address:
134.111.31.1

Node B
IP address:
134.111.31.2

Network
134.111.31.0

IP address:
134.111.31.3
Node C

IP address:
134.111.31.4
Node D

Figure 10-12   Sample IP subnet

the same network. Each of the devices has already received an IP address, but now we must determine what the subnet mask should be. We have determined that the network will grow in the future and need to have enough IP addresses in the subnet for approximately 200 devices. As a result, we will need to use at least 8 bits (1 octet) for the subnet.

The IP addresses used in the sample network are of type Class B. Recall that B Class addresses are in the range of 128–191 and the first two octets are the network address (134.111), while the remaining two (31.1, for instance) are node addresses. The only place we can take bits to use for the subnet is from the host portion of the address. We simply can't use any of the network address because that area of the address is restricted. With this in mind, we need to subdivide the host portion in two, which is where the subnet mask comes into play. By using all ones (1) in the bits of the subnet fields and all zeros (0) in the bits of the node field, we can forge the desired subnet address by converting the IP address and subnet mask into binary:

```
(decimal)          (binary)
134.111.31.1     10000110 01101111 00011111 00000001 (IP address)
255.255.255.0    11111111 11111111 11111111 00000000 (Subnet Mask)
134.111.31.0     10000110 01101111 00011111 00000000 (Subnet Address)
```

Applying the Boolean AND will produce the subnet address of
`134.111.31.0`. After this subnet mask has been configured on every
device within the subnet, every node will do the required AND calculation
to determine the subnet address to which it belongs. On many (if not all)
UNIX systems, this is an automatic task when the system's network services
are started. To summarize, to subnet a network, do the following steps:

1. Determine the IP address class of the network you want to subnet.

2. Determine the number of addresses you require for the subnet.

3. Determine if you can use a full octet (with at least a B Class address)
   for the subnet address.

4. Perform the Boolean AND on one of the device addresses using the
   subnet mask.

5. Apply the subnet mask to all devices that will participate in the subnet.

The subnet mask assignment in this example was relatively straightforward
because a full octet was used for the subnet number. This makes the subnet
calculation (AND) math very simple. However, suppose we change the example
by using a C Class network number instead. The addresses we now need to assign
to the sample network in Figure 10-12 include `199.81.23.1-199.81.23.4`.
With a C Class address, the range of the first octet falls within `192-223`. The
first three octets are the network address (`199.81.23`), while the remaining
octet (4, in this example) is the node address. This example will complicate the
subnet process a bit, because we must now split the host portion and the subnet
address from just one octet. However, the same procedure applies as stated above.

In order to formulate a subnet address from a Class C network address,
we must borrow some number of bits from the host portion of the address to
represent the subnet number. In doing so, we automatically reduce the number
of IP addresses that will be free for each device within the subnet. Therefore,
we need to know exactly how many devices will be installed on the subnet.
To further refine our example, assume we will only need ten IP addresses for
individual nodes on the subnet.

We can determine the subnet mask and other information by hand, but
it is much easier and faster if we use a software program to do the calculations
for us. We use a calculator which provides the ability to subnet any valid IP
address and shows the calculations and steps involved.

10

The first field, `IP Host Address`, requires that we specify the IP address of one of the hosts on our network. In this case, we give it one of the node addresses from our second example (that is, `199.81.23.1`). Next, we provide some information about the subnet by entering information in the third box, labeled `Select One of the Following`. We can do this in one of four ways: by specifying the subnet mask directly (Subnet Mask field), the number of bits for the subnet (Bits field), the maximum number of hosts within the subnet (`Maximum Possible Subnets field`), or the number of possible hosts per subnet (`Possible Hosts per Subnet field`). Changing one of these fields changes the other three automatically. For example, when a subnet mask is changed to `255.255.255.224`, the number of bits becomes 3 and the number of possible hosts per subnet goes to `30`.

Viewing the Calculations window, shown in Figure 10-13, you can see the relationship between these fields. This screen contains five sections. The first shows two lines, each containing three fields: the standard IP Address (`Class C Network` field) class in both decimal and binary format, the `Subnet` and `Host Bits` fields, respectively, and the subnet mask. This is the mask that must be applied to every system that will be involved within the subnet. This subnet mask uses 28 bits and hence can be referred to as a "28-bit subnet mask." The second section contains the subnet number from the logical AND operation of the host address (`199.81.21.1`) and subnet mask (`255.255.255.224`) fields. The third shows the correct subnet mask, inverted subnet mask, and subnet number as expressed in binary. The next section contains the subnet directed address and the broadcast address. The broadcast address directs IP packets to every node on the local subnet. The final section includes the summary that contains the subnet address, the available host addresses specified with a range, and the directed broadcast address. The available host range is important, because it represents the addresses that can be used by all host systems within the subnet.

1-Minute Drill

● What are two major purposes of subnetting?

● Which IP address class has the largest number of possible node addresses per network address?

● One, to distribute administration control of IP address allocation, and two, to permit more effective use of existing addresses.

● Class A.

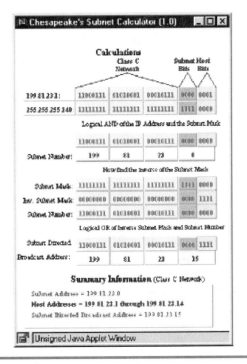

Figure 10-13   Subnet Calculation window

Internet Control Message Protocol

As previously discussed, IP provides a best-effort packet delivery mechanism
that doesn't guarantee data delivery. IP is insulated from the lower-level protocol
details and makes few assumptions about the performance and reliability of the
network. Data delivery is accomplished without any special coordination among
other IP entities and, for the most part, operates quite well. However, conditions
might exist beyond IP's control that makes delivery difficult or impossible. For
example, a remote host could be temporarily removed from the network or a
router could become overloaded when a network-intensive application is started.
IP needs a way to detect these types of problems.

The Internet Control Message Protocol (ICMP) provides a general error
message facility for the IP protocol and related services. ICMP provides a way
for IP entities that encounter errors to report them to the source that caused the
problem. It is the responsibility of the source entity to correct the error. This
might include, for example, reporting the error to a higher-level application.
Table 10-5 lists some of the ICMP message types.

10

Message Type	**Meaning**
Echo request/reply	Determine system reachability
Destination unreachable	Can't reach desired destination
Source quench	Stop sending data
Redirect	Detection of routing error
Time exceeded	Stale IP packet

Table 10-5   ICMP Error Message Types

One of the most popular networking debugging utilities, `ping`, uses ICMP to determine host reachability. `ping` uses the echo request and echo reply primitives that are available within ICMP to determine if a remote host is available and operating correctly on the network. Figure 10-14 shows the basic operation of the echo request and reply. A user wants to determine if Node A is available on the network. From Node B, the user enters a `ping` command that issues an echo request to Node A. If Node A is active, it responds back to Node B using an echo reply. If Node A is not active, then Node B receives no response. In this case, the request from Node B simply times out. When this occurs, the user is presented with a time-out message that indicates that Node A didn't respond to the request.

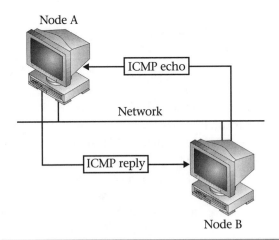

Figure 10-14   ICMP echo request/reply

Destination Unreachable

When a router can't deliver or forward a packet to its destination, it will emit an ICMP destination unreachable message to the sender. Destination unreachable errors usually imply some sort of routing problem or error (that is, incorrect route within a routing table). Destinations may be unreachable due to hardware failures that cause a system to become temporarily unavailable, or when the sender specifies a nonexistent destination address. Sometimes it is impossible to know that a destination is unreachable unless the ping system utility is used. For example, if a user issues a Telnet request to a remote system (which happens to be connected to an Ethernet LAN, for example), and the system has been disconnected from the network, this Telnet request will eventually time out because Ethernet doesn't support any frame acknowledgments. As a result, no destination unreachable messages will be generated, because Ethernet assumes data delivery even for a node that has been temporarily disconnected from the network.

Source Quench

The source quench within ICMP provides a way to handle congestion at the IP packet level. Congestion within a network can be caused by several factors. However, one primary cause is when several systems begin transmission of data that flows through a single router, as shown in Figure 10-15. In this case, the router itself is overburdened by the combined traffic. Another cause of congestion is when a more powerful computer system transmits data to a less powerful system that cannot keep up the pace. If these situations go unchecked, eventually the router and the underpowered system will begin to discard packets, which in turn will cause TCP to retransmit them, thus making the situation worse. In this case, the router and smaller system simply emit a source quench message, which indicates to the sender that it should stop sending data. As a result, the router and smaller system have time to process any outstanding packets.

There is no direct way to reverse the effects of the ICMP source quench message. However, any destination that receives a source quench lowers the rate at which it transmits packets to the destination. After no additional source quench messages are received, the remote system begins to gradually increase the rate of transmission, and eventually normal traffic resumes.

10

Redirect

The ICMP redirect message informs routers of changes to the routing information within the network. One of the basic assumptions with TCP/IP is that routers know

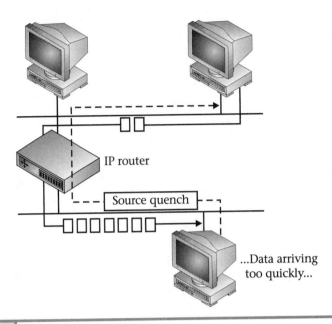

Figure 10-15 ICMP source quench redirect example

the routing topology within a network and this information is shared among participating routers. When a router detects a host using a nonoptimal route, it emits a redirect message informing the host that a better route is available. It is up to the host to incorporate this new information within its routing configuration. In some cases, this is not automatic and must be done by the network administrator. Figure 10-16 shows an example of where a router will send an ICMP redirect message. Assume that Node A wants to talk to Node D. In this case, two paths exist between Node A and Node D, namely R1 and R2. The R1 path is shorter and contains fewer hops between Node A and Node D. The R2 path contains extra links, because it also provides connectivity to other networks that include Node B and Node C. Should Node A attempt to communicate with Node D via R2, then R2 will send the redirect message back to Node A telling it to use R1, which has a shorter path to Node D. Many times the cause of using the incorrect router rests with the configuration on the system itself or incorrect routing information emitted from one or more misconfigured routers. In either event, ICMP redirects help the network administrator track down these sorts of problems.

Redirect messages do not provide a common mechanism for distributing routing information, because they are limited to interaction between hosts and

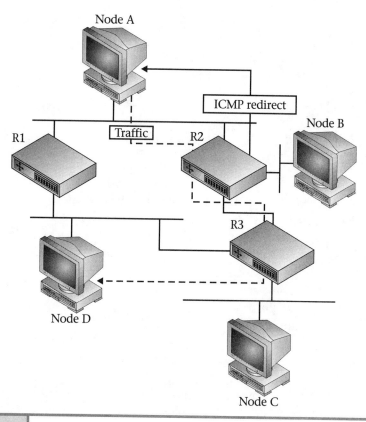

Figure 10-16 | ICMP redirect example

10

routers. Instead, routing protocols such as Routing Information Protocol (RIP) are used to propagate routing information within a network.

Time Exceeded

Each IP packet contains a time-to-live field, which controls how long a packet may exist within the network. When a router processes the packet, it decrements this field before forwarding it. Whenever a router discards a packet because its time-to-live field is zero or because some other time-out occurred with the packet, the router emits an ICMP time exceeded message back to the source of the packet. This is the primary mechanism used to detect routing loops or excessively long routes within a network. The `traceroute` command, for example, uses the time-to-live field to trace the path an IP packet may take between two points and also measures the amount of time required to traverse each router along the path to the destination.

10.3 Discover the Address Resolution Protocol

As we previously discussed, IP imposes a certain structure and format on the addresses used by networking devices. In version 4 of IP, the address is 32 bits in length and is expressed in dotted decimal notation. In version 6, the address is even larger—128 bits. As with any higher-level network protocol such as IP, the requirement exists for a mechanism to translate these addresses into addresses used by such protocols as Ethernet, FDDI, or Token Ring. Known as data link protocols, they each have their own addressing structure and format, which is quite different from IP. For example, Ethernet uses 48-bit addresses and is expressed using the colon hexadecimal notation. Thus, `8:0:20:4:cf:2c` represents a valid Ethernet address. In this case, this data link address doesn't always map easily with addresses used by IP. This is true for many other data link protocols as well. This creates a dilemma because, without a way to map IP addresses to physical interfaces, communication between nodes would not be possible.

It is desirable and very necessary that a simple, flexible, and yet powerful way to map between IP and data link (physical) addresses be available. The Address Resolution Protocol (ARP) has been proven to be a very elegant and robust way to solve the address mapping problem. In particular, ARP was designed to handle address resolution of any network layer protocol to data link protocol—not just between IP and Ethernet.

The basic operation of ARP is simple: When Node A wants to determine the physical address for Node B, Node A will send a special broadcast message requesting the address of Node B to all devices on the network, as shown in Figure 10-17. All hosts receive the message, including Node B and Node C, but only Node B will respond with the correct physical address, as shown in Figure 10-18. The reason only Node B responds is because it examines the ARP packet and determines that its own IP address matches the target IP address that the requester is seeking.

A sister function of ARP—known as Reverse Address Resolution Protocol, or RARP—does the inverse; given a data link address, it finds the corresponding IP address. RARP is primarily used when diskless workstations need to determine their IP addresses during system startup.

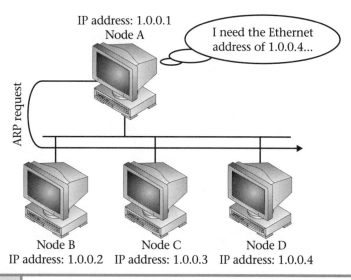

Figure 10-17 | ARP request example

The term *broadcast* in the above example indicates a locally directed packet to all network devices on a particular LAN segment. Certain data-link protocols such as Ethernet provide the facility to transmit broadcast packets to all attached

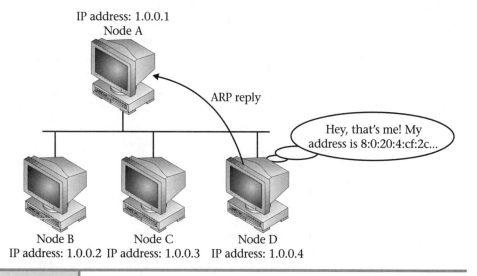

Figure 10-18 | ARP reply example

stations using a special destination address. With Ethernet, all 1s (or FFs in hexadecimal) in the destination address is considered a broadcast. ARP assumes that the details of getting messages to each station will be handled directly by the data link protocol.

As you can see, the ARP is very simple. Yet, despite its simplicity, it has a few profound advantages. First, ARP is dynamic in nature, which obviates the need to statically track and store IP to physical addresses. This dynamic resolution behavior frees the network manager from constantly maintaining and ensuring correct information every time a device is added or removed from the network. With today's networks, it would be impossible to accomplish such a task given the size and growth rate of many networks. Second, ARP is a standard and is available on every device that supports TCP/IP, regardless of datalink protocol. That is why, for example, IP can operate on FDDI and Token Ring. This makes building heterogeneous networks much easier, because ARP hides the data link addressing details, and the network designer need not be concerned about physical address resolution when combining different data link protocols. Third, ARP can be used in IP subnets to provide a very simple way for devices to communicate within a routed network.

Packet Format

Unlike other networking protocols, ARP packet fields are not all fixed-format but rather rely on certain fixed fields near the beginning of the packet. ARP and RARP share the same basic packet format. To make the ARP useful for other datalink protocols, the length of the fields will depend on the type of network. Figure 10-19 shows the standard ARP and RARP message format.

The Hardware Type field defines the hardware interface type for which the sender requires an answer. Standard values include 1 for Ethernet and 2 for FDDI. The Protocol Type field specifies the high-level protocol type the sender is using, which for IP is 0800 in hexadecimal (decimal is 2048). The Operation field notes if the message is an ARP request (1), ARP response (2), RARP request (3), or RARP response (4). The Hlen and Plen fields define the hardware and high-level protocol address field lengths. The Hlen and Plen fields permit ARP to work with any arbitrary data link protocol, because the sizes of the Hardware Type and Protocol Type fields can be determined by inspecting the ARP packet directly. The sending entity will supply, if possible, the Sender HA and/or Sender IP field information when issuing the request. The Sender HA field is used with the ARP request, while the Sender IP field is used with an RARP request. The Target HA field is used when responding to the ARP message; otherwise, the Target IP field is used when responding to RARP.

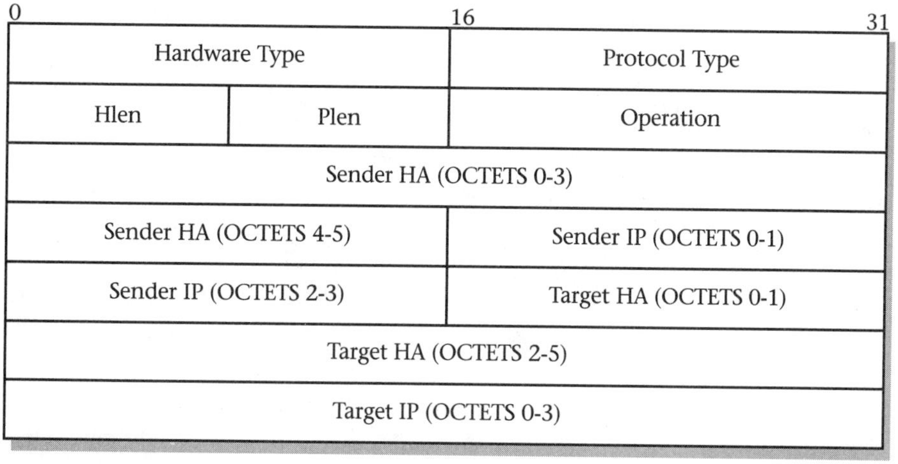

Hardware Type		Protocol Type	
Hlen	Plen	Operation	
Sender HA (OCTETS 0-3)			
Sender HA (OCTETS 4-5)		Sender IP (OCTETS 0-1)	
Sender IP (OCTETS 2-3)		Target HA (OCTETS 0-1)	
Target HA (OCTETS 2-5)			
Target IP (OCTETS 0-3)			

Figure 10-19   ARP/RARP message format

ARP Cache

At first glance, the ARP service may seem inefficient because it will send a broadcast packet each time a device wishes to communicate with another device. However, ARP implementations on many systems include the use of an ARP cache to temporarily store address bindings from previous ARP requests. In fact, before an ARP request is made, the higher-level software scans the ARP cache to see if the required data link address mapping already exists in the cache. If it does, the existing binding is used; otherwise, the ARP request is sent. As a result of the cache, network traffic is reduced because ARP requests are only made when devices are not known. Also, application performance is improved because the sender's ARP request can be satisfied by using the cache instead of transmitting a packet on the network. Finally, the cache provides the administrator with a way to view connectivity between the higher-level protocols and the network hardware. Inspecting the ARP cache can be a powerful way to troubleshoot network and system problems.

Here is one interesting question regarding the ARP cache: When should the bindings be discarded from the cache? The answer is not simple. If we presume to keep the ARP cache populated with entries forever (or until the system is restarted), the possibility exists that the cache will contain invalid information. Consider, for example, a network that contains systems monet and rembrandt, which are in the midst of communicating when the network interface card (NIC)

10

fails on `rembrandt` and is subsequently replaced. The new NIC will contain a new data link address unless the administrator has changed it after the interface was installed. As a result, `monet` can't talk to `rembrandt` any longer because the cache on `monet` contains an invalid data link address for `rembrandt`. On the other hand, we can take the approach that bindings in the ARP cache should expire in a relatively short period of time, say every 30 seconds. Unfortunately, this will adversely affect network performance, because more network broadcasts will be needed because the ARP cache will be very small. However, it will address the problem of the incorrect bindings for NICs that have recently been replaced, because the old entry would have been purged in a reasonable period of time after the new NIC was operational.

Perhaps the best solution to this problem is taking the middle-of-the-road approach. That is to say, the binding expiration shouldn't be so small as to be ineffective but also not too long so that it can address changes in the network within a reasonable time constraint. In general, most UNIX systems will delete ARP entries in approximately 20 minutes. Some versions of UNIX also permit the administrators to change the ARP cache time-out to suit their network requirements and, when necessary, alter it to address other network-related problems.

Data Link Address Format

As indicated, data link addresses are expressed in 48 bits (6 bytes) ando separated by colns. This colon notation is used as the primary method to represent these hardware addresses. Some UNIX network management tools, such as the `ifconfig` and `arp` commands, use this format. Data link protocol addresses for FDDI, Ethernet, and Token Ring contain a vendor code identification number and serial number. This information can be used in node identification for inventory purposes. The IEEE registry authority assigns the vendor portion to those organizations that produce networking hardware and have requested a vendor code. These codes are also referred to as organization unique identifiers (OUIs). The first three bytes of the address represent the manufacturer or vendor of the device, and the remaining three bytes represent the serial number of the unit, as depicted in Figure 10-20.

Often on a multi-homed system, the data link addresses will be shared among all the defined interfaces. This may even be true for systems that contain different network interface types (that is, Ethernet and FDDI). Table 10-6 shows some of the most common vendor codes. Notice that more than one vendor code might be associated with the same vendor. This may be true, for example, when one

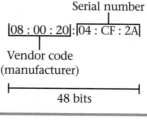

Figure 10-20   Data link address format

company purchases another company and their products. In this case, the vendor code of the company that was purchased now falls under the other company. This is why Table 10-6 contains multiple entries for both 3Com and Cisco. Knowing a few of these addresses can be very handy during network debugging, to help identify the type of device and vendor to which a particular packet belongs. If you are interested in finding a vendor, access the IEEE Web site at `http://standards/ieee.org/regauth/oui/oui.txt`.

Vendor Code	Manufacturer
00:20:AF	3Com Corporation
00-80-3E	Formerly Synernetics, Inc.
00-C0-D4	Formerly AXON, Inc.
(many more)	
00:00:0C	Cisco Systems, Inc.
00-E0-B0	(Includes a large list of former companies)
00-E0-F7	
00-E0-F9	
00-E0-FE	
00-06-7C	
00-06-C1	
00-10-07	
(many more)	
00-60-69	Brocade Corporation
00-E0-B1	Packet Engines, Inc.
08:00:5A	IBM Corporation
08:00:20	Sun Microsystems, Inc.
08-00-09	HP Corporation
00-10-E3	Compaq Corporation

Table 10-6   Sample Vendor OUI Codes

10

Accessing this Universal Resource Locator (URL) will display the entire OUI file. If you're not interested in seeing the entire contents of the OUI file, search for the specific vendor codes you are looking for by accessing the following URL:

```
http:/standards.ieee.org/regauth/oui/index.html.
```

Accessing this URL will display the page shown in Figure 10-21.

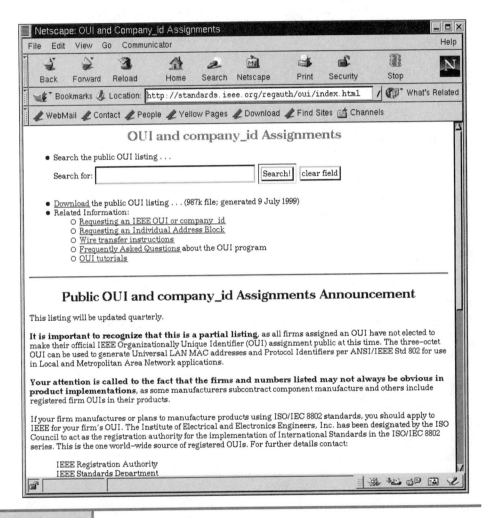

Figure 10-21   IEEE OUI search page

Should you wish to search for a vendor, enter the name of the company in the search text box field. Also, if you know the OUI, but want the vendor, enter the address instead. Next, click the Search button. Figure 10-22 shows the result obtained when the Brocade Company was searched.

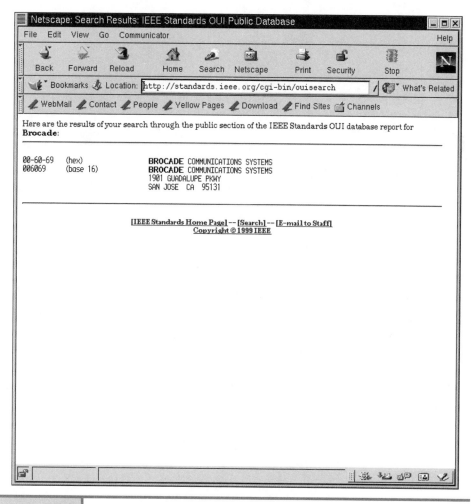

Figure 10-22   OUI search results

✓ *Mastery Check*

1. The most common standard network model is based on _____

2. Which of the following is not a layer in the OSI model?

   A. Application

   B. Session

   C. Interface

   D. Physical

3. Which layer in the OSI model provides services to users that include file transfer, electronic email, remote host access, and many other services?

   A. Application

   B. Session

   C. Data link

   D. Physical

4. Which TCP/IP layer corresponds to the network layer in the OSI model?

5. True or False: Each TCI/IP layer corresponds to one OSI model layer.

6. The _____ maps between hostnames and IP addresses.

7. Which TCP/IP service do clients use to dynamically obtain IP information while booting, thus removing the burden of having to configure each machine?

   A. Rlogin

   B. BootP

   C. DHCP

   D. finger

8. In the TCP/IP model, which layer is responsible for providing a robust data delivery mechanism between different network entities?

☑ Mastery Check

9. What file on UNIX systems contains port numbers for some well-known services?

10. True or False: In the TCP/IP model, the Internet layer provides a reliable flow of information from one network to another.

11. What class does the IP address `198.45.19.151` belong to?

12. _____ is a mechanism used to divide a network into smaller networks.

13. Which UNIX command, invoked on every system interface installed in the system, must include the subnet mask information when executed?

14. Using the Chesapeake subnet calculator and the IP address `198.45.19.151`, what is the subnet mask if you need a subnet with 40 IP nodes?

15. What popular networking debugging utility uses ICMP to determine host reachability?

16. What mechanism translates IP addresses into addresses used by such protocols as Ethernet, FDDI, or token ring?

   A. DNS

   B. ARP

   C. RAPR

   D. OUI

10

Module 11

Basic Network Tools

Critical Skills

11.1 Explore the Network Address Table on a UNIX System Using arp

11.2 Control Network Interfaces Using Ifconfig

11.3 Monitor Network Operations Using Netstat

11.4 Verify Network Connectivity Using Ping

11.5 Gather Network Information with Lanscan

UNIX provides a number of tools for monitoring, debugging, and controlling network services. The programs listed in this section are considered basic networking tools because they are available on many systems that support TCP/IP and provide a minimum amount of monitoring and control. Regular users can invoke many of the TCP/IP system tools. However, certain features of some of the tools (such as ability to disable a network interface) can only be done by the system administrator. The following tools will be reviewed in this section:

- arp
- ifconfig
- netstat
- ping
- lanscan

11-1 Explore the Network Address Table on a UNIX System Using arp

The `arp` command displays and manipulates the network address table on a local UNIX system. The address resolution protocol table, also known as the ARP cache, contains a complete list of all data link protocol to IP address mappings for the local network. The ARP protocol is a dynamic facility that maps data link addresses such as Ethernet to IP addresses. Whenever a system wants to transmit a message, it must first know the low-level (that is, data link) address for the target system. Many networking tools, such as `ssh`, `ftp`, and others, indirectly use the ARP table.

The `arp` command provides the ability to view and modify the ARP cache. Regular UNIX (nonroot) users may display the ARP cache, but cannot make any changes. The reason for this should be obvious: users could make alterations to the cache that would affect connectivity for all users.

Hint
The terms "ARP table" and "ARP cache" can be used interchangeably and refer to the same information. Also, the terms "binding" and "mapping" refer to an ARP entry as well.

With the `arp` command, the system administrator can

● Display the ARP cache

● Delete an ARP entry

● Add an ARP entry

The ARP tool provides a number of command-line options. However, only the most important ones are listed in Table 11-1 and fully discussed and described below. On Linux, each of these options supports either a single command character or keyword, along with two dashes at the beginning. For instance, the `-v` option has an associated `--verbose` keyword. These are equivalent and can be used interchangeably on the command line.

Displaying the ARP Cache

To display the contents of the ARP table, use the `arp -v` command. When the table is displayed, it includes the device name, hardware type, physical address, mask flag, and network interface. A sample from a Linux host is shown here:

```
# arp -a
Address                Hwtype   HWaddress            Flags Mask   Iface
durer.home.com         ether    00:60:97:0E:A3:06      C           eth0
switch.home.com        ether    00:00:1D:0A:5D:01      C           eth0
probe.home.com         ether    00:C0:D4:00:09:40      C           eth0
rembrandt.home.com     ether    08:00:20:82:be:05      C           eth0
rubens.home.com                   (incomplete)                     eth0
monet.home.com         ether    08:00:20:04:cf:2c      C           eth0
Entries: 6 Skipped: 0            Found: 6
```

When the same command is run from a Solaris system, the following is displayed:

```
Net to Media Table: IPv4
Device    IP Address           Mask            Flags   Phys Addr
------    ---------------       ---------------  -----  ---------------
elxl1     dhcpclient-202       255.255.255.255          00:20:78:0e:77:5e
elxl1     didymus.home.com     255.255.255.255          00:60:08:b4:11:89
elxl1     bedrock.home.com     255.255.255.255  SP      00:10:4b:1f:8d:ef
elxl1     224.0.0.0            240.0.0.0        SM      01:00:5e:00:00:00
```

11

Option	Description
-a	Displays the current ARP entry for a specific host (Linux only). Displays all of the entries within the ARP table (Solaris and HP-UX).
-d	Deletes an ARP entry specified after this option.
-f	Loads a file that contains entries to place in the cache.
-i	Displays only those entries for specified interface (Linux only).
-n	Shows numerical addresses instead of hostnames (Linux only).
-s	Creates an ARP entry.
-v	Displays ARP cache using verbose mode (Linux only).

Table 11-1 The ARP Command-Line Options

The Address field (or IP address for Solaris) shows either the hostname or IP address that corresponds to the ARP entry. This is the address that is used to search the ARP table to determine if the desired entry exists. When an IP address (instead of a hostname) is displayed, this indicates that either the IP address couldn't be correctly resolved to a hostname or the -n option (Linux only) was used. This could be the result of an invalid or nonexisting entry within a NIS server or DNS server or /etc/hosts file, a misconfiguration in either of these, or connectivity problems to the DNS server.

The HWType field (The other operating systems don't provides this information) represents the network interface for which the ARP entry was obtained. As you can see, the keyword ether represents entries that were derived from an Ethernet network.

The Flags Mask field (Mask) provides additional details regarding the ARP entry. Table 11-2 shows the available flags and their associated meanings.

The HWaddress (Phys Addr for Solaris), physical address of the Network Interface field, contains the low-level address for each node on the local

ARP Flag	Meaning
C	A completed ARP entry
M or S	A permanent (static) ARP entry (M for Linux, S for Solaris and HP-UX)
P	Publish an ARP entry

Table 11-2 ARP Flag Meaning

network and is expressed in six hexadecimal numbers in colon notation. Colon notation uses hexadecimal number separated by colons, as in

```
00:10:5a:28:5d:7c
```

The `iface` field (`Device` for Solaris) corresponds to the network interface that is attached to the local network, for which the ARP entry was obtained. In practice, most systems contain only a single interface. If a system has more than one active interface, the `arp` command would list all entries, regardless of which interface they came from. The `eth` stands for Ethernet, which is the name of the Ethernet hardware device driver. The zero on the end indicates that this is the first interface defined within the system. For Solaris, the `elxl1` interface represents the second 100-Mbps (Fast Ethernet) LAN connection.

ARP entries that are marked P are permanent (or static) and have been defined outside the normal ARP protocol (for example, manually entered with the `arp -s` command). Static entries are also used to support networked systems that don't support the ARP protocol. Therefore, the address binding must be manually entered in the ARP table. One problem with this approach is that if the IP address or hardware address of any of these system mappings is changed, the ARP information must be manually updated to effect the change. The C flag indicates a normal and complete entry, and most if not all ARP entries should be marked with this flag.

Only the IP addresses associated with genuine interfaces are advertised with ARP. It is interesting to note that ARP information obtained from other network devices is not normally published by third-party systems. It is usually the responsibility of each node on the network to respond to ARP requests with its own information. There is one special case when a system will respond to ARP requests on behalf of others. This is known as proxy ARP, which is used with subnets that use routers, which are special devices that interconnect two or more IP networks, or other special network configurations. ARP entries typically use a timer, which controls how long the entry will remain in the ARP cache. By default, most UNIX systems hold the entry for approximately 20 minutes before removing it. Some systems permit the administrator to alter this timing value.

The `incomplete` string (in the Linux example) indicates that an ARP request is still pending and the mapping is unresolved for the associated host. In the ARP example above, the system `rubens` lacks a physical address because the ARP request didn't obtain a reply. Many things could cause this condition: hardware trouble with the device, network wiring problems, or software

11

configuration issues on the host. The bottom line is that the ARP software wasn't able to communicate with the device to obtain the desired information. The final string that is displayed shows a count of the number of entries in the cache.

In situations where there are many ARP entries, you can use −a (Linux only) followed by a valid hostname to list a specific system. For Solaris and HP-UX, one command option is necessary. The following Linux command will list the ARP mapping for the host called socrates:

```
# arp -a Socrates
socrates.home.com (10.0.2.201) at 00:60:97:0E:A3:03 [ether] on eth0
```

Also, you could have used the IP address instead of the hostname. Thus, the command arp -a 10.0.2.201 would yield the same output.

On Solaris and HP-UX, the arp command also accepts hostnames or IP addresses without the -a option. Without this command option, each of the field labels is displayed along with the ARP entry. Thus, the command

```
# arp bedrock
bedrock (216.155.202.100) at 0:10:4b:1f:8d:ef permanent published
```

provides the ARP information for a specific host. Another command parameter that ARP supports on Linux is −n. This option displays either hostnames or IP addresses within the listings. One reason for choosing to display the ARP entries using IP addresses is that it will be a little faster. Mapping between IP addresses and hostnames is usually done with Domain Name Server, and as a result may take some time to complete. In practice, the delay is negligible in most situations. However, if the name resolution facility (NIS or DNS, for instance) experiences delays or some other operational problem, listing the ARP cache with the −n option will be much faster. The command arp -n will return the output quicker if name resolution is completely nonfunctional, given a fairly large ARP cache. The format of the ARP listings using the first example given in this section will display the following:

```
# arp -n -v
Address        Hwtype     HWaddress          Flags Mask    Iface
10.0.2.10      ether      00:60:97:0E:A3:06        C        eth0
10.0.2.60      ether      00:00:1D:0A:5D:01        C        eth0
```

These numeric IP addresses correspond to the named addresses from the first example.

```
10.0.2.50      ether      00:C0:D4:00:09:40        C        eth0
10.0.2.127     ether      08:00:20:82:be:05        C        eth0
10.0.2.220                (incomplete)                      eth0
10.0.2.126     ether      08:00:20:04:cf:2c        C        eth0
Entries: 6 Skipped: 0       Found: 6
```

As you can see, the IP address of each host has been displayed instead of the actual hostnames.

As previously mentioned, the `arp` command displays the interface name for which the entry was obtained. Given the output above, all of the mappings were from the `eth0` interface. Sometimes a system may contain more than one interface, as previously suggested. This is known as multi-homing. When the ARP cache is displayed on these systems, the output contains entries for each of the interfaces, as in the following example:

```
Address           HWtype      HWaddress           Flags Mask Iface
durer.home.com    ether       00:60:97:0E:A3:06        C       eth0
moster.home.com   ether       00:60:97:0A:B3:09        C       eth1
probe2.home.com   ether       00:80:96:0B:C1:01        C       eth1
switch.home.com   ether       00:00:1D:0A:5D:01        C       eth0
probe.home.com    ether       00:C0:D4:00:09:40        C       eth0
```

These two entries are on a different interface than the other three.

We can see that mapping exists for two interfaces for this system. In this case, `eth0` and `eth1` are listed within the output. Since ARP tracks entries by interface, we can use the `-i` option to display just mappings from a particular interface. The command

```
#arp -i eth1
```

11

will display all ARP listings for the `eth1` interface:

```
Address         Wtype     HWaddress           Flags Mask Iface
moster.home.com   ether   00:60:97:0A:B3:09        C        eth1
probe2.home.com   ether   00:80:96:0B:C1:01        C        eth1
```

Deleting an ARP Cache

It might become necessary to delete one or more entries from the ARP table. For example, should a hardware failure result in the replacement of a network interface card, the network hardware address of the system will change. In this case, the existing ARP entry won't reflect that the low-level address has changed. As a result, messages sent to this host from other devices will not be picked up because the hardware address used will not match that of the interface. It is up to the system administrator to resolve this problem.

To address this, the -d option should be used to delete an ARP entry, as shown in the following. Because removing ARP bindings can cause network problems, only the superuser is permitted to remove them. The arp command expects the -d option to be used with a valid host or IP address. In this example for Linux, the host durer is removed from the ARP table:

```
# arp -d durer
```

If the ARP table were now displayed, the durer entry would not be listed as shown here:

```
Address HWtyp HWaddress Flags Mask  Iface
durer.home.com (incomplete)
```

For Solaris, the same command would show

```
durer.home.com (10.0.2.10) deleted
```

If a nonroot user attempted to remove this host from the table, an error message would be displayed:

```
% arp -d durer
SIOCDARP(priv): Operation not permitted
```

On Solaris and HP-UX:

```
SIOCDARP: Not owner
```

Adding an ARP Cache Entry

Several conditions may warrant manually adding entries to the ARP table. One such situation occurs when communication with a device is needed, but the device for some reason doesn't support ARP, or the implementation is nonfunctional. This might be the case with a very old system that is still in service. Further, should a NIC address change, the table must be manually updated to ensure connectivity. Finally, it may be necessary to add entries to support proxy ARP services.

To add an ARP entry, use the `-s` option followed by the hostname (or address) and the associated physical data link address. For example, let's say we would like to add a system called `bruegel` to the ARP table. The format of the physical data link is represented by 6 bytes separated by colons (`:`) where each byte is a hexadecimal number between `0` and `FF`. To illustrate an example, the following command could be used:

```
# arp -s bruegel 08:00:20:82:be:05
```

If no error message is displayed, it can be assumed that the command was successful. Alternatively, you could list the ARP cache to see if `bruegel` was in fact added:

Solaris/HP-UX:

```
# arp bruegel
bruegel.home.com (216.155.202.100) at 08:00:20:82:be:05 permanent
```

Linux:

```
# arp bruegel
Address              HWtype  HWaddress          Flags Mask   Iface
bruegel.home.com     ether   08:00:20:82:BE:05  CM            eth0
```

Hint

ARP binding on Linux is labeled with the `M` flag while Solaris/HP-UX use the `permanent` keyword, which indicates it is a permanent entry because it was added on the command line. Since permanent mappings are statically defined, they don't time out. Unfortunately, permanent entry types are not saved across system reboots.

11

Ask the Expert

Question   Why is modifying the ARP table restricted to only the superuser?

Answer   Consider that when static ARP entries are defined, no direct linkage exists between this information and the actual devices attached to the network. For example, the entry for `bruegel` was added manually, but no mechanism is available to ARP to ensure that the physical address is indeed correct. The `arp` command assumes the information provided is accurate and that the device is actually attached to the network. Therefore, if normal users had the ability to modify the ARP table, more errors would likely be introduced that would lead to loss of network connectivity. Should the physical address of a critical network resource (like a server) be incorrectly changed, all communication between the local system and the critical system would stop.

1-Minute Drill

● Why can nonroot users only display the ARP table?

● What does an "incomplete" entry in a line in an ARP table indicate?

11.2 Control Network Interfaces Using Ifconfig

The `ifconfig` command is short for "interface configuration" and is used to configure local network interfaces. This command is normally invoked during system startup to set up each interface with a predefined configuration. The `ifconfig` command can also be used to change the network interface parameters after the system has been booted. This command is often used for debugging and/or system tuning activities. This command can be used to do the following:

● Lists the configuration of each defined network interface

● Disables/enables any defined network interface

● Modifies network interface configuration parameters

● Creates pseudo-interfaces

● Because making changes to the ARP table affects connectivity for all users, which is something only the root user should do.
● The incomplete string indicates that an ARP request is still pending and the mapping is unresolved for the associated host. This could be indicative of hardware, network, or software problems with the device.

The ifconfig program provides a large number of options and keywords that are used to configure one or more interfaces. Table 11-3 lists the most important of these options and keywords. The keywords are used as modifiers with other command-line options.

Listing Available Interfaces

To display all system interfaces, use the ifconfig -a command:

```
#ifconfig -a
```

Option	Meaning
-a	Applies to all interfaces presently installed on the system.
arp -arp	Enables the use of the Address Resolution Protocol (ARP) on this interface; disables the use of ARP with the -arp option.
auto-dhcp	Use DHCP to obtain IP address for this interface (Solaris and HP-UX only).
promisc -promisc	(Linux only) Enables promiscuous (that is, listen for all traffic) mode on this interface. The -promisc option disables it.
allmulti -allmulti	(Linux only) Enables all multicast traffic to be received by the interface. The -allmulti option will disable the reception of multicast packets.
broadcast -broadcast	With the argument given, sets or clears the broadcast address for this interface. This is a network layer broadcast address.
pointtopoint -pointtopoint	(Linux only) Enables a point-to-point mode for this interface. The basic assumption is that this is a dedicated link between two devices. If the address argument is provided, it sets the protocol address for the other side of the link. Disables the point-to-point mode with the pointtopoint keyword.
up	Causes the interface to be brought up or activated.
down	Causes the interface to be shut down or deactivated.
netmask	Sets the IP network mask for this interface. The specified argument can be in the form 255.0.0.0 (dotted decimal) or 0xff00000 (hexadecimal).
address	Sets the IP address for this interface. This must be a unique IP address not previously assigned to another system.

Table 11-3   Ifconfig Command-Line Options

11

When this command is run on Linux, the following sample is shown:

```
eth0      Link encap:Ethernet  HWaddr 00:10:5A:28:5D:7C
          inet addr:10.0.2.201  Bcast:10.0.2.255  Mask:255.255.255.0
UP BROADCAST RUNNING PROMISC MULTICAST  MTU:1500  Metric:1
RX packets:822 errors:1 dropped:0 overruns:0 frame:1
    TX packets:108 errors:0 dropped:0 overruns:0 carrier:0
          collisions:0 txqueuelen:100
          Interrupt:10 Base address:0xfc00          Physical hardware interface

lo        Link encap:Local Loopback                 Loopback interface for
          inet addr:127.0.0.1  Mask:255.0.0.0       internal diagnostics
          UP LOOPBACK RUNNING  MTU:3924  Metric:1
          RX packets:92 errors:0 dropped:0 overruns:0 frame:0
          TX packets:92 errors:0 dropped:0 overruns:0 carrier:0
          collisions:0 txqueuelen:0
                                                     Dial-up interface for
ppp0      Link encap:Point-to-Point Protocol        ISP connectivity
          POINTOPOINT NOARP MULTICAST  MTU:1500  Metric:1
          RX packets:0 errors:0 dropped:0 overruns:0 frame:0
          TX packets:0 errors:0 dropped:0 overruns:0 carrier:0
          collisions:0 txqueuelen:10
```

On Solaris:

```
lo0: flags=1000849<UP,LOOPBACK,RUNNING,MULTICAST,IPv4> mtu 8232 index 1
        inet 127.0.0.1 netmask ff000000
elxl1: flags=1000843<UP,BROADCAST,RUNNING,MULTICAST,IPv4> mtu 1500 index 2
        inet 216.155.202.100 netmask ffffff00 broadcast 216.155.202.255
        ether 0:10:4b:1f:8d:ef
lo0: flags=2000849<UP,LOOPBACK,RUNNING,MULTICAST,IPv6> mtu 8252 index 1
        inet6 ::1/128
```

The -a option indicates that all interfaces installed within the system, regardless of their present configuration or operational state, should be shown.

The examples displayed above indicate that a number of interfaces are defined. Note that the system output above is quite similar regardless of which operating system the command was run against. On Linux, the first eth0 entry represents the physical hardware interfaces for 10-Mbps Ethernet using the

3Com Ethernet driver. The second, `lo`, is the loopback interface, primarily used for internal communication and diagnostics. The loopback interface can be used to determine if the TCP/IP software is operating correctly on a local level. For instance, it is possible to ping the loopback address to determine valid responses. The final (`ppp0`) interface represents a point-to-point dial-up link for connectivity to a local Internet service provider (ISP).

For Solaris, the `elxl` interface is shown, which represents the Fast Ethernet interface.

Hint

The Solaris output shows two entries for the loopback interface because one is for IPv4 IP addresses while the second one is for IPv6 IP addresses.

For each interface, the display includes the following fields:

- **Link** encap This specifies the link encapsulation protocol that the interface will use when transmitting data link frames. Supported types include Ethernet, Local Loopback, and Point-to-Point Protocol.

- **HWaddr** This is the data link address for the encapsulation.

- **protocol** Ethernet uses the hexadecimal notation, such as in the entry for the `eth0` interface: `00:10:5A:28:5D:7C`.

- **inet** addr This is the IP address associated with this interface.

- **Bcast** This represents the network layer broadcast address.

- **Mask** This represents the subnet mask address.

In addition, the display includes the operational parameters for the interface. These include `UP`, `BROADCAST`, `RUNNING`, `PROMISC`, and `MULTICAST`. These options show the mode and current state of the interface.

Next, the display includes fields that represent the statistical counters, such as received packets (`RX`), transmitted packets (`TX`), number of collisions (`collisions`), and so forth. These provide a relatively easy way to benchmark the performance of the interface. Finally, the remaining fields show the interrupt number and I/O base address of the interface hardware. Notice, too, that not all interfaces have an associated interrupt number and I/O address. The loopback interface lacks these fields because it uses no specific hardware within the system.

11

Controlling Interface State

With `ifconfig`, it is possible to disable an active interface or enable a disabled interface while the system is running. In the disabled state, no packets will be permitted across the interface. This is equivalent to disconnecting the interface from the network. When an interface is disabled, it is considered down from an administrative standpoint. To place an interface in the down state, invoke the `ifconfig` command with the appropriate interface and the `down` keyword option as shown:

```
# ifconfig eth0 down
```

The administrator can use the `ifconfig` command with the interface name instead of the `-a` option to list an individual interface. The following command displays the configuration of the interface that we shut down with the previous command:

```
# arp eth0
etho       Link encap:Ethernet  HWaddr 08:00:20:04:CF:2C
           inet addr:10.0.3.127  Bcast:10.0.3.255  Mask:255.255.255.0
BROADCAST MULTICAST  MTU:1500  Metric:1
RX packets:3452 errors:0 dropped:0 overruns:0 frame:0
TX packets:3212 errors:1 dropped:0 overruns:0 carrier:1
           collisions:0 txqueuelen:100
           Interrupt:38 Base address:0x3200
```

Keywords UP and RUNNING are gone from here now that we shut this down.

Notice the keywords `up` and `running` are now missing from the output. This is how `ifconfig` indicates that an interface has been disabled and is not available for use. To enable or activate this interface, we simply use the `up` command option:

```
# ifconfig eth0 up
```

When the interface is up, it is available on the network and receiving network information. Without the indication of the `up` flag, the interface is operational and perhaps connected to the network, but no information is flowing to or from the network.

Modifying Interface Parameters

Three methods can be used to modify network interface parameters. First, using `ifconfig` directly, changes can be made on the command line and will take effect immediately. The second approach involves modifying the system startup and/or system files that `ifconfig` uses to configure the interface. This approach ensures that interface changes are made permanently and won't disappear across system reboots. Sometimes both approaches are used. Often, a configuration change must be implemented quickly before the system can be rebooted at a convenient time. As a result, `ifconfig` can be used to make the immediate changes. Normally, when a new interface is installed on a system, this configuration may be handled by the installation procedure. The third method involves using the GUI control panel applications, control-panel for Linux and SAM for HP-UX, to make the changes.

Using `ifconfig`, the following important information can be changed for an interface:

- IP address

- Network mask

- Broadcast address

- Data link address

- MTU

The IP address is specified in the normal dotted decimal notation and represents the unique address for the host on the network to which the system is attached. The network subnet mask (or netmask) specifies the filter used to calculate the network and host portions for the subnet. The broadcast address specifies the IP address to which broadcast packets should be directed. The data link address represents the unique low-level hardware address used by Ethernet or FDDI, and is associated with the hardware itself. The maximum transfer unit (MTU) denotes the maximum message size that the interface can handle. The standard message size is 1500 for Ethernet, 4096 for FDDI, and 2048 for token ring. The MTU is rarely modified, and when it is, it can't be configured to support values higher than what the hardware will support; only lower values may be used.

11

Let's suppose that the IP address of a system must be changed because the system is moved to a different subnet. In this case, the netmask and broadcast information remain the same. The move to the new network involves changing the IP address of the interface only. The old IP address is `128.197.9.10` and the new IP address is `128.197.10.1`. The following command would be used to change the network information on the fly:

```
# ifconfig eth0 128.197.10.1
```

To make this change permanent, we must modify the `/etc/hosts` file. This file contains the mapping between hostname and the associated IP address. On system startup, the IP address is derived from the file and applied to the interface. The netmask and broadcast information are the same; we can use the existing values. The hostname could also be specified on the command line instead of the IP address. Thus, the command

```
# ifconfig eth0 fred
```

accomplishes the same result, assuming that `fred` has been assigned the IP address of `128.197.10.1`, either in the `/etc/hosts` file, DNS, or the NIS hosts database.

As you can see, changing the IP address for an interface is relatively straightforward. However, changing other interface characteristics requires a bit more work. To extend the preceding example, let us now assume that we must change the netmask and broadcast information. To change the interface, the administrator could use

```
# ifconfig eth0 128.197.10.1 netmask 255.255.0.0 broadcast 128.197.255.255
```

In the example above, the `netmask` and `broadcast` keywords must be used to identify the information that follows each keyword. The netmask contains 1s in the bit positions of the 32-bit address that are to be used for the network and subnet (if applicable) parts, and 0s for the host portion. The netmask/subnet portion must occupy at least as many bits as is standard for the particular network class. If no subnets are defined, the standard netmask is used. When using subnets, they require that more bits than what is normally the host portion of the address be reserved to identify the subnet. A netmask can be specified in two different ways: dotted decimal notation and hexadecimal notation.

The dotted decimal notation is expressed in four single-byte numbers separated by dots (for example, `255.255.255.0`). The hexadecimal format includes using the 0x prefix followed by a hexadecimal string value. For example, the hexadecimal value for `255.255.255.0` is `0xffffff00`. Since `ifconfig` supports both formats, they can be used interchangeably. Each of the standard IP class addresses has associated default netmask addresses, as shown in Table 11-4.

Hint

The addresses in Table 11-4 are just the standard ones used if no subnetting is implemented. The specific subnet mask addresses used in many sites will differ from these because the subnets defined use more bits than the standard for that class.

The broadcast address can be specified in the same ways as the netmask address. However, the broadcast address is usually formed by turning all the bits in the host portion of an address to 1s. For example, the broadcast address for the 128.197.0.0 network is 128.197.255.255.

Special Configurations Parameters

The `ifconfig` command supports additional parameters. These include

- arp
- multicast
- promiscuous mode
- media type
- point-to-point

11

Class	Dotted Decimal Notation	Hexadecimal Notation
A	255.0.0.0	0xff000000
B	255.255.0.0	0xffff0000
C	255.255.255.0	0xffffff00

Table 11-4   Standard Netmask Addresses

The `arp` keyword specifies that the interface should support an ARP-style IP address resolution. When an interface is created with `ifconfig`, the default is to support ARP. To disable ARP on an interface, use the `-arp` keyword. On most networks, ARP must be turned on.

The `allmulti` keyword enables or disables (`-allmulti`) all multicast traffic modes. If enabled, multicast packets (that is, packets with Class D network addresses) will be received by the interface. Despite the fact that multicast traffic is available on the interface, an application that supports multicast traffic will need to be running to make use of this type of traffic. Multicast is used by multimedia applications to transport packets that contain real-time video and audio data.

The `promisc` keyword will enable the interface to receive all network traffic. It is known as promiscuous mode when all traffic is read, not just the normal traffic sent to it by other systems on the network. Use the `-promisc` command to disable this mode. Certain networking tools such as `tcpdump` will enable this mode automatically when in operation.

The `media` keyword changes the physical connectivity type for the interface. Not all interfaces support the ability to dynamically change interface media types. For those that do, many of the most common types may be used, such as 10Base2 for thin Ethernet, 10BaseT for twisted pair Ethernet, and AUI which is associated with 10Base5 Ethernet.

The `pointtopoint` keyword enables the use of a point-to-point link layer encapsulation protocol, which generally means that direct connectivity will exist between two systems. The commonly supported protocols, such as PPP or SLIP, can be used.

Logical Interfaces

The `ifconfig` command creates and configures logical (also known as virtual or pseudo) interfaces. These interfaces behave like physical interfaces and can be used to assign multiple IP addresses to the same system. From a configuration standpoint, logical interfaces are configured independently but share the same physical address and interface characteristics as the real physical interface.

To configure a pseudointerface, combine the physical interface with a logical interface reference number, separated by a colon. For example, to configure the first logical interface for `eth0`, use the following command:

```
# ifconfig eth1:1 10.0.2.128 netmask 0xffffff00 broadcast 10.0.2.255
```

Logical interfaces are displayed just like the physical ones using the `ifconfig -a` command. The following output shows one logical interface defined from the physical interface `eth1`:

```
eth1       Link encap:Ethernet  HWaddr 08:00:20:04:CF:2C ◄─────────
           inet addr:10.0.2.127  Bcast:10.0.2.255
 Mask:255.255.255.0
           UP BROADCAST RUNNING MULTICAST  MTU:1500  Metric:1
           RX packets:1810 errors:0 dropped:0 overruns:0 frame:0
            TX packets:1173 errors:0 dropped:0 overruns:0 carrier:0
           collisions:0 txqueuelen:100
           Interrupt:55 Base address:0x3000 ◄───── [Logical interface]──

eth1:1     Link encap:Ethernet  HWaddr 08:00:20:04:CF:2C
           inet addr:10.0.2.128  Bcast:10.0.2.255
 Mask:255.255.255.0 ◄───────
           UP BROADCAST RUNNING MULTICAST  MTU:1500  Metric:1
           Interrupt:55 Base address:0x3000
```

[Physical interface]

Notice the pseudointerface, `eth1:1` contains the same Ethernet hardware address (08:00:20:04:CF:2C) and the same interrupt level (55) as the real interface. These are additional clues that indicate that this interface is the same as the `eth1` interface.

To remove a logical interface, use the `down` keyword. Thus, the command

```
ifconfig -a eth1:1 down
```

will remove the `eth1:1` interface from the system. If this logical interface was created during system startup, the interface will be configured again when the system is restarted.

1-Minute Drill

● Why is the loopback interface useful?
● Explain the use of logical interfaces.

● The loopback address is provided so you can run diagnostics on your own computer.
● A logical interface assigns an additional IP address to a system on the same physical network interface. A logical interface shares all the characteristics of the physical interface except for the different address.

11.3 Monitor Network Operations using Netstat

The `netstat` command provides a wealth of information regarding the present status of network connections, routing information, and other important network-related data. This tool, short for network status, is strictly for monitoring and is one of the most popular debugging aids available on UNIX. Different command-line options control the display behavior of `netstat`. Given this, the functionality can be divided into a number of categories and used to accomplish the following:

- List active network sessions

- Show interface information and statistics

- Display routing table information

This tool also provides specific options that control the operation and output formatting. Table 11-5 contains the major keywords that control the network information that will be displayed. On Linux, some of the command options/keywords have a single-character option and a mnemonic string. For instance, the `-h` and `--help` options, which display command-line summary help, can be used interchangeably.

Option	Description
`-i`	Shows network interface parameters and statistical information (`--interface` Linux only).
`-g`	Displays multicast group membership information (`--groups` Linux only).
`-M`	Lists all sessions that use the masqueraded capabilities within FTP (`--masquerade` Linux only).
`-r`	Shows the network routing tables (`--route` Linux only).
`-P`	Lists connection information for specific network protocol. Supported protocols include `ip`, `ipv6`, `icmp`, `icmpv6`, `igmp`, `udp`, and `rawip` (Solaris and HP-UX).
`-t`	Displays active TCP socket connections. The `-tcp` option will continuously display these connections until interrupted by the user (Linux only).

Table 11-5 Netstat Output Data Options

Table 11-6 contains command-line modifiers that either provide additional information or modify the output when used with the keyword options shown in the previous table.

Displaying Active Network Sessions

One of the significant services provided by netstat is the ability to view active connections between systems. Any TCP session between the local host and any other system can be monitored. Also, any stream sockets that have been created will be displayed. Streams are used as a program-to-program communication channel. To display the currently established connections, issue the netstat command with the -t (Linux only) option as shown here:

```
# netstat -t
Active Internet connections (w/o servers)
Proto Recv-Q Send-Q Local Address          Foreign Address           State
tcp      0      0 110.orlando-11-12r:1052 192.215.123.37:www      ESTABLISHED
tcp      1      0 110.orlando-11-12r:1051 192.215.123.37:www      CLOSE
tcp      0      6 110.orlando-11-12r:1050 postoffice.worldn:pop-3 ESTABLISHED
tcp      0      0 110.orlando-11-12r:1049 www3.yahoo.com:www      ESTABLISHED
tcp      0      0 socrates.home.co:telnet durer.home.com:1033     ESTABLISHED
tcp      0      0 socrates.home.co:telnet durer.home.com:1032     ESTABLISHED
```

Table 11-5 shows that the -t option will display TCP socket activity. As indicated, the output of the above command includes the connections on the local system. Each connection includes information regarding the local and remote

Option	Description
-a	Shows status of all network connections or sockets.
-c	(Linux only) Causes the output to be continuously displayed until the user interrupts the output (--continue is supported as well).
-h	(Linux only) Displays command-line summary information to the user (--help is supported as well).
-n	Displays numeric information (for example, IP addresses) instead of attempting to resolve to a host, port, or username (--numeric Linux only).
-p	(Linux only) Shows the process name and identifier for each network socket listed (--program is supported as well).
-v	(Linux only) Prints additional information (--verbose is supported as well).

Table 11-6   Command Modification Options

11

addresses, statistical information, and connection status. The local and remote addresses are displayed to include hostname and port information in the format:

```
host.port
```

where `host` can either be an assigned hostname from `/etc/hosts` (or from another host resolution mechanism such as NIS or DNS) or a valid IP address. The port represents either a reserved port, as defined in `/etc/services`, or a socket allocated by the system. The local address is the source and the remote address is the destination.

To obtain the same information from either Solaris or HP-UX, use the `-P` option. This option requires adding a network protocol keyword, to be supplied to show connections based on the network protocol. For example, to show all connections based on the TCP transport protocol use the following:

```
netstat -P tcp
TCP: IPv4
   Local Address       Remote Address      Swind Send-Q Rwind Recv-Q  State
-------------------- -------------------- ----- ------ ----- ------ -------
bedrock.home.com.32794 bedrock.home.com.32777 73620      0 73620      0 ESTABLISHED
bedrock.home.com.32777 bedrock.home.com.32794 73620      0 73620      0 ESTABLISHED
localhost.32797      localhost.32792      73620      0 73620      0 ESTABLISHED
localhost.32792      localhost.32797      73620      0 73620      0 ESTABLISHED
localhost.32800      localhost.32799      73620      0 73620      0 ESTABLISHED
```

The other supported protocol keywords are `ip`, `ipv6`, `icmp`, `icmpv6`, `igmp`, `udp`, and `rawip`. As shown above, the output is consistent with the previous Linux output in terms of information that is displayed.

Recall from Module 10 that TCP uses four elements to make up a connection and uses a state machine model as part of TCP's overall transport mechanism. As a result, `monet.telnet` and `rembrandt.1036,` for example, are considered one connection. From the `State` field, we can see that this connection is in the `ESTABLISHED` state, which means that everything is operating normally.

Since TCP uses a state machine to control each of the defined states, we can use the `netstat` command to track and display the state of each TCP connection. Table 11-7 shows the most common states and includes a general description of each.

The preceding `netstat` command only displayed connections that are or were in the `ESTABLISHED` state. Sometimes it is helpful to list all services that are available and active on a system. This can be accomplished by using `netstat`

State	Description
ESTABLISHED	The connection is operational.
LISTEN	A service or application is waiting for a client connection.
SYN_SENT	Local system wants to open a remote connection.
SYN_RCVD	Remote system wants to open a connection.
FIN_WAIT_1	Local system is in the process of closing a connection.
FIN_WAIT_2	Local system is in the process of closing a connection.
CLOSE_WAIT	Remote system wants to close a connection.
LAST_ACK	Final step to CLOSE_WAIT.
TIMED_WAIT	Final step to FIN_WAIT_1 or FIN_WAIT_2.
UNKNOWN	The state of the socket is unknown.

Table 11-7   TCP States Displayed with netstat

with the -a option, as shown below. Please note that the following output
has been reduced to make it more readable. Executing this command on most
systems will produce a larger list because it will include the stream interfaces as
well. However, on Linux, we can use the -t and -u options to further refine the
output to only include TCP and UDP sockets. The following output provides a
list of both UDP and TCP services, regardless of their connection states. This is
useful because it is not always obvious which transport protocol a particular
service uses.

```
#netstat -a -t -u
Active Internet connections (servers and established)
Proto Recv-Q Send-Q Local Address          Foreign Address        State
tcp        0      0 socrates.home.co:telnet durer.home.com:1033    ESTABLISHED
tcp        0      0 110.orlando-11-1:domain *:*                     LISTEN
tcp        0      0 *:1048                  *:*                     LISTEN
tcp        0      0 *:1047                  *:*                     LISTEN
tcp        0      0 *:1046                  *:*                     LISTEN
tcp        0      0 *:1045                  *:*                     LISTEN
tcp        0      0 *:1044                  *:*                     LISTEN
tcp        0      0 *:1037                  *:*                     LISTEN
tcp        0    710 socrates.home.co:telnet durer.home.com:1032    ESTABLISHED
tcp        0      0 *:6000                  *:*                     LISTEN
tcp        0      0 *:nntp                  *:*                     LISTEN
tcp        0      0 *:www                   *:*                     LISTEN
tcp        0      0 *:smtp                  *:*                     LISTEN
tcp        0      0 *:713                   *:*                     LISTEN
tcp        0      0 *:1024                  *:*                     LISTEN
tcp        0      0 *:683                   *:*                     LISTEN
```

11

```
tcp       0      0 *:678                    *:*              LISTEN
tcp       0      0 *:673                    *:*              LISTEN
tcp       0      0 *:652                    *:*              LISTEN
tcp       0      0 *:printer                *:*              LISTEN
tcp       0      0 10.0.2.205:domain        *:*              LISTEN
tcp       0      0 10.0.2.202:domain        *:*              LISTEN
tcp       0      0 socrates.home.co:domain  *:*              LISTEN
tcp       0      0 localhost:domain         *:*              LISTEN
tcp       0      0 *:linuxconf              *:*              LISTEN
tcp       0      0 *:auth                   *:*              LISTEN
tcp       0      0 *:finger                 *:*              LISTEN
tcp       0      0 *:login                  *:*              LISTEN
tcp       0      0 *:shell                  *:*              LISTEN
tcp       0      0 *:telnet                 *:*              LISTEN
tcp       0      0 *:ftp                    *:*              LISTEN
tcp       0      0 *:sunrpc                 *:*              LISTEN
udp       0      0 110.orlando-11-1:domain  *:*
udp       0      0 *:xdmcp                  *:*
udp       0      0 localhost:1119           *:*
udp       0      0 *:800                    *:*
udp       0      0 *:1022                   *:*
udp       0      0 *:714                    *:*
```

Under the TCP heading, not only are the two TCP connections displayed from the previous example, but additional services are included as well. Any services listed in the LISTEN state are waiting for incoming connections and are usually known as server-based resources. When a service is waiting for requests from the network, it is free to access connections from any remote address. That is why *.* is listed under the Foreign Address field. Servers also generally place * in the local host portion to further indicate that the server is free to establish a connection if a client request is made. When a request from a client is sent to a server, the server makes a copy of itself to handle the request and continues listening for additional client requests. Thus when this occurs, netstat displays multiple instances of the same service, as shown here:

```
netstat -a | grep ftp
tcp       0      0 socrates.home.:ftp-data durer.home.com:1034  TIME_WAIT
tcp       0      0 socrates.home.com:ftp   durer.home.com:1033  ESTABLISHED
tcp       0      0 *:ftp                    *:*                 LISTEN
```

The above command issues a netstat and pipes the output into the grep command, which scans the input for the ftp string. As a result, all lines with the ftp string are displayed. In the output above, the FTP server is still listening for incoming connection requests while an FTP session is established to a system called socrates.

Under the UDP heading in the previous output example, only a local address and state field have been displayed; the foreign address is not specified. This is because UDP is a connectionless protocol and therefore doesn't list remote address information. Also, notice that no statistical information is available for UDP. This is another indication that UDP is fundamentally different by design and does not produce this type of information.

Despite the rather large amount of information provided with the -a option, netstat can be used to provide a quick check to ensure that the correct services are running on a given system. By scanning the output of netstat, the network administrator can easily notice any service that shouldn't be running. For example, many organizations consider the finger facility to be a security risk because it can provide user account information to anyone requesting it. Once detected with netstat, the finger service can be disabled by modifying the /etc/inetd.conf (Solaris) or /etc/xinetd.conf (Linux) network configuration file.

If you are interested in displaying the streams defined on the system, issue the netstat command with the --unix option (Linux) or -P with the rawip option (Solaris and HP-UX). The output includes the UNIX streams socket interfaces. Since these connections are mainly used for interprocess communication, their specific use and function won't be described in great detail. Since the number of streams used on a UNIX system can be significant, the output from the netstat command can be rather long. As a result, the following output shows on a Linux system, just a few lines versus what would typically be displayed:

```
unix  1      [ ]         STREAM      CONNECTED     2399    /dev/log
unix  1      [ ]         STREAM      CONNECTED     2384    /tmp/.ICE-unix/963
unix  1      [ N ]       STREAM      CONNECTED     2364    /tmp/.X11-unix/X0
unix  1      [ ]         STREAM      CONNECTED     2220
/tmp/orbit-root/orb-11931020341330722701
unix  1      [ ]         STREAM      CONNECTED     2217
/tmp/orbit-root/orb-2122911451756745208
unix  1      [ ]         STREAM      CONNECTED     2213
/tmp/orbit-root/orb-16956010373298973
unix  1      [ ]         STREAM      CONNECTED     2206    /tmp/.X11-unix/X0
unix  1      [ ]         STREAM      CONNECTED     2202
/tmp/orbit-root/orb-2122911451756745208
```

11

System programs and other applications create streams as a mechanism to communicate between themselves and other programs.

Hint

The -p option is not supported on either HP-UX or Solaris.

One extremely useful feature of netstat on Linux is the -p option, which will show the associated process or program name that has run with the parts opened. The command

```
# netstat -t -p -a
```

produces this output:

```
Active Internet connections (servers and established)
Proto Recv-Q Send-Q Local Address          Foreign Address      State PID/Program
name
tcp        0    285 socrates.home.co:telnet durer.home.com:1032   ESTABLISHED
906/in.telnetd
tcp        0      0 *:1036                 *:*                    LISTEN
846/gnomepager_appl
tcp        0      0 *:1035                 *:*                    LISTEN
843/gen_util_applet
tcp        0      0 *:1034                 *:*                    LISTEN 821/gmc
tcp        0      0 *:1033                 *:*                    LISTEN
823/gnome-name-serv
tcp        0      0 *:1032                 *:*                    LISTEN 812/panel
tcp        0      0 *:1025                 *:*                    LISTEN
766/gnome-session
tcp        0      0 *:6000                 *:*                    LISTEN 738/X
tcp        0      0 *:nntp                 *:*                    LISTEN 685/innd
tcp        0      0 *:www                  *:*                    LISTEN 602/httpd
455/lpd
tcp        0      0 10.0.2.205:domain      *:*                    LISTEN 441/named
tcp        0      0 10.0.2.202:domain      *:*                    LISTEN 441/named
tcp        0      0 socrates.home.co:domain *:*                   LISTEN 441/named
```

Once executed, additional columns are added to the normal output of netstat. They include the PID (process identification) and the Program name fields. As clearly seen from the output above, it is now very easy to track down sockets and find which process and/or program is using them.

Displaying Interface Information

The netstat command can obtain details on the configuration of the network interface and rudimentary packet counts as well. The -i command-line option obtains a list of each defined interface on the system, one interface per line:

Linux:

```
#netstat -I
Kernel Interface table
Iface   MTU Met     RX-OK RX-ERR RX-DRP RX-OVR    TX-OK TX-ERR TX-DRP TX-OVR Flg
eth0    1500  0         0      0      0      0        0      1      0      0 BRU
eth0:   1500  0       - no statistics available -                          BRU
eth1    1500  0      3946      0      0      0      138      0      0      0 BRU
lo      3924  0       192      0      0      0      192      0      0      0 LRU
```

Solaris:

```
Name  Mtu  Net/Dest       Address           Ipkts   Ierrs Opkts   Oerrs Collis Queue
lo0   8232 loopback       localhost        1162897 0     1162897 0     0      0
elx11 1500 216.155.202.0  bedrock.home.com 9663    0     5464    0     12     0

Name  Mtu  Net/Dest                        Address              Ipkts   Ierrs Opkts
Oerrs Collis
lo0   8252 localhost                       localhost            1162897 0
1162897 0      0
```

As you can see, the command displays some of the same information that the ifconfig command provides, plus some basic statistics regarding operating characteristics of each interface—specifically, the name of the interface, the maximum transfer unit (MTU), the network or destination address, and the address of the interface. Also, it displays a count of the total number of input packets, input error packets, input dropped packets, and input overflow counter. It contains the same counters for transmitted packets as well. The Flg field contains a condensed listing of the interface configuration options as enabled and reported by the ifconfig command.

The RX-OK (received) and TX-OK (transmitted) fields (Ipkts and Opkts on Solaris/HP-UX) represent the reception and transmission of valid traffic across the interface, respectively. The next fields, RX-ERR and TX-ERR (Ierrs and Oerrs on Solaris/HP-UX), indicate any input and output error packets that have occurred on the interface; this includes, for example, any runt packets (those that are smaller than the standard size) and other errors. The RX-DRP and TX-DRP fields are counters that represent problems with the transmission of packets on the interface. In the output above, note that the interface eth0 reports a number of output packet errors. In this case, these errors are being generated because the interface is not physically attached to a network, yet the system is attempting to send out packets. Some UNIX systems can't detect when an interface is actually attached to a network. This is also the reason that the RX-OK and TX-OK fields are zero; this indicates that no traffic has been sent or received across this interface.

11

The TX-ERR field indicates the number of collisions (or other transmission errors) that have occurred as recorded by the system. A collision is when two or more devices attempt to transmit packets at nearly the same time. After this happens, a jam signal is sent to inform all devices on the network that a collision has occurred and that any transmission should stop briefly and then, after randomly determined intervals of time, be tried again. This is known as back-off and is the mechanism used by devices to resume normal operations. Collisions only occur on broadcast network technologies such as Ethernet. When the TX-ERR field is nonzero, it indicates that the interface has recorded collisions for which it was directly involved.

Hint

The TX-ERR field does not represent all collisions that have occurred on the network because the system may not always count the number of jam messages transmitted as a result of a collision caused by other systems.

The RX-DRP and TX-DRP fields represent packets that were discarded before being received or transmitted. These fields are useful in situations when the system is performing routing functions where lost or discarded packets could cause connectivity problems between systems or networks. Another instance when it may be important to monitor these counters is when the system is a server, where the network traffic can be significant. In practice, the fields aren't that important for a system that may be used as a single-user workstation. The RX-OVR and TX-OVR fields provide counters for packets that caused overflow conditions for the networking software. Again, these are only critical when the system being monitored is considered critical.

When logical (or pseudo) interfaces are defined on the system, netstat lists each interface as a separate entry. However, you will notice that given the example above, netstat doesn't collect statistical information for these interfaces. As a result, the message "no statistics available" is displayed. In all other respects, netstat shows logical interfaces with the same information as normal interfaces. This includes, for example, the interface (Flg) field codes.

Display Routing Information

The system uses the routing table to determine the path that will be used to send IP packets to particular hosts or networks. Normally, systems are configured with a default router so that routing decisions are straightforward and simple.

However, there may be instances when a machine has more than one interface and each is attached to a different IP network. In this case, the system might also be forwarding IP packets (routing) between these networks. As a result, the routing function becomes a bit more complex. As part of the overall routing system, a routing table is defined that can be displayed as the need arises. One of the primary ways to examine this table is with the -r option:

```
# netstat -r
Kernel IP routing table
Destination     Gateway        Genmask          Flags  MSS Window  irtt Iface
199.70.195.41   *              255.255.255.255  UH      0 0           0 ppp0
10.0.2.201      *              255.255.255.255  UH      0 0           0 eth0
10.0.2.0        *              255.255.255.0    U       0 0           0 eth0
127.0.0.0       *              255.0.0.0        U       0 0           0 lo
default         199.70.195.41  0.0.0.0          UG      0 0           0 ppp0
```

The output above was obtained from a server system that contains two separate network interfaces. In this example, the routing table includes a destination network, gateway (or router), network mask, some status flags, two size fields, a metric value, and the interface with which the route is associated. The Destination field specifies the network for which the route has been established. The Gateway field shows the IP address or hostname of the router that forwards packets to the IP address listed in the Destination column. A * indicates that the router has not been configured for the associated network. If an IP address or hostname is shown in this field, a router has been configured.

The Genmask field shows the network mask that has been configured for this interface. This mask is used like a subnet mask to calculate the network address specified in the Destination column. The Flags field displays status information regarding the route. The U flag indicates that the route is up and active. The H flag shows that the route entry refers to a host system, not an actual router. With UNIX, there is always a route to the local system, which is used internally by the networking software. The G flag indicates that the route is via an external gateway or router.

Hint

The terms "route" and "gateway" are used interchangeably.

When the routing tables are displayed from a workstation that contains a single interface, we may see the following entries:

```
# netstat -r
Kernel IP routing table
Destination     Gateway        Genmask          Flags Metric Ref     Use Iface
```

11

```
199.70.195.41     *              255.255.255.255 UH   0    0    0 ppp0
10.0.2.201        *              255.255.255.255 UH   0    0    0 eth0
10.0.2.0          *              255.255.255.0   U    0    0    0 eth0
127.0.0.0         *              255.0.0.0       U    0    0    0 lo
default           199.70.195.41  0.0.0.0         UG   0    0    0 ppp0
```

In this case, a default route has been set to 199.70.195.41, which happens to be a connection to a local ISP using the Point-to-Point Protocol (PPP). When a system contains a single interface, a default route can be used as a shorthand method to specify the only way out of the local network. Without the default entry, every network for which the system must connect will require a separate routing entry. When the ppp0 link is activated (either manually or automatically), the default route is installed automatically by the PPP software that is used.

The MMS field represents the maximum segment size (MSS) for a TCP session or connection. Normally with netstat, this field contains a zero value. The Window field controls the TCP window size for a connection using this route; typically, this is for certain WAN protocols or other network drivers that have a hard time handling back-to-back frames. Again, this field normally has a value of zero.

The irtt field shows the initial round-trip time (IRTT) for a TCP session or connection—again, used for WAN network protocols. The netstat command shows the value zero. The final field (Iface) shows the network interface to which that route belongs. It is important to note that within the routing tables, many routes could use the same interface. In fact, the previous example shows no less than three routes using the same interface. This is normal and proper because the routing function is concerned with forwarding IP packets from one network to another, regardless of which physical network may be involved or the path that is traversed. This, albeit, in a small way, illustrates the modularity of the TCP/IP protocols and networking software.

Display Multicast Information

Multicast is a mechanism that supports the delivery of high-volume traffic to a network and associated workstations in a very efficient manner. A multicast group is a defined collection of workstations and multicast routers that forward traffic using a special multicast IP address. The -g option displays multicast routing information that is related to the routing groups and interfaces that have been defined on the system. Using this option, the netstat -g command will show the currently configured multicast groups:

```
IPv6/IPv4 Group Memberships
Interface       RefCnt Group
--------------- ------ --------------------
lo              1      224.0.0.1
eth0            1      224.0.0.1
```

In this example, each of the defined interfaces on this system is a member of the default multicast group known as `224.0.0.1` or (`ALL-SYSTEMS.MCAST.NET`, which is defined on some systems). The Solaris and HP-UX system provides the same basic output. This group, which is a standard multicast group, is used to send multicast traffic to all systems on a local network. So, if any application uses the address of `224.0.0.1` to transmit traffic, this system would receive the information. When multicast is deployed using standard multicast applications, additional multicast groups may be defined to restrict the multicast traffic to only those systems for which the information is required.

Display Protocol Statistics

The `netstat` command can be used to display protocol statistics. The `--statistics` option, by itself, will display the supported protocols, including TCP, UDP, and RAW. RAW is a combination of both IP and ICMP packets and can be displayed separately using the keyword `raw`.

```
# netstat -s
Ip:
    3003 total packets received
    0 forwarded
    0 incoming packets discarded
    212 incoming packets delivered
    2847 requests sent out
Icmp:
    489 ICMP messages received
    0 input ICMP message failed.
    ICMP input histogram:
        destination unreachable: 486
        echo replies: 3
    487 ICMP messages sent
    0 ICMP messages failed
    ICMP output histogram:
        destination unreachable: 487
Tcp:
```

11

```
    0 active connections openings
    0 passive connection openings
    0 failed connection attempts
    0 connection resets received
    1 connections established
    2295 segments received
    1700 segments send out
    2 segments retransmitted
    0 bad segments received.
    0 resets sent
Udp:
    171 packets received
    2 packets to unknown port received.
    0 packet receive errors
    657 packets sent:
```

1-Minute Drill

● What's a situation when the routing table for a system will be complex and it's useful to use the `netstat -r` command to display the routing information?

11.4 Verify Network Connectivity Using Ping

The `ping` command provides two basic services. First, it can be used to determine whether a basic level of connectivity is available between one or more endpoints or systems. The `ping` tool can be used to determine if a remote device is reachable on a network from the local system and help debug connectivity problems among systems. Second, it can provide rudimentary network performance statistics, which can be used to diagnose traffic-related network problems. The term "ping" is derived from the phrase packet internet groper. The `ping` tool can be used in one of two ways: by specifying a valid hostname or IP address, or by using command-line options with a hostname or IP address. Using the first form, `ping` provides a handy way to determine that a remote device is available on the network.

● A system with more than one interface connected to separate networks will have a more complex routing table than a single interface system with routing between the two (or more) interfaces.

As discussed in Module 10, `ping` uses the Internet Control Message Protocol (ICMP) to emit ICMP requests and waits for valid ICMP replies. Because ICMP is a required protocol within the TCP/IP family, `ping` can generally be used with every device that supports TCP/IP, and is available on many operating systems and other networking devices. For instance, a Cisco router or UNIX host provides the capability to `ping` other devices on the network. The `ping` program is a client-side application only; no additional software is needed or required for it to function and interact directly with the remote system's protocol layer to accomplish its task.

Determine System Availability

The `ping` tool can be used to determine general availability of any TCP/IP device, even if it doesn't specifically have a general operating system. For example, to determine if the host `durer` is reachable, issue the following `ping` command:

```
#ping durer
PING durer.home.com (10.0.2.10): 56 data bytes
64 bytes from 10.0.2.10: icmp_seq=0 ttl=128 time=0.9 ms
64 bytes from 10.0.2.10: icmp_seq=1 ttl=128 time=0.8 ms
64 bytes from 10.0.2.10: icmp_seq=2 ttl=128 time=0.8 ms
64 bytes from 10.0.2.10: icmp_seq=3 ttl=128 time=0.8 ms

--- durer.home.com ping statistics ---
4 packets transmitted, 4 packets received, 0% packet loss
round-trip min/avg/max = 0.8/0.8/0.9 ms
```

In this case, `ping` displays no packet loss to `durer`, which happens to be a printer. This basically states that `durer` is alive and operating normally from an IP perspective. The default behavior of `ping` on Linux means that the user must type `^c` (CTRL- C) to stop the output. This message generally means that the TCP/IP software is operational. Although alive indicates that the system is visible on the network, it is no guarantee that other network services, such as `ftp` or `telnet`, are available. This is an important distinction. The `ping` tool can only be used to determine basic protocol connectivity—not the availability of higher-level applications or services. In fact, some systems will answer a `ping` request even before they are fully booted. Keep in mind that no single piece of software can determine that every TCP/IP application or service is installed and operating on a system.

11

The Solaris and HP-UX systems display the following:

```
durer.home.com is alive
```

On Linux, if the host `durer` is not reachable, `ping` will display the following message after ^c (CTRL-C)is typed:

```
PING rubens.home.com (10.0.2.220): 56 data bytes
--- rubens.home.com ping statistics ---
2 packets transmitted, 0 packets received, 100% packet loss
```

Normally, the Linux `ping` issues ICMP requests forever, and if no reply is received, it generates the message shown above only after the user has interrupted the command. This is somewhat unfortunate, because other versions of `ping` will eventually time out without the user having to manually interrupt the command. Luckily, a maximum number or count of the total number of requests can be specified, which has the effect of controlling `ping` so that the user doesn't need to manually intervene. On Linux, use the `-c` command-line option with an argument of 1 and the `ping` command will issue a single request to `rubens`:

```
# ping -c 1 rubens
```

and will generate the following output if this host is down:

> 0 packets received and 100% packet loss is an indication the host is down

```
PING rubens.home.com (10.0.2.220): 56 data bytes
--- rubens.home.com ping statistics ---
1 packets transmitted, 0 packets received, 100% packet loss
```

This is useful so that the user can quickly determine reachability of a host without wasting additional time or network bandwidth. Reducing the number of `ping` requests is generally a good thing for the network. Specifying the count in this manner is sometimes preferable when using `ping` within a shell script where issuing a ^c (CTRL-C) would be difficult or inconvenient. Using the count option is an ideal way to obtain a very good round-trip delay average and to determine performance over time.

It is interesting to note that if the host `rubens` isn't on the same subnet as the host issuing the `ping`, it is possible that the host is functioning correctly, but that an intermediate device, such as a network router, is responsible for the lack of connectivity. I term this problem "connectivity fussiness." In this case, `ping` can't determine why `rubens` is not reachable. To further understand this problem, consider the sample network in Figure 11-1.

This network diagram shows several devices attached to two different networks that are interconnected via Router Z. When a `ping` request is issued from node B on network A to node C on network B, the request is passed via router Z. If router Z should stop functioning, the requests will never reach node C. As a result, node C becomes unreachable from the perspective of node B.

Because `ping` can check reachability of any TCP/IP device, we can now issue a `ping` for router Z to further diagnose the problem. By probing the router closest to node C, we will learn that the loss of connectivity is most likely being caused by router Z's network interface to network B, and not node C itself. Also, if we `ping` other devices on network B, this would confirm that all devices are unreachable and lead us to conclude that there is a problem with router Z. This example demonstrates that network problems can be caused by

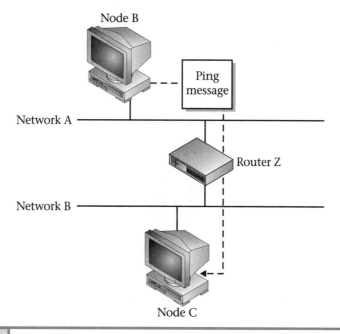

Figure 11-1 | Using ping to determine node availability

devices other than those easily identified as being the problem. Tools such as `ping` help to isolate the sources of routing and many other network failures or problems.

The second form of the `ping` command provides a number of options to control additional functionality. Table 11-8 provides a list of the most popular command-line options available.

Show Basic Network Performance

The `ping` command can be used to measure the amount of time required to transmit a message to a remote destination and the time required to obtain a response. This use of this command in essence measures the relative performance of the path between the two devices at a given point in time. It does not, by any means, provide a detailed analysis of the devices or connectivity between them. Rather, it provides a glimpse of the general condition of the path at the point it is measured. It could be said that network performance is like the stock market. One day it is up and the next it is down. The primary difference with respect to volatility is whether we are talking in terms of days or milliseconds. A large number of factors can cause network performance to vary. These include users that are overly aggressive about using network resources, hardware problems, software configuration problems, and so forth.

Option	Description
-R	Use record route information.
-U	Use UDP packet instead of ICMP packet (Solaris only).
-a	Issue a `ping` to all addresses on a multi-home host (Solaris only).
-c	Send only a certain number of packets (Linux only).
-f	Flood the network with packets.
-i	Delay the number of seconds between each request (Linux only). Specify the outgoing interface (Solaris and HP-UX only).
-n	Show network addresses instead of hostname.
-p	Specify up to 16 bytes to pad a packet with customized data (Linux only). Set the base UDP port to use (Solaris only).
-s	Issue a single ICMP request per second and collect round-trip statistics (Solaris and HP-UX only).

Table 11-8 ping Command-Line Options

The `ping` command provides a means of determining system response times as well, but it takes a little more work to determine if the observed performance problem is related to a specific slow system or a delay in some other network component. The `ping` tool shows output that can be used to measure and report round-trip time and provide packet-loss statistics. By default, `ping` issues an ICMP request every second to the destination supplied on the command line and reports the status of each ICMP reply. Sample output includes the following:

```
# ping -s didymus          Target IP address              Round trip time
PING didymus.home.com (10.0.2.127): 56 data bytes
64 bytes from 10.0.2.127: icmp_seq=0 ttl=255 time=1.2 ms
64 bytes from 10.0.2.127: icmp_seq=1 ttl=255 time=1.1 ms      4 packets sent
64 bytes from 10.0.2.127: icmp_seq=2 ttl=255 time=1.2 ms      and received
64 bytes from 10.0.2.127: icmp_seq=3 ttl=255 time=1.2 ms

--- didymus.home.com ping statistics ---     ICMP sequence number
4 packets transmitted, 4 packets received, 0% packet loss
round-trip min/avg/max = 1.1/1.1/1.2 ms
```
Packet size

This report provides the packet size, the hostname or IP address of the target device, a sequence number, round-trip time value, and a statistical summary. The time value shows the round-trip time in milliseconds (1000ths of a second) for each reply received. The bottom of the report calculates the minimum, average, and maximum trip times for all replies, also displayed in milliseconds. The total length of the ICMP packet transmitted to `didymus` is 64 bytes. This is the default size, which is usually sufficient. However, it might be necessary to increase the packet size to get a better measure of throughput. In this case, a large packet size may be specified using the `-s` command-line option on Linux. For example, the command

11

```
# ping -s 100 didymus
```

issues the ICMP requests with a packet size of 100 bytes to the target host `didymus`. This might be required to obtain a better picture of performance because network throughput may differ for larger packet sizes versus smaller values. When executed, this command shows the following:

```
PING didymus.home.com (10.0.2.127): 100 data bytes
108 bytes from 10.0.2.127: icmp_seq=0 ttl=255 time=2.7 ms
108 bytes from 10.0.2.127: icmp_seq=1 ttl=255 time=1.5 ms
108 bytes from 10.0.2.127: icmp_seq=2 ttl=255 time=1.3 ms
108 bytes from 10.0.2.127: icmp_seq=3 ttl=255 time=1.3 ms
108 bytes from 10.0.2.127: icmp_seq=4 ttl=255 time=1.3 ms
108 bytes from 10.0.2.127: icmp_seq=5 ttl=255 time=1.3 ms
108 bytes from 10.0.2.127: icmp_seq=6 ttl=255 time=1.3 ms
108 bytes from 10.0.2.127: icmp_seq=7 ttl=255 time=1.3 ms

--- didymus.home.com ping statistics ---
8 packets transmitted, 8 packets received, 0% packet loss
round-trip min/avg/max = 1.3/1.5/2.7 ms
```

Packet size equals the 100 bytes specified on the command line plus 8 bytes overhead

On Solaris and HP-UX, use following command to accomplish the same thing:

```
ping -s didymus 100
```

In this case, specifying the size of the packet comes after the hostname.

As you can see from this output above, `ping` adds 8 bytes of overhead for each packet sent; this is determined by subtracting the 100 bytes specified with the `-s` option from the 108 bytes transmitted by `ping`. Notice that the response times didn't change much, despite the fact that we used a large data size. We would need to increase the size significantly to observe a larger delay in processing the packets.

You may have noticed that the hostname `didymus` was used on the command line, but when `ping` echoed back the hostname, it showed a different name, like `didymus.home.com`. The reason for this is that `didymus` is an alias of `didymus.home.com` and using the alias with many UNIX commands results in the official name being used instead.

The `ping` tool uses a sequence number to keep track of requests and replies. Each request is given the next number in sequence and is then matched with the corresponding reply. This sequencing is used to determine packet loss if any requests do not receive an appropriate reply. Generally speaking, packet loss on a small network should be very rare, and if it does occur, it might indicate a network- or system-related problem. However, on a large network or internet (internet with a lowercase i), or on the Internet, packet loss is common and represents a normal state of affairs. Given a popular Internet site as shown below, a certain amount of packet loss may be observed:

```
ping -c 10 www.whitehouse.gov
PING www.whitehouse.com (209.67.27.247): 56 data bytes
64 bytes from 209.67.27.247: icmp_seq=7 ttl=244 time=240.1 ms
64 bytes from 209.67.27.247: icmp_seq=8 ttl=244 time=240.1 ms
64 bytes from 209.67.27.247: icmp_seq=9 ttl=244 time=240.1 ms

--- www.whitehouse.com ping statistics ---
10 packets transmitted, 3 packets received, 70% packet loss
round-trip min/avg/max = 240.1/240.1/240.1 ms
```

The report above indicates that 70 percent of the packets sent to the `www.whitehouse.gov` system did not have corresponding replies! They were lost. In other words, the program sent ten packets, but only received three back; seven out of ten is 70 percent. One possible reason for this noticeable packet loss is that some of the critical Internet routers might be quite busy or even overloaded with network traffic. As a result, some of the ICMP requests might be discarded because the requests expired before they were delivered to the final destination. Also, the relative load of the target device can be a factor because these systems might not have the computing resources to answer all network requests as required. Because of the popularity of this site, it is not unreasonable to think that both the servers and the networks that connect them are all quite busy or even overloaded. An overloaded condition will occur when too many users are using resources from the system or network at the same time.

Sometimes it is desirable to provide additional time for acknowledging each `ping` request instead of using the default value of one second. If additional time is desired between successive ICMP requests, the `-i` option can be used, followed by the desired value. The interval should be long enough to provide the required amount of time for the remote system to respond. When we increase the timeout value as suggested, we will generally notice less packet loss. The command

11

```
ping -c 10 www.whitehouse.gov -i 5
```

adds a five-second delay to each request, thus providing additional time for the processing of the requests through the network and to the destination server. Using the command above, the following was produced:

```
PING www.whitehouse.com (209.67.27.247): 56 data bytes
64 bytes from 209.67.27.247: icmp_seq=1 ttl=244 time=240.1 ms
64 bytes from 209.67.27.247: icmp_seq=2 ttl=244 time=240.1 ms
64 bytes from 209.67.27.247: icmp_seq=3 ttl=244 time=240.1 ms
64 bytes from 209.67.27.247: icmp_seq=4 ttl=244 time=240.0 ms
64 bytes from 209.67.27.247: icmp_seq=5 ttl=244 time=250.1 ms
64 bytes from 209.67.27.247: icmp_seq=6 ttl=244 time=240.1 ms
64 bytes from 209.67.27.247: icmp_seq=7 ttl=244 time=240.1 ms
64 bytes from 209.67.27.247: icmp_seq=8 ttl=244 time=240.2 ms
64 bytes from 209.67.27.247: icmp_seq=9 ttl=244 time=250.1 ms

--- www.whitehouse.com ping statistics ---
10 packets transmitted, 9 packets received, 10% packet loss
round-trip min/avg/max = 240.0/242.3/250.1 ms
```

As noted from the output, the packet loss to this site was reduced to 10 percent. Bear in mind that other factors could have also contributed to the reduction, such as users leaving the site or the network not being used. In general, increasing the amount of time for each request should reduce the overall load on the system. However, this is not guaranteed to always be the case because the system may be overloaded to the point that no additional amount of time would really help.

Additional Command Options

With the -n option, ping displays IP addresses rather than hostnames. This is useful, for example, when network problems involving DNS impact the use of ping. This option instructs ping not to invoke hostname resolution, thus permitting the tool to function while the name service is slow or temporarily disabled.

The -R option enables the record route option with the IP protocol. Toggling the record route informs each router along a path to place its IP address in the IP header. As a result, a list of routers that were used to reach the final destination can be obtained. This is the chief mechanism that the traceroute command utilizes. Another interesting option is flood mode using the -f option, which is available on Linux. This option tells `ping` to attempt to flood the network with ICMP requests approximately 100 times per second or as fast as the remote destination can process each request.

By the way, a note of caution is in order here: The `-f` option can be a dangerous thing. It can consume a significant amount of network bandwidth and cause systems to disappear from the network because they are too heavily loaded to respond to other network requests. It is not recommended that this option be used on a live network when loss of connectivity could impact the business operations of the individuals that use the network. Also, it is not reasonable to flood other networks that you are not associated with.

Having said all this, the command

```
ping -c 100 -f bedrock
```

displays the following output:

```
PING bedrock.home.com (216.155.202.100) from 216.155.202.163 : 56(84) bytes of data.
.
--- bedrock.home.com ping statistics ---
100 packets transmitted, 100 packets received, 0% packet loss
round-trip min/avg/max/mdev = 0.203/0.244/0.427/0.040 ms
```

This sends 100 packets to the host `bedrock`.

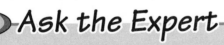

Ask the Expert

Question   Why use the flood capability anyway?

Answer   The reason is simple—attempt to produce a significant amount of traffic on the network and see what happens. You will find that in networking, determining how things work sometimes includes attempting to break things or do things in such a way as to exceed the practical limitations of a device or system. In the case of networking devices such as routers or UNIX systems, industry experts and users want to know what will happen to the device if it is exposed to high-traffic patterns. Measuring performance and other networking characteristics when the network is under tremendous load will help the network manager truly understand the behavior of critical networking devices and systems when they are deployed in their networks. The flood option is one easy way to do this.

11

11-5 Gather Network Information with Lanscan

The `lanscan` command available on HP-UX provides a very quick and easy way to gather network configuration and performance information from all the system network interfaces. Issuing the command

```
# lanscan
```

displays the following:

```
Hardware Station        Crd Hdw   Net-Interface  NM  MAC    HP-DLPI DLPI
Path     Address        In# State NamePPA         ID  Type   Support Mjr#
0/0/0/0  0x00306E060662 0   UP     lan0 snap0      1   ETHER  Yes     119
```

As shown above, the output is very similar to what the `ifconfig` command provides, but in this case more information is given about the low-level data link support (for example, it shows that `lan0` is of type `ETHER`, which represents Ethernet).

Note

Since the HP-UX version doesn't support the `-a` option, this command can be used to determine the name of all the network interfaces on the system. Using the `-v` (verbose) option of the `lanscan` command, additional information can be obtained about the system network interfaces:

```
# lanscan -v
-----------------------------------------------------------------
Hardware Station        Crd Hdw   Net-Interface  NM  MAC    HP-DLPI DLPI
Path     Address        In# State NamePPA         ID  Type   Support Mjr#
0/0/0/0  0x00306E060662 0   UP     lan0 snap0      1   ETHER  Yes     119

Extended Station                         LLC Encapsulation
Address                                  Methods
0x00306E060662                           IEEE HPEXTIEEE SNAP ETHER NOVELL

Driver Specific Information
btlan3
```

This option shows the additional supported data link methods, such as `NOVELL` and also the Ethernet driver information (`btlan3`).

Project 11-1

This project steps you through documenting the network settings on your system and testing your current network connectivity.

Step-by-Step

1. ping your local loopback address to verify that TCP/IP is functional on your system:

```
# ping 127.0.0.1
```

2. Display your ARP table:

```
# arp
```

3. If you are using Linux, display the ARP table in numeric format in verbose mode:

```
# arp -n -v
```

4. List all the available interfaces for your system:

```
#ifconfig -a
```

5. Display all the current network connections:

```
# netstat -a
```

6. Search the results of the netstat command to look for instances of specific services. For example, are you running an FTP server on this system?

```
netstat -a | grep ftp
```

7. ping several major hosts to determine your connectivity to them. For example:

```
ping 198.192.196.56
```

```
ping 4.17.168.6
```

11

☑ Mastery Check

1. The _____ contains a complete list of all data link protocol to IP address mappings for the local network.

2. Which command provides information regarding the present status of network connections, routing information, and other important network-related data?

   A. `ifconfig`

   B. `arp`

   C. `netstat`

   D. `ping`

3. Which command can be used to determine if a remote device is reachable on a network from the local system and help debug connectivity problems among systems?

   A. `ifconfig`

   B. `arp`

   C. `netstat`

   D. `ping`

4. What does this output from the `ping` command tell you about the status of the system pinged?

   `4 packets transmitted, 4 packets received, 0% packet loss`

   A. The system is reachable.

   B. The system is not available.

   C. The system is taking too long to respond to `ping` requests.

   D. No information can be determined from this output.

☑ *Mastery Check*

5. What function is performed with this command?

```
# arp -s bruegel 08:00:20:82:be:05
```

A. Displaying the ARP table for the bruegel system

B. Deleting the bruegel system from the ARP table

C. Changing the hardware address in the ARP table for the bruegel system

D. Adding the bruegel system to the ARP table

6. What is the command to disable the interface `ppp0`?

7. What type of interface does this output from the `ifconfig -a` command indicate?

```
eth1      Link encap:Ethernet  HWaddr 08:00:20:04:CF:2C

          inet addr:10.0.2.127  Bcast:10.0.2.255
```

A. Physical

B. Logical

C. Active

D. Inactive

8. What type of interface does this output from the `ifconfig -a` command indicate?

```
          UP BROADCAST RUNNING MULTICAST  MTU:1500  Metric:1
```

A. Physical

B. Logical

C. Active

D. Inactive

11

 **Mastery Check**

9. What is the command to show all network connections and show them in numeric format?

10. What command would have produced the following two lines of output?

```
tcp        0      0 *:sunrpc                *:*                     LISTEN
udp        0      0 110.orlando-11-1:domain *:*
```

   A. netstat -a | grep ftp

   B. netstat -a -t -u

   C. netstat -a -n

   D. netstat -t -p -a

11. What is the command to record each router's IP address in a ping, similar to the long lines command?

Module 12

Advanced
Network Tools

Critical Skills

12.1 Monitor Network Traffic with the tcpdump Tool

The `tcpdump` command is a general-purpose network traffic monitor that can capture and display packets and their contents. This command can be used as a protocol analyzer, providing one of the best ways to investigate communication and/or connectivity problems among systems and networking devices. Most of the time, network troubleshooting focuses on network configuration problems and diagnosing hardware-related failures. Every once in a while, however, you will be faced with a protocol-related problem and be forced to delve into the heart of the particular networking stack to resolve the problem. With `tcpdump`, the packets scanned will be displayed with information in either a short or long format, depending on the command-line options used. Also, this command has a very powerful filtering mechanism that can search for packets that match a specific string or criteria.

Depending on the installation options selected, this command will be available on Linux by default. On Solaris, this command is available on the Solaris Companion Software CD. When tcpdump is installed from this CD, the default command path is `/opt/sfw/sbin`. For HP-UX, it must be downloaded from the Internet.

Two primary capture modes are provided by this command: promiscuous and nonpromiscuous. In promiscuous mode, every packet transmitted on the network is captured, whether or not the packet was sent to the system on which `tcpdump` is listening. This is the mode, for instance, that network probes use when monitoring network traffic. Network probes listen on the network for traffic and collect protocol information and statistics. Because local area network (LAN) protocols such as Ethernet are broadcast-based, every frame transmitted can be seen by any network interface attached to the LAN. Any device can read every frame transmitted if that device chooses and is configured to do so. When a device or interface reads every frame from the network, it is said to be in promiscuous mode. In practice, the interface must be configured for promiscuous operation and is only used on special occasions when network diagnosis is required. For this reason, only root may enable promiscuous mode on an interface. This is the primary reason that nonroot users are not permitted to invoke `tcpdump`. When the attempt is made by a nonroot user to execute the command, the following message is displayed:

```
tcpdump: socket: Operation not permitted
```

If you want to give a regular user the ability to invoke the `tcpdump` command, you can setuid the program to run as root or install and configure a program like sudo. This utility gives specific users access to privileged programs as deemed appropriate by the system administrator. See Module 7 for more information about the `sudo` command.

With nonpromiscuous mode, only broadcast frames and frames addressed to the local system will be available to the interface. The term "broadcast" actually refers to both normal broadcast (with all 1s in the destination field) and multicast traffic. Under normal circumstances, the interface is in nonpromiscuous mode.

When `tcpdump` is invoked without command-line options, it opens the primary network interface and begins capturing frames from the local network and displaying their contents. Because this command can produce a significant amount of output, the quiet option (`-q`) is used to reduce the amount of output displayed. When executed by `root`, the command

```
# tcpdump -q
```

will display all network frames (packets) in the single-line, nonverbose format. The format of the output will include a timestamp, source and destination hosts (or address), the high-level network protocol, some flags, and additional protocol information, as shown in the following example:

| timestamp | source host | destination host | packet summary |

```
tcpdump: listening on elxl1
15:41:58.055268 durer.home.com.1032 > socrates.home.com.telnet: tcp 0 (DF)
[tos0x50]
15:41:58.055446 socrates.home.com.telnet > durer.home.com.1032: tcp 28 (DF)
15:41:58.274933 durer.home.com.1032 > socrates.home.com.telnet: tcp 0 (DF)
[tos0x50]
15:41:58.275115 socrates.home.com.telnet > durer.home.com.1032: tcp 164 (DF)
15:41:58.494694 durer.home.com.1032 > socrates.home.com.telnet: tcp 0 (DF)
[tos0x50]
15:41:58.494880 socrates.home.com.telnet > durer.home.com.1032: tcp 165 (DF)
15:41:58.544828 socrates.home.com > didymus-gw2.home.com: icmp: echo request
15:41:58.545719 didymus-gw2.home.com > socrates.home.com: icmp: echo
reply5:34:10.601950 socrates.home.com.telnet > durer.home.com.1032: tcp 165
(DF)

8 packets received by filter
0 packets dropped by kernel
```

12

The output includes the time, source/destination, protocol port, protocol contained with the frame, and additional protocol information. In this example, `durer`, the source host, and `socrates`, the destination host, have a Telnet session established. We can tell this by looking at the destination port, which is Telnet. By default, tcpdump captures packets until the user interrupts the program by issuing ^c. Also, `socrates` has issued a ping request to `didymus-gw2`, and it has responded with a reply. The -> string indicates the direction of the communication path. Note that tcpdump always orients the communication path to point to the right, as in the case of the ICMP echo request above. To indicate communication in the other direction, tcpdump reverses the hosts (not the pointer), as shown with the ICMP Echo reply entry. The `tcpdump` command displays the higher-level protocols in lowercase, as in `tcp` and `icmp`, followed by more specific information pertaining to the protocol, which might include ports, additional protocol information, and data. The output also includes a summary of the number of packets obtained before the user terminated the command.

The end of the output includes a count of the number of packets captured by and the number of packets that were dropped. In this case, a total of eight packets were captured and zero packets were discarded.

The `tcpdump` tool provides a large number of command-line options to select capture modes, control output, specify filter specifications, and specify additional operating characteristics. These options are grouped according to their function and include the following categories:

- Operating modes
- Display options
- Packet filter options

Operating Modes

These options are used to control how `tcpdump` will capture and display network traffic. The available options are summarized in Table 12-1 and described fully below.

Normally, `tcpdump` will listen for traffic on the primary network interface. Usually the primary interface has the smallest numeric identifier if the system contains two or more interfaces of the same type. For example, `eth0` is considered the primary when the system contains two Ethernet interfaces: `eth0` and `eth1`. However, if you want to run `tcpdump` on a different

Option	**Description**
-c	Captures specified number of packets and then quits
-F	Uses file as source for filter expression
-I	Captures packets using alternate network interface
-p	Disables capturing in promiscuous mode
-r	Reads capture file instead of network interface
-w	Saves raw packets to file

Table 12-1 | tcpdump Operating Mode Common Options

interface, use the -i option and the device name to specify the alternate interface. For example, to select the point-to-point (ppp0) interface, use the following command:

```
# tcpdump -i ppp0
tcpdump: listening on ppp0
```

As previously indicated, tcpdump will capture packets until ^c is typed from the controlling terminal (or if placed in the background, until the process is terminated with the kill command). If you wish to specify the number of packets to be captured, use the -c option followed by a packet count value. To capture ten packets from the eth1 interface, use the following command:

socrates initiates snmp query

10 lines captured corresponds to 10 packets

```
tcpdump -t -q -i eth1 -c 10
tcpdump: listening on eth1
chips.home.com > didymus-gw2.home.com: icmp: echo request
didymus-gw2.home.com > chips.home.com: icmp: echo reply
chips.home.com > didymus-gw2.home.com: icmp: echo request
didymus-gw2.home.com > chips.home.com: icmp: echo reply
socrates.home.com.1032 > switch.home.com.snmp: udp 44
switch.home.com.snmp > socrates.home.com.1032: udp 111
socrates.home.com.1032 > switch.home.com.snmp: udp 51
switch.home.com.snmp > socrates.home.com.1032: udp 61
socrates.home.com.1032 > switch.com.snmp: udp 51
switch.com.snmp > socrates.home.com.1032: udp 54
```

12

In this case, tcpdump has captured a ping session between socrates and didymus-gw2, as detected by the first four lines. Also, socrates was querying a device called switch using SNMP, as denoted by the SNMP port and the UDP protocol used (the remaining lines). We can confirm the number of captured packets by counting the number of lines displayed. Specifying the number of packets to capture is useful when the intent is to monitor a critical network transaction that uses a fixed number of packet exchanges. This option is also useful when monitoring packets within a shell script because you don't have to be concerned about stopping tcpdump after it has been started. The -t option, which removes the packet timestamp information, was used in this example as well.

As previously indicated, tcpdump, by default, opens the network interface in promiscuous mode to capture all network traffic. Promiscuous mode means that all network traffic, regardless of the destination of the packet, will be captured. Sometimes, it is more effective to examine packets delivered to a specified host than it is to read all packets on the network. If we want to capture those packets addressed to the host that tcpdump is running on, the -p option is used to disable promiscuous mode capture. You will see later that we can tell tcpdump to capture packets coming from or going to a particular host using filters.

```
# tcpdump -p
tcpdump: listening on eth0
```

Unfortunately, the tcpdump command doesn't confirm the use of the -p option. As a result, the user has no way of knowing after the command was executed which mode it is capturing with, except to examine the output to see the destination addresses. In other words, any packet that isn't a broadcast or sent to a local address indicates that tcpdump is capturing with promiscuous mode enabled.

On a very active network or a busy system, and when using certain command-line options, tcpdump can produce a large amount of output. To help manage this, the -w option can be used to redirect the captured information into a file. One reason to use a file is to save the captured data for later inspection and analysis. This could include manipulating the data in other ways, possibly using the data to build specialized reports, and the like.

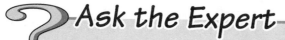

Ask the Expert

Question   Why would you disable promiscuous mode with the -p option anyway?

Answer   Sometimes it becomes necessary to examine just the traffic that arrives normally at a particular system. With this option, we can see every packet that is destined by the local system, and nothing more. This can be used to easily detect (by monitoring the incoming packets), for example, whether a request for a particular service is reaching the system. Given a client/server environment, we can determine if requests from client systems are reaching the server (by running tcpdump on the server) or if a particular client is transmitting requests in the first place (by running tcpdump on the client). It is true that we can use filters to accomplish the same thing, but it is more efficient and easier to just reduce the number of packets in the first place.

To capture network traffic and save it to a file called traffic-data, use the following command:

```
# tcpdump -w traffic-data
tcpdump: listening on eth0
```

The file, traffic-data, is created in the local directory once the command above is invoked. However, the data captured isn't written to the file until the user interrupts the program or the -c option is used. Once the user does this, the following is displayed:

```
48 packets received by filter
0 packets dropped by kernel
```

Hint

The traffic-data file created is not an ordinary text file, but rather a specially formatted data file that only tcpdump and certain other programs understand. One such program, called tcpslice, can cut out or splice different tcpdump files together.

To learn a little bit more about the `tcpdump` file, use the UNIX `file` command. If this is run against the `traffic-data` file, it reports that it is associated with the `tcpdump` command, the version of the software, and that the data contains packets that are of type Ethernet, with a frame length of 68 bytes. It is not a human-readable text file. The UNIX command

```
# file traffic-data
```

shows the following:

```
traffic-data: tcpdump capture file (little-endian) - version 2.4 (Ethernet,
capture length 68)
```

As previously mentioned, it is interesting that `tcpdump` labels the frame types that are contained with the data file. In the previous example, the label indicates that Ethernet frames are stored in this file. Additional types include raw IP, FDDI, and others. Thus, if a packet capture were done on a point-to-point link, as in the `ppp0` interface, the raw IP packet type would be displayed. If you were trying to view the file, it would appear to be a long series of strange characters. However, this file can be read by such programs as the `ethereal` tool, which provides a GUI-based approach to protocol capture and analysis.

The `tcpdump` command does a reasonable job of compressing data stored in files. For instance, over 3,000 packets consume approximately 260K worth of disk space. If you are going to save a significant amount of captured data, it may be necessary to compress the data further using either compress or gzip. The compress utility manages to reduce the size of this data file to a little over 33K, while the gzip program reduces the byte count down even more to just over 18K. Not bad from a byte size of over 260K!

To display the packets that have been saved in a data file, use the `-r` option followed by the name of the packet capture file. For instance, to replay the packets saved within the `traffic-data` file, issue the following command:

```
# tcpdump -r traffic-data
```

Display Options

These options control how `tcpdump` will display packets from the network. The list of the available options under this category is summarized in Table 12-2.

Option	Description
-e	Prints link-level header information on each line
-v	Specifies verbose mode
-q	Specifies quick mode, displays short packet information
-t	Disables printing of the timestamp
-s	Limits the size of packets captured
-x	Displays both hexadecimal and ASCII format

Table 12-2   Display Options for tcpdump

Sometimes it is useful to determine the length of data link frames. This can be helpful, for example, when investigating performance problems related to higher-level applications. The tcpdump tool provides a way to obtain the size of each frame, including both the header and data portion, with the -e command-line option. The following sample command and output show a file transfer session using FTP and ARP broadcasts:

```
# tcpdump -t -e                                        Length field
0:10:5a:28:5d:7c Broadcast arp 42: arp who-has
didymus-gw2.home.com tell socrates.home.com
0:10:5a:28:5d:7c Broadcast arp 42: arp who-has
didymus-gw2.home.com tell socrates.home.com
0:10:5a:28:5d:7c Broadcast arp 42: arp who-has
didymus-gw2.home.com tell socrates.home.com
0:10:5a:28:5d:7c 0:60:97:e:a3:6 1514: socrates.home.com.ftp-data
durer.home.com.1036: tcp 1448 (DF) [tos 0x8]
0:10:5a:28:5d:7c 0:60:97:e:a3:6 1514: socrates.home.com.ftp-data
durer.home.com.1036: tcp 1448 (DF) [tos 0x8]
```

As you can see, the length field is displayed next to the protocol, or if no protocol is shown, after the destination address. It shows the total size of the frame in bytes. The reason the packets from socrates to durer are greater than 1,500 bytes is because FTP fills the packet with as much data as it can hold. Ethernet has a data capacity of approximately 1,500 bytes, not including the header portion of the frame.

The -x option provides a way to display a hexadecimal dump of network frames. It displays link-level header information such as source and destination

12

address. Consider the series of packet exchanges when the host `rembrandt` attempts to open an FTP session to a system called `durer`. The `tcpdump` command

```
tcpdump -d le1 -x 0 tcp and port 21
```

will capture any FTP activity on the network. When this command is executed and an FTP session is started, the packets will be captured and displayed as follows:

TCP source port

Datalink destination address

Datalink source address

IP Destination Host

```
0:60:97:e:a3:6|0:10:5a:28:5d:7c|ip 78: durer.home.com.1044 >
socrates.home.com.ftp:
S 9262138:9262138(0) win 8192 <mss 1460,nop,wscale
0,nop,nop,timestamp[|tcp]
(DF) [tos 0x1d] (ttl 128, id 19970)
                        451d 0040 4e02 4000 8006 93c6 0a00 020a
                        0a00 02c9 0414 0015 008d 543a 0000 0000
                        b002 2000 a43e 0000 0204 05b4 0103 0300
                        0101 080a 0000
0:10:5a:28:5d:7c 0:60:97:e:a3:6 ip 74: socrates.home.com.ftp
durer.home.com.1044: S 1087677057:1087677057(0) ack 9262139 win 32120 <mss
1460,sackOK,timestamp> 1106589[|tcp]> (DF) (ttl 64, id 490)
                        4500 003c 01ea 4000 4006 2000 0a00 02c9
                        0a00 020a 0015 0414 40d4 a281 008d 543b
                        a012 7d78 92b7 0000 0204 05b4 0402 080a
                        0010 e29d 0000
0:60:97:e:a3:6 0:10:5a:28:5d:7c ip 66: durer.home.com.1044 >
socrates.home.com.ftp: .ack 1 win 8760 <nop,nop,timestamp 84320 1106589>
(DF) [tos 0x1d] (ttl 128,id 20226)
                        451d 0034 4f02 4000 8006 92d2 0a00 020a
                        0a00 02c9 0414 0015 008d 543b 40d4 a282
                        8010 2238 d35b 0000 0101 080a 0001 4960
                        0010 e29d
0:10:5a:28:5d:7c 0:60:97:e:a3:6 ip 163: socrates.home.com.ftp
durer.home.com.1044: P 1:98(97) ack 1 win 32120 <nop,nop,timestamp 1106595
84320> (DF) [tos 0x10] (ttl 64, id 493)
                        4510 0095 01ed 4000 4006 1f94 0a00 02c9
                        0a00 020a 0015 0414 40d4 a282 008d 543b
                        8018 7d78 b4a1 0000 0101 080a 0010 e2a3
                        0001 4960 3232
0:60:97:e:a3:6 0:10:5a:28:5d:7c ip 66: durer.home.com.1044
socrates.home.com.ftp: . ack 98 win 8663 <nop,nop,timestamp 84323 1106595>
(DF) [tos 0x1d] (ttl 128, id 20994)
                        451d 0034 5202 4000 8006 8fd2 0a00 020a
                        0a00 02c9 0414 0015 008d 543b 40d4 a2e3
                        8010 21d7 d352 0000 0101 080a 0001 4963
                        0010 e2a3
```

Please note that some unwanted information has been manually removed from the output to make it more readable.

As you can see, the output shows a summary lines that contains the Datalink Source Address, Datalink Destination Address, Highlevel Protocol, Frame Size, IP Source Host, TCP Source Port, IP Destination Host, and TCP Destination Port in the first packet in the preceding example.

After the TCP destination port, we see the TCP packet flags. These map to the standard TCP packet types listed in Module 10. The S indicates that the packet is a SYN, or start of a TCP connection, while the P means it is a push of data. The ack indicates an acknowledgment. The next part of the listing shows the entire frame in hexadecimal. Unfortunately, it doesn't do a good job of showing us the ASCII version of the frame where appropriate. For instance, when a user starts an FTP session to a host, some valuable information is displayed along with a login prompt:

```
# ftp Socrates
220 socrates.home.com FTP server (Version wu-2.4.2-VR17(1) Mon Apr 19 09:21:53 E
DT 1999) ready.
Name (socrates:root):
```

This information is contained within the frames shown above, but tcpdump doesn't show us this information in ASCII.

Using Packet Filters

One very important aspect of network protocol debugging involves the use of packet filters. A packet filter is a predefined pattern that is compared to incoming packets and consists of a series of one or more primitives that may be combined with operators such as and, or, and not. When the pattern is matched, that packet is captured and displayed, or else the packet is discarded and not displayed. Packet filters are useful in searching for a particular protocol type or any other specific information available within the packet. We first used a packet filter in the previous example by telling tcpdump that we were interested in displaying packets that were related to a file transfer.

The tcpdump command supports user-defined packet filters. A filter is installed by tcpdump when a filter expression is given on the command line. This filter is placed in memory and will filter according to the rules that have been defined using the keywords and primitives. Every packet is compared to the filter, and when a match is found, the packet is displayed. Otherwise, the packet is discarded. Figure 4-1 shows a high-level overview of a packet filter.

12

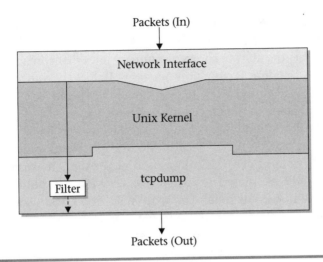

Packets (In)

Network Interface

Unix Kernel

tcpdump

Filter

Packets (Out)

Figure 12-1   Packet filter diagram

Normally, network packets are read from the network interface by the associated driver on behalf of the kernel. Next, tcpdump requests the information from the kernel using system calls. The tcpdump tool provides a large number of predefined expressions or primitives that can be used to build very powerful packet filters. These expressions can be divided into three groups. The first group, called address primitives, operates on packets using address information such as IP or data link addresses; the second group, known as protocol primitives, operates on packets that use different protocols, including IP, AppleTalk, and others. The final group includes Boolean and arithmetic primitives (or operators) that can be used with the first two expression types to produce compound filters. Compound filters include more than one expression type separated by reserve words such as and, not, and or. These filters can also include arithmetic operators such as +, -, *, and others. These expressions are evaluated to be either true or false, and the result will determine what action tcpdump will take. A description of the primitives follows.

Address Primitives

Expressions that operate on the addressing portions of a packet are listed in Table 12-3 and described in more detail next.

Primitive	Description
gateway	Selects packets that have been used by a specified host acting as a gateway
host ipaddr	Select packets from a specified host or IP address
etheraddr	Selects packets from either IP or data link addresses
broadcast	Selects broadcast packets that contain all 1s or Fs in either source or destination fields
multicast	Selects packets that are sent to multicast addresses
net	Selects packets that contain specified network portions used with the IP protocol
port	Selects packets that contain specified port addresses used with the IP protocol

Table 12-3   Address-Related Primitives

The `gateway` primitive selects packets that have been forwarded by a router. This indicates that the data link address of the packet (either source or destination) matches that of the router, while the IP address matches that of the host. Normally, a router will not change the IP address information when forwarding packets, but the data link address will match the device that forwards the packet.

The `host` primitive followed by a valid hostname can select packets that are either sent to or received from the specified hostname. The `host` keyword is mainly used to avoid ambiguity that might arise if you were to specify a hostname that just happens to be the same as one of the `tcpdump` existing keywords. For example, when monitoring the host called `gateway`, the `host` keyword must be used because the `gateway` keyword will be interpreted as a keyword rather than as a valid hostname. Thus, the `tcpdump` command listed next produces an error because the `gateway` string is assumed to specify a local gateway:

```
# tcpdump gateway
tcpdump: parse error
```

The way to specify the capture of packets from a host called `gateway` would be the following:

```
# tcpdump host gateway
```

12

The `ipaddr` and `etheraddr` options specify actual IP addresses and data link addresses in dotted and colon formats, respectively. For example, to capture all packets from the IP address 10.0.2.100, the following command would be used:

```
# tcpdump ipaddr 10.0.2.100
```

The `ipaddr` and `etheraddr` primitives will match either the source or destination address. Some data link addresses begin with a letter and will cause `tcpdump` to misinterpret these as hostnames rather than true addresses. To avoid this problem, insert a zero in front when specifying these types of addresses.

To capture broadcast packets, use the `broadcast` primitive. A broadcast is a special address that designates that all devices should receive the message. Several network protocols and services such as ARP, NIS, and RIP use broadcasts to propagate information across the network. Using broadcast will result in the capture of broadcast packets from the data link level. This means that any address that contains 255 or FF values within the source or destination field will be captured. This includes data link packets that contain broadcasts (such as ARP requests) and high-level protocol broadcasts (such as an IP broadcast). This primitive could be used to capture routing data from the Routing Information Protocol (RIP) because routers periodically broadcast routing updates.

Also, to obtain multicast traffic such as Internet radio, use the multicast primitive. The standard multicast address of 224.0.0.1 supports this type of traffic as defined by the multicast standard. Additional addresses (both physical or IP) can be used at your site. It may be necessary to determine the exact multicast addresses before you start filtering these types of packets.

Protocol Primitives

The `tcpdump` application provides protocol primitives as a shorthand way to select specific network traffic, without requiring or knowing the low-level protocol information. For example, the `ip` primitive can be used to capture all IP traffic. Without this keyword, you would need to use the IP type of `x0800`, which is harder to remember. These primitives support the TCP/IP, AppleTalk, and DECnet family of protocols. Table 12-4 lists and describes these protocol keywords.

Protocol Primitive	Description
apple	AppleTalk protocol family
arp	Address Resolution Protocol—includes both request and reply
fddi	FDDI data link protocol
ethertype	Another protocol type (used with a type code)
decnet	DECnet protocol family
ip	Internet Protocol
icmp	Internet Control Message Protocol—includes both echo and reply
rarp	Reverse Address Resolution Protocol—includes both request and reply
tcp	Transmission Control Protocol
udp	User Datagram Protocol

Table 12-4   Protocol Primitives Supported by tcpdump

To select a protocol family or type that isn't provided directly by tcpdump, use the ethertype primitive along with the type code for the desired protocol. For example, to monitor Novell NetWare packets, which have a type code of 0x8137, use the following command:

```
# tcpdump ethertype 0x8137
```

Please note that because tcpdump doesn't support the Novell protocol family directly, no packet information can be displayed beyond the data link layer. If tcpdump finds packets that contain a Novell header, it will list the data link information only. However, despite this disadvantage, tcpdump is still useful for identifying certain packet types and providing rudimentary packet count information.

Operators

The tcpdump command supports several expression (or operator) types and can be combined with primitives and qualifiers to produce compound filters.

12

These expressions include the arithmetic and Boolean operators listed in Table 12-5. Operators can build powerful expressions to search for specific packets. Expressions can be composed of numbers, packet field selections, length primitives, and arithmetic operators. To use the value of a field in an expression within a packet, use the following syntax:

```
primitive [offset [: size] ]
```

where the word `primitive` is replaced with ether, `ip`, `udp`, `tcp`, or `icmp`. The offset is used in the base of the protocol primitive, and the size specifies the length of the field. If not supplied, they default to 1.

Packet field sections can be used in a variety of ways. Consider the following example:

```
tcpdump "ether[1:4]&0xffffffff = 0xffffffff"
```

In this example, `tcpdump` will display all broadcast packets transmitted on the local network—this means all frames with a destination address of all

Operator	Description
>	Greater than
<	Less than
>=	Greater than or equal to
<=	Less than or equal to
=	Equal to
!=	Not equal
+	Plus
–	Minus
*	Multiply
/	Divide
&	Bitwise AND
|	Bitwise inclusive OR
^	Bitwise exclusive OR
and or &&	Concatenation
or or ||	Alternation
not or !	Negation

Table 12-5   tcpdump Arithmetic Operators

1s (255 in decimal, 0xff in hexadecimal). The 1 in `ether[1:4]` indicates the first addressable byte of the frame (the destination address), and the 4 value specifies the length of this field. Despite the fact that Ethernet addresses are six bytes, we can examine the first four bytes to determine if it is a broadcast address.

To display all packets that originate from a particular Sun system, for example, use this command:

```
tcpdump "ether[6:4]&0xffffffff = 0x08002004"
```

This tells tcpdump to examine the sixth byte of the frame (the source frame address) and compare it to the 0x08002004 addresses using the & (and) operator. This data link address represents the address of a local system called `monet`. Recall that Ethernet addresses are six bytes in length, and we can use the first four bytes to identify the system desired. As a result, all packets transmitted from `monet` will be displayed. To identify another system, obtain the data link address of the system, convert it to hexadecimal, and place it on the right side of the preceding command.

Miscellaneous Primitives

A few additional primitives are also available from tcpdump that can't be classified as either address or protocol primitives. These include the following:

- greater
- less
- length

The `greater` and `less` primitives are used in conjunction with other tcpdump commands to filter, based on the total length of the packet. For example, to display all packets that are greater than 56 bytes, invoke the following command:

```
# tcpdump greater 56
```

To display all packets that are less than 60 bytes, use the `less` primitive:

```
# tcpdump -x less 60
```

12

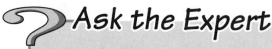

Ask the Expert

Question   Why would you use the `greater` or `less` commands?

Answer   The primary reason is to search for packets based on size, rather than content. Another primitive, `length`, can also be used to handle capturing packets based on their exact size. The length can be used when the need to capture packets is based on some calculation. For example, the following command will display any packet that is not equal to 56:

```
# tcpdump length != 56
```

This command will display all frames that are less than 60 bytes. For instance, ARP (Address Resolution Protocol) request frames are smaller than 60 bytes. Executing this command will display any ARP messages, as shown here:

```
tcpdump: listening on eth0
23:45:29.240364 arp who-has durer.home.com tell socrates.home.com
0001 0800 0604 0001 0010 5a28 5d7c 0a00
02c9 0000 0000 0000 0a00 020a
```

Qualifiers

Three qualifiers may be used in conjunction with the primitives listed in the preceding tables. A qualifier can further define search characteristics to pinpoint specific network traffic. These qualifiers include the following:

- `from` or `src`
- `to` or `dst`

The `from` and `src` qualifiers are used with the `host`, `net`, `ipaddr`, `etheraddr`, `port`, or `rpc` primitives to filter based on a specific destination address or network port. The qualifiers `to` or `dst` modify the primitives just mentioned, but will result in the captured packets going to a particular address or port. The `ether` modifier resolves a name to a data link address when used with the `host` primitive. To illustrate the use of the `host` keyword, let's suppose we want to capture traffic from a particular host only. The following `tcpdump` command could be used:

```
# tcpdump from host monet
```

Contrast the command above with the following:

```
# tcpdump host monet
```

In the latter example, all the traffic involving `monet`, which includes packets being sent to and received from `monet`, will be displayed. In the former example, only traffic received from `monet` will be displayed. As you can see, this can make a big difference when attempting to isolate a network problem.

Tcpdump Command Examples

Listed below are command examples and associated descriptions of actual `tcpdump` command syntax. It is hoped that these commands will provide a quick reference on using `tcpdump` in real-world situations.

```
tcpcumpd -w data-file host 216.155.43.1
```

Captures traffic sent or received by the host with the IP address of 216.155.43.1 and saves that packet information to the file called. `data-file`.

```
tcpdump host barney
```

Will capture and display traffic sent from or delivered to the system called `barney`. This command examines both the source and destination address fields of the IP header.

```
tcpdump host not barney
```

Will capture and display traffic from all hosts on the network, except the system called `barney`.

```
tcpdump host barney and host fred and \ (not pebbles\)
```

12

Will capture and display traffic from hosts `barney` and `fred`, but not from the system called `pebbles`. The parentheses were added to make the command more readable. However, each of the `tcpdump` arithmetical and Boolean operators has precedence and the parentheses can be used to define command interpretation ordering.

Hint

Because the parentheses are special to some shells, they must be escaped using the backslash (\).

```
tcpdump arp
```

Will capture and display all Address Resolution Protocol (ARP) packets. This includes both requests and replies.

```
tcpdump host durer and tcp
```

Will capture and display all Transmission Control Protocol (TCP) packets from/to the host `durer`.

```
tcpdump host vectra and port 23
```

Will capture and display all packets using port 23 from or to host `vectra`. This amounts to inspecting all Telnet packets going to this system from others on the network. Recall that port 23 is the Telnet service port for all incoming packets.

```
tcpdump ether multicast
```

Will capture and display multicast packets. See the next command for alternatives.

```
tcpdump 'ip[16] >= 224'
```

Will capture and display all packets that use the multicast address. This command compares the 16th byte (which is the destination address) of the IP packet to the value of 224. This prefix is for the standard multicast address of 224.0.0.1, which means all hosts within the default multicast group.

```
tcpdump 'ether[0] & 1 = 1'
```

Will capture and display all broadcast packets. The sequence ether[0] provides access to the first field of the Ethernet data link destination field and is compared to the value of 1. If the destination fields contain all 1s (which will be true if broadcast address, when expressed in binary) and when the and (&) operator is applied to a positive value, it will yield a value of 1. In this case, the expression is true and the packets are displayed.

```
tcpdump 'ip[2:2] > 512'
```

Will capture and display all IP packets that are larger than 512 bytes. The sequence ip[2:2] identifies the second byte of the IP header (which is the size of the packet) and compares this value of 512. The 2: indicates the offset of the IP packet, while the remaining 2 is the number of bytes within that field.

1-Minute Drill

● When reading tcpdump output, what direction is the communication between the source and destination oriented in the output lines?

● What are the three main groups of predefined expressions or primitives for filtering tcpdump results?

● The source and destination are always read left to right and indicated by the > character. If the communication direction between systems is reversed, the source and host will swap order on the output line and you still read left to right.
● Address, protocol, operators.

12

12.2 Execute the traceroute Command to Show Network Connectivity

The traceroute command examines and records the path to a specified network destination. Within a traditional IP network, one or more routers are used to provide connectivity between different IP networks. IP routers come in different shapes and sizes, from a simple multi-homed UNIX system with two interfaces to an industrial-strength Cisco router series that contains a large number of interfaces. In each of these cases, the routing function is primarily the same; it forwards IP packets from one interface to another based on established routing information.

The traceroute command uses the Time-To-Live (TTL) field contained within an IP packet and attempts to obtain an ICMP TIME_EXCEEDED message from each host along the route to the destination. Coupled with an attempt to attach to the destination at an unreachable port, it will cause a systematic response from every router along the path to the ultimate destination. It accomplishes this task by sending out requests (or probes) with a TTL of 1 and increases the TTL by 1 until it either reaches the desired host or exceeds the maximum TTL value. By default, the TTL is set to 30 hops, but this can be changed.

This command has a large number of command-line options, but the only required argument is either a hostname or an IP address of the destination. For example, to display the IP path between the local system running traceroute and the destination system called vermeer, issue the following command:

```
# traceroute vermeer
```

Figures 12-2 and 12-3 show a sample network that consists of one router and two network nodes. When the above traceroute command is executed on monet, the following output will be displayed:

```
# traceroute Vermeer
traceroute to vermeer (128.197.2.200), 30 hops max, 40 byte packets
 1  Router-Z (10.0.2.129)  4.256 ms *  2.899 ms
 2  vermeer (128.197.2.200)  7.340 ms  7.433 ms  7.526 ms
```

By default, `traceroute` sends a total of three probes, each with a different TTL value, to every hop. The first line of the output includes the destination along with the IP address, the default number of hops used, and the size of the packets being sent. The second line (with a 1) displays the first hop encountered by traceroute (see Figure 12-2).

Because `vermeer` is on a different physical network than `monet`, a router must be used to reach this system. Because the default router in this example is `Router-Z`, the first packet is sent there. The first packet sent is an ICMP request packet with the TTL field set to 1. With IP, any packet that reaches the router decrements the TTL by 1, which makes it zero. When a router gets a packet and the TTL is zero, it is supposed to discard the packet and notify the sender. This forces the router to respond with a `TIME_EXCEEDED` message back to `monet`. After this happens, `traceroute` measures the amount of time between when it sent the packet and when it obtained the reply. This is known as the round-trip time, or RTT, and is displayed in milliseconds (1,000th of a second) as shown after the hostname and IP address information. This implies that the RTT of the first series of probe packets took 4.25 milliseconds (or .004 seconds), and the third series took 2.89 milliseconds (or .028 seconds).

The second line details the second routing hop and shows that `traceroute` reached the destination system `vermeer` with slower RTT times than the first (see Figure 12-3). When the second probe was sent, the router decremented the

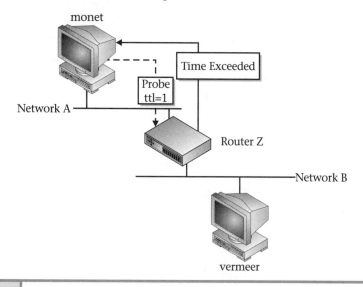

Figure 12-2   Using traceroute with single hop in network

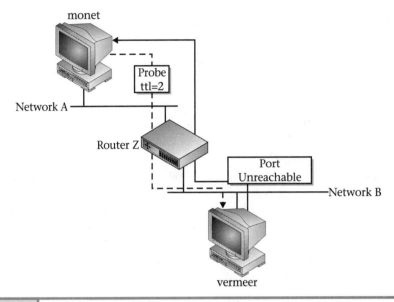

Figure 12-3 Using traceroute with two hops in network

TTL, and then passed this packet to `vermeer`. Because traceroute is attempting to access an unused port, `vermeer` responds with the `PORT UNREACHABLE` error. In fact, as a general rule on large (and sometimes small) networks, performance between systems and networks can (and will) vary a significant amount even from one moment to the next.

There is no restriction on what constitutes a destination; it can be any kind of device that ranges from a simple host system to an Internet router. The only requirement is that it must support IP.

Reading Output

Due to variations and problems with router devices along certain paths, the general fluctuations of network routes can lead to unpredictable and strange `traceroute` output. As a result, certain codes might appear after the timing information is displayed. Table 12-6 lists these codes and their associated meanings.

Code	Meaning
*	No response to probe packets.
!	TTL in the received packet is set to 1.
!H	Destination host is unreachable.
!N	Destination network is unreachable.
!P	Destination protocol is unreachable.
!S	The source route option has failed. In practice, this shouldn't happen, and if it does, it indicates a bug or problem with the router that generated the error.
!F	Fragmentation was needed for a probe packet. In practice, this shouldn't happen, and if it does, it indicates a bug or problem with the router that generated the error.
!X	The path is blocked due to communication being disabled from an administrative standpoint. In other words, the path is shut down or blocked from a software standpoint.
!N>	An ICMP error code where N is that number.

Table 12-6 Display Codes for Traceroute

Some of these display codes come in handy when you debug network problems. For example, if a destination is not reachable (like www.whitehouse.gov) by the system that is running the traceroute command, executing

```
monet# traceroute www.whitehouse.gov
```

will produce

```
traceroute to www.whitehouse.gov (198.137.240.91), 30 hops max, 40 byte
packets
1  monet (10.0.2.126)  4.281 ms !N *  1.896 ms !N
```

In this example, the network 198.137.240 can't be reached from the local system, and traceroute displays the error string !N to indicate this problem. In this particular case, monet can't send any packets to 198.137.240 because no route to that network exists. The * means that the particular probe packet never received a response; the * is used as a time-out indicator. To further

12

verify these results, use the `ping` command with the same destination. Thus, the command

```
monet# ping www.whitehouse.gov
```

will show the same problem, except the error is a little more descriptive:

```
ICMP Net Unreachable from gateway monet (10.0.2.126)
for icmp from monet (10.0.2.126) to www.whitehouse.gov
```

In the same way, both `!H` and `!P` error codes are also used to debug general network problems. However, in these two cases `!H` reports when a host is unreachable and the `!P` reports when the protocol is unreachable. The host unreachable message will be displayed, for example, when the network is also unreachable.

Given the fact that at any point in time the performance or RTT between networks and systems can change significantly, a trace to the Web site of the Louvre Museum first reveals the following:

```
# traceroute 198.137.240.91
traceroute to 198.137.240.91 (198.137.240.91), 30 hops max, 40 byte packets
 1   10.0.2.76 (10.0.2.76)  19.906 ms   9.801 ms   8.174 ms
 2   199.70.195.38 (199.70.195.38)  197.460 ms  188.000 ms  181.029 ms
 3   12.77.194.1 (12.77.194.1)  166.802 ms  184.713 ms  185.857 ms
 4   12.127.12.205 (12.127.12.205)  245.026 ms  270.253 ms  266.718 ms
 5   12.127.15.145 (12.127.15.145)  215.191 ms  211.920 ms  208.979 ms
 6   192.205.31.165 (192.205.31.165)  217.875 ms  232.610 ms  222.274 ms
 7   204.6.117.65 (204.6.117.65)  266.797 ms  239.000 ms  215.671 ms
 8   38.1.4.69 (38.1.4.69)  235.431 ms  225.447 ms  301.119 ms
 9   38.1.25.5 (38.1.25.5)  235.369 ms  236.134 ms  263.557 ms
10   38.1.25.5 (38.1.25.5)  252.172 ms  238.984 ms  263.013 ms
11   38.146.148.45 (38.146.148.45)  241.956 ms  248.091 ms  243.300 ms
12   198.137.240.33 (198.137.240.33)  249.361 ms  228.717 ms  252.927 ms
13   198.137.240.91 (198.137.240.91)  238.799 ms  259.967 ms  236.384 ms
```

When the trace is repeated later, it shows the following:

```
traceroute to 198.137.240.91 (198.137.240.91), 30 hops max, 40 byte packets
 1   10.0.2.76 (10.0.2.76)  7.619 ms   5.863 ms   6.206 ms
 2   199.70.195.42 (199.70.195.42)  177.685 ms  177.691 ms  177.842 ms
 3   12.77.242.129 (12.77.242.129)  170.712 ms  177.096 ms  173.517 ms
 4   12.127.12.205 (12.127.12.205)  260.239 ms  248.072 ms  252.829 ms
 5   12.127.15.145 (12.127.15.145)  219.767 ms  215.645 ms  232.399 ms
```

```
 6  192.205.31.165 (192.205.31.165)  232.259 ms  225.243 ms  219.236 ms
 7  204.6.117.65 (204.6.117.65)  228.997 ms  218.067 ms  219.365 ms
 8  38.1.4.69 (38.1.4.69)  445.758 ms  232.797 ms  276.249 ms  ◀─── Significant
 9  38.1.25.5 (38.1.25.5)  245.674 ms  443.611 ms  577.309 ms  ◀─── RTT delays
10  38.1.25.5 (38.1.25.5)  432.994 ms  222.527 ms  242.844 ms
11  38.146.148.45 (38.146.148.45)  257.668 ms  249.923 ms  263.074 ms ◀───
12  198.137.240.33 (198.137.240.33)  276.658 ms  242.361 ms *
13  198.137.240.91 (198.137.240.91)  248.266 ms  245.006 ms  251.071 ms
```

As you can see, most of the response times are very close. However, significant delays can be observed with hops 8, 9, and 11. In these cases, the RTT is almost doubled, which further indicates that performance on a large routed network (such as the Internet) can and does vary over time.

Changing Characteristics

The traceroute command contains a number of operational parameters that can be used to affect how it traces a path to the specified destination. Each of these parameters has an associated command-line option that can alter its default values. Table 12-7 lists these options.

Option	Meaning
-I	Specifies an alternate interface
-p	Sets the alternate port to send probe packets
-g	Specifies a router for loose source routing
-f	Sets the initial TTL value to be used (Linux only)
-s	Uses the specified address as the source address in transmitting probe packets
-q	Sets the number of probe queries
-m	Sets the maximum hops
-d	Enables debug flag (SO_DEBUG)—this enables socket-level debugging
-F	Specifies not to fragment
-t	Sets the type of service (TOS) flag
-w	Sets the wait time for probe packets
-x	Specifies not to calculate checksums
-v	Enable verbose mode

Table 12-7   traceroute Operational Command-Line Options

12

When the `traceroute` command is executed on a system that is multi-homed (that is, a system that contains more than one network interface), it selects the first interface it encounters. Unfortunately, this might not be the desired action because the destination network can only be accessed from another interface. To address this issue, the `-i` option can be used to force `traceroute` to send probe packets using the interface specified with this option. Thus, the command

```
traceoute -i hem0
traceroute: Warning: Multiple interfaces found; using 10.0.2.126 @ hme0
```

will cause traceroute to use the Fast Ethernet interface instead of the default interface.

In certain situations, the default TTL value of 30 is not enough to reach a destination that might contain a larger number of routes. When this occurs, traceroute will never reach the destination. In this situation, use the -m option to increase the hop count.

When you do a traceroute to certain devices, it might sometimes fail, despite the fact that the path to the device is operational. Further, using the `ping` command against the device will indicate that it is working correctly as well. Why? Before we answer this question, let's look at an example:

```
# traceroute -m 5 128.197.2.200
traceroute to 128.197.2.200 (128.197.2.200), 5 hops max, 40 byte packets
1  rodin (10.0.2.129)  10.193 ms *  2.158 ms
2  * * *
3  * * *
4  * * *
5  * * *
```

This traceroute produces no response to the probe packets. Note the use of the -m option to keep the number of probe packets small.

The answer to this problem lies in the fact that, by default, `traceroute` sends probe packets based on the UDP protocol. It is most likely that the destination in question does not support this protocol directly or can't handle the UDP destination port used. Also, there could be a firewall device that is blocking the probe packets. From a TCP/IP standpoint, not all devices are required to support UDP, and if they do support UDP, they do not necessarily support the port number used by `traceroute`.

When `traceroute` sends out probe packets, it uses, by default, the UDP port of 33434 and assumes that this port isn't being used by any other application or network service. It uses this high port number in hopes that the destination will respond with a port unreachable message, thus terminating the route tracing. On the other hand, if that port is being used, it will cause problems for `traceroute`. If this happens, use the -p option followed by another port number, and `traceroute` will use that port instead of the default.

```
# traceroute -p 10 -m 5 128.197.2.200
traceroute to 128.197.2.200 (128.197.2.200), 5 hops max, 40 byte packets
1  rodin (10.0.2.129)  10.193 ms *  2.158 ms
2  * * *
3  * * *
4  * * *
5  * * *
```

If this still doesn't do the trick, attempt to use the -I option, which will instruct traceroute to use the ICMP protocol instead of UDP when sending probe packets. So, the command

```
monet# traceroute -m 5 -I 128.197.2.200
```

with the -I option produces the correct results:

```
traceroute to 128.197.2.200 (128.197.2.200), 5 hops max, 40 byte packets
1  rodin (10.0.2.129)  4.412 ms *  2.235 ms
2  vermeer (128.197.2.200)  6.875 ms  6.955 ms  6.935 ms
```

As you can see, this took a bit of trial and error to obtain the desired result. However, this is not a contrived example; rather, `vermeer` represents an actual device—a laser printer. The real point here is that when tracing the route to a particular destination, there can be many reasons why `traceroute` fails to reach a destination. Failure might not mean that the device is down or disconnected from the network.

Display Options

Two options are available to modify the output of `traceroute`. The first, -v, displays for each hop the size and destination of the response packets. The following shows an example:

```
# traceroute -v rembrandt
traceroute to rembrandt (10.0.2.75), 30 hops max, 40 byte packets
1  rembrandt (10.0.2.75) 56 bytes to 10.0.2.1 3.450 ms 2.085 ms  2.094 ms
```

12

The second option, -n, displays addresses in numerical form rather than using the symbolic name. This removes the added task from traceroute of having to resolve each router's hostname.

12.3 Verify Basic Operations Using the landiag Command

The landiag command, which is available only on HP-UX, provides a quick and easy way to test and verify basic operations of the local network interfaces on the system.

To run the command, use the following:

```
# landiag
```

As a result, the following output will be displayed:

```
        LOCAL AREA NETWORK ONLINE ADMINISTRATION, Version 1.0
                    Sat, Feb 9,2002  18:02:05

            Copyright 1994 Hewlett Packard Company.
                    All rights are reserved.
Test Selection mode.

        lan     = LAN Interface Administration
        menu    = Display this menu
        quit    = Terminate the Administration
        terse   = Do not display command menu
        verbose = Display command menu

Enter command:
```

A list of menu items is presented to the administrator. To review additional features for LAN interfaces, type the lan command and the following will be shown:

```
LAN Interface test mode. LAN Interface PPA Number = 0

        clear   = Clear statistics registers
        display = Display LAN Interface status and statistics registers
        end     = End LAN Interface Administration, return to Test Sele
        menu    = Display this menu
        ppa     = PPA Number of the LAN Interface
        quit    = Terminate the Administration, return to shell
        reset   = Reset LAN Interface to execute its selftest

Enter command:
```

Use the `display` option to show detailed information about the configuration and operation state of the system interfaces:

```
                    LAN INTERFACE STATUS DISPLAY
                    Sat, Feb 9,2002  18:02:36

PPA Number                         = 0
Description                        = lan0 Hewlett-Packard 10/100 TX Full-Duplex Manual TT = 1
500
Type (value)                       = ethernet-csmacd(6)
MTU Size                           = 1500
Speed                              = 100000000
Station Address                    = 0x306e060662
Administration Status (value)      = up(1)
Operation Status (value)           = up(1)
Last Change                        = 21486
Inbound Octets                     = 3271707541
Inbound Unicast Packets            = 338351587
Inbound Non-Unicast Packets        = 6257857
Inbound Discards                   = 0
Inbound Errors                     = 60
Inbound Unknown Protocols          = 256
Outbound Octets                    = 1179449614
Outbound Unicast Packets           = 312586275
Outbound Non-Unicast Packets       = 167
Outbound Discards                  = 0
Outbound Errors                    = 0
Outbound Queue Length              = 0
Specific                           = 655367

Press <Return> to continue
Ethernet-like Statistics Group

Index                              = 1
Alignment Errors                   = 0
FCS Errors                         = 0
Single Collision Frames            = 0
Multiple Collision Frames          = 0
Deferred Transmissions             = 0
Late Collisions                    = 0
Excessive Collisions               = 0
Internal MAC Transmit Errors       = 0
Carrier Sense Errors               = 0
Frames Too Long                    = 0
Internal MAC Receive Errors        = 0
```

Due to the length of the output, the administrator is prompted to continue to display the information. The command output above reveals important information about the configuration of the interface. For instance, the type of Ethernet hardware is shown in the description field. Also, important statistics are shown such as the number of bytes read (`Inbound Octets`) and written (`Outbound Octets`) on the network.

12

Project 12-1

This project familiarizes you with using `tcpdump` and `traceroute` on your system.

Step-by-Step

1. Use the `tcpdump` command, configured in nonpromiscuous mode, to capture all the packets to your system's Web port 80.

```
# tcpdump -p port 80
```

2. Open a Web browser and let it load your default home page.

3. Switch to the `tcpdump` window and examine its output.

4. In the Web browser, navigate to another Web site such as `www.whitehouse.gov` and again examine the output in the `tcpdump` window.

5. Stop the `tcpdump` capture with ^c.

6. Perform a `traceroute` without converting the addresses to hostnames from your system to each of these systems: `sans.org` and `cert.org`.

```
# traceroute -d sans.org
# traceroute -d cert.org
```

7. Examine the number of hops in the output for each to see which of these sites your system is more closely connected to on the Internet. Also, compare them to see if the RTT values for one are significantly slower than the other. You can use this method to compare other resources—for example, if you are considering a hosting provider and want to see how well connected you are to their server compared to another server.

☑ *Mastery Check*

1. What is the `tcpdump` command to run in quiet mode capturing 15 packets from the `ppp0` interface?

2. True or False: By default, nonroot users are not permitted to invoke `tcpdump`.

3. The _____ command examines and records the path to a specified network destination.

4. What is the command to display `tcpdump` data captured to a file named `dump-data`?

   A. `file dump-data`

   B. `tcpdump -r dump-data`

   C. `tcpdump -F dump-data`

   D. `tcpdump -x dump-data`

5. Which of the following is not an address primitive for `tcpdump` filtering?

   A. `etheraddr`

   B. `ipaddr`

   C. `ethertype`

   D. `port`

6. What is the `tcpdump` syntax to capture traffic from all hosts on the network, except the system called `fred`?

7. The _____ primitives group operates on packets that use different protocols including IP, TCP, FDDI, UDP, and others.

8. What is the command to display the IP path between the local system and the destination system called `barney`?

9. What is the command to display the IP path between the local system and the destination system called `www.whitehouse.gov` using a maximum of 20 hops?

12

☑ Mastery Check

10. In the LAN Interface Test Mode of the HP-UX command, what is the command to show detailed information about the configuration and operation state of the system interfaces?

A. display

B. lan

C. ppa

D. interface

11. What tcpdump address primitive filter selects packets that contain all 1s or Fs in either source or destination fields?

12. True or False: The only restriction for a traceroute destination is that the device must support TCP/IP.

Module 13

Overview of SNMP

Critical Skills

The Simple Network Management Protocol (SNMP) provides the low-level framework for many network management systems. SNMP is widely implemented and can be found in a large variety of different networking devices and systems. Today, SNMP is considered the management protocol of choice for system administrators, network hardware vendors, network management vendors, software application developers, and many others that are required to manage UNIX and other networked systems.

SNMP is popular for several reasons and continues to be enhanced as time goes on. SNMP is simple to implement compared to other network management architectures or protocols. The protocol, MIBs, and associated framework can be run on anything from low-end personal computers (PCs) to high-end mainframes, servers, and network devices such as routers and switches. An SNMP agent component doesn't need to occupy a large footprint in terms of memory and doesn't require significant processing power. SNMP can generally be developed very quickly on target systems, thus increasing the time to market for new products and enhancements. When SNMP was first introduced, other management mechanisms were available, but SNMP proved to be more flexible and easier to implement. It is true that SNMP lacks certain features found in other network management protocols (such as OSI, for example), but its simple design, extensibility, and ease of use minimize any possible drawbacks.

SNMP is free and in the public domain. As a result, no single vendor can claim ownership of the protocol, nor can it be copy protected by any company or individual. The only way to influence or change SNMP is to engage in the standards process of the Internet Engineering Task Force (IETF). The IETF is one of the standards bodies for the Internet. Vendors may choose to make proprietary changes to SNMP. Such changes may prove futile, however, because these vendors must lobby other vendors and users to support their nonstandard enhancements, which defeats the purpose of having a standard in the first place.

SNMP is well documented (via RFCs, articles, and textbooks) and well understood in the networking and systems industry. This provides an established foundation for continued enhancement and adoption. Finally, SNMP can be used to control a variety of devices. It is even finding its way into nontraditional equipment such as telephone systems, environmental control equipment, and just about anything else that can be attached to a network and requires management or control.

13.1 Discover SNMP Basics

SNMP defines the packet format and information exchange between a network manager and associated agents. At its core, SNMP manipulates objects within the MIB of the agent and, as a result, can manage a variety of tasks defined within the agent. The SNMP protocol and related components are described in a number of RFCs. Any SNMP-compliant agent can communicate with any network management system that supports SNMP. The management system is responsible for asking questions of the agents. This is also known as "polling the agent." If the agent supports standard MIBs, then the management system simply requests one or more objects from the agent. If the agent supports nonstandard MIBs (that is, vendor-specific MIBs), the manager must have a copy of the agent MIB to correctly interpret the supported agent objects.

One of the reasons SNMP is considered simple is because it provides three general-purpose operations that can be applied to agent objects. These operations, or functions, are at the heart of SNMP; they are *set*, *get*, and *trap*:

- **Set** A management system may update or change the value of an object that is contained in an agent. The set operation is a privileged command because, for example, it can be used to alter a device configuration or control its operating state.

- **Get** A management system may obtain or read the value of an object that is contained within an agent. The get function is the most common SNMP operation because this is the primary mechanism used to obtain management information from devices.

- **Trap** An agent may send an unsolicited message to a network manager. The purpose of the trap service is to notify a network management system of a special condition or problem without the management system specifically requesting this information.

SNMP defines the relationship and message flow between manager and agent with respect to communications, as shown in Figure 13-1. As you can see, in most instances the SNMP manager directs the message exchange with the agent. This is accomplished via either the get or set function. A management application requests information; the message is translated to SNMP using the SNMP layer, passed to the network interface layer, and eventually transmitted

13

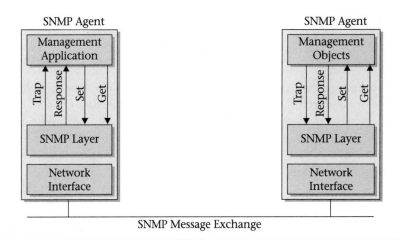

Figure 13-1 Relationship of SNMP agent and manager

on the network. The agent receives the message on the network interface layer, passes the message to the SNMP for translation, and accesses the desired object information. The reverse process is used when the agent sends the reply to the manager.

SNMP provides the ability for the agent to send the manager asynchronous messages without specifically being polled. This is known as a *trap*. The trap provides a convenient and important way for agents to communicate without specifically being asked, and also to communicate important information, or special circumstances or events.

SNMP doesn't define any additional mechanisms outside of the above-listed SNMP commands to control or issue commands to device agents. The only actions that can be applied to MIB objects are to set or get a value. For instance, there is no reboot function defined in SNMP. Instead, agent software can implement specific commands by associating MIB objects with the internal commands supported within the device. To reboot a device, the management station would alter (via the set operation) a specific MIB object to 1, for example. This would signal the agent to reboot the device and reset the MIB reboot object to its previous state. Note that no standard set of interfaces (or MIB objects) are currently available that can manipulate all aspects of device control. Instead, each vendor is responsible for providing this access using his or her own collection of MIB objects.

SNMP Applications

There are a number of both commercial and public domain SNMP applications that are available on many different platforms including UNIX and MS Windows. Several of the commercial SNMP packages are geared toward providing a host of SNMP management tools for both small and large network enterprise environments. For example, HP OpenView provides a wide range of functions that includes management of hosts, network devices such as switches and routers, and other devices such as printers. On the public domain side, a large number of tools are available that address many system and network management functions. For example, the University of California at Davis (UCD) SNMP agent is available. The SNMP application tools are described in Module 16.

Many of the UNIX operating system vendors provide one or more SNMP agents that support both standard and vendor-specific MIBs. For example, on the Solaris system, the Sun SNMP agent is provided and supports both MIB-II and the Sun enterprise-specific MIBs. For Linux, the UCD SNMP agent is available and supports standard MIBs like MIB-II. These SNMP agents are described in Appendix C.

1-Minute Drill

● What are some advantages to SNMP over other network management protocols?

● What is a disadvantage of SNMP compared to some other network management protocols?

13.2 Uncover MIBs

As previously mentioned, the Management Information Base (MIB) is a storehouse of information related to configuration, performance, and other data contained within an agent. MIBs have an organization and common structure, and may contain a large number of objects separated into groups.

MIB objects are organized in a hierarchical tree structure in which each branch has a unique name and numeric identifier. Figure 13-2 shows the

13

● SNMP is free and in the public domain. It is simple to implement. It runs on a wide variety of computers, network devices, and even devices not traditionally associated with computing such as telephones that are now increasingly networked. Its memory and processor requirements are small and it is easy to develop applications for SNMP. SNMP is well documented.

● Some other network management protocols offer more features than SNMP.

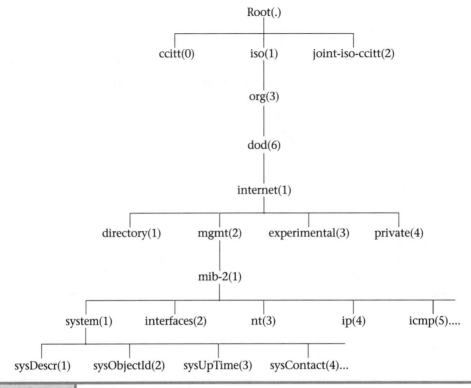

Figure 13-2   MIB organization and structure

standard MIB organization from the root to additional branches. The branches of the tree serve as logical groupings of related objects. The leaves, or *nodes* as they are often called, represent individual objects. Also, subtrees are formed and represent both additional intermediate branches and connecting leaves. Objects within a MIB can be referenced by specifying each of the numeric identifiers starting with the top of the tree (or root) and proceeding to the individual leaf or object. The root of the branch is commonly written with a "."(dot).

Hint

Accessing MIBs is similar to referencing files within the UNIX operating system. However, one key difference is that UNIX pathnames can be expressed in absolute or relative terms. MIB objects can only be accessed in an absolute manner; the relative format is not available.

For example, Figure 13-2 shows `root (.)` at the topmost position of the tree and `sysDescr(1)` as the leaf. The common method of expressing object identifiers is to use the *dotted notation*. This notation requires that a dot separate each branch name or identifier. Often the `root` is not expressed, as it is implied. To access the `sysDescr(1)` object, the fully qualified identifier would be written as

```
iso.org.dod.internet.mgmt.mib-2.system.sysDescr
```

This identifier is read from left to right. Objects can also be expressed in a short form by substituting the branch name with the numeric identifier associated with each identifier name. Thus, `iso.org.dod.internet.mgmt.mib-2.system.sysDescr` can also be expressed as `1.3.6.1.2.1.1.1`. These two expressions are functionally equivalent and reference the same MIB object.

Hint

The reason to choose one identifier form over the other is a matter of preference, although the numeric identifier is much more concise. However, MIB browsers can display MIB objects in either format, thus making it easy to convert from one format to the other. After using SNMP and MIBs for a short while, you will become familiar with both methods and have the opportunity to choose which style is best for you.

By using the structure shown in the figure, an SNMP manager (or MIB browser tool) can drill down into the MIB in an easy yet concise manner. A MIB browser is a software application that traverses a MIB tree, usually showing a graphical display of branches, leaf objects, and associated values. MIB browsers are great for probing an agent for specific information or learning the structure and format of new MIBs.

Object Types

Within a MIB, different object types represent data structures or values contained in an agent. The objects can represent physical agent attributes, configuration information, or other data. These object types are derived from the Abstract Syntax Notation (ASN.1) standard rules. ASN.1 provides a detailed standard for the implementation and encoding of basic data types that are machine independent and can be transmitted over the network in an unambiguous way.

13

Ask the Expert

Question Why are machine independence and unambiguous network transmission important to SNMP or network management?

Answer Because network management must address a heterogeneous network environment, a standard way must be provided to ensure that SNMP messages can be transmitted and understood on different systems and devices. Because various computer platforms store information differently, ASN.1 provides a common format. For example, an integer on one system can be expressed with the most significant digit first, while on others it might be expressed with the least significant digit first. Also, ASN.1 data types are found in MIBs.

Question Why is it so important to learn the MIB details in this module?

Answer The sections in the succeeding modules will focus on using network management tools that manipulate MIB objects. So it seems reasonable to present the types of objects that might be encountered. It is important that the reader understands the different types of objects and why values from these objects are in a certain format or structure. Of equal importance is the access mode of MIB objects, which is discussed in the next section, "Sample MIB Object."

For us to understand network management, we must be able to read and understand MIB objects. Without a good grasp of MIBs, it will be difficult to use SNMP tools and software to manage a network effectively.

Two object data type classes are defined using ASN.1:

- Universal types

- Application types

The universal class consists of primitive types that can be used to build additional data types of objects within a MIB. Table 13-1 lists some of the available simple data types found in the universal class.

ASN.1 Data Type	Description
INTEGER	A data type representing a cardinal number, where no limitation is made on the level of precision that might be required to represent an integer value.
OCTET STRING	A data type representing zero or more octets, where each octet may take any value from 0 to 255.
NULL	A data type meant as a placeholder, but currently not used.
OBJECT IDENTIFIER	A data type representing an authoritatively named object that consists of a sequence of values that specify a MIB tree.
SEQUENCE SEQUENCE OF	A data type used to denote an ordered list of zero or more elements that contain other ASN.1 types. SEQUENCE OF contains an ordered list of the same ASN.1 type.

Table 13-1   SNMP Universal Data Types

SNMP derives some application data types from the universal class type. These application types define additional sub-types that can be used to represent specific values customized for use within the network management environment. Table 13-2 describes some of the application data types presently available in the application class.

ASN.1 Data Type	Description
Counter Counter32	A data type that represents a non-negative integer that increases until it reaches a maximum value and then resets to zero. A counter is an INTEGER that can take a value between 0 and 4294967295. A counter has no defined starting value.
Counter64	Just like a counter object except that a counter64 is an INTEGER that can take a value between 0 and 18446744073709551615.
DisplayString	A data type representing zero or more octets, where each octet may take any value from 0 to 255. A DisplayString is like an OctetString object.
Gauge Gauge32	A data type that represents a non-negative integer that may increase or decrease and will trigger at a maximum value. A gauge is like a counter in every other aspect.
IpAddress	Represents an OCTET STRING that has a length of 4 bytes (32 bits) and where each of the four octets relates to the four bytes of a standard IP address.

Table 13-2   SNMP Application Data Types

13

ASN.1 Data Type	Description
Opaque	A data type that provides the ability to pass arbitrary information that uses the OCTET STRING data type.
NetworkAddress	Represents an address from one of several network protocol address standards. Presently, it is the same as IpAddress.
TimeTicks	Represents a non-negative integer that counts time in hundredths of a second since some established epoch. TimeTicks is like a counter in every other aspect.

Table 13-2   SNMP Application Data Types *(continued)*

Sample MIB Object

MIB objects are important components of network management, and some of the modules in this book specifically describe MIB definitions as they relate to system agents and network management tools. Therefore, when discussing MIBs, the common format shown below will be used:

● **Object Name** sysDescr

● **OID** system.1

● **Object Type** Octet String

● **Access Mode** read-only

● **Status** current

● **Description** A description of the agent device or entity. This value should include the full name, identification of the system, hardware type, operating system, and network software. It is mandatory that this object type contain only printable ASCII characters. A sample of this object includes the following obtained for a Solaris system: Sun SNMP Agent.

This format includes the object name, OID string, object type, access mode, status, and description. The object name is the name used when querying an agent for this particular object. In this example, the sysDescr object is a string that contains a general description of the device or agent contained within the device. The object identifier string, or OID string, shows which group the object is contained in and its logical position in that MIB hierarchy.

In this case, it is the first object in the `system` group. This group can be found within the standard MIB-II definition.

The object type is `OctetString` and can be as long as 255 characters. Recall that Table 13-2 lists the definitions of these ASN.1 types. The access mode indicates how the manager or other tools may manipulate the object.

Hint

It is very common for those new to SNMP to attempt to alter nonwritable objects. In this case, attempting to alter the `sysDescr` object will cause the agent to respond with `not writable` or another error message.

The status field indicates the current status of the object, for example, current or historic. The `current` status means that the object is presently available within the agent as described within the MIB. That is, if the MIB represents that agent, then all objects labeled as `current` will be implemented within that agent. Other values can also be used to indicate additional states of the objects. For example, the `obsolete` reference indicates that the object is no longer supported within the MIB. The `deprecated` reference can be used to aid interoperability with older versions or implementations of the agent.

The description field provides an overview of the object, purpose, and a sample value if appropriate. In the above example, when the `sysDescr` object is queried, it returns the agent operating system (for example, Solaris), the hostname the agent resides within (`socrates`), operating system version information, and date information.

Another way this book describes MIBs is with a hierarchical graph showing each of the objects laid out in a tree structure. Figure 13-3 shows the general format that represents a MIB tree. In particular, it shows the MIB-II objects found under the `system` group. As you can see, the formatting includes the use of closed circles (⊙⊙●) and closed squares (■). The squares represent discrete objects such as `INTEGER` and `OCTET STRING`, but not tables or other groups of objects. The circles represent groups of objects or tables. Also, gray lines and objects that are peripheral further indicate the structure needed to navigate to the group in question. These objects and associated lines that are of interest are drawn in black. Included with these objects is the member index (in parentheses) that shows the relative position of each object within the tree structure. Thus, `sysContact(4)` is the fourth object within the `system` group.

13

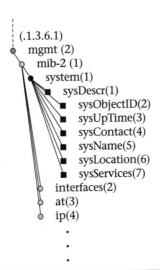

(.1.3.6.1)
mgmt (2)
mib-2 (1)
system(1)
sysDescr(1)
sysObjectID(2)
sysUpTime(3)
sysContact(4)
sysName(5)
sysLocation(6)
sysServices(7)
interfaces(2)
at(3)
ip(4)

Figure 13-3   General MIB format

SNMP Tables

As noted above, an MIB may contain objects that represent physical characteristics of a device or other information contained within an agent. These objects can either be in the form of discrete elements (i.e., individual objects like `sysDescr`) or, in some cases, two-dimensional tables. Tables store related information that might contain several instances or copies of an MIB object. The best way to illustrate the use of a table is by examining a table within an actual MIB.

Defined in the MIB-II standard is the `interface` group that has the object identifier defined as `1.3.6.1.2.1.2` or `iso.org.dod.internet.mgmt .mib-2.interface`. Objects within this group represent physical network interfaces and related information installed within a networking device. Performance-related information is also collected and stored within this group.

For each interface within a network device, the following information is used to describe the characteristics of the interface and associated configuration:

- **Description**   General description of the interface

- **Type**   The type of interface, such as Ethernet or token ring

- **Mtu**   The maximum transmission size

- **Speed**   The transmission speed of the interface

- **Physical address**   The data link protocol or hardware address

- **Administration status**   The current administrative status of the interface

- **Operational status**   The actual operating status of the interface

- **Last change**   The time when the interface became operational

Additional objects within the table store the following performance-monitoring information:

- Number of octets (bytes) received or sent

- Number of unicast packets delivered to or sent from higher-level software

- Number of non-unicast packets delivered to or sent from higher-level software

- Number of inbound/outbound packets discarded

- Number of inbound/outbound packets containing errors

- Number of inbound/outbound packets discarded due to bad protocol

- Length of the output packet queue

Figure 13-4 shows the structure of the `interface` group. Tables are used to contain interface information because networking devices can contain more than one interface. For example, a router or switch device can contain literally dozens of interfaces, often supporting different network protocols such as Ethernet, ATM, or FDDI. Using a table provides a straightforward and convenient way to access individual objects within a given interface definition.

The `interface` group includes the `ifNumber` object, which contains the total number of network interfaces within the networking device. Using the sample data contained in Table 13-3, the `ifNumber` value would be 2. In this case, the device reports two interfaces: one defined as a pseudointerface and the other defined as an Ethernet. It is common for networking UNIX systems to contain a pseudointerface for internal diagnostic purposes.

The rest of the `interface` group consists of a table called `ifTable`, which contains a row for each interface defined within the device. This table is

13

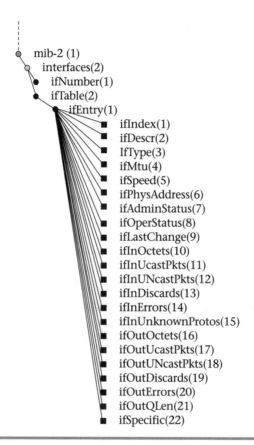

mib-2 (1)
  interfaces(2)
    ifNumber(1)
    ifTable(2)
      ifEntry(1)
        ifIndex(1)
        ifDescr(2)
        IfType(3)
        ifMtu(4)
        ifSpeed(5)
        ifPhysAddress(6)
        ifAdminStatus(7)
        ifOperStatus(8)
        ifLastChange(9)
        ifInOctets(10)
        ifInUcastPkts(11)
        ifInUNcastPkts(12)
        ifInDiscards(13)
        ifInErrors(14)
        ifInUnknownProtos(15)
        ifOutOctets(16)
        ifOutUcastPkts(17)
        ifOutUNcastPkts(18)
        ifOutDiscards(19)
        ifOutErrors(20)
        ifOutQLen(21)
        ifSpecific(22)

Figure 13-4   Interface group from MIB-II

indexed by ifIndex, which contains a value between the range of 1 and the value of ifNumber. The ifIndex object uniquely addresses each column of the table that represents the interface.

Table 13-3 shows the entire interface group in the first column and associated values taken from an actual network device in the remaining columns. Each row corresponds to each of the specific MIB objects contained within the ifEntry table. Each ifEntry instance represents an interface defined in the table. To access the object ifDescr for the first interface, one would use the following object identifier (OID)

```
1.3.6.1.2.1.2.2.1.1
```

MIB Objects	IfEntry (1.3.6.1.2.1.2.2.1)	IfEntry (1.3.6.1.2.1.2.2.2)
IfIndex	1	2
ifDescr	Pseudo Interface	Ethernet
ifType	1	6
ifMtu	1500	1500
IfSpeed	10000000	10000000
ifPhysAddress	None	0x00040010ee5d
IfAdminStatus	1	1
IfOperStatus	1	1
IfLastChange	0	0
IfInOctets	0	42617
IfInUcastPkts	445	680
IfInNUcastPkts	0	19
IfInDiscards	0	0
IfInErrors	0	5
IfInUnknown-Protos	0	0
IfOutOctets	0	42600
IfOutUcastPkts	445	570
IfOutNUcastPkts	0	94
IfOutDiscards	0	0
IfOutErrors	0	87
IfOutQLen	0	0
ifSpecific	null	null

Table 13-3   Interface Group Instance Table

or

```
iso.org.dod.internet.mgmt.mib-2.interface.ifTable.ifEntry.ifDescr
```

The ifDescr object provides a general description of the interface.
The objects starting from IfInOctets to IfOutQLen represent traffic
counters for device interfaces and can be used to measure network and system
performance.

13

Accessing Objects

MIB objects are defined with access control information that specifies what kind of operation can be performed on the object. SNMP includes the following access control information for MIB objects:

- Not-accessible

- Accessible-for-notify

- Read-only

- Read-write

- Read-create

Not-accessible objects defined within the MIB usually reference object definitions, or other object descriptions that are not objects themselves, that can be manipulated by an SNMP manager. One good example is the table data structure, where an object describes the shape or size of the table but not the actual rows or columns.

Accessible-for-notify objects are only available via a notification to a network manager or another agent. No direct polling of the object is permitted. Read-only objects are not alterable by the network management system, but values may be obtained via a get or trap operation.

Read-write access is necessary when a particular object must be altered to accomplish some specific goal or must be configured in a certain way. For example, it might be necessary to disable a router port due to a large number of errors detected on one of its interfaces. In this case, the network management system must change the operational status of the interface to 0, thus shutting down the physical connection until the cause of the errors is determined.

Read-create objects have the same access permission as read-only and read-write objects. Read-create access is used for objects that may be created on the fly. Such objects may include table row (also called conceptual row) instances, for example.

Standard and Private MIBs

As previously mentioned, MIBs are organized under a hierarchical tree structure, and a number of standard MIBs have been developed and placed under the mgmt (2) branch. Many of these MIBs were developed via the RFC process. Many different individuals or vendors assisted with their development but don't actually own them, nor can they arbitrarily make changes to them. However, many vendors and third-party software developers have developed additional MIBs to address specific functionality or services for their particular products. Many of these MIBs, known as enterprise MIBs, start under the private(4) branch of the standard MIB tree. Figure 13-5 shows several popular MIBs that can be found under this branch.

The Internet Assigned Numbers Authority (IANA; www.iana.org) maintains a list of assigned enterprise numbers. Those wishing to obtain a number make a request to this organization and obtain a valid number. Table 13-4 shows a small sample of the numbers that have already been assigned.

SNMP Communities

Typically, a network management system will be deployed in a large network environment that contains a collection of many different groups of networks and devices. Thus, it is reasonable for an enterprise network to be divided into

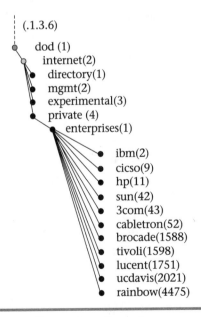

| **Figure 13-5** | Enterprise tree from private branch |

13

Number	Vendor
2	IBM
9	Cisco Systems
11	Hewlett-Packard
42	Sun Microsystems
43	3Com Corporation
52	Cabletron Systems
1588	Brocade Communications Systems
1598	Tivoli Systems
1751/3729	Lucent Technologies
4475	Rainbow Software Solutions

Table 13-4   Assigned Enterprise MIB Numbers

zones or communities of users in order to partition responsibility. As a result, a community name can be assigned to a class of devices and provide a security boundary that helps to implement the desired communities or zones. SNMP supports this kind of security model based on community string information, which is physically added to each device within the selected community. Some practical examples include selecting a community that represents all the Cisco backbone routers or selecting another community that includes devices in just the sales department.

The current SNMP community-based authentication model is considered very weak and poses a significant security problem. The major reason is that older SNMP versions don't provide any encryption facilities or other mechanisms to ensure that the community information is not simply copied from the network during an SNMP packet exchange. Using a packet capture tool, the entire SNMP packet could be decoded, thus revealing the community name. As a result of this limitation, many sites disable set operations to many of the agent devices. This has the unfortunate side effect of limiting SNMP usefulness because it can then only monitor object values and not alter them.

13.3 Explore SNMP Versions

SNMP became generally available in 1988. Since then, it has seen widespread use and been implemented in virtually all local area networking (LAN) devices

Ask the Expert

Question   Why would a change to an MIB object be prohibited?

Answer   Certain MIB information will never change during the life of a product. For example, the MIB object `sysDescr`, which stands for system description, contains vendor information for the agent. An SNMP manager should not modify this information because it would disassociate the device with the actual product vendor, thus making agent identification difficult. Also, it can adversely affect the accuracy of any software-based network inventory mechanisms. Another reason to make objects read-only is to ensure that performance information or other statistical data remains accurate rather than getting altered unintentionally.

Read-write access is necessary when a particular object must be altered to accomplish some specific goal or must be configured in a certain way. For example, it might be necessary to disable a router port due to a large number of errors detected on one of its interfaces. In this case, the network management system must change the operational status of the interface to 0, thus shutting down the physical connection until the cause of the errors is determined.

Question   Why develop enterprise MIBs?

Answer   Many vendors do so because they may need specific objects for their devices that may not be defined or available within the standard MIBs. Also, vendor-specific MIBs don't need to become standards, since only that vendor and their customers actually need to use the MIBs. It only makes sense to develop standard MIBs when many vendors can implement the same collection of MIBs across a large number of different devices.

and on many computer operating systems. This popular version, known as SNMPv1, accounts for a significant portion of the installed base of agents today. Despite its popularity, SNMPv1 has several fundamental problems. First, because it lacks a robust security mechanism, it can't be used to its full potential.

13

As a result, many vendors limit the set operations on agents to minimize the potential risk of a security breach. Second, SNMPv1 doesn't optimize the processing of large amounts of information, thus further restricting the use of SNMP. Third, SNMPv1's relationship between network manager and agent are well defined— agents play only a single, simplistic role of accepting commands from more management systems. This significantly limits SNMPv1 when smart agents are needed to address specific requirements for distributed network management functions. SNMPv1 also specifies a collection of MIB objects known as MIB-II. The goal of MIB-II was to provide a collection of objects that all SNMP agents can support, regardless of which vendor implemented the agent. To summarize, SNMPv1 provides

- Basic network management framework

- Definition of the MIB-II standard

- Descriptions of the Protocol Data Units (PDUs), which include GetRequest, GetNextRequest, SetRequest, GetResponse, and Trap

- Description of ASN.1 encoding language

To address some of the deficiencies in SNMPv1, a significant amount of effort has been made over the past few years to enhance SNMP. The first series of improvements came in 1993 when a series of 12 RFCs (1441–1452) was introduced, proposing to add PDUs and enhancements to the SNMP architecture and security model. This collection of RFCs was known as SNMPv2 Classic. At that time, many users of SNMP were anticipating these improvements and planned to implement the new version as soon as it became available.

Unfortunately, there was still much debate about SNMPv2 security and remote configuration. When it became apparent that not all the original SNMPv2 proposals were going to be widely adopted, additional work was done to define SNMP security and remote configuration management components. This led to additional proposals that included a new protocol and new MIB structure elements (documented in RFCs 1901–1908). These proposals were more popular than SNMPv2 Classic and became known as community-based SNMPv2 or SNMPv2c. The problem with SNMPv2c was that, though it was endorsed by the IETF, it lacked robust security and administration facilities.

Additional improvements to the remote management capability of SNMPv1 resulted in proposals known as SNMPv2usec and SNMPv2, documented in

RFCs 1909–1910 and RFC 2222, respectively. The SNMPv2usec recommends a robust security model and administrative framework. One of the problems with SNMPv2usec is that it lacks endorsement of the IETF, which relinquished the proposal to a nonstandard. The major functions of SNMPv2 include

- Expanded data types, such as 64-bit counters
- Improved performance and efficiency with the get-bulk PDU
- Event notification with the inform PDU
- Better error handling
- More efficient row creation and deletion

Finally, in an attempt to reach some agreement between the various remote management and security proposals, another series of RFCs was written, which later became known as SNMPv3. These RFCs (2271–2275) have been put forth by the IETF as Proposed Standards, which means that they are available to the general public for review and discussion. SNMPv3 is SNMPv2c plus provisions for robust security and administration; it draws upon the SNMPv2c RFCs (1902–1908). At a high level, the SNMPv3 proposal attempts to

- Put forth a security model based on DES, MD5, and other authentication protocols
- Define a view-based access control model
- Redefine some of the SNMP concepts and terms

SNMPv3 has enjoyed a certain level of success in the industry at this point, but the protocols are still quite new. Major networking hardware and software companies already support SNMPv3. However, SNMPv3 has yet to be deployed widely within the industry; this is perhaps just a matter of time. One of the major delays for adoption of this new protocol is the cost-to-benefit ratio. For those sites that require better security today, they can upgrade to the new protocols as vendors make their implementation available. However, it may not be justifiable for everyone to upgrade all existing equipment to support SNMPv3. The most likely approach will be to migrate slowly over time as newer products that contain SNMPv3 support are deployed. Eventually, new products will replace the older ones, and deploying the new management protocols will simply be a matter of configuration.

13

SNMP Protocol Operation

An SNMPv1 message contains three major components: a version field, a
community field, and an SNMP protocol data unit (PDU) field. Unlike other
TCP/IP protocols, SNMP packets are not of a fixed length and, instead, rely
on ASN.1 formatting. Figure 13-6 shows this basic SNMP packet structure
and a description of the fields (and sizes) follows.

The format includes field names, shown in bold text, and formatting labels
(type), as shown on the top in gray text. The type shows the basic format for
each of the fields. For instance, the version information is an INTEGER object.
The field names are defined as follows:

- **version**   This field indicates which version of the SNMP protocol is being
  used. Presently, version 1 is the most widely implemented and supported
  SNMP protocol.

- **community name**   The community is used as the primary security
  mechanism to establish authentication from a network manager to agents
  within the SNMP. The community name or string is used as a password
  for access to objects. This is based on the condition that the network
  manager knows the agent's password. If the agent has been configured
  to emit traps, an authenticationFailure trap is generated when a network
  manager queries an agent with an invalid community string.

- **protocol data units**   SNMPv1 PDUs can be one of five different types and
  consist of request and response components. They include

  - GetRequest
  - GetNextRequest
  - SetRequest
  - GetResponse
  - Trap

Integer	Octet string	Sequence
Version	Community Name	SNMP Protocol Data Unit

Figure 13-6   SNMP master/subagent diagram

SNMPv2 defines these additional PDUs:

- GetBulkRequest

- InformRequest

Each of the GetRequest, GetNextRequest, and SetRequest components elicits from the responding agent a GetResponse that might contain valid data or an error status.

GetRequest

The GetRequest PDU is issued by an SNMP manager or application to obtain one or more MIB objects from an SNMP agent. The fields for this packet type include

- **pdu type**   Indicates the PDU type is a GetRequest.

- **request-id**   Unique identifier that permits the SNMP manager to match paired requests and responses. It also aids in detecting duplicate messages that may be received when using an unreliable transport service.

- **variable-bindings**   A list of requested MIB objects.

The GetRequest operation is the primary way to obtain information from agents when the objects in question are known beforehand. For example, should the network manager decide to retrieve sysDescr and sysUpTime objects from an agent, we can think of the request as simply a function to include

```
GetRequest (sysDescr, sysUpTime)
```

In this case, both of these objects are placed within the variable-binding field when sent. The sysDescr object represents a string that contains a general description of the agent, and sysUptime reflects the amount of time that an agent has been running.

When the agent receives the above message and no errors have occurred, it will respond with the values of the MIB objects requested via a GetResponse PDU. The GetRequest operation is atomic. That is, either all the values requested are returned or no values are returned. When the receiving entity responds to the GetRequest, it includes the values in the GetResponse variable-binding field. If, for some reason, at least one of the values cannot be supplied, no values will be provided.

13

If the values requested from a manager cannot be returned by the agent, the agent will respond with an error. For example, the management system might have requested an MIB object that isn't implemented in the agent. In this case, the agent can't possibly satisfy the request, and thus an error is returned. Also, in certain situations, returning the value of a requested object fails because it might be too large to be processed by the manager.

The variable-bindings field includes a list of objects for which values are requested. When the agent responds via GetResponse, the variable binding includes the requested objects and associated values. Given the example above, the following GetResponse would be sent by the agent:

```
GetResponse(sysDescr="3Com Enterprise Monitor", sysUpTime=0000154477)
```

In this example, the agent is a 3Com enterprise RMON monitor (or network probe), as indicated by the `sysDescr` field. This device collects network performance and packet contents information for later analysis and reporting. The `sysUpTime` object contains the amount of time the agent has been up and running. The value shown in the example indicates that the device was running for approximately 15 minutes and 44 seconds.

GetNextRequest

The GetNextRequest PDU is similar to the GetRequest PDU, and the packet formats are identical. However, the GetNextRequest PDU has one difference: It is used to retrieve objects when the structure of the MIB tree is unknown. The GetNextRequest can be a great asset when it is used to discover the exact MIB structure of an agent. Why would an agent's MIB structure be unknown to an SNMP manager? SNMP provides no direct way to determine which MIBs or MIB structures are supported within an agent. Vendors are, of course, are free to implement whichever MIBs their devices need. Therefore, the network manager must discover the supported MIBs by walking the MIB tree in an automated fashion. When the GetNextRequest is sent with a particular object, the GetResponse returns the requested object's value, plus the instance of the next lexicographic object in the MIB tree. As a result, each GetNextRequest will reveal the next object within the MIB without the manager knowing what the next object will be. The GetNextRequest operation also provides a more efficient mechanism to retrieve objects from an agent than GetRequest because it requires fewer request/response exchanges.

SetRequest

The SetRequest operation is used to alter agent information such as the value of a MIB object. The packet format is the same as GetRequest and GetNextRequest. Unlike GetRequest or GetNextRequest, SetRequest is used to alter the value of a MIB object. As mentioned before, the SetRequest requires security privileges, which are presently mapped via the community string for the SNMPv1 protocol. Therefore, the agent must validate the SetRequest community string provided before the operation is permitted. The SetRequest is also atomic; either all the values can be altered or none can. If the SetRequest is successful, a GetResponse is returned and the variable-binding list contains the objects with their new values. This is how the network manager can determine that the set operation was successful. If the SetRequest was unsuccessful, an error is returned in the GetResponse.

GetResponse

Each of the SNMP operations, with the exception of the trap, receives a GetResponse from the agent of the GetResponse packet, which includes the following fields:

- **pdu type**   Indicates the PDU type, which is GetResponse.

- **request-id**   Unique identifier that permits the pairing of requests and responses.

- **error-status**   Indicates that an exception condition occurred while processing the request.

- **error-index**   When an error occurs, indicates which object variable in the variable-binding list caused the error.

- **variable-bindings**   A list of MIB objects that are involved in the operation.

Trap

A Trap is an unsolicited message from an agent directed to a network management station that represents a significant event or condition for which notification to the manager is considered necessary. This type of communication from the agent is asynchronous as compared to the polling from the manager. The Trap PDU is quite different from that of the other PDUs defined in SNMP. Unlike the

13

other SNMP PDUs, Trap does not warrant a response from the receiving network. The fields from a Trap include

- **PDU type** Indicates that the PDU type is a Trap.

- **Enterprise** Contains the MIB object sysObjectID of the sending agent. The sysObjectID object includes information regarding the vendor of the agent that sent the Trap.

- **Agent-address** Represents the IP address of the sending agent.

- **Generic-trap** One of the predefined Trap values listed in Table 13-5.

- **Specific-trap** More detailed information about the Trap. This is usually zero unless the generic-trap is an enterpriseSpecific Trap. Enterprise Traps are vendor specific and may contain additional agent information about the condition that caused the Trap in the first place.

- **Time-stamp** The amount of time between the generation of the Trap and when the device was last initialized, expressed in tenths of a millisecond.

- **Variable-binding** Vendor-specific information related to the Trap.

Table 13-5 lists the seven predefined general Trap types. The enterpriseSpecific Trap type is provided as a mechanism to define custom or proprietary traps that do not fit within the other generic types.

Trap Type	Description
ColdStart (0)	The device is restarting or reinitializing itself such that the agent or configuration may be changed. Usually, this indicates a crash or other reboot condition.
WarmStart (1)	The device is restarting or reinitializing itself such that no changes are made to the agent or configuration. Usually, this implies a simple refresh or reboot of the operating system environment.
LinkDown (2)	Indicates a failure on one of the device's communications (interface) links.

Table 13-5 SNMP Predefined Trap Types

Trap Type	Description
LinkUp (3)	Indicates that a device's communication (interface) link is now up and running.
AuthenticationFailure (4)	An authentication or security failure has occurred on the device. Typically, this indicates that an invalid SNMP community string has been used.
EgpNeighborLoss (5)	Indicates that External Gateway Protocol (EGP) neighbor, of which the device is a peer, has been labeled down and the relationship no longer is valid.
EnterpriseSpecific (6)	Indicates that some vendor-specific event has occurred. Vendors use this generic trap type to represent their own proprietary traps.

Table 13-5   SNMP Predefined Trap Types (*continued*)

GetBulkRequest

This PDU is issued by an SNMPv2 manager or application to minimize network interaction and permit the agent to return larger packets (as compared to GetNextRequest or GetRequest), thus improving the efficiency of obtaining a large number of objects from an agent. This uses the same PDU format as most other SNMPv1 operators. The only difference is the renaming of the error-status and error-index (from the Response PDU) fields to non-repeaters and max-repetitions, respectively. These fields are defined as follows:

- **non-repeaters**   The number of MIB objects that should be retrieved once at most

- **max-repetitions**   The maximum number of times other MIB objects should be retrieved

InformRequest

The InformRequest PDU is issued by an SNMPv2 entity acting in a manager role to another SNMPv2 entity acting in the same role for the purpose of providing network management information. The major function of this PDU is to provide distributed SNMP management capabilities. Thus, an agent can implement this PDU to provide management-like services and functions. The format of this PDU is the same as for GetRequest and other related PDUs.

13

1-Minute Drill

● What are the advantages of SNMPv3 over previous versions and what are its major current limitations?

● Why is a trap message useful?

SNMP Response Codes

The error codes returned from an SNMPv1 agent are very limited. For example, if an SNMP manager requested the set operation on a MIB object, and the agent can't perform the operation as requested, the agent replies with `noSuchName`. With the addition of more error codes in SNMPv2, the agent will reply with `notWritable` in this situation. Table 13-6 lists the SNMP response codes.

Response Code	Description
SNMPv1	
`tooBig`	Returned by the agent if the response to a request would be too large to send.
`noSuchName`	Returned by the agent in either of these two cases: 1) if a set operation is attempted for an object that is not in the MIB view, or 2) if a set operation is attempted for an object that is in the MIB view, but its object is read-only.
`badValue`	Returned by the agent that has detected an error in the PDU variable binding list.
`Read-only`	Returned by the agent.
`genError`	Returned by the agent when processing of a PDU fails for a reason other than what is listed in this table.

Table 13-6   SNMP Response Codes

● SNMPv3 increases security over older standards.

● A trap message can inform a network management station about an unexpected problem that the agent might not otherwise find out about in a timely fashion.

Response Code SNMPv2/v3	Description
noAccess	The variable is outside the defined MIB view for this operation to succeed.
notWritable	The variable exists within the agent, but the agent is unable to modify the object.
WrongType	The value supplied is of the wrong data type, as defined by ASN.1.
WrongLength	The value supplied is of the wrong length.
WrongEncoding	The value supplied was not encoded correctly.
WrongValue	The value supplied is not within the range required for the object type.
NoCreation	The object doesn't exist and the agent is unable to create an instance of this object.
InconsistentName	The object doesn't exist and the agent is unable to create an instance of this object because the name is inconsistent with the values of other related objects.
InconsistentValue	The object provided is inconsistent with the values of the managed objects.
resourceUnavailable	A needed resource within the agent can't be reserved to complete the request.

Table 13-6   SNMP Response Codes (*continued*)

Hint

These codes are important because they can help you track down problems and issues when using SNMP agents and tools that communicate with agents. Determining the solution to SNMP problems is aided by knowing these message codes and understanding the difference between configuration errors with the agent versus connectivity problems between the manager and agent.

Transmission of an SNMP Message

The following series of events occurs when a network manager formulates an SNMP message:

1. The basic PDU is constructed.

2. The PDU is passed to the security service layer if available.

13

3. The protocol layer formats the message, including the version and community information.

4. The entire message is now encoded using ASN.1 rules.

5. The message is passed to the transport service so that it will be delivered to the receiving entity.

The following series of events occurs when an agent device receives an SNMP message:

1. A basic check is performed to ensure the message is formatted correctly. The message is discarded if any errors are encountered.

2. The protocol version information is verified. If there is a mismatch, the message is discarded.

3. The security service attempts to verify the sending entity. If this fails, a trap is generated and the message is discarded.

4. The PDU is decoded.

5. The PDU is processed.

Connectionless Protocol

SNMP is a connectionless protocol, which means that it doesn't support the concept of establishing and controlling a dedicated connection like Telnet or FTP. SNMP transmits information between an agent and a manager by the use of requests and return responses. This removes the burden from agents of having to support additional protocols and processes associated with connection-based schemes. Therefore, SNMP provides its own mechanism to address reliability and error detection.

13.5 Investigate SNMP Master and Subagent

When deploying network management software, it is common to have a single agent installed on each system that will be managed. In the case of networking devices such as network routers and switches, usually only a single agent is available. In either case, the agents will communicate with one or more network managers using the standard SNMP port of 161. For most needs, a single agent approach makes sense and is appropriate. However, there are instances when more than one agent is necessary to achieve the desired level of manageability. For example, workstation manufacturers will often provide an SNMP agent within their operating system. In the case of both Solaris and HP-UX, the vendor provides a master agent and one or more subagents. A single agent is available on the Linux platform.

Most system agents will usually support a limited number of operating system functions and parameters. If we wish to manage database services on this same system via SNMP, this will require that we install another agent to specifically monitor the database functions. This poses a problem because both agents will typically be accessed by the SNMP manager using the same SNMP standard port. Further, when the agents are started by the system, the first agent will start and open the port 161 and will operate normally. However, when the second agent starts and attempts to do the same, it will get an error stating that the port is busy and it should abort operation.

Two possible approaches can be taken to address this port contention problem. First, one of the agents can be configured to use an alternative port instead of the standard 161. This solution will work if the agent can be made to support another port when it is started by the system. Many system agents do support alternative ports, but this is by no means the rule. The major drawback to this solution is that any SNMP managers used to poll the agent must now be configured to use this new port as well. This doesn't pose a significant problem when only a small number of nonstandard ports are used. However, if this solution is used on a large scale—say, with many agents using all nonstandard ports across a large number of systems—the approach loses its appeal because of the administrative burden it introduces.

The other solution might be considered more elegant because it involves using a master agent and one or more subagents. A master agent solves the port conflict problem by becoming the keeper of the standard SNMP port and forwards all the SNMP traffic to the appropriate subagent. Subagents are normal SNMP agents, but they are registered with the master agent and assigned nonstandard ports that are used to communicate with the master agent. SNMP messages from managers are sent to the master agent, who in turn delivers the messages to the correct subagent using the port it assigned to the subagent. Figure 13-6 shows a diagram of the master/subagent architecture. One major benefit of this solution is that it alleviates the administration task of modifying the SNMP managers

13

cited in the first solution. Also, this solution can scale very well because new subagents can be added in a straightforward manner.

On the negative side, the master agent can pose a problem because it can crash or otherwise become inoperative. This would have the adverse effect of disabling the connectivity to all the subagents. Because this particular problem can be said of other software systems as well, the risk (although not zero) isn't necessarily a significant factor. Also, because the master agent is responsible for delivering the SNMP to the appropriate subagent, it takes a certain amount of processing time and overhead. This might be a factor in time-critical management functions.

☑ *Mastery Check*

1. Which MIB object class consists of primitive types that can be used to build additional data types of objects?

2. Which SNMP function notifies a network management system of a special condition or problem without the management system specifically requesting this information?

   A. Get

   B. Set

   C. Trap

   D. MIB

3. Which class does the IpAddress data type belong to?

4. Which of the following elements does SNMPv1 not provide?

   A. Basic network management framework

   B. Robust security model

   C. Definition of the MIB-II standard

   D. Description of ASN.1 encoding language

5. What are the three main components of a SNMPv1 message?

6. In the MIB hierarchical tree structure, the _____ represent individual objects.

7. What type of objects are not alterable by the network management system, but allow their values to be obtained with a get operation?

   A. Not-accessible

   B. Accessible-for-notify

   C. Read-only

   D. Read-write

13

☑ *Mastery Check*

8. What does an SNMP manager or application issue to obtain one or more MIB objects from a SNMP agent?

9. What does an SNMP manager or application issue to obtain a MIB object from a SNMP agent when the structure of the MIB tree is unknown?

10. Match each of the data types in the first list (A-D) with its description from the second list (i-iv):

   A. INTEGER

   B. NULL

   C. OBJECT IDENTIFIER

   D. SEQUENCE

   i. A data type used to denote an ordered list of zero or more elements that contain other ASN.1 types

   ii. A data type representing a cardinal number

   iii. A data type meant as a placeholder, but currently not used

   iv. A data type representing an authoritatively named object that consists of a sequence of values that specify a MIB tree

11. Which of the following is information that would be contained in an SNMP table for each interface within a network device to describe the nature of the interface and associated configuration? (choose all that apply)

   A. Desciption

   B. MTU

   C. Protocol data unit

   D. Physical address

12. A _____ is an unsolicited message from an agent directed to a network management station that represents a significant event or condition for which notification to the manager is considered necessary.

☑ *Mastery Check*

13. What might you assign to a class of devices to provide a security boundary for a desired group of devices?

    A. Boundary name

    B. Community name

    C. Security model

    D. Encryption facilities

14. Which SNMP operation doesn't receive a GetResponse from the agent?

15. Which SNMPv2 operation helps minimize network interaction and permits the agent to return larger packets relative to GetRequest or GetNextRequest?

16. What response code will an SNMPv2 agent receive if the object doesn't exist and the agent is unable to create an instance of this object?

13

Module 14

Using the Domain Name System

Critical Skills

One major issue with TCP/IP networking is how to provide mappings between system names and their corresponding network addresses. UNIX provides several ways to facilitate the mapping between hostnames and IP addresses.

14.1 Discover How the Domain Name System Works

First, the traditional method involves the use of the `/etc/hosts` file. When a network application wishes to resolve a name, it invokes a standard library routine that looks up the name from this file. The file provides simple mappings of hostnames on the local level; this particular method has several problems. The chief issue is that it doesn't scale well; in other words, it would be impossible for the system administrator to maintain an `/etc/host` file that contains all the possible systems that one would need. When the Internet was much smaller, it used the `/etc/host` file approach for name resolution. However, because of operational problems it became clear that another mechanism was needed.

The second approach is to use Network Information Services (NIS). Today, this method is deployed within many companies, largely to handle internal name resolution for a company. This approach, too, suffers from the same basic problem as `/etc/hosts`—scalability. NIS doesn't provide for host resolution for a significant number of hosts, such as that contained on the Internet.

The third method uses DNS for name resolution. DNS provides a hierarchical namespace that contains domains, subdomains, and hostnames. A domain is a collection or grouping of hostnames strategically defined within the namespace so that no conflicts arise among different domains. For example, it is possible that two different companies may have picked identical hostnames for some of their systems. However, this doesn't represent a problem because the both companies are in different domains; thus, the system name overlay is negated.

The Domain Name System (DNS) provides a very critical element for the Internet—it provides mappings between hostnames and their corresponding Internet Protocol (IP) addresses. For example, when the URL of the form `http://www.whitehouse.gov` is entered within a Web browser, the browser in turn requests the IP address of this host from a DNS server in order for the communication between the user's system (browser) and the remote Web site to commence. Why does the browser do this? Because communication between systems on the Internet, for example, must use an Internet Protocol address. This is true for any TCP/IP network and must include the use of IP addresses when specifying systems. The term that refers to converting from a hostname to an IP address is known as *host resolution* and is completely transparent for the user. The DNS system available on most UNIX versions is known as the Berkeley Internet Name Domain (BIND) package and is used quite extensively on the Internet. BIND has been placed in the public domain and is freely available at www.isc.org.   This module is based on the BIND version of DNS.

The DNS namespace can be clearly explained by using an inverted tree structure, which is similar to a UNIX file system. The UNIX file system starts at the base or root, which is represented with a leading "/". Within DNS, a dot "." is used to represent the base of the tree. Figure 14-1 shows a sample of the DNS namespace. As you can see from the figure, several of the common DNS domains are defined that include edu, com, and net. These are known as "top level" or root domains, and any objects defined below these top levels are known as subdomains. The placement of companies, corporations, or institutions largely depends on the type of business the organization is engaged in. For instance, if a university called Zippy wants to join the Internet, a new subdomain called zippy will be defined under the edu domain because it is an education establishment. Standard DNS domains are listed in Table 14-1.

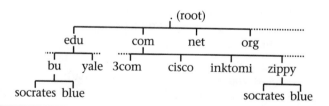

Figure 14-1   DNS namespace

14

Domain	Purpose
edu	Educational: universities, colleges, prep schools, etc.
com	Institutions and other organizations that engage in commercial activities
gov	Government organizations and institutions
int	International organizations
mil	Military organizations or those that work with such organizations
net	Internet service providers and other network support centers
org	Organizations that are noncommercial in nature, such as a nonprofit institution
country code	Each country code based on geographic location

Table 14-1   Top-Level DNS Domains

   Note that two systems have been assigned the name socrates; one in the edu domain and the other in the com domain. This is a perfectly acceptable and reasonable thing to do; that is, there is no conflict. The UNIX file system works the same way; two files with the same name can be defined within two different directories. One reads or interprets a domain and hostname in the opposite order as a UNIX file and pathname—from right to left. For example, the host

```
socrates.mis.zippy.edu
```

reads as follows: within the edu root domain, an organization called zippy defines a subdomain called mis, which contains a host called socrates. The DNS character separator is the dot (" . "), and a dot is implied after each top-level domain. However, in practice the rightmost dot is not used.

   DNS consists of two major elements: the server and the client. The server provides DNS services to one or more client systems. Whenever the client must obtain the IP address of a host, it makes a request to a DNS server. The server responds with a valid answer and the client continues to process the transaction. Typically, several servers are deployed so that should a failure occur with a particular DNS server, other backup systems will respond to the client request. This approach works well and provides a reasonable amount of fault tolerance.

14.2 Explore Both DNS Server and Client Components

A DNS server contains the following elements:

- Domain files
- Processes
- Tools

Domain Files

A DNS server is configured to service one or more domains. A domain is a collection of individual hosts that are grouped according to some arbitrary criteria. For example, all the systems within a particular department or team can be defined within a DNS domain. When a new domain is defined on the DNS server, a new domain file is created that contains records for each host. When the DNS server is started, it reads each domain file and then knows how to resolve mapping between names and IP addresses for that domain.

DNS Example

One of the best ways to understand the DNS system is to review an example configuration. The following listing contains a sample (but fully functional) domain file for the fictitious home.com domain. Comments can be placed with the file using the "//", "#" or " /* */" characters.

```
1   //
2   // home.com DNS named.conf file
3   //
4   options {
5           directory "/var/named";
6           allow-transfer {
7                   216.155.202.163;
8                   216.155.202.100;
9           };
10
11  };
```

Specifying the allow transfer option means only the two nodes listed here are allowed to query this server

The directory option specifies which UNIX directory the DNS server will use to find additional configuration files and zone information

14

```
12  //
13  // Our Primary DNS Information
14  //
15  zone "home.com" {
16          type master;
17          file "home.com";
18  };
19  zone "202.155.216.in-addr.arpa" {
20          type master;
21          file "reverse-home.com";
22  };
```

This listing represents a minimal DNS configuration that would be placed in the named.conf file. By default the DNS server will look for this file within the /etc directory, but this can be changed by using the -c command-line argument. The basic syntax of this DNS configuration includes

```
statement_keyword "string" {
    option keyword;
    option Keyword;
};
```

The statement keywords include high-level directives that define DNS services and control operational aspects of the server. Table 14-2 lists the supported keywords.

The basic named.conf file (as shown earlier) includes several sections that include configuration options, basic initialization, and individual zone

Statement Keyword	Meaning
acl	Provides an access control mechanism to form an IP address match list
include	Includes another file
logging	Controls server logging
options	Specific and control global server configuration options
controls	Determines how to communicate with the rndc utility
server	Defines a new server for a particular
zone	Defines a DNS zone. May contain either master or secondary keywords

Table 14-2   DNS Server Statement Keywords

configurations. The `option` section includes operational aspects of the DNS server. For example, use the `directory` (lines 4–9) option to specify which UNIX directory the DNS server will use to find additional configuration files and zone information. Some of the most common configuration keywords supported by the DNS server are listed in Tables 14-3 and 14-4. The DNS server options are divided into two groups: those options that control how the server interacts on the network (Table 14-3) with other systems, and configuration options (Table 14-4), which control how the server operates on the local system.

The configuration includes support for two zones: the `home.com` and the associated reverse IP domain. The `home.com` domain is defined within lines 15–18; the reverse domain, `202.155.216.in-addr.arpa` is contained within lines 19–22. Defining a new domain is very simple; all that is required is

Option Keyword	Meaning
`allow-query IP Addresses`	Determines which IP addresses are permitted to query the server. The default is all hosts are allowed.
`allow-transfer` IP Addresses	Determines which IP addresses are permitted to do a zone transfer from the DNS server. By default, any node can do a zone transfer.
`auth-mxdomain yes/no`	The default value is `yes`; this tells the server to answer authoritatively for domain queries on domains that have SOA records.
`check-names type action`	Tells the server to verify the integrity of domain names.
`fake-iquery yes/no`	The default value is `no`; the server will simulate the support for the `IQUERY` option type.
`fetch-glue yes/no`	The default value is `yes`; tells the server to query and cache the necessary DNS records about domains to which is it not authoritative
`forward first only`	The default value is `first`; this causes the server to forward to another DNS server when a client's query can't be resolved.
`forwarders ip list`	Provides a list of IP addresses for the DNS server to query when it doesn't have information about a client request.
`multiple-cnames yes/no`	The default value is `no`; this permits the server to support CNAMES and point to other CNAMES.
`notify yes/no`	The default value is `yes`; this tells the server to emit a notify message to all secondaries when a zone has been updated on the server.
`recursion yes/no`	The default value is `yes`; this instructs the server to query other DNS servers to resolve a client DNS request.

14

Table 14-3   Server Interaction Options

Option Keyword	Meaning
`directory path`	Specifies the working directory for the DNS server.
`name-xfer path`	Specifies the path for the `name-xfer` program. This program is responsible for doing a zone transfer.
`dump-file path`	Specifies the path name for where the DNS server should write database information when it receives a special signal.
`memstatistics-file`	Specifies the name of the file to dump usage statistics when the DNS server exits, when the `deallocate-on-exit` option is set to `yes`. The default filename is `named.memstats`.

Table 14-4   Server Operational Options

the name of the domain to determine the relationship between the domain and the DNS server and the resource file, which contains the specific hosts for that domain.

In this example, the `zone` keyword is used to tell the server that a new domain (zone) is being defined. The `zone` keyword defines a forward mapping between IP addresses and names. This specific configuration information is contained within the `home.com` file. The brackets (`{}`) are used to delimit or include additional optional keywords for that domain. The `type` keyword defines the relationship between the domain and the DNS server, and in this case the `master` word is used.

When a DNS server is a master for a domain, no other DNS server anywhere will answer authoritative requests for that domain. In other words, the master DNS server is supposed to be the definitive source for the

Hint
"Zone" is another term that means DNS domain.

domain. However, there are cases when additional DNS servers appear to be answering requests for a domain for which they are not the master. A DNS server need not be a master for a domain, but rather can be a secondary server. A secondary DNS server is one that obtains DNS records from a master, but can answer DNS client queries for that domain. This approach is a great way to address performance factors in a larger network and by adding load-balancing features into the DNS namespace.

Next, the reverse map is defined and is called the `202.155.216.in-addr.arpa` domain. The specifics of this zone are contained within `reverse-home.com` file. The reverse map is used to convert from an IP address to hostname. This domain is simply the IP address of a network for the forward domain plus the `in-addr.arpa` extension tacked on the end. Although this domain isn't strictly required to operate a DNS server, other sites require the ability to review maps from a particular host to ensure that an individual system is from a particular domain. This forms the basis of a rudimentary security policy for DNS servers.

Certain security measures can be implemented using the `allow-transfer` keyword (lines 6–9) to control which other systems can "talk" to the DNS server to obtain wholesale information about one or more domains. In this case, two nodes (216.155.202.163 and 216.155.202.100) have permission to query the DNS server.

Hint

`allow-transfer` is not for generic DNS resolver (client) queries, but for other systems that may wish to interrogate the DNS server. Later in this module, you will learn to use debugging tools to query DNS servers for a variety of useful and important information.

DNS Records

A DNS server contains one or more host records, which contain information so that correct mappings between hostnames and IP addresses can be done and also records to provide mappings in the opposite direction. Further, the DNS server can be used to provide additional information to clients that include additional fields about host records. For example, the DNS server can provide the name of the mail server that should be used when attempting to send mail to a system contained within the DNS namespace. The standard DNS record types are listed in Table 14-5.

Digging Deeper

At this point, both of the associated zone files listed in the example above haven't been discussed. In the previous example, lines 17 and 21 refer to external files: `home.com` and `reverse-home.com`. The `home.com` file contains the forward DNS records of this domain, while the `reverse-home.com` contains the reverse mappings. It is typical to place each zone within a separate file; this

14

DNS Record Type	Description
A	An address record; used to provide a mapping between a hostname and IP address
CNAME	A conical name record; used to designate an alias for an A record
NS	Name server records define a new DNS server that will provide authoritative information about a particular domain
MX	Mail exchanger record; used to indicate the mail server for a particular domain
PTR	A pointer record; used to provide reverse mapping between an IP address and hostname
RP	Responsible person record; specifies the contact information about a particular host
TXT	A text record; can be used to provide additional information about a host

Table 14-5 | DNS Record Types

makes administration of the domain that much easier. The home.com file contains the following:

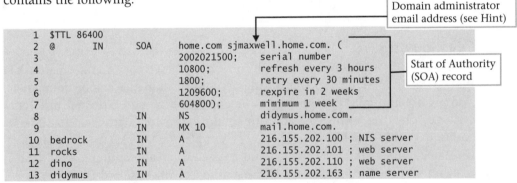

```
 1  $TTL 86400
 2  @        IN    SOA    home.com sjmaxwell.home.com. (
 3                        2002021500;   serial number
 4                        10800;        refresh every 3 hours
 5                        1800;         retry every 30 minutes
 6                        1209600;      rexpire in 2 weeks
 7                        604800);      mimimum 1 week
 8                 IN     NS     didymus.home.com.
 9                 IN     MX 10  mail.home.com.
10  bedrock        IN     A      216.155.202.100 ; NIS server
11  rocks          IN     A      216.155.202.101 ; web server
12  dino           IN     A      216.155.202.110 ; web server
13  didymus        IN     A      216.155.202.163 ; name server
```

Whenever a DNS server is master for a particular domain, it must contain a Start of Authority (SOA) record. The SOA record is contained within lines 2–7 in the example above and is used to specify the operational parameters for the domain, such as the email address for the administrator and other important timing elements. The SOA records contains the following:

● Email address of domain administrator

● Serial number of the domain

● Zone refresh metric

- Zone retry metric

- Zone expiration metric

Hint

In the email address, the @ that is usually in the address is replaced by a period (.), so in this example the email address `sjmaxwell.home.com` corresponds to `sjmaxwell@home.com`.

This information controls the interface between the primary DNS server and any secondary servers that have been configured.

The `reverse-home.com` file contains the following:

```
 1  $TTL 86400
 2  @        IN      SOA     202.155.216.in-addr.arpa  sjmaxwell.home.com (
 3                           2002021500;    serial number
 4                           10800;         refresh every 3 hours
 5                           1800;          retry every 30 minutes
 6                           1209600;       rexpire in 2 weeks
 7                           604800 ) ;       mimimum 1 week
 8                   IN      NS   didymus.home.com.
 9  100              IN      PTR  bedrock.home.com.
10  101              IN      PTR  rocks.home.com.
11  110              IN      PTR  dino.home.com.
12  163              IN      PTR  didymus.home.com.
```

As you can see, the format used is the same as the forward mapping `home.com` file, but instead of using `A` records, `PTR` records are used. Also, the name of each record is the last byte of the IP address, not the hostname of the system.

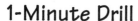

1-Minute Drill

- What benefit does the Domain Name System (DNS) provide for mappings between system names and their corresponding network addresses that both a UNIX `/etc/host` file approach and Network Information Service (NIS) lack for a system like the Internet?

- What is the DNS reverse map used for?

- Explain a DNS master server.

- Scalability
- The DNS reverse map converts from an IP address to hostname.
- When DNS server is a master for a domain, that means that no other DNS server anywhere will answer authoritative requests for that domain by clients.

Processes

On the DNS server, a program listens on port 53 and waits for DNS client requests. For Linux, the server is called `named`, but on both Solaris and HP-UX the server is known as `in.named`. Despite the name difference, each of the servers provides the same basic functions and also each of the programs supports many of the command-line options. The DNS servers are available by default for each platform; however, this will depend on the type of installation that was performed. To ensure that DNS server has been installed, do the following:

Linux: `ls -al /usr/sbin/named`

Solaris/HP-UX: `ls -al /usr/sbin/in.named`

If the DNS server program is not found within these locations, the package hasn't been installed. Use the native installation programs to install the DNS package—for Linux, use gnoprm; for Solaris, use pkgadd; and for HP-UX use swinstall. See Module 4 for additional information on these tools.

When the system is started and DNS services have been installed, the DNS server is typically started as one of the standard processes. On Linux, `/etc/rc.d/init.d/named` is the primary startup script. Symbolic links are placed within each of the run-level directories to this script; this includes both S and K scripts. Thus, the following (for example) should be installed:

```
/etc/rc.d/rc5.d/K45named
/etc/rc.d/rc5.d/S45named
```

On Solaris and HP-UX, the script `/etc/init.d/inetsvc` brings up the DNS server when the system boots and contains the following linked files:

```
/etc/rc0.d/K42inetsvc
/etc/rc2.d/S72inetsvc
```

Verify DNS Server Is Running

As the administrator, you can verify that the server is running and listening on the correct network port.

To verify that the server is running on the system, use the `ps` command (Linux):

```
# ps -ef | grep name
named        867     1  0 21:53 ?        00:00:00 named -u named
named        869   867  0 21:53 ?        00:00:00 named -u named
named        870   869  0 21:53 ?        00:00:00 named -u named
named        871   869  0 21:53 ?        00:00:00 named -u named
named        872   869  0 21:53 ?        00:00:00 named -u named
```

The named process for Linux is multithreaded, which when listed with the `ps` command, shows the command with multiple processes. However, only a single process is actually running.

For Solaris/HP-UX, use the following:

```
# ps -ef | grep in.named
    root    220     1  0 23:53:10 ?         0:00 /usr/sbin/in.named
```

To show which ports the DNS server is listening on, use the following commands (Linux):

```
# netstat -p -a | grep name
Proto Recv-Q Send-Q Local Address           Foreign Address         State
PID/Program name
tcp        0      0 didymus.home.com:domain *:*                     LISTEN
867/named
tcp        0      0 localhost:domain        *:*                     LISTEN
867/named
udp        0      0 didymus.home.com:domain *:*
867/named
udp        0      0 localhost:domain        *:*
867/named
```

The output above may suggest that several different named processes are running when, in fact, only a single process is running. Examine the PID field—it shows a single process ID, which in this case is 867. Using the `netstat` command, both the port and DNS process can be listed. In the output above, processes are listed for both TCP and UDP ports. This means that DNS requests are available using both TCP and UDP transport protocols. The string `didymus.home.com:domain` contains both the local address hostname (or address) and port component. In this example, `domain` refers to port 53, which is mapped in the `/etc/services` file.

14

The `Foreign Address` indicates which remote address the network connection is attached to. Here we see that "`*:*`" is used, and this means that any remote address will be accepted.

> ## Hint
> On Linux, the `-p` option is available, which gives the name of the program that is listening on a specific port. The other versions of UNIX don't support this option.

For Solaris/HP-UX, use the following:

```
# netstat -a | grep domain
localhost.domain                       Idle
bedrock.home.com.domain                Idle
localhost.domain          *.*        0    0 65536    0 LISTEN
bedrock.home.com.domain   *.*        0    0 65536    0 LISTEN
```

The output for both Solaris and HP-UX systems looks different from the Linux output, but the same basic information is provided, just using a modified format.

DNS Tools

The BIND package includes several useful tools for debugging and verifying DNS server operations. The tools include

- nslookup

- dig

- host

nslookup

The `nslookup` command provides a mechanism to query a DNS server from the command line. The `nslookup` command is available across a wide number of UNIX systems; however, on Linux it is being depreciated and will be replaced by other tools such as `host` and `dig`. On Solaris and HP-UX `nslookup` ships with the basic operating system and is the standard DNS debugging tool for these platforms. The command has two basic modes: simple query and complex command interface mode. To use simple query mode, provide a hostname for DNS resolution as an option to the command (Linux):

```
# nslookup dino.home.com
Note:  nslookup is deprecated and may be removed from future releases.
Consider using the `dig' or `host' programs instead.  Run nslookup with
the `-sil[ent]' option to prevent this message from appearing.
Server:         216.155.202.163
Address:        216.155.202.163#53

Name:    dino.home.com
Address: 216.155.202.110
```

On Linux, we get a warning message about the fate of the nslookup command, but on Solaris and HP-UX, the following is displayed:

```
# nslookup dino.home.com
Server:  didymus.home.com
Address:  216.155.202.163

Name:    dino.home.com
Address:  216.155.202.110
```

In the examples above, we obtain the same basic information about the dino.home.com host: the IP address of the host called dino.home.com. This is the fundamental purpose of simply query mode.

To use complete query mode; issue the nslookup command without any options:

```
# nslookup
Default Server:  didymus.home.com
Address:  216.155.202.163

>
```

As a result, the command displays the default DNS server, associated IP address of the DNS server, and a command prompt (>). At this point, nslookup will

14

accept command options that control how and what to query from the DNS
server. Typing the ? command (help) will show all the supported commands:

```
> ?
Commands:          (identifiers are shown in uppercase, [] means optional)
NAME               - print info about the host/domain NAME using default server
NAME1 NAME2        - as above, but use NAME2 as server
help or ?          - print info on common commands; see nslookup(1) for details
set OPTION         - set an option
    all            - print options, current server and host
    [no]debug      - print debugging information
    [no]d2         - print exhaustive debugging information
    [no]defname    - append domain name to each query
    [no]recurse    - ask for recursive answer to query
    [no]vc         - always use a virtual circuit
    domain=NAME    - set default domain name to NAME
    srchlist=N1[/N2/.../N6] - set domain to N1 and search list to N1,N2,
etc.
    root=NAME      - set root server to NAME
    retry=X        - set number of retries to X
    timeout=X      - set initial time-out interval to X seconds
    querytype=X    - set query type, e.g.,
A,ANY,CNAME,HINFO,MX,PX,NS,PTR,SOA,TXT,WKS
    port=X         - set port number to send query on
    type=X         - synonym for querytype
    class=X        - set query class to one of IN (Internet), CHAOS, HESIOD or
ANY
server NAME        - set default server to NAME, using current default server
lserver NAME       - set default server to NAME, using initial server
finger [USER]      - finger the optional USER at the current default host
root               - set current default server to the root
ls [opt] DOMAIN [> FILE] - list addresses in DOMAIN (optional: output to
FILE)
    -a             -  list canonical names and aliases
    -h             -  list HINFO (CPU type and operating system)
    -s             -  list well-known services
    -d             -  list all records
    -t TYPE        -  list records of the given type (e.g., A,CNAME,MX, etc.)
view FILE          - sort an 'ls' output file and view it with more
exit               - exit the program, ^D also exits
```

Although the list of command-line options appears complicated, using
nslookup in this mode is quite easy. At the command prompt, a hostname
can be typed to obtain DNS resolution:

```
> bedrock
Server:  didymus.home.com
Address:  216.155.202.163

Name:    bedrock.home.com
Address:  216.155.202.100

>
```

As the output shows, the `nslookup` command displays the DNS server information and the resolution for a host called `bedrock.home.com`. Two very useful features of `nslookup` are that another DNS server can be queried and different types of information can be obtained from the specified server. To change the DNS server while in command mode, do the following:

```
> server 216.155.202.100
Default Server:  bedrock.home.com
Address:  216.155.202.100
```

Either the IP address or the hostname of an alternate DNS server can be specified using the `server` command. The example above shows the IP address. To instruct `nslookup` to display the SOA record for a particular domain, change the query type:

```
> set type=soa
>
```

This tells the server to request the Start of Authority record instead of a host record. Then, type a domain name:

```
> home.com
Server:  bedrock.home.com
Address:  216.155.202.100

home.com
        origin = home.com
        mail addr = sjmaxwell.home.com
        serial = 2002021500
        refresh = 10800 (3H)
        retry   = 1800 (30M)
        expire  = 1209600 (2W)
        minimum ttl = 604800 (1W)
home.com           nameserver = didymus.home.com
didymus.home.com           internet address = 216.155.202.163
```

The information obtained about the SOA record will match what has been placed with the zone file for this domain.

dig

The `dig` command provides a mechanism to query a DNS server from the command line, just like the `nslookup` command. However, it provides much

14

more information about the underlying interaction between the client and DNS server. This command is available with the BIND package, but it doesn't come standard on either Solaris or HP-UX. It is available out of the box for Linux:

```
# dig dino.home.com

; <<>> DiG 9.1.3 <<>> dino.home.com
;; global options:  printcmd
;; Got answer:
;; ->>HEADER<<- opcode: QUERY, status: NOERROR, id: 19633
;; flags: qr aa rd ra; QUERY: 1, ANSWER: 1, AUTHORITY: 1, ADDITIONAL: 1

;; QUESTION SECTION:
;dino.home.com.                  IN      A

;; ANSWER SECTION:
dino.home.com.          86400   IN      A       216.155.202.110

;; AUTHORITY SECTION:
home.com.               86400   IN      NS      didymus.home.com.

;; ADDITIONAL SECTION:
didymus.home.com.       86400   IN      A       216.155.202.163

;; Query time: 22 msec
;; SERVER: 216.155.202.163#53(216.155.202.163)
;; WHEN: Mon Feb 18 23:30:55 2002
;; MSG SIZE  rcvd: 85
```

host

The host command is relatively new to the DNS community and comes with the basic Linux operating system. It provides the same basic services as both nslookup and dig. However, it provides a few handy command-line options to make it easier to obtain DNS information. For example, it supports the -1 option that will list all the hosts within a specified domain. It also supports basic hostname resolution. Thus, using this command with a valid DNS name yields

```
# host dino
dino.home.com. has address 216.155.202.110
```

Typing the host command without any arguments causes a listing of the command-line arguments to be displayed:

```
# host
Usage: host [-aCdlrTwv] [-c class] [-n] [-N ndots] [-t type] [-W time]
            [-R number] hostname [server]
       -a is equivalent to -v -t *
       -c specifies query class for non-IN data
       -C compares SOA records on authoritative nameservers
       -d is equivalent to -v
       -l lists all hosts in a domain, using AXFR
       -n Use the nibble form of IPv6 reverse lookup
       -N changes the number of dots allowed before root lookup is done
       -r disables recursive processing
       -R specifies number of retries for UDP packets
       -t specifies the query type
       -T enables TCP/IP mode
       -v enables verbose output
       -w specifies to wait forever for a reply
       -W specifies how long to wait for a reply
```

Explore DNS Client Components

In order for a UNIX client to use a DNS server, two files must be configured correctly. The first is the /etc/nsswitch.conf file and the second is the /etc/resolv.conf file. The nsswitch.conf file determines how the system should obtain important information such as login information and host information. Consider a partial file listing from the default nsswitch.conf file from Solaris:

```
passwd:     files
group:      files
hosts:      files
```

The file includes a string label, which represents a network or system service (or system database) and a number of associated arguments. The arguments include the directives that tell the system to use one or more mechanisms to obtain the needed information. For example, the entry passwd: files means that when login information is needed (when a user logs in to the system, for instance), the system should consult the local files for user authentication. The entry passwd: nisplus files now means that the system should first attempt to authenticate the user using NIS+ services, and if that fails use the local files. Table 14-6 lists all the supported nsswitch.conf directives.

14

Directive	Meaning
files	Consult the local database files that include /etc/passwd, /etc/group, /etc/shadow, and /etc/hosts.
nis	Query a NIS server for authentication or other database information.
nisplus	Query a NIS+ server for authentication or other database information.
ldap	Query an LDAP database for authentication or other database information.
dns	Use a DNS server when attempting to resolve hostnames or IP addresses.
compat	Used with both the /etc/passwd and /etc/group files that support the "+" and "-" directives.

Table 14-6 The nsswitch.conf Directives

In the same way, before the UNIX client will use a DNS server, the hosts; entry must include a dns directive:

```
hosts; dns files
```

The /etc/resolv.conf file is used to provide specific information about the DNS configuration for the local machine. The basic syntax of the file includes adding which domain the client is a member of and one or more nameservers to query. The example

```
domain home.com
nameserver 216.155.202.163
```

indicates that the local machine should use the home.com domain when making queries to the DNS server with the IP address of 216.155.202.163. In practice, usually two DNS server entries are added to this file so that the client may query the second server should the first one be unavailable.

Hint

The nameserver command must be accomplished by a valid IP address of the DNS server and not the hostname of the server. Why? Because if the hostname of the DNS were supplied, there would be no way to resolve the name to an IP address since this entry is supposed to provide DNS resolution for the system. When nslookup or other DNS tools are invoked, they consult this file for nameserver and domain information.

You can place one or more nameserver entries in the file so that should one of the primary DNS servers fail, another one may be used so that client request will be answered. Typically, each client system should have at least two nameserver definitions to ensure a reasonable amount of redundancy.

Project 14-1

In this project, you will examine the DNS configuration on your system and practice using DNS tools.

Step-by-Step

1. Display the contents of your system's DNS configuration file:

```
# more /etc/named.conf
```

2. Identify the directory where additional DNS configuration files are stored on your system by looking for a `directory` option line.

3. Display the contents of your system's master zone file and reverse zone file, substituting your correct directory for `/var/named` and your correct domain name and reverse domain name for `sjmaxwell.org` and `192.168.1.in-addr.arpa`, remembering to use the IP address for your network in the latter:

```
# more /var/named/sjmaxwell.org
# more /var/named/192.168.1.in-addr.arpa
```

4. Verify that your system's DNS server is running. For Linux systems, use

```
# ps -ef | grep name
```

For Solaris, use

```
# ps -ef | grep in.named
```

5. Display the ports your system's DNS server is listening on. For Linux systems, use

```
# netstat -p -a | grep name
```

For Solaris, use

```
# netstat -a | grep domain
```

6. Display the hostname and IP address for your system:

```
# nslookup
```

14

✓ *Mastery Check*

1. DNS provides a _____ namespace that contains domains, subdomains, and hostnames.

2. True or False: If two companies with different domains choose the same hostnames for some of their systems, one of the companies will need to change the hostnames to avoid DNS conflicts.

3. Converting from a hostname to an IP address is _____.

4. What are the domain, organization, subdomain, and host in this hostname?

   `www.athletics.indiana.edu`

5. Which command provides a mechanism to query a DNS server from the command line?

6. When using `nslookup` in command mode, what is the command to change the DNS server to the DNS server at 192.168.1.215?

7. What two commands might you consider using instead of `nslookup` that both provide the same information as `nslookup` as well as additional DNS information?

8. Which DNS configuration file provides specific information about the DNS configuration for the local machine?

9. Which DNS configuration file determines the how the system should obtain important system information such as login information and host information?

Module 15

Using NIS

Critical Skills

In previous modules, the administration of user accounts was reviewed with particular emphasis on manipulation of text files on stand-alone UNIX systems. In this section, the Network Information Services (NIS) facility, which was developed by Sun Microsystems, is explored and discussed. NIS supports a centralized management approach to such things as account management and hostname resolution. The NIS service provides a distributed database for UNIX accounts as well as other important services. NIS is a general text file lookup facility. In general, NIS provides a namespace domain where objects elements are defined on a server and are then made available across a network in a distributed fashion. The information can be stored on several servers to build a robust, mission-critical database service that can be used across a large enterprise of systems. Clients make requests for objects (such as a UNIX login) from the network and one of the NIS servers answers and responds with the correct information.

15.1 Overview of Network Information Services

A NIS server can be configured to serve a variety of database files that include `/etc/hosts`, `/etc/passwd`, and `/etc/group`. A default list of NIS services is shown in Table 15-1 along with any associated configuration files. The NIS databases are derived from the standard UNIX configuration files.

To support these NIS services, one or more NIS servers are installed on the network and are used to support a cluster or domain of machines, which consist of servers and clients. When NIS systems are set up, a NIS domain must be defined, which determines the scope of machines involved. For example, if the engineering department wishes to deploy a number of NIS servers and clients, a domain call `eng` can be defined on each of the machines. A NIS domain is simply a collection of machines that have something in common.

Each server is configured to support one or more NIS domains that service requests for information from NIS clients within that domain. However, a NIS server may support more than one NIS domain, but there should be only a single NIS master as primary per domain. A NIS master is simply a machine that acts as an authoritative server for a partner NIS domain. In a typical

> ## Hint
> A NIS server doesn't necessarily have to serve all of the database files listed in the table, but rather only those deemed required by the administrator. It will be up to the administrator to determine which databases are needed within the NIS domain.

When NIS was first introduced, it was called "Yellow Pages," but due to a conflict with a company that already has the right to that name, Sun changed the service to NIS. However, many of the tools and software programs still contain the "`yp`" string, which stood for "Yellow Pages."

Hint
This section describes version 2 of the NIS system; a newer version of NIS is available, but not reviewed in this module. The new version of NIS (called NIS+) provides increased security, the ability to scale to larger networks, and enhanced administrative functions.

configuration, at least two NIS servers are deployed for each domain: one as a primary master and the other as secondary. The secondary contains the exact same information as the primary, but all changes are made on the primary.

Services	Description
Hostname resolution	Maps name to IP addresses and IP addresses to names; replaces the local `/etc/hosts` database file; reverse mapping that replaces the local `/etc/ethers` file.
UNIX account authentication	Provides UNIX login services with central account authentication; replaces the `/etc/passwd`, `/etc/group`, and `/etc/shadow` local files.
Group level security	Provides rudimentary authentication based on groups.
IP network masks	Provides a mapping between subnet networks and their corresponding network masks; replaces the `/etc/netmasks` file.
IP networks name	Maps network names to IP networks; replaces the local `/etc/networks` file.
Mail aliases	Supports mail aliases, which are obtained from the local `/etc/aliases` file.
Network protocols	Maps network protocol names to numbers.
Network services	Maps network services to network ports.
Time zone definition	Contains the time zone of the local network; uses the `/etc/timezone` file.

Table 15-1 NIS Services and Associated UNIX Files

15

When a change is made on the primary NIS server, the information is "pushed" to the secondary automatically.

When a client system boots, it binds to one of the NIS servers within the client's domain. All requests for database information, such as UNIX authentication or host resolution, are sent to the server for which the client is bound.

15.2 Discover NIS Components

A NIS server contains the following:

- Databases

- Processes

- Tools

Databases

The NIS server maintains a database for each type of file or network service available on UNIX. For example, for name resolution, the /etc/hosts file is used and NIS database files are constructed from this file. When the NIS server is set up, each of the local files on the NIS server is used as the basis for the NIS databases. Each NIS database served by a NIS server is known as a NIS map and these maps are located within the /var/yp directory. For each NIS service, one or more DBM database files are created to provide very quick access to the contents. For instance, for the /etc/hosts file, the following DBM files are created:

```
-rw-------   1 root     1           4096 Feb 25 22:06 hosts.byaddr.dir
-rw-------   1 root     1           4096 Feb 25 22:06 hosts.byaddr.pag
-rw-------   1 root     1           4096 Feb 25 22:06 hosts.byname.dir
-rw-------   1 root     1           3072 Feb 25 22:06 hosts.byname.pag
```

These files support key/content pairs that make up the database. The .dir files contain a bit map of the file data, while the actual data is stored with the .pag files. In the case of the /etc/hosts file, two separate database files are maintained: one that sorts the database by IP address (hosts.byaddr), while the other does so by hostname (host.byname).

To determine which services and/or files are supported by a particular NIS server, examine the /var/yp/<domain> directory, where <domain> is the NIS domain—for example, home.com. Thus, the command

```
ls -l /var/yp/home.com/*.pag
```

shows all the maps for the home.com domain:

```
/var/yp/home.com/auto.home.pag
/var/yp/home.com/auto.master.pag
/var/yp/home.com/group.bygid.pag
/var/yp/home.com/group.byname.pag
/var/yp/home.com/hosts.byaddr.pag
/var/yp/home.com/hosts.byname.pag
/var/yp/home.com/ipnodes.byaddr.pag
/var/yp/home.com/ipnodes.byname.pag
/var/yp/home.com/mail.aliases.pag
/var/yp/home.com/mail.byaddr.pag
/var/yp/home.com/netgroup.byhost.pag
/var/yp/home.com/netgroup.byuser.pag
/var/yp/home.com/netgroup.pag
/var/yp/home.com/netid.byname.pag
/var/yp/home.com/netmasks.byaddr.pag
/var/yp/home.com/networks.byaddr.pag
/var/yp/home.com/networks.byname.pag
/var/yp/home.com/passwd.byname.pag
/var/yp/home.com/passwd.byuid.pag
/var/yp/home.com/protocols.byname.pag
/var/yp/home.com/protocols.bynumber.pag
/var/yp/home.com/publickey.byname.pag
/var/yp/home.com/rpc.bynumber.pag
/var/yp/home.com/services.byname.pag
/var/yp/home.com/services.byservicename.pag
/var/yp/home.com/timezone.byname.pag
/var/yp/home.com/ypservers.pag
```

Processes

A NIS server is a machine that has been configured to run NIS server software and contains one or more NIS databases files. The configuration of a NIS server involves the `ypinit` script which builds NIS databases and starts the appropriate NIS processes. On a standard NIS server, the following processes are necessary:

- `ypserv`
- `ypxfrd`
- `ypbind`
- `rpc.yppasswdd`

A NIS client will typically run a subset of these processes. The programs are started automatically when the NIS server is configured. Thus, manual

15

manipulation of these processes is not normally necessary. However, on Solaris and HP-UX, a script called `/usr/lib/netsvc/yp/ypstart` is provided to start the NIS server manually. To stop the server, use `ypstop`. On Linux, use the `/etc/rc.d/init.d/ypbind` script with the `stop` option.

ypserv

This is the main NIS server process; it listens on the network for NIS requests and performs database lookups on objects, and returns responses to clients. The interaction between the client and server are by means of remote procedure calls (RPCs).

ypxfrd

When it becomes necessary to transfer an entire NIS map from one host to another, the `ypxfrd` process is the most efficient means of doing so. It is typically run when the `ypserv` is started to handle any transfer of database maps between the primary and any secondary servers.

ypbind

This process is typically run on client systems and is the vehicle by which clients talk to NIS servers. A client system is said to be *bound* to a particular NIS server when the `ypbind` process is started; this is usually at system startup. A client may bind to a specific server or whichever server responds to a bind request.

rpc.yppasswdd

This program is used to handle UNIX password changes across the NIS domain. This program is run on each client system (and any NIS server if necessary) to process `passwd` requests on the behalf of normal UNIX users.

Tools

NIS provides a standard set of tools for managing NIS servers, verifying NIS operations, and debugging problems. Table 15-2 show the most important and relevant NIS tools sorted by generic functional types.

ypcat

The `ypcat` command is used to retrieve a NIS map from a server. When supplied with a name of a map filename, it obtains the latest copy of the NIS map from the

NIS Tools	Description
Verification and Lookup	
ypcat	Retrieves the contents of a NIS map.
ypwhich	Shows to which NIS server a client is bound.
ypmatch	Displays the values of the keys from one or more NIS maps.
General Operations	
yppasswd	Changes a user's NIS password.
ypmake	Updates the NIS maps across all NIS servers.
ypxfr	Transfers a entire NIS map.
ypset	Forces a NIS client to bind to a specific server.
yppush	Pushes out update maps to all NIS servers.
Debugging	
yppoll	Determines information about a specific NIS map.

Table 15-2   Standard NIS Tools

server to which the local system is bound. For example, the following command can be used to obtain the passwd map from the NIS server:

```
# ypcat passwd
```

The sample output includes

```
anonymou:*LK*:102:1::/home/anonymou:/bin/sh
nobody:ZVgYQwi9shwvI:60001:60001:Nobody:/:
daemon:NP:1:1::/:
anitat::1001:10:Ms. Anita Tognazzini:/home/anita:/bin/sh
nuucp:NP:9:9:uucp Admin:/var/spool/uucppublic:/usr/lib/uucp/uucico
root:gFcK3fd1xU8K6:0:1:Super-User:/:/sbin/sh
adm:NP:4:4:Admin:/var/adm:
noaccess:NP:60002:60002:No Access User:/:
jjwalker:*LK*:25000:1:Mr JJ Walker:/home/jj:/bin/sh
nobody4:NP:65534:65534:SunOS 4.x Nobody:/:
stevem:2OsoeRO1KBFLQ:20001:10:Mr. Steve
Maxwell:/homes/stevem:/usr/bin/bash
listen:*LK*:37:4:Network Admin:/usr/net/nls:
billc:88kn2zz5.roeE:20002:10:Mr. Bill
Clinton:/homes/billc:/usr/bin/bash
```

15

```
uucp:NP:5:5:uucp Admin:/usr/lib/uucp:
samc::20110:10:Mr Sam Clinton:/homes/samc:/bin/sh
sys:NP:3:3::/:
bin:NP:2:2::/usr/bin:
lp:NP:71:8:Line Printer Admin:/usr/spool/lp:
```

This NIS map will contain all the UNIX accounts that have been established on the NIS server. Assuming this command was run on a NIS client, the fact that the transfer was successful means that the NIS server is able to deliver this particular NIS map to the requesting system.

Hint

Being able to retrieve a particular map from the NIS server does indicate that the server is functional. However, it doesn't mean that other maps can be retrieved or that a map contains correct information.

ypwhich

The ypwhich command is used to show to which NIS server a client is bound; it provides a handy way to determine if the client is connected to a NIS server. The command

```
ypwhich
```

will show the name of a valid NIS server if the client was able to bind to a NIS server during the boot process or if the bind was invoked after booting. This command can also be used to list all the defined NIS map nicknames. A NIS nickname is simply another name for the NIS map. The −x option displays all the defined NIS nicknames:

```
# ypwhich -x
Use "ethers"    for map "ethers.byname"
Use "aliases"   for map "mail.aliases"
Use "services"  for map "services.byname"
Use "protocols" for map "protocols.bynumber"
Use "hosts"     for map "hosts.byname"
Use "networks"  for map "networks.byaddr"
Use "group"     for map "group.byname"
Use "passwd"    for map "passwd.byname"
```

These nicknames are found in the /var/yp/nickname file. On Linux, this file by default contains the above mapping, while on Solaris and HP-UX the file is empty.

yppasswd

The yppasswd command is used to change a UNIX account password on the NIS master server. Actually, on Solaris this command is a link to the passwd command. Normally, when the passwd command is used it will change the user's password on the local system. This is not what is needed since the password change is only for the local machine. As the administrator, it will be your job to instruct users to use the yppasswd command to change their passwords for the NIS environment. The following example shows the output when the NIS user stevem changes his password:

```
# yppasswd stevem
New password:
Re-enter new password:
NIS passwd/attributes changed on bedrock
```

In this case, bedrock is a NIS master server.

ypmake

The ypmake command doesn't actually exist; it is just a shorthand reference to update the NIS maps on the NIS master. The administrator must invoke the make command within the /var/yp directory. Executing the make command within this directory causes the NIS Makefile to be parsed, which results in NIS maps being updated and pushed to secondary (slave) NIS servers.

   This command would be run after one or more of the UNIX system files have been updated on the NIS master so that the changes can take effect and be pushed out to the other NIS servers. For example, when a new user is added to the /etc/passwd file on the NIS master and the make command is executed, the following would be displayed:

```
# make
updated passwd
pushed passwd
```

   The output of this command means the passwd NIS map was updated successfully.

ypxfr

The ypxfr command is used to retrieve one or more NIS maps from a NIS server to another host on the network. Typically, this command is run from the root crontab file to transfer NIS maps automatically on a periodic basis. Several scripts

15

are provided with NIS to aid in automating the NIS map transfer function. The scripts are located within the /usr/lib/netsvc/yp directory.

ypset

The ypset command is used to force a client to bind to a particular NIS server. This command is used in situations where no NIS server exists on the local network and the NIS broadcast option is not used or the network infrastructure doesn't support broadcast facilities.

yppush

This command is used to push or update all secondary NIS servers with changes from the master. It is not normally invoked by the administrator; instead, the make command via the NIS update process invokes this command.

yppoll

The yppoll command is used to determine the order number for a NIS map. This can be used to determine when maps are being updated either on the NIS master or any secondary. For example, the command

```
# yppoll group.byname
```

shows the following:

```
Domain home.com is supported.
Map group.byname has order number 1014880132.
The master server is bedrock.
```

The order number is used like a serial number so that a new version of NIS maps can be detected. In this example, the order number for the group map is 1014880132. Thus, when this map is updated on the NIS master, such as

```
# touch /etc/group
# cd /var/yp;make
updated group
pushed group
updated netid
pushed netid
```

and we again run the yppoll command, we see that the order number has been incremented:

```
# yppoll group.byname
Domain home.com is supported.
```

```
Map group.byname has order number 1014880550. ◄─────
The master server is bedrock.
```

> Order number is
> incremented from
> first example

1-Minute Drill

● If you are a system administrator using NIS on your network for account authentication, what is something you need to let users know about their accounts?

● What three components does a NIS server have?

15.3 Setting Up a NIS Server

When configuring one or more NIS servers, use the `ypinit` command to configure the NIS server. This command is used to set up both NIS master and secondary servers. This command creates the `/var/yp` directory structure and the NIS database files.

Project 15-1

In this project, you'll set up a NIS server. You should substitute the names of your domains and NIS servers for the NIS domain `home.com` and the NIS servers `bedrock` and `dino` used in the example.

Step-by-Step

1. Set the system domain name:

On Solaris and HP-UX, edit the `/etc/defaultdomain` file and add the NIS domain name. In this case, the `home.com` name is added to this file. On Linux, add the `NIS_DOMAIN` variable to the `/etc/sysconfig/network` file.

Hint

Certain versions of Linux don't support this method. As a result, add the command `nisdomainname` with the appropriate domain string to the `/etc/rc.d/init.t/ypserv` file. For example, the line `nisdomainname home.com` added to the beginning of the `ypserv` script ensures that when this startup script is executed during system boot, the NIS domain name is set automatically.

● You need to let them know to change their password with the `yppasswd` command instead of `passwd`.
● Databases, processes, tools

2. Execute the `ypinit -m` command on the NIS master machine. When done, similar output will be displayed:

```
In order for NIS to operate sucessfully, we have to construct a list of the
NIS servers.  Please continue to add the names for YP servers in order of
preference, one per line.  When you are done with the list, type a <control D>
or a return on a line by itself.
        next host to add:  bedrock
        next host to add:

The current list of yp servers looks like this:

bedrock

Is this correct?  [y/n: y]

Installing the YP database will require that you answer a few questions.
Questions will all be asked at the beginning of the procedure.

Do you want this procedure to quit on non-fatal errors? [y/n: n]
OK, please remember to go back and redo manually whatever fails.  If you
don't, some part of the system (perhaps the yp itself) won't work.
The yp domain directory is /var/yp/home.com
Can we destroy the existing /var/yp/home.com and its contents? [y/n: n]  yes
There will be no further questions. The remainder of the procedure should take
5 to 10 minutes.
Building /var/yp/home.com/ypservers...
Running /var/yp /Makefile...
updated passwd
updated group
updated hosts
updated ipnodes
updated ethers
updated networks
updated rpc
updated services
updated protocols
updated netgroup
/var/yp/home.com/mail.aliases: 4 aliases, longest 25 bytes, 80 bytes total
/usr/lib/netsvc/yp/mkalias /var/yp/`domainname`/mail.aliases
/var/yp/`domainname`/mail.byaddr;
updated aliases
updated publickey
updated netid
/usr/sbin/makedbm /etc/netmasks /var/yp/`domainname`/netmasks.byaddr;
updated netmasks
updated timezone
updated auto.master
updated auto.home

bedrock has been set up as a yp master server without any errors.

If there are running slave yp servers, run yppush now for any data bases
which have been changed.  If there are no running slaves, run ypinit on
those hosts which are to be slave servers. Enter the NIS server and answer
the remaining questions.
```

3. Reboot the NIS server, or on Solaris and HP-UX, run the command `/usr/lib` `/netsvc/yp/ypstart`. For Linux, run the `/etc/rc.d/init.d/ypserv` command. When executed, the following will be displayed:

Solaris:

```
starting NIS (YP server) services: ypserv ypbind ypxfrd rpc.yppasswdd done.
```

Linux:

```
Starting YP server services:                              [  OK  ]
```

Errors may be encountered when the `ypinit` command is executed, such as the following:

```
make: Warning: Don't know how to make target `/etc/ethers'
make: Warning: Target `all' not remade because of errors
Current working directory /var/yp
*** Error code 1
make: Fatal error: Command failed for target `k'
Error running Makefile.

bedrock has been set up as a yp master server with errors.  Please remember
to figure out what went wrong, and fix it.
```

This error is displayed because one of the local files (`/etc/ethers`, in this case) can't be found on the system. However, the administrator can choose which files are maintained by the NIS server; thus, it is not necessary to have the `/etc/ethers` file. The problem can be fixed in one of two ways: create a dummy `/etc/ethers` file or edit the NIS `Makefile` that is located within the `/var/yp` directory and strip out the `ethers` entry.

4. Verify NIS server functionality. On a NIS client system, execute the following commands: `ypwhich` and `ypcat`. Thus,

```
dino# ypwhich
bedrock
```

This command shows to which NIS server the client is bound, and in this example the client `dino` is bound to the NIS server called `bedrock`. The `ypcat` command displays the contents of a NIS map that is located on the NIS primary server. For example, to view the contents of the group map database, use the following command:

```
ypcat group
```

If the `ypwhich` command shows the correct server and the `ypcat` command yields the correct contents, the NIS server is functional. Note that any NIS map database name can be supplied with the `ypcat` command.

15

15.4 Configure a NIS Client

Many versions of UNIX support NIS client functionality. In particular, the setup of clients for HP-UX and Solaris is the same. However, the configuration needed for Linux is different. In general, the configuration of a NIS client system is a very straightforward procedure as compared to the server setup. The process includes the following for Solaris and HP-UX:

1. Set the NIS domain.

2. Make sure the client can talk to the NIS server via `ping`.

3. Modify the `/etc/nsswitch.conf` file to use NIS services.

4. Execute the `ypinit` script—just run the `ypinit` script with the `-c` option for Solaris and HP-UX. Thus, the command

```
# ypinit -c
```

shows the following:

```
In order for NIS to operate sucessfully, we have to construct a list of
the
NIS servers.  Please continue to add the names for YP servers in order of
preference, one per line.  When you are done with the list, type a
<control D>
or a return on a line by itself.
        next host to add:  bedrock          Add a server name as
        next host to add:                    here when prompted

The current list of yp servers looks like this:    Type control D here to
                                                    end adding list entries
bedrock

Is this correct?  [y/n: y]  y
```

For Linux, do the following:

1. Modify the `/etc/yp.conf` file and set the NIS domain and server.

2. Modify the `/etc/nsswitch.conf` file to use NIS services.

3. Execute `lete/rc.d/init.d/ypbnd`.

To ensure that the NIS client can talk to the NIS server, do the following:

● Execute the `ypwhich` command to ensure that the correct server is reported.

15.5 Setting Up a Secondary NIS Server

Although a NIS secondary or slave server is not specifically required, it is highly recommended that at least one secondary system be set up to ensure that no single point of failure causes NIS clients to become inoperable should a NIS server fail. In practice, it is common to deploy several secondary NIS servers within a corporate enterprise network to increase resiliency and to handle rudimentary load balancing for NIS clients.

To set up a NIS secondary, do the following:

1. Make sure the NIS domain has been set up on the NIS secondary server.

2. Make sure that the secondary can talk to the primary NIS server via `ping`.

3. Execute the `ypinit` script on the NIS secondary server and supply the NIS master machine using the `-s` option:

```
# ypinit -s bedrock ◄──────            bedrock is the NIS master server

Installing the YP database will require that you answer a few questions.
Questions will all be asked at the beginning of the procedure.

Do you want this procedure to quit on non-fatal errors? [y/n: n]
OK, please remember to go back and redo manually whatever fails.  If you
don't, some part of the system (perhaps the yp itself) won't work.
The yp domain directory is /var/yp/home.com
Can we destroy the existing /var/yp/home.com and its contents? [y/n: n]  yes
There will be no further questions. The remainder of the procedure should take
a few minutes, to copy the data bases from bedrock.
Transferring auto.home...
Transferring auto.master...
Transferring timezone.byname...
Transferring netmasks.byaddr...
Transferring netid.byname...
Transferring mail.byaddr...
Transferring mail.aliases...
Transferring netgroup.byhost...
Transferring netgroup.byuser...
Transferring netgroup...
Transferring protocols.byname...
Transferring protocols.bynumber...
Transferring services.byservicename...
Transferring services.byname...
Transferring rpc.bynumber...
Transferring networks.byaddr...
Transferring networks.byname...
Transferring ethers.byname...
Transferring ethers.byaddr...
```

```
Transferring ipnodes.byaddr...
Transferring publickey.byname...
Transferring ipnodes.byname...
Transferring hosts.byaddr...
Transferring hosts.byname...
Transferring group.bygid...
Transferring group.byname...
Transferring passwd.byuid...
Transferring passwd.byname...
Transferring ypservers...

dino's nis data base has been set up
without any errors.
```

In this example installation, the machine called `dino` has been set up as a NIS secondary server for the `home.com` domain. All of the NIS maps have been transferred to the secondary, as shown by the "`Transferring`" messages.

4. Finally, on the NIS master, add the hostname of the NIS secondary to the `ypservers` file, which on Solaris and HP-UX is located in the `/var/yp/binding/<domainname>/` directory, while on Linux the location of the file is `/var/yp`. This file contains a list of all the NIS servers (including the master itself) that the master should push updates to when NIS maps are modified. For the `home.com` domain, the file contains the following:

```
bedrock
dino
```

Hint

By default, when the NIS master has been set up (when the `ypinit -m` command has been executed), this file is automatically created and contains the name of the NIS master server; thus, when adding NIS secondary servers, the file should already be available for editing.

Mastery Check

1. True/False: The `ypmake` command updates the NIS maps on the NIS master.

2. What command is used to change a UNIX account password on the NIS master server?

3. For NIS database files, the actual data is stored within _____ files.

4. For NIS database files, the _____ files contain a bit map of the file data.

5. What is the command that shows which server a client is bound to?

6. What is the command to configure a secondary NIS server if the secondary server is named `barney` and the master server is `fred`?

   A. # `ypinit -s fred`

   B. # `ypinit -s barney`

   C. # `ypinit -m barney`

   D. # `ypinit -m`

7. What is the command to configure a NIS client named `barney` if the master NIS server is named `fred`?

   A. # `ypinit -c fred`

   B. # `ypinit -c barney`

   C. # `ypinit -m barney`

   D. # `ypinit -c`

8. What command discussed in this module produces the following line of output?

   ```
   Use "protocols" for map "protocols.bynumber"
   ```

15

Mastery Check

9. What command discussed in this module produces the following line of output?

   ```
   Transferring protocols.byname...
   ```

10. The _____ is used in situations where no NIS server exists on the local network and the NIS broadcast option is not used or the network infrastructure doesn't support broadcast facilities.

Module 16

SNMP System Management Tools

Critical Skills

When addressing system management from a more global or even group basis, it is important that robust and scalable solutions be available to handle the many different aspects of system management. For example, consider the potential impact of a UNIX server failure, which means that an important system is unusable until it can be fixed and brought back in service.

16.1 Discover Elements of System Management

Every moment the system is down, it can financially impact the company. If the failed system went down in the middle of the night, this might not be detected until the next morning when users attempted to access the system. In this case, a significant amount of time has gone by and the problem should have been detected much earlier (just as the system went down). This is the job of a system or network management application.

As previously mentioned, SNMP is a powerful protocol that provides both system and network management functions. However, SNMP by itself is just a set of rules for how to obtain information and provide control for systems and network devices; the administrator needs specific tools to help manage systems that support SNMP. Due to the popularity of SNMP, several robust and functional SNMP applications are available for UNIX. These tools can be used to provide system management functions such as system heartbeat, system up/down messages, system process activity, network information (protocol statistics, interface performance, and routing information), system information, and configuration control.

Although the subject of the book is centered on UNIX system administration, it is helpful to review some elements of networking that involve other devices, since more and more system administrators are called upon to manage networking components as well. Thus, some of the examples provided involve configuration of networking devices such as routers.

Hint

From a network management standpoint, the management of UNIX systems is very similar to the management of networking devices such as routers, switches, and other networking components that support SNMP.

Hint

The SNMP tools described here come standard on Linux, but must be installed on other UNIX versions such as Solaris and HP-UX.

System Heartbeat

A system heartbeat is used to determine the general health of a system. In the case of SNMP, a system manager application uses a get request message to determine the general reachability of an agent and the system. For example, the system administrator may poll the system clock MIB variable of the agent to determine that each successive poll is more recent than the previous one. Each successive poll should indicate that time is moving forward. The MIB variable that may be polled is the `unixTime` object, which is part of the `sunSystem` group

Hint

Specific MIB agent information is available in Appendix C under "Using UNIX SNMP Agents."

of the Sun system agent. As an alternative, the `sysUpTime` object may be polled from the MIB-2 system group, which should be supported on all SNMP agents.

Hint

Polling a single SNMP MIB object can serve as the means by which a system heartbeat can be established. Thus, when a series of polls fail, either the SNMP agent isn't working or the system is having trouble communicating on the network.

System Up/Down Messages

Should the system be brought down and rebooted for any reason, a message will be sent to the designated network management system in the form of an SNMP trap. Recall that a trap is an unsolicited message emitted from the agent indicating some special condition or event. By receiving these messages, the manager is informed (for example) of system outages and can take appropriate action. The Linux agent, for example, uses a configuration file, and additional tools can be used to forward trap messages to one or more network management systems.

System Process Activity

The SNMP agents support the management of critical system activities and other aspects of system administration. With the Sun MIB and the UCD agent, the monitoring of system processes is possible. Thus, with the SNMP agent, the administrator may obtain a detailed list of processes on the system. This functionality is analogous to executing the `ps` command remotely. Additional agent functions can establish the overall health of the system or the condition of an individual component by monitoring critical processes and other related information.

Network Information

Many SNMP agents support the MIB-II standard, which means that protocol performance monitoring and basic system monitoring are possible. This includes monitoring of IP, ICMP, TCP, SNMP, network interface counters, and additional agent system performance objects. Also, additional network protocol MIBs are supported by the agents, which provide even greater information and control of the network and system elements. For example, route-monitoring MIB objects can report the routing configuration of a system and report any errors found. Or, if an organization has determined that each UNIX workstation must have a default route, this can be verified by probing the SNMP agent within these systems. Agents also provide objects that contain performance information for each of the network interfaces installed within the system. With this information, it is possible to report on network performance of all active interfaces.

System Configuration Control

Many networked systems (for example, UNIX workstations, printers, and so forth) must be configured before they can be effectively used. For example, the configuration of important services like DNS client configuration can be managed with an SNMP agent. Also, as network requirements change, so too the configurations within these systems must change. SNMP tools can be used to alter system configuration in an automated fashion, thus reducing the interaction and tasks from the system administrator's point of view. Today, most versions of UNIX support one or more SNMP agents. With Linux, the UCD package is provided by default, while on Solaris the Sun SNMP agent is available. On HP-UX, the Emanate SNMP agent is provided.

Hint

All of these agents support MIB-II objects.

16.2 Explore the UCD SNMP Package

The University of California at Davis (UCD) package provides not only a robust and powerful SNMP agent, but it also provides a series of handy tools that can be used to manage SNMP-enabled systems and query any SNMP agent. These tools support SNMPv1, SNMPv2, and SNMPv3 management protocols, and each SNMP version is available using command-line options. These command-line tools can be used to build scripts or other programs to accomplish management functions or other customized tasks. For example, the `snmpget` command can monitor critical server network interfaces to determine if one or more of them become inoperable. In such a case, the system administrator can be notified automatically should a failure occur. The UCD package includes tools

Hint
Only the most common UCD package tools are fully described in this module.

that obtain MIB information and also tools to alter MIB objects. Table 16-1 lists all the commands that are provided by the UCD package.

Command	Description
snmpconf	Configures SNMP agent based on configuration file.
snmpdelta	Monitors changes of SNMP variables.
snmpget	Obtains one or more MIB object values.
snmpgetnext	Continuously walks an SNMP MIB tree and obtains MIB object values.
snmpnetstat	Obtains agent interface configuration information.
snmpset	Sets one or more MIB objects to specified value.
snmpstatus	Obtains important MIB object information.
snmptable	Obtains a complete SNMP table.
snmptest	Communicates with an SNMP agent entity.
snmptranslate	Converts MIB objects into more meaningful information.
snmptrap	Sends SNMP trap messages to one or more managers.
snmptrapd	Retrieves SNMP traps from the network.
snmpwalk	Obtains a group of related MIB objects.
snmpbulkwalk	Obtains a MIB object with SNMP bulk request.

Table 16-1   UCD SNMP Applications

---Hint---

Instead of using the native SNMP agents from different vendors, and because the UCD SNMP package is functional on many different releases of UNIX, it is recommended that this agent can be deployed across most (if not all) of the important systems. Using a single agent will simplify many aspects of system management and configuration.

The basic syntax of most of the UCD tools includes the following:

```
snmpcmd protocol_version [additional_options] hostname community object [object]
```

The snmpcmd is a placeholder and represents one of the commands listed in Table 16-1. The word protocol_version determines which SNMP protocol version should be used and can be 1, 2c, or 3. The command-line option 1 represents the standard SNMPv1 format, which includes the use of a simple password for authentication. The 2c option indicates differences within the supported SNMP protocol data units, but uses the same community-based approach as in SNMPv1. The final option, 3, indicates the use of the SNMPv3 security model, which provides the most advanced security model available for SNMP.

The additional_options placeholder represents options that control both display attributes and operational behavior of the tools. The most commonly used command-line options are described next. Luckily, most of the tools support these common options. The hostname can be replaced with the name of any system on the network that contains an SNMP agent that matches the protocol_version information specified on the command line. Also, a valid IP address, expressed in dotted notation, may be used instead of a hostname. The community represents the password strings for authentication if version 1 or 2c is used.

The object represents the MIB OID that should be retrieved (in the case of an SNMP get request) or altered (in the case of an SNMP set request). It may be expressed in either dotted numeric or dotted named notation. In the case of an SNMP set request operation, additional object information will be required.

Note that one or more MIB objects may be specified on the command line.

Common Command-Line Options

UCD tools share a number of common command-line arguments. Having a core set of options makes them easier to remember and use. The arguments supported by all the commands are divided into two categories: operational options and display options. The operational options control the behavior of each of the tools, while the display options control how the MIB objects, associated values, and other information are displayed.

Application Display Options

Table 16-2 lists the display arguments that control some aspect of the output. Note that the table does not fully describe each of the available options. For instance, the –h option, which displays a help string of the command-line arguments, is not described because it is fairly intuitive.

Three of these options provide control over how MIB object path information is formatted and displayed: -f, -s, and -S. The -f option displays the full object identifier path information. Thus, this option will display the object

```
system.sysContact.0
```

with the full MIB path

```
.iso.org.dod.internet.mgmt.mib-2.system.sysContact.0
```

The -s option permits only the suffix component of the OID to be printed; the last symbolic portion of the MIB object identifier will be shown. For example, the –s option will display the object

```
.iso.org.dod.internet.mgmt.mib-2.system.sysName.0
```

in the following format:

```
sysName.0
```

Option	Description
-D	Displays debugging information.
-S	Displays both suffix identifiers and MIB name.
-V	Displays version information for the tools.
-d	Dumps SNMP packets to the display.
-f	Displays the full object identifier path.
-h	Displays a help message.
-q	Makes the output easier to parse for programs.
-s	Displays only suffix identifiers.

Table 16-2 Common UCD Application Command-Line Options

Finally, the `-S` option requests that the MIB object be printed with both suffix and the MIB name. Thus, when this option is displayed,

```
.iso.org.dod.internet.mgmt.mib-2.system.sysUpTime.0
```

the following will be shown:

```
SNMPv2-MIB:sysUpTime.0
```

Note

In this example, the `sysUpTime` object is found within the SNMPv2-MIB; this is true when the UCD tools are used. Traditionally, however, this object is found in the MIB-II tree.

Hint

Use the `-q` option to format the output so that it will be suitable as input to other UNIX tools and programs.

If you need to collect SNMP information from a system and use this information as input into another program, the `-q` option will come in handy. Normally, MIB object information is displayed as shown:

```
system.sysObjectID.0 = OID: enterprises.9.1.17
system.sysUpTime.0 = Timeticks: (139494644) 16 days, 3:29:06.44
system.sysContact.0 = Matthew Maxwell
system.sysName.0 = remote-gw5
system.sysLocation.0 = Remote Sales Office (San Jose)
system.sysServices.0 = 6
```

This option, which stands for quick format, causes the output from the UCD tools to be formatted differently. First, the equal sign (=) is removed; this makes it easier to parse because the data is now in columnar format. Second, notice that both the `sysObjectID` and `sysUptime` formats have been altered. The information for these two objects in the preceding example is interpreted, while, in the following example, only the raw data is displayed:

```
system.sysObjectID.0 enterprises.9.1.17
system.sysUpTime.0 16:3:24:11.44
system.sysContact.0 Matthew Maxwell
```

```
system.sysName.0 remote-gw5
system.sysLocation.0 Remote Sales Office (San Jose)
system.sysServices.0 6
```

To display debugging information, use the -d option. This shows the packet information, including the size and destination, and also provides a hexadecimal and ASCII dump of the packet. The output shown here is the result of an SNMP get request of the system.sysContact MIB object:

```
sending 51 bytes to 10.0.2.220:161:
0000: 30 82 00 2F  02 01 00 04  06 70 75 62  6C 69 63 A0   0../.....public.
0016: 82 00 20 02  04 41 C9 4A  92 02 01 00  02 01 00 30   .. ..A.J.......0
0032: 82 00 10 30  82 00 0C 06  08 2B 06 01  02 01 01 04   ...0.....+......
0048: 00 05 00                                             ...

received 60 bytes from 10.0.2.220:161:
0000: 30 82 00 38  02 01 00 04  06 70 75 62  6C 69 63 A2   0..8.....public.
0016: 2B 02 04 41  C9 4A 92 02  01 00 02 01  00 30 1D 30   +..A.J.......0.0
0032: 1B 06 08 2B  06 01 02 01  01 04 00 04  0F 4D 61 74   ...+........Mat
0048: 74 68 65 77  20 4D 61 78  77 65 6C 6C                thew Maxwell
system.sysContact.0 = Matthew Maxwell
```

The first part of the output is the request packet, as indicated by the string sending 51 bytes to 10.0.2.220:161, which are in the standard SNMP packet format. Note the echoing of the community string of public. The receiving packet is the response from the agent and it, too, uses the standard SNMP packet format. In this case, we see both the community string public and the sysContact object string. The second part is the response, which starts with the string receiving 60 bytes from 10.0.2.220:161.

Operational Options

Table 16-3 lists many of the available operational arguments for the UCD applications.

Hint

Some of the options in Table 16-3 are not fully described because their use is somewhat limited. For instance, the -c option, which controls the ability to define the clock values with SNMPv2 authentication messages, is not a critical function for using the tools and is not described. However, some of the more useful options are described.

Option	Description
-R	Requests random access to the agent MIB table.
-c	Sets the clock values.
-m	Specifies a list of MIB modules to load.
-M	Specifies a list of directories in which to search for MIB files.
-p	Uses the specified port to communicate with the agent.
-r	Specifies the number of retries.
-t	Specifies the time-out between retry attempts.
-v	Specifies the protocol version.

Table 16-3 SNMP Application Operational Options

By default, MIB objects are located in standard, well-known places within the MIB tree. Consider, for example, the `system.sysContact.0` MIB object, which is normally found within the following tree:

```
.iso.org.dod.internet.mgmt.mib-2 tree
```

The UCD tools support a concept of random access MIBs. Using this approach, the `system.sysContact` MIB object may be entered as `sysContact`—without the `system` group name prefix. To specify a single search of a MIB object, because it might appear more than once, specify the name of the MIB followed by the object, such as `SNMPv2-MIB:sysContact.0`. To enable random access, use the `-R` command-line option. This feature is most useful when searching for MIB objects that are not located in standard places and when more than one instance of the same object name exists within the agent.

As with any software tool that communicates with an SNMP agent, some method must be provided to convert the numeric dotted notation (such as `.1.3.6.1`) of the MIB object tree into the notation that uses names (such as `.iso.org.dod.internet.mgmt.mib-2`). Normally, without the MIB files, the UCD tools display MIB information using the numeric form. This is because these tools obtain only the numeric form from the agent; they don't know how to map these identifiers into the corresponding string names. For example, when an SNMP get request is done against an agent with the MIB files not available, the following output snippet may be displayed:

```
.iso.3.6.1.2.1.1.1.0 = "Linux didymus 2.4.7-10 #1 Thu Sep 6 17:27:27 EDT 2001 i686"
.iso.3.6.1.2.1.1.2.0 = OID: .iso.3.6.1.4.1.2021.250.10
.iso.3.6.1.2.1.1.3.0 = Timeticks: (219939) 0:36:39.39
.iso.3.6.1.2.1.1.4.0 = "Anita Maxwell"
.iso.3.6.1.2.1.1.5.0 = "didymus"
```

```
.iso.3.6.1.2.1.1.6.0 = "Graphics Lab"
.iso.3.6.1.2.1.1.8.0 = Timeticks: (0) 0:00:00.00
```

This output is from a query of a UNIX server, and, as you can see, the MIB object path information contains numeric strings only after the iso name. This string was included in the output because the UCD tools know only the starting point of the MIB tree. When it comes to nonstandard or vendor-specific MIBs, only the numeric form is available. To address this issue, the -m and -M options are provided. The -m option specifies a list of MIB modules that should be loaded before the UCD tool attempts any SNMP queries on an agent. When more than one MIB module is listed, the modules must be separated by a colon (:). A MIB module is just a file that contains the MIB definitions for an agent. Using the -m option, we can supply the correct MIB modules so that our output snippet above will contain all string names. This option helps because we can supply a list of directories in which to search for MIB files. Thus, the command

```
# snmpwalk -M /var/mibs cisco-gw1 public system
```

will search the directory /var/mibs. Assuming that it finds the standard MIB files, it will display the following:

```
system.sysDescr.0 = Cisco Internetwork Operating System Software
IOS (tm) 4500 Software (C4500-J-M), Version 11.1(5), RELEASE SOFTWARE (fc1)
Copyright (c) 1986-1996 by cisco Systems, Inc.
Compiled Mon 05-Aug-96 13:17 by mkamson
system.sysObjectID.0 = OID: enterprises.9.1.50
system.sysUpTime.0 = Timeticks: (99487614) 11 days, 12:21:16.14
system.sysContact.0 = Nita Maxwell
system.sysName.0 = remote-gw
system.sysLocation.0 = Remote Sales Office (Florida)
system.sysServices.0 = 78
```

There is also a shorthand way to specify all MIB modules (as opposed to supplying a list)—by using the all command. This overrides the MIBS environment variable, which is discussed in the next section.

1-Minute Drill

● What is a system heartbeat used for?

● What are the two categories of arguments supported by all the UCD tool commands?

● To determine the general system health
● Operational and display

Environment Variables

Each of the UCD applications uses a small set of environment variables that help establish global values for certain operating parameters and shortcuts for command-line options. These include the following variables:

- MIBS
- MIBDIR
- PREFIX
- SUFFIX

The MIBS and MIBDIR variables provide a way to load in additional MIB modules. The variable MIBS provides the same function as the -m command-line option. The MIBDIR variable functions the same as the -M option. Both are convenient because they work with all UCD management applications.

The SUFFIX variable toggles the -s command-line option, which displays the suffix, or last, component of the MIB object path. The PREFIX variable provides a standard way to define the prefix of MIB object identifiers. The default value is

```
.iso.org.dod.internet.mgmt.mib-2
```

If this variable is defined, the contents of the variable are added to the beginning of the MIB object being referenced when using one of the UCD tools. Defining this value will help in situations where nonstandard MIBs are used.

16.3 Use the UCD Magement Tools

The following tools are provided within the UCD package; these applications make up the bulk of services provided by the UCD software.

Snmpdelta Command

The snmpdelta command collects changes in MIB integer values from an SNMP agent entity. This command monitors the specified integer objects and displays changes to the objects that occur over time. This is very useful in tracking networking errors. It might be necessary, for example, to determine the number of packets discarded from an interface—as with the ifInDiscards

MIB-II object. When the number of discarded packets is high on an interface, this could indicate trouble for the system. To monitor this object from the device called `bedrock`, the following command may be used:

```
# snmpdelta -IR bedrock public ifInDiscards.1
```

When invoked, this command will produce the following:

```
ifInDiscards.1 /1 sec: 12
ifInDiscards.1 /1 sec: 0
ifInDiscards.1 /1 sec: 0
ifInDiscards.1 /1 sec: 0
ifInDiscards.1 /1 sec: 3
ifInDiscards.1 /1 sec: 0
ifInDiscards.1 /1 sec: 0
ifInDiscards.1 /1 sec: 8
ifInDiscards.1 /1 sec: 2
```

Without user interaction, the above command continually polls the agent until a CTRL-C (^c) is issued by the user. Note that in the command we have used, the -IR option activates random access to the agent MIB. This makes it easy to obtain the desired MIB objects. A high discard rate may indicate trouble with the interface. This trouble could be caused by a hardware problem related to cabling or even a software configuration error. In the example above, the discard rate is changed and is not zero, thus indicating a problem.

Snmpget Command

The `snmpget` command retrieves information from an SNMP agent entity. It uses the SNMP get request with one or more MIB object names as arguments and returns their associated MIB values. If an error occurs, a descriptive message will be shown to help pinpoint the problem. If a list of objects is specified on the command line, only those objects that are contained within the agent's MIB will be returned.

The command syntax is as follows:

```
snmpget [common arguments] host community_string MIB-object [MIB-object]
```

To retrieve the MIB objects `sysDescr` and `sysContact` from a Solaris system, the following command could be used:

```
# snmpget bedrock public system.sysDescr.0 system.sysUpTime.0
```

Depending on the model and configuration, this command would display output like the following:

```
system.sysDescr.0 = Sun SNMP Agent, Netra 1 Server
system.sysUpTime.0 = Timeticks: (69212467) 8 days, 0:15:24.67
```

In this example, the system bedrock is a Netra server and has been up for the last eight days.

Sometimes when accessing objects from certain devices, errors may be encountered that might lead us to believe that the device is not working, For example, consider the following command that is executed against a Linux system called monet:

```
# snmpget monet private-write system.sysDescr.0
```

The command produces the following:

```
system.sysDescr.0 = Linux monet 2.4.7-10 #1 Thu Sep 6 17:27:27 EDT 2001 i686
```

However, running the same command against the same system but using a different community string produces the following:

```
# snmpget monet bad-password system.sysDescr.0
Timeout: No Response from monet
```

In the last example, the error message isn't clear about what is going on; the message suggests that the object being requested does not exist within the agent. Obviously, from the first example, the object (system.sysDescr.0) does exist and has an associated MIB value. This error message is displayed because when the community string doesn't match the password configured within it, an SNMPv1 agent disregards the request. If authentication traps are enabled, it then sends an associated trap. The important thing to remember is that when polling for specific objects, don't assume that objects are not available despite the generation of error messages suggesting that they are unavailable. It might be helpful to execute an snmpwalk against the agent if questions come up regarding which objects are indeed supported by the agent.

Hint

When querying a device that doesn't respond to SNMP requests, try to ping the device to see if it is reachable on the network. If the device responds with ping, but not with SNMP, then either the agent isn't running or you are using the wrong SNMP authentication—such as an incorrect community string.

Snmpgetnext Command

The snmpgetnext command retrieves one or more MIB objects using the SNMP getnext request. For each object specified on the command line, snmpgetnext gets the next lexicographical MIB object found in the MIB tree. This tool is very useful for returning a series of objects when the exact structure of the MIB object that is being retrieved is unknown. For example, the SNMP command

```
# snmpgetnext probe public system.sysContact.0
```

will obtain the next MIB object after the sysContact.0 object:

```
system.sysName.0 = "AXON" Hex: 41 58 4F 4E
```

The sysName.0 object is displayed because it is lexicographically next to the sysContract.0 object. How do we know this for sure? Well, the simplest approach is to display the entire system group. An snmpwalk of the group displays the following:

```
system.sysDescr.0 = "AXON LANServant - Ethernet (4.16)"
system.sysObjectID.0 = OID: enterprises.370.2.2
system.sysUpTime.0 = Timeticks: (868306) 2:24:43.06
system.sysContact.0 = "3Com Corporation"
system.sysName.0 = "AXON" Hex: 41 58 4F 4E ◄——— next object
system.sysLocation.0 = ""
system.sysServices.0 = 15
```

The primary purpose of the snmpwalk command is to retrieve an agent table in a more effective manner. Consider the udp table from MIB-II, which contains information related to any open sockets using the User Datagram Protocol. Polling this SNMP table on a Linux system displays the partial output shown here:

```
1  udp.udpInDatagrams.0 = 860
2  udp.udpNoPorts.0 = 5
3  udp.udpInErrors.0 = 0
4  udp.udpOutDatagrams.0 = 911
5  udp.udpTable.udpEntry.udpLocalAddress.0.0.0.0.111 = IpAddress: 0.0.0.0
```

Note that the line numbers in this output were not generated by the same command.

```
 6  udp.udpTable.udpEntry.udpLocalAddress.0.0.0.0.161 = IpAddress: 0.0.0.0
 7  udp.udpTable.udpEntry.udpLocalAddress.0.0.0.0.162 = IpAddress: 0.0.0.0
 8  udp.udpTable.udpEntry.udpLocalAddress.0.0.0.0.177 = IpAddress: 0.0.0.0
 9  udp.udpTable.udpEntry.udpLocalAddress.0.0.0.0.517 = IpAddress: 0.0.0.0
10  udp.udpTable.udpEntry.udpLocalAddress.0.0.0.0.518 = IpAddress: 0.0.0.0
11  udp.udpTable.udpEntry.udpLocalAddress.0.0.0.0.624 = IpAddress: 0.0.0.0
12  udp.udpTable.udpEntry.udpLocalAddress.0.0.0.0.635 = IpAddress: 0.0.0.0
13  udp.udpTable.udpEntry.udpLocalPort.0.0.0.0.111 = 111
14  udp.udpTable.udpEntry.udpLocalPort.0.0.0.0.161 = 161
15  udp.udpTable.udpEntry.udpLocalPort.0.0.0.0.162 = 162
16  udp.udpTable.udpEntry.udpLocalPort.0.0.0.0.177 = 177
17  udp.udpTable.udpEntry.udpLocalPort.0.0.0.0.517 = 517
18  udp.udpTable.udpEntry.udpLocalPort.0.0.0.0.518 = 518
19  udp.udpTable.udpEntry.udpLocalPort.0.0.0.0.624 = 624
20  udp.udpTable.udpEntry.udpLocalPort.0.0.0.0.635 = 635
```

The listing above includes table objects that contain related information, but don't have an associated index to retrieve each object when needed. As you can see, the objects are referenced by the IP address (0.0.0.0) being used—as shown on line 5, for example. This entry contains the local IP and port address for this socket. The IP is used as an index into the object listed in line 13, which contains the UDP port information. The ability to retrieve MIB objects based on lexicographical ordering is the only way to discover each object in order as indexed from the MIB.

Snmpnetstat Command

The snmpnetstat command is similar to the UNIX netstat utility and provides some of the same basic information about attached device interfaces and routing. What is remarkable about this tool is that it provides an easy way to obtain interface information from any SNMP-compliant system. This includes, for example, devices such as UNIX workstations and servers, printers, networking devices, and other devices that support the MIB-II standard. This is a very powerful tool because interface information can be collected without the use of complicated command sequences. Also, it removes the barrier requiring the use of vendor-specific interfaces when a network consists of a large number of different vendor products. In other words, regardless of the vendor system or device, the information obtained is similar and in the same format.

Like its UNIX counterpart, snmpnetstat supports a number of command-line options that control basic operations and output. Table 16-4 lists the available command options. As you can see, many of these options are consistent with those of the netstat command.

16

Option	Description
-I	Displays information on the specified network interface.
-a	Shows the state of all socket connections.
-i	Shows the state of all interfaces defined on the system.
-o	Displays an abbreviated status of interfaces.
-n	Displays network addresses as numbers.
-p	Shows statistics sorted by the network protocol.
-r	Displays routing table information.
-s	Shows per-protocol network statistics.

Table 16-4   Command-Line Options for the snmpnetstat Command

Displaying Interface Information

To show the configuration of all the functional network interfaces on the system, use the -i option. In the following example, the snmpnetstat command queries a HP-UX system called nfs-server:

```
# snmpnetstat -i nfs-server public
Name    Mtu     Network    Address    Ipkts        Ierrs Opkts Oerrs Queue
Ethern  1500    10.0.2     10.0.2.1      13377        315  132503  501    15
```

The output should be familiar; it mirrors the UNIX netstat command output. The only major differences are the names of the interfaces and the removal of the column that represents the total number of collisions on the interface.

To list the available interfaces in an abbreviated form, use the -s option. As you can see from the following output, only the columns of incoming and outgoing octets (bytes) are listed. Compare this to what is displayed with the -i option in the previous example.

```
# snmpnetstat -o nfs-server public
Name    Network    Address    Ioctets    Ooctets
Ethern  10.0.2     10.0.2.1   487708     12778317
```

The nfs-server device contains a single interface: called Ethern, which represents an Ethernet interface. If we query a network device such as a network router, we might see a large number of interfaces. Typically, Cisco routers and switches (and other vendor devices, too) may contain a large number of interfaces. For example, executing the above `snmpnetstat` command on a Cisco 7000 router will yield the following:

Name	Network	Address	Ioctets	Ooctets
Fddi0/	10.10.1	10.10.1.1	3723440280	1783534532
Fddi1/	10.11.2	10.11.2.1	2560994642	2783361340
Ethern	10.0.2	10.0.2.254	2141819815	1555401237
Ethern*	none	none	0	0
Ethern*	none	none	0	0
Ethern*	none	none	0	0
Ethern*	none	none	0	0
Ethern*	none	none	0	0
Fddi3/	10.14.1	10.14.1.1	2248945512	2083011069
Serial	10.250.10	10.250.10.1	1401691701	870256641
Serial*	none	none	592331671	3226921185
Serial*	none	none	0	0
Serial*	none	none	0	0
FastEt	19.80.8	19.82.8.1	4086327200	421590301
FastEt	19.80.9	19.82.9.1	4017448469	3080615899
FastEt	19.80.10	19.82.10.1	269162560	1781784403
FastEt*	none	none	0	0

The actual number of interfaces will depend on the model of the router and installed interface cards. In this example, 17 interfaces have been listed. In the output, four different interface types have been listed: Serial, Ether, Fast, and FDDI. This output was polled from a core backbone router, which explains the high utilization on many of the interfaces.

To list an individual interface, use the -I option followed by the interface name. This option is also used in conjunction with the interval option. When snmpnetstat is invoked with the interval argument, it shows a running count of network statistics relating to the interface specified. The information displayed includes one column for the specified interface and another column summarizing information for all other interfaces. The first line of output presents a summary of information since the device was last rebooted. All additional lines represent values that are changing over the specified interval. The command

```
# snmpnetstat -I Ethernet cisco-gw3 public 10
```

will show the following:

input	(Ether)				output	input	(Total)	output	
packets	errs	packets	errs	colls	packets	errs	packets	errs	colls
68355	39800	131733	198	0	499131	3924	648945	730	0
178	62	93				68	0	376	255
	236	22		0					
	46	58		142			84	0	172
	167	268	42	0					
	93	63		67			60	0	210
	134	359	14	0					
	119	49		169			85	0	326
	187	385	18	0					

This display includes a running count of packet activity on the `Ether` interface contained in the `cisco-gw3`. The command will continue displaying this output until a CTRL-C (`^c`) is typed. The first two columns represent the number of input packets and input errors, while the next two represent the number of output packets and output errors. The fifth column provides the number of collisions. The remaining five columns are cumulative totals for all interfaces defined within the device.

Display Routing Information

To display the routing information from the same device, use the `-r` option, as in the following example:

```
# snmpnetstat -r cisco-gw3 public
```

The option will display the following:

```
Routing tables
Destination          Gateway        Flags Interface
default              161.135.59.1   UG    if0
155.161.75/25        161.135.59.9   U     Serial0
155.161.114.128/26   rembrandt      U     Ethernet0
161.135              161.135.59.1   UG    if0
161.135.59/26        161.135.59.9   U     Serial0
161.135.59.64/26     161.135.59.8   UG    if0
161.135.59.128/26    rembrandt      U     Ethernet0
170.5                161.135.59.1   UG    if0
```

The statistics for each network protocol are supported with this command. Thus, the -s (shows statistics for each protocol) and -P (shows statistics sorted by each protocol) options can be used to show detailed protocol performance data. To see just the statistics for each protocol, use the following command:

```
# snmpnetstat -s monet public
```

This command will produce the following sample output:

```
udp:
        8606737 total datagrams received
        7727372 datagrams to invalid port        This unusually high
        1 datagram dropped due to errors          number of datagrams
        851929 output datagram requests           to an invalid port
tcp:                                               indicates some kind
        0 active opens                             of problem
        8 passive opens
        0 failed attempts
        1 reset of established connections
        0 current established connections
        645 segments received
        476 segments sent
        0 segments retransmitted
icmp:
        9741 total messages received
        0 messages dropped due to errors
        10042 ouput message requests
        0 output messages discarded
        Output Histogram:
                Destination unreachable: 310
                Echo Reply: 9732
        Input Histogram:
                Destination unreachable: 9
                Echo Request: 9732
ip:
        22222667 total datagrams received
        0 datagrams with header errors
        0 datagrams with an invalid destination address
        0 datagrams forwarded
        0 datagrams with unknown protocol
        0 datagrams discarded
        22222673 datagrams delivered
        0 output datagram requests
```

```
0 output datagrams discarded
0 datagrams with no route
0 fragments received
0 datagrams reassembled
0 reassembly failures
0 datagrams fragmented
0 fragmentation failures
0 fragments created
```

This output provides a quick snapshot of the network performance and the activity of each of the networking protocols. Many of the counters appear to represent normal network usage. However, one metric value, 7727372 datagrams to an invalid port, may represent a significant problem. For some unknown reason, data is arriving into this system, from possibly several other machines, to one or more UDP ports that are invalid. One possible cause for this situation is that an application that should receive data from another source is not running, but the other end hasn't been able to detect this condition. Another reason might be that a remote application is attempting to send information to this system but is misconfigured and attempting to send information to a nonexistent port.

One positive way to track down the cause of this problem is to capture traffic on the same network as this system and attempt to learn which remote device is sending the traffic. Once you get the identity of the remote system, investigating which application is causing this problem is simply a matter of notifying the owner of the system. It is easy to see why using the snmpnetstat command is a good way to determine potential network problems before they get out of hand.

Snmpset Tool

The snmpset command is one of the most useful and powerful commands within the UCD package. Many of the tools in this module focus on obtaining object values from an SNMP agent. However, this tool is used to alter modifiable (writable) MIB agent objects. The ability to alter a MIB object is profound in its implications because doing so changes the configuration or operating state of a system.

This tool represents a power mechanism for controlling agents on a global scale. The ability to change the configuration of a large number of devices provides an important facility that every network manager or system administrator must have. Having the power to control many devices can represent a liability as well. Consider, for example, a router with several interfaces that serve as remote connection points between important distant office networks. A single `snmpset` command (with the appropriate security password) executed against one or more interfaces on this router could disable network connectivity between the local network and the remote office(s). Obviously, this could have disastrous consequence for business, to say nothing of your reputation. This same problem can happen for a cluster of UNIX systems; a single setting could result in some loss of system service.

Hint

When attempting to configure a service or object using SNMP, use a test system or test agent before attempting to implement the management function on a production or live system.

Another liability is related to making a global change to a series of systems when the new configuration is incorrect or causes some service outage due to the nature of the change. Because the `snmpset` command is powerful, exercise caution when using this command on an active network. It can never be said too often that the first rule of thumb in networking is to review the proposed changes in a test environment first. That way, when the changes are deployed on the real network, failures and other nasty surprises are kept to a minimum.

The basic syntax of the `snmpset` command is as follows:

```
snmpset [common arguments] MIB-objectID type value [MIB-objectID type value]
```

The MIB-objectID is the MIB object that will be given a new value. The `type` argument represents the type of object that should be altered, and the value represents the new object value. The type is a single character that represents one of the object types listed in Table 16-5.

Hint

Module 13 presents and discusses these object types.

From a system administration or general networking standpoint, SNMP can be used to handle a variety of management tasks. For example, SNMP can be used to

- Disable or enable a network interface.

- Update a device with new administration information (`sysContact`, for example).

- Reset certain network traffic counters.
- Restart a device or agent.
- Modify some configuration parameter.
- Monitor critical processes.
- Monitor system logs

You may recall an earlier scenario in which a disabled interface caused a network problem. There are also situations when not disabling an interface can cause additional network problems. For example, during a broadcast storm or when a cracker is attempting to penetrate a UNIX system, shutting down a network or interface might be the only way to prevent the problem from spreading to other parts of the company. However, before resorting to turning off interfaces, watch out for the "*set of no return*" syndrome. Consider the sample network shown in Figure 16-1.

In this sample network, we have two routers, R1 and R2. R2 is located in the San Francisco Office, while the other is located in the Chicago Office. Our only access to R2 is via router R1, using the serial1 interface. From device Node A, we issue an `snmpset` command to disable the serial of R1 interface. This stops the broadcast storm but also causes a connectivity loss from the remote office. The problem is now: How do we enable the interface on R1 after the broadcast storm has been fixed? The "set of no return" means that the only means of access to the device has been cut off. Remote access to the router has been lost, unless some out-of-band management capability such as dial-up can be used.

Code	Object Type
I	INTEGER
s	STRING
x	HEXADECIMAL STRING
d	DECIMAL STRING
n	NULL OBJECT
o	OBJECTID
t	TIMETICKS
a	IPADDRESS

Table 16-5   Snmpset Object Types

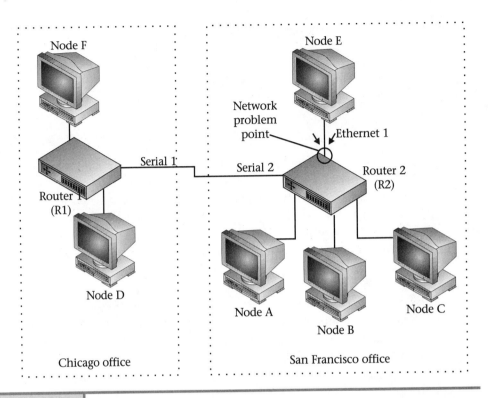

Figure 16-1 Problem of SNMP "Set of no return"

In this case, the port must be enabled from the local side, which could require instructing an assistant to enable the port or reboot the device to reset the port.

The best way to avoid the "set of no return" is to disable the local serial2 interface on R2 or the remote ethernet1 interface on R1. This way, the broadcast problem is contained, yet we still maintain access to the devices. To disable a serial interface on router R1, a modification to the `ifOperStatus` object must be made. This includes setting the object to zero (0) to disable the interface from an administrative perspective. Set this object using the following command:

```
# snmpset router1 private interfaces.ifTable.ifEntry.ifAdminStatus.2 i 0\
interfaces.ifTable.ifEntry.ifAdminStatus.3 = 0
```

16

When executed, the command will disable the flow of traffic to and from this interface. With most agents, this object change is not permanent, meaning that a system reboot will reset this object back to the default (enabled) value. However, without a system reset, the only other way to restore network connectivity will be to enable the interface using the snmpset command.

The snmpset command can alter other MIB objects within the agent. For example, consider the sysContact and sysLocation objects that are contained with one of the UNIX SNMP agents. Let's assign new values to these objects using a single snmpset command:

```
# snmpset bedrock private system.sysContact.0 s "NCC Support"\
system.sysLocation.0 s "3rd Floor Closet"
```

Due to the nature of UNIX SNMP agents, the MIB assignments made above may not be permanent and thus, when the system is rebooted, these values may pick their default values.

When the above command has been executed, it returns the following:

```
system.sysContact.0 = "NCC Support"
system.sysLocation.0 = "3rd Floor Closet"
```

Hint

These MIB objects can also be assigned values using the SNMP agent configuration file.

1-Minute Drill

● Name three useful features of the snmpnetstat tool.

● What is the "set of no return" problem?

● 1) It provides an easy way to obtain interface information from any SNMP-compliant system. 2) Interface information can be collected without the use of complicated command sequences. 3) It makes it easier to work with multi-vendor networks.

● "Set of no return" means making a change to a network device remotely via SNMP such as disabling an interface that prevents you from further communicating with the device remotely, thus requiring local access to make additional configuration changes.

Snmpstatus Tool

The `snmpstatus` command obtains important information from an SNMP network entity using the SNMP get request operation. The syntax of the command is as follows:

```
snmpstatus host community
```

When the remote agent utilizes the generic community string of `public`, the string need not be specified from the SNMP commands because `public` is used by default. By the way, the use of the `public` community string is highly discouraged, because it is very unsecure.

When the `snmpstatus` command is used against a device, it displays the following information:

- IP address of the device

- `sysDescr` MIB object

- `sysUpTime` MIB object

- Number of packets received and transmitted on all active interfaces (that is, the sum of `ifInUCastPkts.*` and `ifInNUCastPkts.*` objects)

- Number of IP packets received and transmitted (that is, `ipInReceives.0` and `ipOutRequests.0`)

- Number of active interfaces

- Number of interfaces that have been disabled

Thus, running the command

```
# snmpstatus didymus private
```

on the UNIX system called `didymus` displays the output as shown below:

```
[216.155.202.100]=>[Sun SNMP Agent, Netra 1 Server] Up: 11 days, 7:13:30.52
Interfaces: 2, Recv/Trans packets: 1177200/1144224 | IP: 89044/65055
```

Using this command is a good way to obtain a quick snapshot of a network device without knowing a lot about the node or some of the specific MIB objects to poll. The device has been running for over 10 days. Notice that `snmpstatus` has detected two interfaces, which is common for the Netra series of systems.

Snmptable Tool

The `snmptable` command probes an agent and displays a MIB table using the SNMP getnext request operation. The syntax of the command is as follows:

```
snmptable [common options ] [additional options] host community tableID
```

The minimum required arguments include `host`, `community`, and `tableID`. The `tableID` must be a real SNMP table, such as `interfaces.ifTable`. The `ifTable` table contains a series of MIB objects that contain performance information and other characteristics of the interfaces within a device. The basic purpose of this command is to give the user the ability to display SNMP tables and import the data into other programs for additional reporting and manipulation.

Snmptest Tool

The `snmptest` command provides a simple shell-like facility that makes it easy to communicate with a network entity using SNMP. Unlike most other SNMP tools, this command is interactive, prompting for information to accomplish one or more tasks.

The software supports three operating modes—snmp-get, snmp-getnext, and snmp-set—and uses a simple command structure to issue tasks. Issuing the `$N` command will place `snmptest` in snmp-getnext mode, while using the `$S` puts the command in snmp-set mode. To get back to snmp-get mode, use the `$G` command. By default, `snmptest` is placed in snmp-get mode, in which the user is prompted for a MIB object to retrieve from an SNMP agent.

For example, the following command sequence will obtain the `sysUpTime` object from a system called `monet`:

```
# snmptest monet stevewrite
Variable: system.sysUpTime.0
Variable:
Received Get Response from monet
requestid 0x4362F60A errstat 0x0 errindex 0x0
system.sysUpTime.0 = Timeticks: (379613) 1:03:16.13
Variable: ^c
```

Clearly, this is a rudimentary interface for issuing basic SNMP operations to SNMP agents. It is somewhat useful if a large number of tasks must be performed against the same network target. Note that to exit the program, you simply use the CTRL-C (^c) command sequence.

Snmptranslate Tool

The `snmptranslate` tool translates SNMP MIB objects into a more user-friendly and readable format. When this command is run with a MIB object, it will translate the object into either the SMI value or symbolic form. When no options are specified, it defaults to displaying the SMI value. The primary use of the command is to help display the full characteristics of MIB objects, without resorting to reading the appropriate MIB definition files.

By default, `snmptranslate` displays the numeric dotted object notation. Thus, translation of the `system.sysDescr` MIB object can be accomplished with the command

```
# snmptranslate system.sysDescr
```

which results in the following:

```
.1.3.6.1.2.1.1.1
```

To display a fairly complete description of a MIB object, use the `-Td` option. For example, consider the following command:

```
# snmptranslate -Td system.sysDescr
```

When executed, the command will produce the following:

```
.1.3.6.1.2.1.1.1
sysDescr OBJECT-TYPE
  -- FROM       SNMPv2-MIB, RFC1213-MIB
  -- TEXTUAL CONVENTION DisplayString
  SYNTAX        OCTET STRING (0..255)
  DISPLAY-HINT  "255a"
  MAX-ACCESS    read-only
  STATUS        current
  DESCRIPTION   "A textual description of the entity.  This value should
                include the full name and version identification of the
                system's hardware type, software operating-system, and
                networking software."
::= { iso(1) org(3) dod(6) internet(1) mgmt(2) mib-2(1) system(1) 1 }
```

16

As shown, a complete reference of the MIB object can be obtained. This information is taken from the MIB definition files that the agent references. In this case, the file `RFC1213-MIB.txt`, which is located in the `/usr/share/snmp/mibs` directory, was used.

Snmptrap Tool

The `snmptrap` command will emit an SNMP trap to one or more designated SNMP manager applications or systems. This tool is very useful when embedded within a shell script or other program that handles traps. One or more object identifiers can be specified on the command line, plus the type and value must accompany each object. Recall that an SNMP trap is an unsolicited message sent by an SNMP agent to a network manager application or system. The basic syntax of the command is as follows:

```
snmptrap -v 1 [command arguments] enterprise-oid agent generic-trap\ specific-trap
uptime [object ID type value]
```

The `enterprise-oid` field identifies the network management subsystem that generated the trap. The agent is the host that emits the trap. The generic-trap corresponds to one of the predefined SNMP traps listed in Module 13. The `specific-trap` value indicates more specifically the nature of the trap. The `uptime` field is used as a timestamp between the last initialization of the device and the issuance of the trap. The `object ID, type`, and `value` fields provide additional information relating to the trap. These additional fields are known as the variable binding and may contain any type of information that is related to the trap.

The `enterprise-oid, agent`, and `uptime` fields need not be specified on the command line. Instead, the empty character sequence " may be used to specify the default values for these fields. The default agent value is the hostname of the machine running the `snmptrap` command. The uptime is obtained from the local system's MIB object `system.sysUpTime.0`.

Consider, for example, that we would like to emit a link-down trap to a network management system called `rembrandt`. Further, if we want to communicate that a particular port has gone down, we include the port within the variable bindings of the trap. We can use the following command:

```
# snmptrap -v 1 public '' monet 2 0 '' interfaces.iftable.ifentry.\
ifindex.1 i 1
```

In this example, we use the default values for the `enterprise-oid` and `uptime` fields. Also, we specify the particular interface (`ifindex.1`) and set the value to 1 (which indicates the second interface with the device). The 2 represents the link-down trap, and 0 provides a null value for the `specific-trap` value.

If we review the traps on `rembrandt`, we will see output like the following:

```
Feb 24 17:51:27 monet snmptrapd[385]: 10.0.2.201: Link Down
Trap (0) Uptime:2:26:59, interfaces.ifTable.ifEntry.
ifIndex.1 = 1
```

In practice, most link-down messages are not that meaningful or interesting. However, when they come from critical devices, such as core routers or switches, a disabled interface could spell disaster for the network.

Care should be taken when configuring traps from network devices because doing so can cause a trap flood. This condition occurs when a large number of traps are sent in response to a particular recurring event. For example, within a LAN Ethernet switch, a port's link state may bounce up and down many times per second due to a hardware malfunction. This type of problem can yield a large number of traps. In practice, trap notification should be enabled only on critical devices or UNIX systems. In this case, if possible, traps should be disabled for linkup/link-down events from generic network devices.

Snmptrapd Server

The `snmptrapd` server will receive and log SNMP traps obtained from other devices. Traps that are sent on port 162 are either logged to the UNIX syslog facility or displayed on the terminal. These messages are sent using `LOG_WARNING` and the `LOG_LOCAL0` logging levels. The `snmptrapd` command must be run as superuser because it listens on a reserved system port. Executing the command without any options will cause it to be placed in the background and detached from the calling shell.

The `snmptrapd` command supports several command-line arguments, including -P (display trap), -D (more debugging), -d (detailed packet information), and -q (verbose output). The -P option will instruct `snmptrapd` to display any traps received on the standard output, and the -d option will display a detailed dump of the trap packet. Thus, to show received traps and display the contents of trap packets, use the following command:

```
# snmptrapd -P -d
```

Executing this command, using the previous example on the host rembrandt, will display the following output:

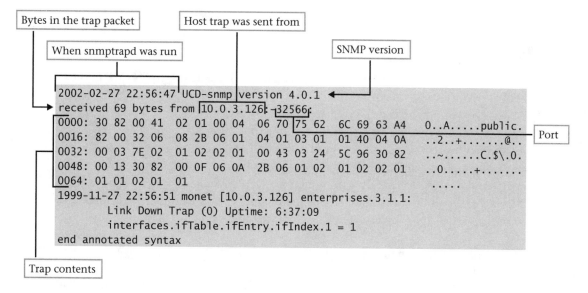

The first line shows the current version and when the snmptrapd process was run. Next, the output displays the number of bytes in the trap packet, the host the trap was sent from (monetIP:10.0.3.126), and the UDP port (32566, in this case). The contents of the trap include both hexadecimal and ASCII characters. Finally, the trap information, including the variable-binding information, is shown.

The -D option will display additional debugging information that includes the parsing of MIB files. The -q option provides a more verbose output.

The snmptrapd command can be used as a focal point for reception of traps for a large number of UNIX systems. However, it must be running continuously in order to receive traps from the network. By default, this tool is not started by the system. To enable this command on system startup, you should add it to the existing UCD agent startup script called `snmpd`.

1-Minute Drill

● What does the `snmptrapd` server do?

● What command provides a good way to obtain a quick snapshot of a network device without knowing a lot about the node or some of the specific MIB objects to poll?

Snmpwalk Tool

The `snmpwalk` command will walk an agent MIB tree using the SNMP getnext request. Why use this command instead of the `snmpget` tool? Well, the `snmpwalk` command can discover the entire MIB store contained within the agent automatically. With `snmpget`, you need to explicitly specify an object to obtain a value. With the `snmpwalk` command, you can start at a given point and move through the agent's MIB to the end. An object variable may be given on the command line to specify with which portion of the MIB space the search will begin. Without a MIB object argument, `snmpwalk` searches and starts with the MIB-II object store. Thus, the command

```
# snmpwalk monet public
```

will walk the entire system agent on the device `monet`. Since MIB-II contains a large number of objects, the command will produce a rather long listing. Instead of listing every object supported by the agent, we can limit the search and display only a single group of objects. Thus, we can list all the objects found within the MIB-II `system` group using the following command:

```
# snmpwalk bedrock public system
```

● It receives and logs SNMP traps obtained from other devices.

● `snmpstatus`

Executing this command against a UNIX system generates the following
sample output:

```
system.sysDescr.0 = Linux didymus 2.4.7-10 #1 Thu Sep 6 17:27:27 EDT 2001 i686
system.sysObjectID.0 = OID: enterprises.ucdavis.ucdSnmpAgent.linux
system.sysUpTime.0 = Timeticks: (168468) 0:28:04.68
system.sysContact.0 = Steve Maxwell (sjmaxwell@worldnet.att.net)
system.sysName.0 = didymus
system.sysLocation.0 = Graphics Lab
system.sysORLastChange.0 = Timeticks: (0) 0:00:00.00
system.sysORTable.sysOREntry.sysORID.1 = OID: ifMIB
system.sysORTable.sysOREntry.sysORID.2 = OID:
.iso.org.dod.internet.snmpV2.snmpModules.snmpMIB
system.sysORTable.sysOREntry.sysORID.3 = OID: tcpMIB
system.sysORTable.sysOREntry.sysORID.4 = OID: ip
system.sysORTable.sysOREntry.sysORID.5 = OID: udpMIB
system.sysORTable.sysOREntry.sysORID.6 = OID:
.iso.org.dod.internet.snmpV2.snmpModules.snmpVacmMIB.vacmMIBConformance.vacmMIBGroups
.vacmBasicGroup
system.sysORTable.sysOREntry.sysORID.7 = OID: .iso.org.dod.internet.snmpV2.snmpM
odules.snmpFrameworkMIB.snmpFrameworkMIBConformance.snmpFrameworkMIBCompliances.snmpF
rameworkMIBCompliance
system.sysORTable.sysOREntry.sysORID.8 = OID: .iso.org.dod.internet.snmpV2.snmpM
odules.snmpMPDMIB.snmpMPDMIBConformance.snmpMPDMIBCompliances.snmpMPDCompliance
system.sysORTable.sysOREntry.sysORID.9 = OID: .iso.org.dod.internet.snmpV2.snmpM
odules.snmpUsmMIB.usmMIBConformance.usmMIBCompliances.usmMIBCompliance
system.sysORTable.sysOREntry.sysORDescr.1 = The MIB module to describe generic o
bjects for network interface sub-layers
system.sysORTable.sysOREntry.sysORDescr.2 = The MIB module for SNMPv2 entities
system.sysORTable.sysOREntry.sysORDescr.3 = The MIB module for managing TCP impl
ementations
system.sysORTable.sysOREntry.sysORDescr.4 = The MIB module for managing IP and ICMP
implementations
system.sysORTable.sysOREntry.sysORDescr.5 = The MIB module for managing UDP
implementations
system.sysORTable.sysOREntry.sysORDescr.6 = View-based Access Control Model for SNMP.
system.sysORTable.sysOREntry.sysORDescr.7 = The SNMP Management Architecture MIB.
system.sysORTable.sysOREntry.sysORDescr.8 = The MIB for Message Processing and D
ispatching.
system.sysORTable.sysOREntry.sysORDescr.9 = The management information definitions
for the SNMP User-based Security Model.
system.sysORTable.sysOREntry.sysORUpTime.1 = Timeticks: (0) 0:00:00.00
system.sysORTable.sysOREntry.sysORUpTime.2 = Timeticks: (0) 0:00:00.00
system.sysORTable.sysOREntry.sysORUpTime.3 = Timeticks: (0) 0:00:00.00
system.sysORTable.sysOREntry.sysORUpTime.4 = Timeticks: (0) 0:00:00.00
system.sysORTable.sysOREntry.sysORUpTime.5 = Timeticks: (0) 0:00:00.00
system.sysORTable.sysOREntry.sysORUpTime.6 = Timeticks: (0) 0:00:00.00
system.sysORTable.sysOREntry.sysORUpTime.7 = Timeticks: (0) 0:00:00.00
system.sysORTable.sysOREntry.sysORUpTime.8 = Timeticks: (0) 0:00:00.00
system.sysORTable.sysOREntry.sysORUpTime.9 = Timeticks: (0) 0:00:00.00
End of MIB
```

To walk the entire MIB within a given agent and save the output to a file, use the following command:

```
# snmpwalk bedrock public .1 > walk.out
```

This command uses the .1 as the starting point to begin listing objects. Doing this ensures that every object will be displayed because .1 is the root of the entire MIB tree and all objects are accessible from this point. Walking the entire MIB tree with an agent helps identify certain MIB objects or gives you an idea of exactly how many objects a particular agent may support. To see the approximate number of objects that the Linux agent supports, count the number of lines in the file. Because the snmpwalk command displays each MIB object on its own line (unless the line is longer than the maximum number of characters for a line), we can then use the UNIX wc command to total the number of lines within the walk.out file. Thus, the command

```
# wc -l walk.out
```

produces the following output:

```
2242 walk.out
```

This command output shows that the agent contained within the Linux agent supports roughly 2242 MIB objects. When no object is specified with the snmpwalk command, it will search the MIB-II object tree by default. When the snmpwalk command reaches the end of the MIB within the agent, it will display the message End of MIB.

Note that the use of this command is a rather inefficient means to obtain a large number of MIB objects from an agent. This is because the command continuously queries a single MIB object to obtain an associated value. It is recommended that the snmpbulkwalk command be used whenever possible to reduce network traffic and load on the agent system. This command significantly reduces the work involved, from a lower-level standpoint, to obtain a large amount of information from an agent. See the following snmpbulkwalk section for additional information.

Snmpbulkwalk Tool

The `snmpbulkwalk` tool communicates with a network entity using the SNMPv2 bulk request. Like the `snmpwalk` tool, `snmpbulkwalk` will walk a MIB tree until the end of the MIB is reached or an error occurs. The bulk request provides a more efficient mechanism to transfer a large amount of data than the regular SNMPv1 get request. For example, assume we would like to retrieve the entire MIB-II `interface` group from a Linux server. We would issue the following command:

```
# snmpwalk monet public interfaces
```

This command will result in a series of SNMP getnext requests to the interface's MIB `group` against a network node called `monet`. The SNMPv1 `snmpwalk` (which uses a normal get request) command will obtain the information using 136 packets. How do we know this? Just before the `snmpwalk` command was executed, a packet capture was started using the following command:

```
# tcpdump host monet -w output.file
```

The `tcpdump` command, which is described in Module 12, will capture all packets coming from or going to the host called `monet`. These packets are saved in the file called `output.file`. Once the `snmpwalk` command has finished, the `tcpdump` command is manually stopped. Next, we simply count the number of packets that were captured within the `output.file` file. Thus, with

```
# tcpdump -r output.file | wc -l
    136
```

we see that a total of 136 packets were captured. This is the number of packets needed to retrieve the `interfaces` table. Please note that depending on the number of interfaces defined within a device, more or fewer packets would be required. However, if we query the same device using the `snmpbulkwalk` command instead,

```
# snmpbulkwalk -v 2c monet public interfaces
```

we will poll the same interface's `group` information but only use two packets!

This is a tremendous savings in terms of network bandwidth and increased SNMP performance for both the agent and manager. The SNMP bulk-request option is efficient because it attempts to place as many MIB OID values as possible within the `variable-binding` field of the SNMP response packet(s). The only limit to the amount of data that can be placed within the SNMP packet is the maximum packet size of the underlying protocols.

To walk the entire MIB tree of the device called `cisco-gw1`, use the following command:

```
# snmpbulkwalk -v 2c CISCO-gw1 public
```

The `snmpbulkwalk` command only works with SNMPv2 or SNMPv3 agents. This is because the bulk-request facility specification came after the widespread deployment of SNMPv1. Using this command on an SNMPv1 agent will, therefore, generate an error.

For instance, the following command attempts to walk the MIB tree of a device called `-gw` starting from the `system` group. In this example, `monet` supports only the SNMPv1:

```
# snmpbulkwalk -v 2c monet public system
```

Since this device doesn't understand the SNMP bulk request, it eventually times out, and the following message is displayed following the `snmpbulkwalk` command:

```
Timeout: No Response from monet
```

A timeout error condition occurs because the requests are issued to the device, but the agent residing in the device doesn't understand the SNMP bulk-request format. As a result, the packet is not answered by the agent and the command simply times out. In practice, many networking devices have been upgraded to support the bulk-request operation. Therefore, this problem will diminish over time as older devices are replaced or upgraded.

Note that `snmpbulkwalk` requires that you use either the 2c or 2p security options. If you attempt to invoke `snmpbulkwalk` without specifying which version of the SNMP protocol is to be used, the following error will be displayed:

```
snmpbulkwalk: Cannot send V1 PDU on V2 session
```

16

By default, the `snmpbulkwalk` command will search the entire MIB-II tree if a MIB object or group isn't specified on the command line. From a practical standpoint, this makes the tool a little easier to use if the complete MIB-II objects store is desired.

✓ *Mastery Check*

1. In the following command example, what is the `-M /var/mibs` option used for?

   ```
   # snmpwalk -M /var/mibs cisco-gw1 public system
   ```

   A. Specifies a list of MIB modules to load.

   B. Supplies a list of directories for the command to search for MIB files.

   C. Directs output to the specified directory.

   D. Runs the SNMP scripts found in the specified directory.

2. The _____ command collects changes in MIB integer values from an SNMP agent entity.

3. If a device doesn't respond to SNMP requests, what command might you try to see if the device is reachable on the network?

   A. `snmpwalk`

   B. `snmptrap`

   C. `snmpnetstat`

   D. `ping`

4. What command is similar to the UNIX `netstat` utility and provides some of the same basic information about attached device interfaces and routing information?

☑ *Mastery Check*

5. Which of the following management tasks isn't something SNMP is useful for?

   A. Reset a user password

   B. Disable or enable a network interface

   C. Restart a device or agent

   D. Monitor critical processes

6. What is the correct syntax for the `snmpstatus` command?

   A. `snmpstatus host community`

   B. `snmpstatus community host`

   C. `snmpstatus interface community`

   D. `snmpstatus community interface`

7. The snmptrapd server will receive and log SNMP _____ obtained from other devices.

8. What command option is used to generate output shown in the second example line instead of the first, using the same input command?

```
system.sysUpTime.0 = Timeticks: (139494644) 16 days, 3:29:06.44
system.sysUpTime.0 16:3:24:11.44
```

   A. `-S`

   B. `-s`

   C. `-f`

   D. `-q`

9. True/False: It might be helpful to execute an `snmpwalk` against the agent if questions come up regarding which objects are indeed supported by the agent.

16

☑ *Mastery Check*

10. The _____ tool will walk a MIB tree until the end of the MIB is reached or an error occurs and provides a more efficient mechanism to transfer a large amount of data than the `snmpwalk` tool.

11. True/False: `snmpnetstat` only works with Unix workstations and servers.

Module 17

Using Network File System

Critical Skills

The Network File System (NFS) is a service that provides file sharing across a network of systems. NFS was first implemented by Sun Microsystems and was supported only on the Sun version of UNIX, which at the time was called SunOS. Today, it is supported across most, if not all, versions of UNIX that are available today. Also, NFS is supported on a number of non-UNIX platforms such as Windows and Macintosh. On UNIX systems, NFS behaves and is configured in much the same way regardless of which version of UNIX is used. In recent years, network appliance servers have been developed, which are systems that provide NFS services on dedicated, high-performance hardware platforms. Typically, these servers are built to support only a smaller number of services (such as NFS) and are not meant to support a wide range of additional network services.

File sharing is a concept that has been around for quite some time; it means that one or more files may be shared across a number of different systems and by any number of users. The basic premise is that read-only file access can be shared by any number of users when the file in question is stored within NFS. Updating or writing to a file with multiple users is an entirely different issue, and NFS provides the same services that are available with the operating system. NFS files appear to the system as if they were stored locally. In other words, NFS is implemented in such as way as to provide the same facilities for files as if they were stored on the local file system.

NFS can be divided into two broad sections: the server and client. The server component consists of several elements that include server processes and configuration files. The client component includes a single-server process. The details of the server and client are described below.

Versions of NFS

NFS has seen some important improvements since it was first introduced back in 1984. The features and improvements of the protocols are presented here:

- **Version 1** This version only existed within Sun Microsystems and was never actually released as a product.

- **Version 2** The first official release of the protocol was shipped with SunOS 2.0, and it had the following limitations:

  - Didn't support files greater than 2GB

  - Maximum transfer rate of only 8K

  - Limitation on performance due to client/server interaction

  - Poor security features

17

- **Version 3** This version has been out for a number of years and addresses some of the most important issues that plagued version 2. In addition, version 3 handles the following:

  - Reliable asynchronous write

  - Reduces protocol overhead

  - Maintains backward compatibility with version 2

  However, security remained a significant problem for the earlier versions of NFS.

- **Version 4** Back in 1999, Sun published a technical brief describing new features for NFS. Also, RFC3010 was developed, which described technical details regarding this new version. Basically, version 4 will provide better security, improve operation over WAN networks, provide better cross-platform interoperability, and include extensions to the protocol.

17.1 NFS Server Uncovered

The NFS server consist of several programs and services, which include

- `nfsd`

- `lockd`

- `statd`

- `mountd`

Also, the server contains a standard NFS configuration file, which lists all the file systems that are made available to NFS clients. The process of making one or more file systems available to NFS clients on the network is called "file system exporting" or "sharing."

The nfsd Process

The `nfsd` process handles NFS remote file system requests from client systems. Typically, this process is started automatically on system startup. On Solaris, the `/etc/init.d/nfs.server` startup script is used, while on Linux the `/etc/rc.d/init.d/nfsd` script is used. For HP-UX, the `/etc/init.d/nfs.server` is used. By default, NFS servers use both TCP and UDP transport protocols. However, depending on site requirements, the transport protocol may be selected using the -p option, followed by the protocol (such as `tcp` or `udp`).

One of the most important aspects of the NFS server configuration is the number of concurrent requests that it can handle from clients. In large networks or otherwise demanding computing environments, where many systems will access NFS servers, it is important to ensure that each server is operating in the most efficient manner possible. One way to increase server performance is to set the maximum number of parallel NFS servers that should be run to handle NFS requests. The number of NFS servers that are used is derived from the command-line parameter within the server startup script. By default, only a single server instance is started.

Note

Depending on the implementation of the NFS server, it may use lightweight processes (kernel threads) which, when the `ps` or `top` commands are used to inspect processes, system usage will not appear for the NFS server. Thus, either zero CPU or a smaller amount than was actually used may be displayed. In general, it is not uncommon to have as many as 10 or more NFS processes in a demanding environment.

To increase the number of NFS server instances, edit the startup script and place the desired number of instances after the `nfsd` process command line. For example, to instruct the NFS server to start with eight instances, the following would be used:

```
nfsd 8
```

To have this change take effect, restart the NFS process using the appropriate startup script.

The *lockd* Process

The `lockd` process implements record locks for NFS files. Record locking is a mechanism to restrict access to an individual file record or the entire file when changes are being made. This is necessary when more than one user or application is updating a file. The `lockd` process is also known as the lock manager and handles lock requests from the `fcntl` system call, which is issued from client systems.

The *statd* Process

The `statd` process is used in conjunction with the `lockd` process to handle cases when the NFS server crashes and requires recovery. The `statd` process keeps track of clients that spawn processes that hold locks on files from the NFS server. Should the NFS server reboot after a crash, `statd` sends a message to each client indicating that the NFS server has rebooted. Then, the `lockd` process on the client attempts to reclaim any pending locks from the server.

The *mountd* Process

The `mountd` process is used to handle remote NFS mount requests from clients. It is responsible for determining which file systems are available and interacts with the client to provide file and directory information. By default, this service is running when NFS services are activated.

If the system supports auto-mounting, such as in Solaris, the `automountd` process is also active and provides the same basic services for clients as `mountd`. The auto-mount facility provides a way to set up automatic mounting of file systems when users access one or more files or directories.

17.2 Mounting Remote File System

One very interesting aspect of NFS is that it provides complete transparency of remote file systems for the average user. In fact, from a file system perspective, there is no difference between a remotely mounted file system and one that is mounted from a local disk. For example, consider the following listing from `/usr/docs` directory:

```
drwxr-xr-x   6 root      root       4096 Apr  1 22:01 .
drwxr-xr-x   6 root      1           512 Apr  1 23:03 ..
drwxr-xr-x   2 root      root       4096 Apr  1 22:01 html
drwxr-xr-x   2 root      root       4096 Apr  1 22:00 man
drwxr-xr-x   2 root      root       4096 Apr  1 22:00 pdf
drwxr-xr-x   2 root      root       4096 Apr  1 22:00 postscript
```

In the list above, four directories are shown using the `ls -al` command. Can you identify which directories are stored locally versus those that are actually stored on a remote NFS server? From this listing, it is impossible for anyone to determine which directories are made available via NFS—they all appear as if they are from the local file system.

To show which file systems are mounted locally versus remotely using NFS, use the `df` command. This command shows interesting file system information for all mounted file systems on the system. For example, issuing this command on the system that contained the above `/usr/docs` directory shows

```
Filesystem            kbytes      used    avail  capacity  Mounted on
/dev/dsk/c0d0s0       480815     39338   393396    10%     /
/dev/dsk/c0d0s6      1587078    811771   727695    53%     /usr
/dev/dsk/c0d0s1       384847    117108   229255    34%     /var
/dev/dsk/c0d0s5       480815    337833    94901    79%     /opt
didymus:/docs        2522552   1665304   729108    70%     /usr/docs/pdf
```

As you can see from the output, the `pdf` directory is a remotely mounted NFS file system from the system called `didymus`.

Just as when mounting a file system that is stored on a local disk, the `mount` command can be used to connect NFS volumes to the local system. To mount the file system called `/share` from the NFS server `bedrock` on the local directory called `/files`, use the following command:

```
mount bedrock:/share /files
```

The `mount` command shown here does provide only a temporary mount of this volume. This means that the `/share` volume will not be mounted automatically when the system is rebooted; thus, this NFS volume will go away should the system called `didymus` be restarted. To address this issue, the NFS mount must be defined within the standard NFS configuration file, such as `/etc/exports`. Review the next section, "Share/Export File Options," to find out how to set up permanent NFS mounts.

The dfstab/export Files

In order for a UNIX NFS server to make local files available to clients, each file system must be exported or shared on the network. On Solaris, the `/etc/dfs/dfstab` is used to specify that the file systems should be made available to clients on a permanent basis. On Linux and HPUX, the `/etc/exports` file is used instead. Both of these files contain pretty much the same information; however, the supported command options do differ.

For example, the way to indicate if the file system access should be read-only would be to use the string –o ro for dfstab, while (ro) is used for exports file. A file system is exported or shared when it is made available to other systems for mounting across the network. The process of exporting or sharing a file system includes adding the designated file system to the exports or dfstab and then issuing a command to make the file system "live" on the network.

A sample /etc/dfs/dfstab file is shown below:

```
share -F nfs -o rw /usr
share -F nfs -o ro /docs
```

In this example, two file systems, /usr and /docs, are being exported. Note that the share string is included, which is the actual command that makes the file system available. The share command on Solaris is used to provide access to the file system resource for remote clients. The /usr file system contains the file access option of rw. This indicates that both read and write file access will be granted to NFS clients. The /docs file system is made available read only due to the ro option.

A sample /etc/exports file includes the following:

```
/ (rw)
/docs (ro)
```

Share/Export File Options

Both the /etc/dfs/dfstab and /etc/exportfs configuration files are used to provide automatic setup of NFS volumes to client systems. Each of these files supports a number of similar options and also some unique ones. Table 17-1 shows some of the most important command line options.

Option	Description
anon=uid	Sets the UID on the server to be the effective user ID of any unknown users. By default, all unknown users are given the UID of 60001.
-F	(dfstab) Specifies the type of file system for the NFS volume. Use the keyword nfs for NFS-type file systems.
-d	(dfstab) Provides a descriptive string of the NFS volume.
log	(dfstab) Enables NFS logging for the given file system.

Table 17-1   Share/Export NFS Options

Option	Description
rw	(Both) The associated pathname is read/write to all clients; this is the default behavior if no option is provided (This default behavior is for Solaris)
rw=client_host	(dfstab) A client system name may be specified with the NFS volume permission. For Linux, the syntax includes client(rw).
ro	(Both) The associated pathname is read-only to all clients.
ro=client_host	(dfstab) A client system name may be specified with the NFS volume permission. For Linux, the syntax includes client(rw).
root_squash	(exportfs) Maps any requests from the root user (UID of 0) to the anonymous UID.
secure	(dfstab) Requires that NFS client requests originate on a network port that is less than 1024. By default this option is enabled. Disable by using the insecure option.
sync	Requests that all file write transactions be completed to the underlying hardware before the write request has been completed. This means that requests are buffered before the write requests are returned.

Table 17-1 Share/Export NFS Options (*continued*)

In order to gain a better understanding of some possible dfstab and exports configuration options, a series of examples are provided in Table 17-2. Each example shows the necessary options for both configuration files.

/etc/dfs/dfstab **Configuration**   /etc/exports **Configuration**

/usr   didymus(ro) chips(rw)   share -F nfs -o rw=chips,ro=didymus /usr

Explanation Provide read-only access to the client called didymus and read-write access to the client called chips for the /usr file system.

/src   (rw,anonuid=70000)   share -F nfs -o rw,anon=70000 /src

Explanation Provide read-write access to all clients for the /src file system and also map the anonymous users to the UID of 70000.

/home   (rw,log,root=bedrock)   share -F nfs -o rw,log,root=bedrock /home

Explanation Provide read-write access to all clients for the /home file system, enable NFS logging, and also permit root access from the host called bedrock.

Table 17-2 Configuration File Options

17.3 Exploring NFS Tools

UNIX provides additional tools for monitoring and controlling NFS services.
These tools include

- exportfs
- share/unshare
- showmount
- nfsstat

exportfs

The exportfs command is provided on Linux to make one or more file
systems available to clients on an NFS server. The file systems must be specified
within the /etc/exports file. The command supports a few command-line
options and they are shown in Table 17-3.

To export all file systems contained within the /etc/exports file, issue
the following command:

```
exportfs -a
```

If you wanted to unexport all the file systems, issue the above command
again; this will assume that file systems have already been exported. If not, it

Option	Description
-a	Export or unexport all file systems contained within the /etc/exports file.
-o	Specify a list of options when exporting file systems. See Table 17-1 for additional information.
-r	Reexport all file systems contained within the /etc/exports file.
-u	Unexport one or more file systems.
-v	Provide verbose output when exporting or unexporting file systems.

Table 17-3 Export Command-Line Options

simply exports them. The other approach is to use the –u option. You can also specify the individual file systems that you want to export without having to add them to the /etc/export file. Just list the file system as an option to the exportfs command. For example, to provide NFS access to the /prod file system to the client didymus, use the following command:

```
exportfs didymus:/prod
```

To display a list of all exported file systems, just issue the exportfs command without any options. Note that issuing this command doesn't make the export permanent. In order to make it last across reboots, the lete/export file must be updated. Thus, the command

```
exportfs
```

will show all file systems that are available to clients:

```
/docs          dino.home.com
/              bedrock.home.com
/prod          *.home.com
```

In this example, the * character is shown; this is a shorthand notation to specify a wildcard, which is interpreted as all hosts within the home.com domain.

share/unShare (Solaris Only)

Use the share command on the Solaris system to make NFS volumes available over the network to client systems. To make NFS volumes available on a permanent basis, use the /etc/dfs/dfstab file. To remove shared file systems, use the unshare command.

Issuing the share command without any arguments shows the currently available NFS volumes that are being shared. For example, the command

```
share
```

shows the following sample file systems:

```
-    /usr   rw    "user home directories"
-    /docs  ro    "system documentation"
-    /src   rw    "source tree"
```

To share a particular volume, specify it on the command line with the `share` command. Also, the `shareall` command is provided to share all the NFS volumes currently defined within the `/etc/dfs/dfstab` configuration file.

Note

Sharing a file system without it being defined within the `dfstab` file means that it will not be shared when the NFS server is rebooted.

To remove or unshare a volume, use the `unshared` or `unshareall` commands. Thus, either command would prohibit NFS client access. If one or more client's systems were accessing an NFS volume when it was unshared, the client would get a `stale NFS file handle` and the operation would not complete; thus, care should be taken when removing NFS access from critical file systems.

showmount

The `showmount` command is used to provide information about clients that have mounted any file systems on the NFS server. For example, to display all the clients that have mounted the file systems on a Solaris system called `bedrock`, issue the following command:

```
showmount -a
```

The `-a` option formats the output to show `hostname: directory` for each file system and client. The sample output

```
didymus.home.com:/usr
didymus.home.com:/docs
chips.home.com:/usr
chips.home.com:/src
```

shows two client systems that have mounted file systems from `bedrock`. The first client, `didymus`, has mounted both the `/usr` and `/docs` file systems. The second system, called `chips`, mounted the `/usr` and `/src` file systems, respectively. The `showmount` command can also be used to show the available mounted file systems on the local NFS server. For example, if the `showmount` command is run with the −d option, on the system bedrock, the following would be shown:

```
/docs
/usr
```

The output above shows all the file systems that have been made available to NFS clients. In this case, the output is similar to what is provided with the share command.

nfsstat

The nfsstat command provides NFS server-based statistic and performance information on NFS activities. The following categories of information can be displayed:

- Server RPC statistics

- Server NFS statistics

- Client RPC statistics

- Client NFS statistics

The statistics that are displayed are determined by the command-line options, which are listed in Table 17-4. Issuing the command without any parameters will result in the−csnrc options being activated and the corresponding output displayed for each statistic.

Option	Description
−a	Show NFS access control list (ACL) information.
−c	Show client-side information for NFS, RPC, and ACL.
−m	Show configuration and stats for each NFS mounted file system.
−n	Show both client and server NFS information.
−r	Show only remote procedure call (RPC) information.
−s	Show only server information.
−z	Reset all statistic counters. This can only be run by the superuser.

Table 17-4 The nfsstat Command-Line Options

The output of `nfsstat` is not that user friendly, but it does contain some important information on the activities and configuration of the NFS server. For example, the `-m` option displays statistical information on each mounted file system, such as

```
/mnt/bedrock/docs from bedrock:/docs
Flags:
vers=3,proto=tcp,sec=sys,hard,intr,link,symlink,acl,rsize=32768,\
    wsize=32768,retrans=5,timeo=600
Attr cache: acregmin=3,acregmax=60,acdirmin=30,acdirmax=60
```

In this example, the `/mnt/bedrock/docs` file system is mounted from the server called `bedrock` and the associated file system configuration information is also displayed. The Flags fields shows specific configuration (either by default or manually configured) from the NFS server. From the output we notice that, for instance, this file system is mounted with the `hard` option on the client. A hard mount is one that ensures that a client system will block any pending NFS activity should the file system become unavailable. This is meant to ensure a certain level of file system integrity on the client system.

The Attr field contains file system cache attributes, which are used to control the amount of time certain file elements (such as file's owner) are stored in the NFS server cache. The remaining mount flag options and associated descriptions are listed in Table 17-5.

NFS Mount Options	Description
vers	The version of the NFS protocol.
proto	The NFS lower-layer transport protocol. Can be either Transmission Control Protocol (TCP) or User Datagram Protocol (UDP).
sec	The security model used; values include `none` (no authentication), `sys` (standard UNIX authentication based on UID and GID), `short` (alternative UNIX-style authentication), `dh` (DES-based authentication), and `kbr` (Kerberos v4, v5, or v5i).
hard	Hard NFS mount; ensures that should the NFS server not respond due to some kind of failure, the client will block file transactions until the server file system is restored.
soft	soft NFS mount; does the inverse of a hard mount; instructs the client to not block NFS transactions to the server, but lets them time out, instead.

Table 17-5   The nfsstat Mount Options

NFS Mount Options	Description
intr	Permits the client to interrupt a process when a transaction is pending on the server.
link	The server supports file links.
acl	Access control list (ACL) that applies to the file system; no assignment means no authentication is used.
rsize	The size of the read buffer.
wsize	The size of the write buffer.
retrans	The retransmission delay in tenths of a second.
timeo	The transaction timeout in tenths of a second.
acregmin	The minimum amount of time (in seconds) to store cached file attributes.
acregmax	The maximum amount of time (in seconds) to store cached file attributes.
acdirmin	The minimum amount of time (in seconds) to store cached directory attributes.
acdirmax	The maximum amount of time (in seconds) to store cached directory attributes.

Table 17-5   The nfsstat Mount Options (*continued*)

Note

With regard to hard versus soft mounts, when hard mounts are used on client systems, and the server experiences a problem that causes an interruption of NFS services, the client can lock up until the server problem has been fixed. The solution to address this is to use soft mounts. However, although using soft mounts will help with the lockup problem, it doesn't specifically address any server problem since any pending NFS activity will simply time out. When a timeout occurs, the client system will generate one or more error messages. This could result in application-related problems.

To show specific NFS activity, use the following command:

```
nfsstat -n
```

The −n option displays NFS stats for both clients and the server. Sample output is shown below and can be divided into two broad categories: specific stats from the NFS server and from the client standpoint. The first part of the listing includes server information that contains stats for both versions 2 and 3 of the NFS protocol. For each type of activity received by the server, a counter is maintained. Also, for each counter, the percent of the total number of transactions received is calculated. For example, the `getattr` attribute consists of 35 percent of the total number of transactions received by the server. The `getattr` is used when the specific file information is needed by a NFS client system.

```
Server nfs:
calls          badcalls
478088         5
Version 2: (14 calls)
null           getattr        setattr        root           lookup         readlink
0 0%           5 35%          0 0%           0 0%           0 0%           0 0%
read           wrcache        write          create         remove         rename
0 0%           0 0%           0 0%           0 0%           0 0%           0 0%
link           symlink        mkdir          rmdir          readdir        statfs
0 0%           0 0%           0 0%           0 0%           3 21%          6 42%
Version 3: (478074 calls)
null           getattr        setattr        lookup         access         readlink
1 0%           23 0%          0 0%           57321 11%      414682 86%     2058 0%
read           write          create         mkdir          symlink        mknod
0 0%           0 0%           0 0%           0 0%           0 0%           0 0%
remove         rmdir          rename         link           readdir        readdirplus
0 0%           0 0%           0 0%           0 0%           3943 0%        1 0%
fsstat         fsinfo         pathconf       commit
24 0%          21 0%          0 0%           0 0%
```

A listing and description of the individual counter fields are provided in Table 17-6.

```
Client nfs:
calls          badcalls       clgets         cltoomany
79             1              79             0
Version 2: (63 calls)
null           getattr        setattr        root           lookup         readlink
0 0%           55 87%         0 0%           0 0%           7 11%          0 0%
read           wrcache        write          create         remove         rename
0 0%           0 0%           0 0%           0 0%           0 0%           0 0%
link           symlink        mkdir          rmdir          readdir        statfs
0 0%           0 0%           0 0%           0 0%           0 0%           1 1%
Version 3: (15 calls)
null           getattr        setattr        lookup         access         readlink
0 0%           3 20%          0 0%           0 0%           1 6%           0 0%
read           write          create         mkdir          symlink        mknod
0 0%           0 0%           0 0%           0 0%           0 0%           0 0%
remove         rmdir          rename         link           readdir        readdirplus
0 0%           0 0%           0 0%           0 0%           0 0%           1 6%
fsstat         fsinfo         pathconf       commit
8 53%          2 13%          0 0%           0 0%
```

Field	Description
calls	The total number of NFS calls received.
badcalls	The total number of NFS call that were rejected.
null	The total number of times an NFS call was made but not received.
getattr	The total number of file attribute lookup calls that were made. For example, obtaining information about the size of a file.
setattr	The total number of file set attribute calls that were made. For example, updating the modification date of a file.
root	The total number of root user requests that were made.
lookup	The total number of file/directory lookup requests that were made.
readlink	The total number of readlink (file link) requests that were made.
read	The total number of read requests that were made.
wrcache	The total number of write to cache requests that were made.
write	The total number of write requests that were made.
create	The total number of create (file or directory) requests that were made.
remove	The total number of remove requests that were made.
rename	The total number of rename requests that were made.
link	The total number of link (hard) requests that were made.
symlink	The total number of link (symbolic) requests that were made.
mkdir	The total number of create directory requests that were made.
rmdir	The total number of delete directory requests that were made.
readdir	The total number of read directory requests that were made.
statfs	The total number of file system status requests that were made.
readdirplus	The total number of read directory requests that were made.
fsstat	The total number of file status operation requests that were made.
fsinfo	The total number of file system status queries that were made.
pathconf	The total number of read path requests that were made.
commit	The total number of commit requests that were made.

Table 17-6   The nfsstat NFS Field Descriptions

17.4 Configuring NFS Clients

The client component consists of a single background process, standard UNIX directories for the mounts, and a configuration file. The mountd process must be running on the client systems that issue NFS mount requests to the NFS server. In order for the client to use the remote file system, it must be mounted onto an existing UNIX directory and the client has to have the associated permission on the NFS server to access the remote file system. Finally, a configuration file is needed to have the NFS mounts remembered between system reboots.

Typically, the administrator doesn't need to worry about any associated processes for client NFS systems, because any required services are started automatically when client requests are issued. Instead, the main area of concern are making sure a client can access the NFS server if security has been enabled and that the client is configured to mount one or more file systems automatically.

The mounting of a file system on a standard UNIX client from an NFS server involves several simple steps. These steps are described in the following procedure. In particular, the example shows the /docs file system being mounted on the client system called chips, from the NFS server called bedrock.

Note

Assume the system chips has already been installed on the network and network connectivity and services are fully operational. For example, chips has been placed within the NIS or DNS services and can talk to the NFS server bedrock using such tools as ping.

1. Create the target directory that will be used for the associated mount point from the remote file system. For example, the remote file system is called /docs. As the administrator, you must determine the name of the local directory that will be used to access the files from the docs directory. In our example, let's assume we are going to use the new target directory called /usr/docs.

   Thus, the UNIX command mkdir /usr/docs must be executed on the client system; this will create the target directory mount point for the client.

2. Attempt to mount the file system manually using the UNIX command line. The following command would be used:

```
mount bedrock:/docs /usr/docs
```

   When mounting an NFS file system, the hostname is specified in front of the name of the remote file system, followed by the target directory. In this example, bedrock:/docs specifies the name of the NFS server, plus the file system name.

3. Verify access to the newly mounted system by listing the files using the `ls-1/usr/docs` command. If you see files, the mount was successful.

4. Edit the associated system configuration file to make the NFS mount permanent across system reboots. For Linux, the `/etc/fstab` file is used, and for both Solaris and HP-UX, the `/etc/vfstab` is used. Regardless which operating system is involved, the NFS mount entry is very similar. Consider the file syntax depending on the UNIX system:

● Linux (`/etc/fstab`):

```
bedrock:/docs          /mnt/bedrock/docs      nfs      bg,soft        0 0
```

● Solaris/HP-UX (`/etc/vfstab`):

```
didymus:/docs -  /mnt/didymus/docs          nfs      -      yes bg,soft
```

Review the section "Controlling the File System Mount Table" below for additional information on the syntax of these files.

17.5 Controlling the File System Mount Table

The syntax of the file system table is used to indicate which local and remote file systems should be mounted when the system is brought from single-user mode to multi-user mode or when the system is rebooted and brought to normal operational status. For Linux, the `/etc/fstab` file is used, while on both Solaris and HP-UX, the `/etc/vfstab` file is used. In both cases, the contents of these files are static by nature and will be maintained by the system administrator. When new file systems are added to the system, or when new NFS volumes are made available on the network, these files must be updated for the client system to use these new file systems.

The file system mount table consists of several fields, which describe the file systems that are either mounted locally or from remote NFS servers. In the case of NFS, additional options are used to control how the file systems are mounted. In general, the mount table consist of the following fields:

● `file_system [NFS host:file system] mount_point type additional_options` Some fields may contain one or more optional parameters or keywords. The fields include

● `file_system` This represents the name of the file system or partition name—for example, the entry `/dev/dsk/c1d0s2`. With

NFS, this contains the name of the NFS server followed by the name of the remote file system—for instance, the entry `bedrock:/usr`.

17

Note

The colon character (`:`) is needed as a string separator.

- **mount_point**   The mount point represents the directory that the file system will be mounted on—for instance, `/usr/docs`. The target directory should be empty and the administrator should check to determine the status of an existing directory before mounting.

Note

If a file system is mounted onto a directory that contains additional directories or files, these become invisible while the new file system is mounted. Thus, to gain access to these files or directories, the file system should be unmounted.

The mount point is the directory that the file system will be associated with and that is used by the users to navigate the mounted file system. The purpose of the target directory is the same regardless if the file system is local or from an NFS server.

- **type**   The type field represents the type of file system that should be mounted. For example, the keyword `ufs` represents a local file system, while the `nfs` keyword is used for remote NFS file systems. Additional keyword types are supported, and the most common ones are listed in Table 17-7.

- **additional_options**   The additional options section represents a few fields that further control the mounting of file systems. For example, for NFS file systems, the client can mount the volume using

File system	Description
auto	(Linux only) File systems that are mounted via the automounter (for example, floppy disk).
ext3	(Linux only) Extended file system.
proc	The process file system, which maps both system and process information onto directories and files.
nfs	Network File System.
swap	Swap file.
ufs	Universal File System—this file system will be local to the system.

Table 17-7   File System Types

either hard or soft modes. The NFS hard mode instructs the client system to cause any pending process to sleep when the NFS volume becomes unavailable. This might be necessary, for example, to ensure that a critical transaction will complete when the NFS volume is made available again. The soft mode causes the inverse to occur—any pending process will simply time out due to an NFS volume that becomes unavailable. In general, the soft mode can be used in most cases and computing environments.

A sample /etc/fstab that was obtained from a Linux system contains the following:

```
LABEL=/                 /                   ext3    defaults        1 1
/dev/fd0                /mnt/floppy         auto    noauto,owner    0 0
none                    /proc               proc    defaults        0 0
none                    /dev/shm            tmpfs   defaults        0 0
none                    /dev/pts            devpts  gid=5,mode=620  0 0
/dev/hda5               swap                swap    defaults        0 0
bedrock:/docs           /mnt/bedrock/docs   nfs     bg,soft         0 0
bedrock:/usr            /mnt/bedrock/usr    nfs     bg,soft         0 0
```

A sample /etc/vfstab file that is available on a Solaris system contains the following:

```
#device        device       mount      FS    fsck   mountmount
#to mount      to fsck      point      type  pass   at boot options
#
#/dev/dsk/c1d0s2 /dev/rdsk/c1d0s2 /usr          ufs   1      yes       -
fd       -       /dev/fd fd       -    no     -
/proc    -       /proc   proc     -    no     -
/dev/dsk/c0d0s3 -         -       swap  -     no     -
/dev/dsk/c0d0s0 /dev/rdsk/c0d0s0     /     ufs   1      no     -
/dev/dsk/c0d0s6 /dev/rdsk/c0d0s6     /usr  ufs   1      no     -
/dev/dsk/c0d0s1 /dev/rdsk/c0d0s1     /var  ufs   1      no     -
/dev/dsk/c0d0p0:boot    -        /boot pcfs  -     no     -
/dev/dsk/c0d0s7 /dev/rdsk/c0d0s7     /export/home ufs   2      no -
/dev/dsk/c0d0s5 /dev/rdsk/c0d0s5     /opt  ufs   2      yes    -
swap     -       /tmp    tmpfs    -    yes    -
didymus:/      - /mnt/didymus/root      nfs   -      yes bg,soft
didymus:/docs -  /mnt/didymus/docs      nfs   -      yes bg,soft
```

☑ *Mastery Check*

1. What command would you use in the NFS startup script to start the server with four processes?

2. The _____process restricts access to an individual file record or the entire file when changes are being made.

3. True/False: From a file system perspective there is a difference between a remotely mounted file system and one that is mounted from a local disk.

4. On a Solaris NFS server, what configuration file specifies which file systems should be made available to clients on a permanent basis?

   A. /etc/dfs/dfstab

   B. /etc/exports

   C. /etc/fstab

   D. /etc/vfstab

5. What command provides NFS server-based statistics and performance information on NFS activities?

6. On a Linux system, what is the file system table used to indicate which local and remote file systems should be mounted when the system is brought from single-user mode to multi-user mode or when the system is rebooted and brought to normal operational status?

   A. /etc/dfs/dfstab

   B. /etc/exports

   C. /etc/fstab

   D. /etc/vfstab

Please refer to the following output for questions 7-8:

```
Server nfs:
calls        badcalls
478088        5
Version 2: (14 calls)
null          getattr     setattr     root        lookup      readlink
```

☑ *Mastery Check*

0 0%	5 35%	0 0%	0 0%	0 0%	0 0%
read	wrcache	write	create	remove	rename
0 0%	0 0%	0 0%	0 0%	0 0%	0 0%
link	symlink	mkdir	rmdir	readdir	statfs
0 0%	0 0%	0 0%	0 0%	3 21%	6 42%

Version 3: (478074 calls)

null	getattr	setattr	lookup	access	readlink
1 0%	23 0%	0 0%	57321 11%	414682 86%	2058 0%
read	write	create	mkdir	symlink	mknod
0 0%	0 0%	0 0%	0 0%	0 0%	0 0%
remove	rmdir	rename	link	readdir	readdirplus
0 0%	0 0%	0 0%	0 0%	3943 0%	1 0%

fsstat	fsinfo	pathconf	commit
24 0%	21 0%	0 0%	0 0%

7. How many version 3 read directory requests were made?

8. What percent of the total version 2 requests were write to cache requests?

Please refer to the following configuration file for questions 9-11:

```
LABEL=/              /                    ext3    defaults           1 1
/dev/fd0             /mnt/floppy          auto    noauto,owner       0 0
none                 /proc                proc    defaults           0 0
none                 /dev/shm             tmpfs   defaults           0 0
none                 /dev/pts             devpts  gid=5,mode=620     0 0
/dev/hda5            swap                 swap    defaults           0 0
bedrock:/docs        /mnt/bedrock/docs    nfs
bg,soft        0 0
```

9. What is the system name of the device that is being mounted with NFS?

10. What is the mount point for the file system mounted with NFS?

11. Is the NFS mount in this example a hard or a soft mount?

Module 18

File Transfer Protocol

Critical Skills

The File Transfer Protocol (FTP) is a widely implemented file transfer mechanism that provides access to files on a central server from one or more FTP client applications. FTP itself is a collection of rules on how to physically transfer files (either text or binary) from one system to another, without the worry about file system differences or the operating systems involved. For example, a Windows PC can transfer a file from a UNIX system, despite that fact that both operating systems involved catalog and store files differently.

The FTP server consists of one or more FTP server processes that handle requests for each FTP session. A session is one that has been issued by an FTP client to a server; there is a corresponding match between the number of clients and the FTP server process. Every time a client makes a new session, a new FTP process is started to handle the client connection.

The FTP server and client application are built using the standard client/ server model, where the client issues one or more requests and the server attempts to fulfill those requests. The basic FTP interaction includes the following:

1. A user invokes a client FTP application that requests to log in to an FTP server; the application opens a connection to the server.

2. The user specifies the authentication parameters (such as login name and password) to the server.

3. The server validates the authentication information, and if acceptable, permits the user to access the server.

4. The user accesses the files on the FTP server and can list, retrieve, or place files on the server, depending specific permissions and configuration options.

5. The user logs off the FTP server and closes the session connection.

Many FTP sites that support FTP provide general anonymous login access, which basically means that any user can access files on the server when they use the *anonymous* username. This is done to provide a general server without the need of defining specific user accounts.

Note

In general, anonymous FTP access can be dangerous. It is important that anonymous FTP access be set up correctly; otherwise, the server can be more susceptible to increased security-related problems from malicious Internet users.

The Linux FTP server software is from Washington University and is typically referred to as `wu.ftpd`. However, on later releases of Linux (such as Red Hat 7.2), the server is simply called `ftpd`. On Solaris and HP-UX, the FTP server is called `in.ftpd` and comes directly from the operating system provider. However, it is quite common for the system administrator to download the `wu-ftpd` software to run on these environments instead of the default packages.

Hint

On many (if not all) UNIX systems, the FTP server is not started automatically when the system boots, like other network services such as DHCP. Instead, the FTP server is invoked from the `inetd` network master service found on both HP-UX and Solaris (or `xnetd` on Linux). Once a client FTP session is activated, a server process is started to handle the client connection, and when the client closes the connection, the server exits and no longer runs. Configuration of the FTP server using either `inetd` or `xnetd` is discussed later in this module.

1.1 Explore a Sample FTP Session

To further understand the basic operation of FTP services, a sample FTP session has been provided. In this example, a FTP server is running on a system called `bedrock`, while the client session is invoked from a system called `didymus`. This is shown in Figure 18-1.

In this example, both systems are UNIX systems, but it doesn't always have to be that way; the client system can be running any software that supports FTP client software. For example, Windows ships with an FTP client. On the server side, again, any operating system can be used provided that an FTP server is running on the system.

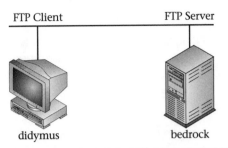

FTP Client   FTP Server

didymus   bedrock

Figure 18-1   Sample FTP session

On the client side (`didymus`), the user invokes the FTP session to the server (`bedrock`) using the standard UNIX `ftp` client program:

```
[root@didymus /]# ftp bedrock
Connected to bedrock (216.155.202.100).
220 bedrock FTP server (Eng Server) ready.
Name (bedrock:root): root
331 Password required for root.
Password:
230 User root logged in.
Remote system type is UNIX.
Using binary mode to transfer files.
ftp>
```

In the example above the `ftp` command includes the name of the FTP server to access. Once the connection has been made, the server responds with some server-side information to include the name of the server (for instance, `Connected to bedrock (216.155.202.100).`) and a login prompt (`Name (bedrock:root):`). At this point, it is up to the user, via the client software, to provide authentication information (login name and password) to gain access to the FTP server.

In the output above, the `root` account and associated password was used to gain access to the FTP server. This demonstrates that the FTP server works with the standard UNIX account login procedures. Typically, it you are going to provide FTP over the Internet, you will set up an anonymous account access; otherwise, you will need to create accounts for FTP only users.

Note

By default, many UNIX systems permit users to access FTP services without additional configuration or setup. Configuring anonymous access for FTP will be discussed later in this module.

18

Once the user has been authenticated to the FTP server, it echoes a message indicating the user has been logged in like the following:

```
230 User root logged in.
```

At this point, the FTP server indicates the type of system the server is running on (Remote system type is UNIX.) and provides some additional configuration information on the connection (Using binary mode to transfer files.). The "binary mode" message indicates that any file transfer will be done in such a way as to ensure that binary data is transferred accurately.

Finally, the standard FTP server prompt is provided: ftp>, which indicates the FTP client shell. This informs the user that the server is ready to accept FTP commands. At the prompt, the user may list available FTP commands, obtain a directory listing of either the remote or local current directories, get a remote file from the server, or put a local file on the server. Some of these activities depend on having certain privileges or configuration parameters set on the FTP server side.

Obtaining a Directory Listing

The FTP service provides the ability to navigate the directories on the remote FTP server using the dir FTP command. For example, the following output shows this command:

```
ftp> dir
227 Entering Passive Mode (216,155,202,100,128,164)
150 ASCII data connection for /bin/ls (216.155.202.163,1048) (0 bytes).
total 28
drwxrwxr-x   7 root      sys           512 Feb  2 13:37 .
drwxr-xr-x  32 root      root         1024 Apr 19 12:39 ..
drwxr-xr-x   6 root      sys           512 Nov 11 16:37 SUNWebnfs
```

```
drwxrwxr-x    3 bin      bin          512 Nov 11 16:11 SUNWits
drwxr-xr-x    3 root     1            512 Feb  2 13:37 answerbooks
drwx------    2 root     root        8192 Nov 11 16:00 lost+found
drwxr-xr-x   20 root     sys          512 Jan 24 23:20 sfw
-r--r--r--    1 root     1            916 Apr 20 17:09 xtrace
-r--r--r--    1 root     1           1016 Apr 20 15:10 yellow
226 ASCII Transfer complete.
ftp>
```

The output generated is from the `/bin/ls` command; thus, this file listing should be familiar to the reader at this point. The `ftp` client program supports wildcard matching and other regular expressions characters such as "`[]`", "`*`", and "`?`". The `dir` command can be combined with UNIX expressions to list only certain files and/or directories. Thus, the command

```
ftp> dir SUN*
```

will yield the following output, which is based on the directory listing from above:

```
227 Entering Passive Mode (216,155,202,100,128,172)
150 ASCII data connection for /bin/ls (216.155.202.163,1049) (0 bytes).
SUNWebnfs:
total 524
drwxr-xr-x    6 root     sys          512 Nov 11 16:37 .
drwxrwxr-x    7 root     sys          512 Feb  2 13:37 ..
drwxr-xr-x    4 root     sys          512 Nov 11 16:37 JFileChooser-patch
drwxr-xr-x    4 root     sys          512 Nov 11 16:37 demos
drwxr-xr-x    3 root     sys          512 Nov 11 16:37 javadoc
drwxr-xr-x    2 root     sys          512 Nov 11 16:37 sample
-rw-r--r--    1 root     sys       122052 May 28  1999 webnfs.zip
-rw-r--r--    1 root     sys       121613 May 28  1999 xfilechooser.jar
SUNWits:
total 6
drwxrwxr-x    3 bin      bin          512 Nov 11 16:11 .
drwxrwxr-x    7 root     sys          512 Feb  2 13:37 ..
drwxrwxr-x    3 bin      bin          512 Nov 11 16:11 Graphics-sw
226 ASCII Transfer complete.
ftp>
```

As you can see, the contents of the directories named SUNWebnfs and SUNWits were listed. In addition, other expressions are supported, such as listing just certain files using file range name matching. The command

```
ftp> dir [x-y]*
```

will show only those files (or any directories) that start with x through y characters:

```
227 Entering Passive Mode (216,155,202,100,128,184)
150 ASCII data connection for /bin/ls (216.155.202.163,1061) (0 bytes).
-r--r--r--   1 root     1        916 Apr 20 17:09 xtrace
-r--r--r--   1 root     1       1016 Apr 20 15:10 yellow
226 ASCII Transfer complete.
ftp>
```

In this case, both the xtrace and yellow files were listed. The "?" character is used to match a single character within a filename.

Configuration Options

The FTP client application in conjunction with the remote FTP service can negotiate certain file transfer options or configuration parameters. For example, the client can request that a file transfer should be done in binary mode versus text (ASCII) mode. Binary mode file transfer means that the contents of a file are sent to the remote server without any conversion of characters. This mode is also called raw or image mode, and is used to transfer files that contain programs or other files that must not be converted to the ASCII character set. By default, most FTP servers configure the connection to support ASCII transfer mode. Thus, to set the connection to binary mode, use the binary command:

```
ftp> binary
```

Once executed, the ftp client issues a response indicating that its transfer mode is now image:

```
200 Type set to I.
```

To go back to ASCII mode, use the ascii command.

Retrieving a File

When obtaining or retrieving files from the server, it is helpful to think of the server as the "remote" end of the FTP connection, while the client side is the "local" end. In our example above, the remote end is bedrock, while the local end is didymus. With FTP, to transfer a file from the remote end to the local end, you would use the get FTP command. Thus, to transfer the file yellow from the bedrock server to the local system, use the following command while in the FTP shell:

```
ftp> get yellow
```

The client session will show the following:

```
227 Entering Passive Mode (216,155,202,100,128,206)
150 ASCII data connection for yellow (216.155.202.163,1047) (916 bytes).
226 ASCII Transfer complete.
938 bytes received in 0.000418 secs (2.2e+03 Kbytes/sec)
ftp>
```

As you can see, the output includes the name of the file, the size of the file, and the amount of time it took to transfer the contents of the file. Also, the relative network performance was shown.

To verify that the file was actually transferred, inspect the local system by using the !ls -l yellow command. The ! (bang) character is supported on many UNIX FTP client programs, which permits the execution of a local command (in this case, the ls -l command, which lists files and/or directories). Thus, when this command is run within the FTP client shell, and when no errors were generated during the file transfer, the following should be displayed:

```
-rw-r--r--   1 root     root         916 Apr 25 02:03 yellow
```

Note

The byte counts for the file yellow match the number of bytes transferred with the FTP program.

Sending a File

To send a local file to the remote host, use the put FTP command. Thus, to place a new file called steve.dat onto the bedrock system, use the following command:

```
ftp> put steve.dat
```

When the command is executed, the following is displayed by the client program:

```
local: steve.dat remote: steve.dat
227 Entering Passive Mode (216,155,202,100,128,208)
150 ASCII data connection for steve.dat (216.155.202.163,1050).
226 Transfer complete.
18396 bytes sent in 0.0124 secs (1.5e+03 Kbytes/sec)
ftp>
```

Again, much of the same information is shown as in the previous transfer example. To verify the file was sent (which, in most cases, is not necessary), use the dir command with the filename:

```
ftp> dir  steve.dat
227 Entering Passive Mode (216,155,202,100,128,210)
150 ASCII data connection for /bin/ls (216.155.202.163,1052) (0 bytes).
-rw-r--r--   1 root     1            17884 Apr 24 15:23 steve.dat
226 ASCII Transfer complete.
ftp>
```

As you can see, the file is listed on the remote end, confirming the transfer.

Monitoring File Transfers

When transferring very large files, it is hard to determine if the transfer is progressing or has stopped for some reason. As a result, most FTP clients support the hash command. When enabled, the hash command tells the FTP client to echo a "#" character every time a block of information was successfully retrieved. For example, the command

```
ftp> hash
```

shows the following:

```
Hash mark printing on (1024 bytes/hash mark).
```

Thus, when each chunk of the file is transferred, a new pound sign is displayed. Here is what will be shown when a file called records.dat is transferred:

```
ftp> put record.dat
local: record.dat remote: record.dat
```

```
227 Entering Passive Mode (216,155,202,100,128,213)
150 ASCII data connection for record.dat (216.155.202.163,1055).
######################################################################
######################################################################
######################################################################
######
226 Transfer complete.
240902 bytes sent in 0.257 secs (9.1e+02 Kbytes/sec
```

Due to the size of the file, a number of hash characters were displayed—thus providing a visual way to see the FTP activity. Use the `byte` command to close the FTP session. This logs you off the server and exits the FTP client program.

18.2 Discover FTP Commands

The FTP facility supports a large number of commands. However, the most important and popular ones are listed and described in Table 18-1. Note, too, that some of the listed commands may or may not be supported on either the FTP client or server end. Typing the "?" (or `help`) command will provide a list

FTP Command	Description
ascii	Enable ASCII transfer mode; this mode is used to copy regular text files.
binary	Enable binary transfer mode; this is used to copy programs and other data files—for example, `tar` or `gzip` archive files.
bye	Log off the FTP server.
cd	Change working directory.
chmod	Change the mode of a file or directory.
close	Close the FTP session.
delete	Delete a file or directory.
debug	Enable debug mode, which will display more information about each transaction.
dir	Display the current directory listing or individual file.
exit	Same as `bye`.
get	Transfer a file from the remote server to the local client.
glob	Enable specific character matching for files and directories.

Table 18-1 Command FTP Commands

FTP Command	Description
hash	Enable hash mode; displays a # character for each 8K block of data that has been transferred.
help	Display a list of FTP commands.
image	Same as `binary` command.
lcd	Change working directory on local client system.
ls	Like `dir` command.
mdelete	Delete multiple files and directories.
mget	Transfer multiple files from the remote server to the local client.
mput	Transfer multiple files from the client to the server.
open	Open a new FTP session.
prompt	Toggle the prompting of confirmation before transfer begins. When enabled, it will prompt for each file before transfer begins.
pwd	Print the working directory.
quit	Same as `bye`.
rmdir	Remove a directory on the server side.
send	Same as `put`.
status	Show the FTP session status.
verbose	Display additional information for each transaction (like `debug`, but not as much information).

Table 18-1   Command FTP Commands (*continued*)

of supported commands for the client side, but these may not all be available on the server side.

18.3 Controlling FTP Access

On the FTP server, the /etc/ftpusers file can be used to control access to the FTP server.

Note

On Linux, this file is replaced by the /etc/ftpaccess configuration file.

On Solaris, by default, the file contains the following entries:

● daemon

● bin

- sys

- adm

- lp

- uucp

- nuucp

- listen

- nobody

- noaccess

- nobody4

Each of the login names defined within this file is blocked from using the FTP facility. Note that each name is on a separate line by itself and there is no special ordering—the file is simply processed from beginning to end whenever a user accesses the FTP server. If a user that is listed within this file attempts to access the FTP server, they get a `login incorrect` message. When a change is made to the /etc/ftpuser file, it takes effect immediately and no additional steps are necessary to restrict users.

When the wu-ftpd server is deployed, the /etc/ftpaccess file can be used to replace the function of the /etc/ftpusers file. Also, the /etc/ftpaccess provides additional configuration options as well. The wu-ftpd server comes standard with Linux. The /etc/ftpaccess configuration file can be used to control the following:

- Access to the FTP server

- Which command a user may execute

- The logging of FTP access

- General FTP configuration

The default entries for this file are shown here:

```
# This file controls the behavior of the wu-ftpd
# ftp server.
```

```
#
# If you're looking for a graphical frontend to
# editing it, try kwuftpd from the kdeadmin
# package.

# Don't allow system accounts to log in over ftp
#deny-uid %-99 %65534-
#deny-gid %-99 %65534-
allow-uid ftp
allow-gid ftp

# The ftpchroot group doesn't exist by default, this
# entry is just supplied as an example.
# To chroot a user, modify the line below or create
# the ftpchroot group and add the user to it.
#
# You will need to setup the required applications
# and libraries in the root directory (set using
# guest-root).
#
# Look at the anonftp package for the files you'll need.
guestgroup ftpchroot

# User classes...
class   all    real,guest,anonymous   *

# Set this to your email address
email root@localhost

# Allow 5 mistyped passwords
loginfails 5

# Notify the users of README files at login and when
# changing to a different directory
readme   README*     login
readme   README*     cwd=*

# Messages displayed to the user
message /welcome.msg            login
message .message                cwd=*

# Allow on-the-fly compression and tarring
compress        yes             all
tar             yes             all
```

```
# Prevent anonymous users (and partially guest users)
# from executing dangerous commands
chmod          no             guest,anonymous
delete         no             anonymous
overwrite      no             anonymous
rename         no             anonymous

# Turn on logging to /var/log/xferlog
log transfers anonymous,guest,real inbound,outbound

# If /etc/shutmsg exists, don't allow logins
# see ftpshut man page
shutdown /etc/shutmsg

# Ask users to use their email address as anonymous
# password
passwd-check rfc822 warn
```

18.4 Configure Anonymous FTP

On the Internet, many sites offer free FTP access to the public; this is known
as anonymous FTP. Basically, anyone can log in an FTP service using a generic
login and password. This type of access can be dangerous, since you really don't
know the true identity of the user accessing the server.

Here is an anonymous login session using the "ftp.cisco.com" server:

```
# ftp ftp.cisco.com
Connected to ftp.cisco.com.
220-
220-  Cisco Connection Online    |         |    Cisco Systems, Inc.
220-  Email: cco-team@cisco.com  |||       |||    170 West Tasman Drive
220-  Phone: +1.800.553.2447  .:|||||:...:|||||:. San Jose, CA 95134
220-
220-  You may login with:
220-      + Your CCO username and password, or
220-      + A special access code followed by your e-mail address, or
220-      + "anonymous" followed by your e-mail address for guest access.
220-
220-
220 ftp-poc-2 FTP server (CIOESD #422 Wed May 1 14:15:23 PDT 2002) ready.
```

At this point, the anonymous username is entered and the FTP server responds with the standard password which is typical of the e-mail address of the user:

```
User (ftp.cisco.com:(none)): anonymous
331 Guest login ok, send your complete e-mail address as password.
Password:
```

If the login name and password are accepted, the FTP server grants access to the system, and displays a welcome message.

18

Note

Not all FTP servers display these types of informative messages.

```
230-  <======[+]> FTP.CISCO.COM <[+]=======>
230-
230-Welcome to the Cisco Systems CCO FTP server.
230-
230-Local time is currently Wed May  8 23:03:09 2002.
230-
230-There are currently 20 users out of 120 maximum logged in.
230-
230-This server has a number of restrictions.  If you are not familiar
230-with these, please first get and read the /README or /README.TXT file.
230-
230-If you have any odd problems, try logging in with a minus sign (-) as
230-the first character of your password.  This will turn off a feature that
230-may be confusing your ftp client program.
230-
230-Please send any questions, comments, or problem reports about this
230-server to cco-team@cisco.com.
230-
230-You are logged in with guest (anonymous) level access.
230-
230-
230-Please read the file README
230- it was last modified on Mon Jul  5 21:31:32 1999 - 1037 days ago
230 Guest login ok, access restrictions apply.
```

Once logged into the system, you can retrieve or place files according to the corresponding site permissions and/or directory structure.

Setting Up Anonymous Access

Configuring anonymous FTP access on a server is a fairly straightforward process. However, having said that, care must be taken to ensure that every step is executed correctly and that no configuration-related problems result.

Note

Providing anonymous FTP on the Internet or even locally can be a potential security risk. The risk is even compounded when the configuration is not complete or has not been done correctly. One good way to minimize problems is to have other knowledgeable people help test the final configuration before going live. Also, continuously consult the relevant security web sites (such as www.cert.org) about FTP security issues and problems. Using these approaches, you may help to reduce the number of problems that would-be hackers might exploit.

The basic process for anonymous account setup includes the following:

1. Create the FTP login in the /etc/passwd and /etc/shadow files.

2. Make sure the FTP account name does not appear in the /etc/ftpusers file.

3. Set up the required FTP environment.

4. Test the account.

Some of the above procedure need not be executed manually. For example, the setup of the FTP environment can be done with an automated script. On Solaris, the ftpd manual (that is, man ftpd) gives a listing of a script to handle all the required steps. Just copy this output and save it to a file for execution. Other operating systems such as Linux provide a list of steps via the ftpd man page and provide an RPM (anonftp-4.0.9.i386.sp) to handle the details of setting up the correct configuration.

Once the anonymous account and configuration has been set up, test the account to ensure that basic FTP services are functional and work as expected (such as retrieving files). Next, make sure that the anonymous user can't do things such as remove system files or execute unauthorized commands. Finally, monitor the FTP log file for any suspicious activities, such as a larger number of requests for login within a short period of time. This could indicate that someone is attempting to log in to the server using a program or script, which may indicate an attempted denial service attack being done against your server.

18.5 Log FTP Activity

One important aspect of system administration is keeping track of activity on your systems. That is why, for example, critical services like FTP should be monitored on a continued basis. As a result, FTP activity should be logged to a special file so that later inspection and monitoring can be done in the most efficient manner. Most of the available FTP servers support robust logging facilities. In particular, the ability to monitor each FTP session is important. Also, some FTP servers (for example, the Linux wu-ftpd server) provide a way to view each FTP command executed by a FTP user. With this capability, it becomes much easier to identify possible nonfriendly behavior toward your FTP services.

To activate FTP logging, the following will need to be done:

1. Enable FTP server logging.

2. Enable logging via the syslog facility.

3. Test that logging is functional.

Enable FTP logging

To activate FTP logging, the proper command-line argument(s) must be supplied to the FTP server process when it is invoked by the system. For example, on Solaris, the in.ftpd FTP server supports the −l option, which tells the server to record every active session when a user logs into the FTP server. Typically, the FTP server will send this monitoring information to the general-purpose system logging process via the syslogd process. See below for additional details about syslog logging facility.

To enable logging on Solaris and HP-UX, edit the /etc/inetd.conf network services configuration file and modify the in.ftpd entry. For example, the default FTP entry on Solaris contains the following:

```
ftp   stream tcp6   nowait  root  /usr/sbin/in.ftpd      in.ftpd
```

In order to have logging, place a -l option in front of the in.ftpd command. Thus, the new entry should be

```
ftp    stream tcp6  nowait  root  /usr/sbin/in.ftpdin.ftpd -l
```

In order for this change to take effect, the inetd process must be told to reread its configuration file. Thus, to find the process identification of the inetd process, issue the following command:

```
ps -ef | grep inetd | grep -v grep
```

This will show

```
root   209    1  0 14:48:39 ?         0:00 /usr/sbin/inetd -s
```

Then, when you have the process ID, issue the following:

```
kill -SIGHUP 209
```

Thus, any changes made to the inetd.conf file should now be active.

To activate logging on Linux, edit the /etc/xinetd.d/wu-ftpd configuration file and alter the relevant line as shown here:

```
server_args            = -a
```

Note

Depending on the version of Linux you have, the -l option may already be in this file. If that is the case, you are all set for session logging. However, if you want more detailed logging in addition to session logging, add the -L option. The -L option will provide logging for each FTP command that is typed by the user after they log into the server. Thus, the new wu-ftpd configuration should be as follows:

```
server_args             = -a -l -L
```

In order for this change to take effect, the xinetd process must be told to reread its configuration file. Thus, to find the process identification of the xinetd process, issue the following command:

```
ps -ef | grep inetd | grep -v grep
```

Note

The Linux `xinetd` program requires the `SIGUSR2` signal to be issued to reread its configuration file.

Then, determine the process identification and supply it on the command line as shown here:

```
kill -SIGUSR2 [pid]
```

Enable the syslog Facility

Now that the FTP servers are configured to log activity, we need to set up the system to support FTP activity from a `syslog` facility point of view. This is because the FTP servers will forward logging information onto `syslog` automatically, but unless we set up the `syslog` configuration to specifically process FTP messages, we may not see the logging output.

The `syslog` logging facility is a general-purpose log aggregator, which funnels messages from many different operating system components on to small number of log files, with both the component name and time stamp information included. For example, a typical FTP session message might include the following:

```
Apr 17 14:55:46 bedrock in.ftpd[605]: [ID 373804 daemon.info] connection
from didymus.home.com at Wed Apr 17 14:55:46 2002
```

The `syslog` server (`syslogd`) handles the processing of messages that have been sent by other programs; in the example above, the message was sent by the `in.ftpd` server. As you can see from the message, the relevant information includes the date and time that the transaction was initiated and also the systems involved.

The `syslogd` process uses the `/etc/syslog.conf` configuration file for how to funnel messages. The logging of messages is divided into different categories and levels depending on the type of message and associated severity. Table 18-2 shows the logging categories and their associated meanings.

The `syslog` facility includes severity or levels of priority for each category; these range from emergency (`emerg`) to debug (`debug`), and can be thought of as the type of message. For example, the `emerg` category is used to denote very critical panic types of conditions, which informs the administrator of some important event. Additional types include `alert` for situations that should be

Category	Meaning
auth	Messages related to system authorization from such programs as `login`, `su`, and `getty`. (`getty` is used on Solaris and HP-UX, and `agetty` is used on Linux.)
cron	Messages related to `cron` or `at` services from such programs `crontab`, `at`, and `cron`.
daemon	Messages related to server processes `in.ftpd` and `in.dhcpd`.
kern	Messages generated by the kernel
lpr	Messages generated by the printer spooler system from programs as `lpr`, `lpc`, and `lpd`.
mail	Messages related to the mail system.
news	Messages related to the news system.
local0-7	Message levels for custom applications.
uucp	Messages related to the uucp system.

Table 18-2   Syslog Message Categories

corrected immediately; `crit` for warnings about important conditions, such as hardware errors; `err` for other types of errors, and `warning` messages about important problems; `notice` messages that reflect an important situation, but may require special handling; `info`, which are information types of messages; `debug` messages that represent debug information within a program; and `none` messages, where no types of messages are sent.

To make it easier to identify FTP and other related activities with the logging facility, group FTP server (and related daemon processes) messages into a single file. For example, the `syslog.conf` file, which has been configured to capture FTP transactions, can include the following:

```
daemon.notice                        /var/adm/services
daemon.info                          /var/adm/services
```

In this case, the `/var/log/services` file is used to store messages that come from the `daemon` message category, using both `notice` and `info` messages types. To verify that messages are flowing to this file, access the FTP server from another client and then inspect the file for log activity. Thus, the command

```
grep ftp /var/log/services
```

will show lines containing FTP transactions, like the following:

```
May 11 14:51:07 bedrock in.ftpd[1395]: [ID 373804 daemon.info]
connection from socs.home.com at Sat May 11 14:51:07 2002
May 11 14:56:00 bedrock in.ftpd[1399]: [ID 373804 daemon.info]
connection from socs.home.com at Sat May 11 14:56:00 2002
May 11 14:56:28 bedrock in.ftpd[1402]: [ID 373804 daemon.info]
connection from socs.home.com at Sat May 11 14:56:28 2002
May 11 15:18:28 bedrock in.ftpd[1453]: [ID 373804 daemon.info]
connection from socs.home.com at Sat May 11 15:18:28 2002
May 11 15:23:00 bedrock in.ftpd[1461]: [ID 373804 daemon.info]
connection from socs.home.com at Sat May 11 15:23:00 2002
May 11 15:23:11 bedrock in.ftpd[1464]: [ID 373804 daemon.info]
connection from bedrock.home.com at Sat May 11 15:23:11 2002
May 11 15:38:11 bedrock in.ftpd[1464]: [ID 639925 daemon.info]
User unknown timed out after 900 seconds at Sat May 11 15:38:11 2002
```

Project 18-1

This project will help you check your FTP server configuration and also help you make sure it is current with the latest versions and security patches.

Step-by-Step

1. Is there an FTP server currently running on your system? To check, do:

```
# ps -ef | grep ftp
```

2. If you don't want FTP running on this system, comment out or remove the FTP line in /etc/inetd.conf so that it won't run the next time you restart the system.

3. If there is an FTP server running, check to see if anonymous access is enabled by using another system and attempting to FTP anonymously to your system.

4. If anonymous FTP access is enabled and you don't want it to be, add

```
ftp
```

on a line by itself in the /etc/ftpusers file (or in the /etc/ftpaccess file in Linux).

5. If you are using the FTP server supplied with your operating system, check your operating system's vendor's Web site to ensure you have the latest version and patches. If you have installed a different FTP server, such as wu-ftpd, check frequently for updates and check security sites for new vulnerabilities you need to patch for.

18

☑ *Mastery Check*

1. What type of FTP server access allows access without requiring a specific account?

2. What is the FTP command syntax to list the files and directories that start with the letters J-M?

3. What FTP command do you use to send a file from a client to an FTP server?

   A. send

   B. get

   C. put

   D. ascii

4. The _____ command tells the FTP client to echo a "#" character every time a block of information was successfully retrieved.

5. What is the purpose of each entry in the Solaris /etc/ftpusers file?

   A. Grant access to that user

   B. Deny access to that user

   C. Define that user's account

   D. Define user groups

6. With the wu-ftpd server, what configuration file controls access to the FTP server, determines commands a user may execute, and specifies FTP access logging?

7. What does the -l entry at the end of this Solaris /etc/inetd.conf network services configuration file do?

   ```
   ftp     stream tcp6    nowait  root    /usr/sbin/in.ftpd
   in.ftpd -l
   ```

8. What syslog category do login messages belong to?

Module 19

Important System
Administration
Tasks/Information

Critical Skills

Unlike many of the other modules contained within this book that focus on a specific topic or area, this module provides solutions to specific UNIX system tasks and administrative problems.

19.1 Communicate with Users on the System

As the system administrator, you will need to, on occasion, communicate with users on the system, using the `talk`, `wall`, or `write` commands. The `talk` command provides a visual mechanism to "talk" to a single user, the `wall` command can send a message to a number of users at once, and the `write` command can also be used to talk to an individual user, using line-by-line mode.

The `talk` syntax includes

```
talk user [@hostname]
```

where `user` is an existing UNIX user currently logged into the system. If `user` is on a different system as compared to local originator, the user's hostname must be specified.

Assuming the `root` user would like to talk with the user `billc` that is currently on the local system, the following command would be used:

```
talk billc
```

Once this command has been executed, the following will be displayed:

```
[Waiting for your party to respond]
```

The command clears the screen and places a line in the middle of display to divide the screen. The top portion is use to contain the text that `root` will send to `billc`, while the bottom part is for `billc`'s responses to `root`.

On `billc`'s terminal, the following is displayed:

```
Message from Talk_Daemon@socrates at 11:27 ...
talk: connection requested by root@socrates.
talk: respond with:  talk root@socrates
```

Once `billc` responds using the above comand, his screen is updated and the message [Connection established] is displayed to indicate that communication is now possible.

Here is what the `root`'s screen will look like when the question is asked "How are you?"

```
How are you?
```

Bill responds with:

```
I'm fine! and you?
```

19

Note

Either party may close the talk session by issuing a control-c (^-c).

To communicate to all users on the system at the same time, use the `wall` command. For example, the command

```
wall -a
system needs to be rebooted; back in 20 minutes....
(^d) ◄────── Issue Control D to end the wall session.
```

The administrator types the above message after the `wall` command, followed by control-c (^-c).

The −a option tells `wall` to send the message to all users attached via pseudo-terminals and to the system console. When this command is run, the following will be displayed to all users logging in:

```
Broadcast Message from root (pts/8) on bedrock Mon May 27 19:40:55...
system needs to be rebooted; back in 20 minutes....
```

Note

You must end the `wall` command with a CONTROL-d (^D) to tell the command you entered the desired message.

19.2 Increase System Swap Space

A file system or swap file represents a location on a disk drive that is used to support swap space and other important temporary storage functions for UNIX. In many instances, the swap area was defined when the system was first installed and configured. It is quite common for the system administrator to increase the amount of swap space for a system after it has been set up. In fact, sometimes the sizing of critical resources like swap space are much more accurate only after the system has been deployed and is actively being used.

For most versions of UNIX, the requirements for swap space are the same; the versions discussed all require a minimum amount of space for the system to operate. The actual size of the swap area is highly dependent on the number of users of the system and the actual services or applications being supported. Also, the tools used to manage swap space are somewhat different. Table 19-1 shows the relevant swap management commands for each operating system.

List Swap Space

It is important to know how much swap space is actually being used. Use either the swapon command for Linux or the swap command for Solaris. For HP-UX, use the swapinfo command. Each of these commands will show information about how much space has been defined on the system and any associated use. For example, the Solaris swap command will show the following when used with the −s option:

> Total kbytes swap space currently used

```
total: 39488k bytes allocated + 12520k reserved = 52008k used,
1062656k available
```

> Total kbytes space configured as swap space

Function	Linux	Solaris	HP-UX
Add swap space	swapon −a	swap	swapon −a
Create swap area using a regular file	mkswap	mkfile	
List swap usage	swapon −s	swap −l	swapinfo -ta
Delete swap area	swapoff	swap −d	

Table 19-1 UNIX Swap Commands

This shows the total amount of swap space currently used on the system—in this case, 52,008K (or 52008000 bytes). The total amount of configured swap on the system is 1,062,656K. When the used space approaches the total amount of available space on the system, it is time to increase the amount of swap space. Also, it is not uncommon to increase swap space even if the currently used space is quite a bit smaller than that available—perhaps because the system administrator wants additional performance gains, one or more additional drives are configured to support swapping. In this way, the swap activities are spread across additional physical disk drive, thereby increasing system performance.

Using the `swapon -s` command on Linux shows the available and swap space sizes:

19

```
Filename                         Type        Size    Used   Priority
/dev/hda5                        partition   740840  14048  -1
```

Add More Swap Space

To add more space to the system, use either the `swapon` or `swap` commands, depending on the system in question. Adding more swap space can be accomplished by increasing the size of the current swap area or by adding an additional swap file or disk partition. In general, the installation procedures for most UNIX systems describe implementing swap space using a separate disk partition. For example, given the snippet of the `/etc/fstab` file from a Linux system, we see the following:

```
none               /proc                proc    defaults        0 0
none               /dev/shm             tmpfs   defaults        0 0
none               /dev/pts             devpts  gid=5,mode=620  0 0
/dev/hda5          swap                 swap    defaults        0 0
bedrock:/docs      /mnt/bedrock/docs    nfs     bg,hard         0 0
bedrock:/usr       /mnt/bedrock/usr     nfs     bg,soft         0 0
```

The swap partition is defined by `/dev/hda5`, and it is possible to use tools such as `fdisk` (for Linux, for instance) to increase the size of the partition, assuming that extra unused space is available on the disk.

Another approach to increasing the swap space is to define another partition that should be used for swap and simply add the partition to the mounted file

Hint

The system should be placed in single-user mode when attempting to adjust the size of the swap partition; this precaution should be standard procedure for making critical types of changes to the system.

system table, such as /etc/vfstab (Solaris). Using this approach, the system would need to be rebooted before the new swap area could be used. On the other hand, if you want to use the space without rebooting the system, use the swap command. For example, assume that you would like to use the /dev/dsk/ c0d0s0 partition for swapping. Thus, this command (on Solaris) could be used:

```
# swap -a /dev/dsk/c0d0s0
```

When the swap −l command is run, it shows the total mount of swap space allocated and used, and we see additional swap has been added to the system:

```
swapfile              dev  swaplo  blocks    free
/dev/dsk/c0d0s3      102,3       8 2048248 2048248
/dev/dsk/c0d0s7      102,7       8 4194288 4194288 ◄─────── New swap allocated
```

The final approach to increasing swap space is to create a simple UNIX file using the mkfile (on Solaris) command, which creates a file the size of the swap space that is needed. Once this has been done, issue the swap command with the file as the argument instead of the disk partition.

19.3 Control Root Access

Most versions of UNIX have a mechanism to control when the root user can access the system from the network versus just from the system console. For example, by default, it is not possible for the root user to access a Solaris system over the network when first installed. In other words, when attempting to telnet to a Solaris system and log in as root, this account is blocked. Why? Well, there are those who believe that accessing the root account over the network represents a security concern. There are a few ways to handle this problem. First, one solution is to install the SSH package and use the ssh program to provide remote connectivity for root access. Second, connect the system to a terminal server and access the console over the network as supported by the terminal server. Third, enable root access to the system over the network by modifying the /etc/default/login file. This file contains a single-line parameter that controls if root can access non-console ports.

A portion of this file is shown here:

```
# If CONSOLE is set, root can only login on that device.
# Comment this line out to allow remote login by root.
#
CONSOLE=/dev/console
```

As you can see from the comments, the CONSOLE variable should be commented out with a # character, should the administrator desire to enable remote login for the root user.

19.4 Display System Configuration Information

19

Sometimes, when attempting to debug system problems or if it is necessary to determine a specific software version and/or other system information, it will be necessary use one or more system tools. Also, with many newer versions of UNIX, the /proc file system has been introduced, which makes it very easy to probe the system for a host of configuration and operating information. On Solaris, the prtconf tool can be used, which provides both low-level and operating system configuration information. When the tool is run without any command-line arguments, the following is produced:

```
System Configuration:  Sun Microsystems   i86pc         System Info. (system
Memory size: 128 Megabytes                              architecture and memory)
System Peripherals (Software Nodes):
i86pc
    +boot (driver not attached)
        memory (driver not attached)
    aliases (driver not attached)
    chosen (driver not attached)
    i86pc-memory (driver not attached)
    i86pc-mmu (driver not attached)
    openprom (driver not attached)
    options, instance #0
    packages (driver not attached)
    delayed-writes (driver not attached)
    itu-props (driver not attached)
    isa, instance #0
        motherboard (driver not attached)
        asy, instance #0 (driver not attached)
        lp (driver not attached)
        asy, instance #1 (driver not attached)
        fdc, instance #0
            fd, instance #0
            fd, instance #1 (driver not attached)
        i8042, instance #0
```

```
            keyboard, instance #0
            mouse, instance #0
        bios (driver not attached)
        bios (driver not attached)
    pci, instance #0
        pci8086,7190 (driver not attached)
        pci8086,7191, instance #0
            display, instance #0
        pci8086,7110 (driver not attached)
        pci-ide, instance #0
            ide, instance #0
                cmdk, instance #0
            ide, instance #1
                sd, instance #0
        pci8086,7112, instance #0
        pci8086,7113 (driver not attached)
        pci10b7,9050, instance #1
    used-resources (driver not attached)
    objmgr, instance #0
    cpu, instance #0 (driver not attached)
    pseudo, instance #0
```

Not all the information generated from this command is really useful. However, the command does provide some general information about the system architecture and installed memory, and detailed information about the number of different devices installed on the system. In general, the message "driver not attached" indicates that no device was found and thus no driver was loaded to handle the hardware component. The `prtconf` tool provides a fair number of command-line options, but only the most common options are listed in Table 19-2.

Command Option	Description
-B	Shows device driver information.
-F	Shows frame buffer information.
-v	Enables verbose mode.

Table 19-2   prtconf Command-Line Options

Another very useful Solaris command is `showrev`. This is the output of this command:

```
Hostname: bedrock
Hostid: 1e056f4b
Release: 5.8
Kernel architecture: i86pc
Application architecture: i386
Hardware provider:
Domain: home.com
Kernel version: SunOS 5.8 Generic 108529-07 February 2001
```

19

As seen from the output, this command provides some useful information about the system. In addition, one very good command-line option with this command is `-c`. This instructs the command to list detailed version information about a particular UNIX command when specified. For example, the command

```
showrev -c ls ◄──────── Determine information about a UNIX command.
```

shows the following:

```
PATH is:
/usr/sbin:/usr/bin:/usr/dt/bin:/usr/openwin/bin:/bin:/usr/ucb
PWD is:
/
LD_LIBRARY_PATH is not set in the current environment

File: /usr/bin/ls
=================
File type: ELF 32-bit LSB executable 80386 Version 1, dynamically linked, stripped
Command version: SunOS 5.8 Generic February 2000
File mode: r-xr-xr-x
User owning file: root
Group owning file: bin
Library information:
        libc.so.1 =>     /usr/lib/libc.so.1
        libdl.so.1 =>    /usr/lib/libdl.so.1
Sum: 43151

File: /bin/ls
=============
File type: ELF 32-bit LSB executable 80386 Version 1, dynamically linked, stripped
Command version: SunOS 5.8 Generic February 2000
File mode: r-xr-xr-x
User owning file: root
Group owning file: bin
Library information:
        libc.so.1 =>     /usr/lib/libc.so.1
```

```
        libdl.so.1 =>    /usr/lib/libdl.so.1
Sum: 43151


File: /usr/ucb/ls
=================
File type: ELF 32-bit LSB executable 80386 Version 1, dynamically linked, stripped
Command version: SunOS 5.8 Generic February 2000
File mode: rwxr-xr-x
User owning file: root
Group owning file: bin
Library information:
        libc.so.1 =>     /usr/lib/libc.so.1
        libdl.so.1 =>    /usr/lib/libdl.so.1
Sum: 42882
```

This might be more information than most people want, but when tracking down problems, having this kind of detail can be quite invaluable.

The /proc Directory

The /proc directory or file system is another very good way to obtain important configuration and other information from the system. The /proc directory is a tree hierarchy, which contains both additional subdirectories and individual files that represent some aspect of the system or running process. When the ls command is used to list the contents of the /proc file system on Linux, you may see something like this:

> Each number in this list corresponds to a PID for a currently running process (which you can see with the ps command)

1	1267	1456	1589	1662	512	680	922	ide	mounts
1102	1268	1458	1593	1663	517	681	940	interrupts	mtrr
1121	1269	1460	1622	1664	537	682	975	iomem	net
1139	1270	1462	1624	1919	565	683	982	ioports	partitions
1185	1271	1464	1629	1921	589	7	bus	irq	pci
12	1272	1466	1630	1923	6	710	cmdline	kcore	self
1214	1279	1469	1631	1924	664	8	cpuinfo	kmsg	slabinfo
1254	1280	1470	1632	2	669	87	devices	ksyms	stat
1255	1291	1471	1633	2077	674	880	dma	loadavg	swaps
1256	1417	1472	1654	2102	675	897	driver	locks	sys
1257	1419	1473	1655	2108	676	899	execdomains	mdstat	sysvipc
1258	1432	1474	1656	3	677	900	fb	meminfo	tty
1259	1450	1475	1657	4	678	901	filesystems	misc	uptime
1266	1454	1481	1658	5	679	902	fs	modules	version

What is shown is a series of directories (for example, `1102`), which represent the currently running processes on the system. These are the directories that have numbers as the names. Naturally, when you examine the `/proc` directory on your system, you will see different directories. Other directories—such as `mounts`, for instance—show specific system configurations instead of running processes.

To see how the `/proc` directory can be useful, let's examine several examples The directory `2120` represents a system process. When we list the contents of this directory using the `ls -l` command, we see the following files:

Hint

The `/proc` directory on Solaris only shows processes, not system configuration files, like other versions of UNIX.

19

```
total 0
dr-xr-xr-x    3 root      root         0 May 16 11:37 .
dr-xr-xr-x  112 root      root         0 May 16 01:16 ..
-r--r--r--    1 root      root         0 May 16 11:42 cmdline
lrwxrwxrwx    1 root      root         0 May 16 11:42 cwd -> /etc/default
-r--------    1 root      root         0 May 16 11:42 environ
lrwxrwxrwx    1 root      root         0 May 16 11:42 exe -> /bin/vi
dr-x------    2 root      root         0 May 16 11:42 fd
-r--r--r--    1 root      root         0 May 16 11:42 maps
-rw-------    1 root      root         0 May 16 11:42 mem
lrwxrwxrwx    1 root      root         0 May 16 11:42 root -> /
-r--r--r--    1 root      root         0 May 16 11:42 stat
-r--r--r--    1 root      root         0 May 16 11:42 statm
-r--r--r--    1 root      root         0 May 16 11:42 status
```

If we wanted to see which command was running, the `cmdline` command can be examined. Thus, using the command

```
more cmdline
```

will show the following:

```
vi/etc/ftpusers
```

As shown, the process `2102` represents an edit session for the `/etc/ftpuser` file. If it was necessary to validate this process, to really see what was running, the `ps` command followed by the process ID (which in the case is `1102`) could be used.

Thus, the command

```
ps 1102
```

shows

```
  PID TTY       STAT   TIME COMMAND
 1102 pts/5     S      0:00 vi /etc/ftpusers
```

which is exactly what would be expected.

Additional information can be obtained about processes such as the shell environment that the command has been run in, the status of the process, and so on.

To view the process status, which is similar to what can be obtained with the ps command, examine the status file.

This file contains the following:

```
Name:    vi
State:   S (sleeping)
Pid:     1102
PPid:    1923
TracerPid:      0
Uid:     0        0        0        0
Gid:     0        0        0        0
FDSize: 256
Groups: 0 1 2 3 4 6 10
VmSize:      2216 kB
VmLck:          0 kB
VmRSS:        968 kB
VmData:       208 kB
VmStk:         20 kB
VmExe:        332 kB
VmLib:       1364 kB
SigPnd: 0000000000000000
SigBlk: 0000000000000000
SigIgn: 8000000000003000
SigCgt: 000000004f804eff
CapInh: 0000000000000000
CapPrm: 00000000fffffeff
CapEff: 00000000fffffeff
```

Hint

Many of the directories and files, with few exceptions, show a byte size greater than 0; this is because these are not really normal directories or files in the typical file system sense. Instead, they represent pointers to where specific information is stored.

As far as system configuration is concerned, the /proc directory provides a generous amount of information. Table 19-3 lists some of the most useful directories and/or filenames and their corresponding information. Note that all versions of UNIX support each to the file or directories.

By way of example, the /proc file system can show some very interesting information. For example, the interrupts file shows all the system's devices and their associated interrupt vectors:

```
           CPU0
  0:     1340342     XT-PIC  timer
  1:         525     XT-PIC  keyboard
  2:           0     XT-PIC  cascade
  3:       39351     XT-PIC  3c574_cs
  5:        1904     XT-PIC  usb-uhci, Allegro
  8:           1     XT-PIC  rtc
  9:           0     XT-PIC  Texas Instruments PCI1410 PC card Cardbus Controller
 14:       40799     XT-PIC  ide0
 15:      293668     XT-PIC  ide1
NMI:           0
ERR:           1
```

Directory/File	Description
devices	Shows a detailed list of all the installed devices.
ioports	Contains a listing of all the memory vectors used by each system device.
interrupts	Shows the low-level device interrupts for the system.
meminfo	Provides a detailed breakdown of system memory.
partitions	Shows a detailed listing of the defined partition maps on system.
swaps	Shows swap information.
version	Displays system version information.

Table 19-3   Subdirectories of the /proc Directory

Another example is the `partitions` file, which shows all the defined disk partitions on the system:

```
major minor  #blocks  name     rio rmerge rsect ruse wio wmerge wsect wuse running use aveq
  3     0    5866560 hda 28345 16900 361900 461290 12600 22212 279128 1546840 0 520430 2008490
  3     1    2562808 hda1 8 0 16 110 0 0 0 0 0 110 110
  3     2    2562840 hda2 28162 15377 348354 454620 12388 19340 254456 1444150 0 517910 1899130
  3     3          1 hda3 0 0 0 0 0 0 0 0 0 0 0
  3     5     740848 hda5 172 1517 13512 6500 212 2872 24672 102690 0 14960 109190
```

Project 19-1

In this project you'll familiarize yourself with your system and the toolbox of commands presented in this module.

Step-by-Step

1. List your current swap space configuration and usage.

Linux:

```
# swapon -s
```

Solaris/HP-UX:

```
# swap -l
```

2. Check your `/etc/default/login` file. Unless you have a specific reason to allow remote root access, ensure that the `CONSOLE=/dev/console` line exists and is not commented out.

3. You may find it helpful to keep some basic system information handy in printed form in case you ever have major system problems and need to know, for example, your kernel version. Print the results of this command and keep it in a safe place:

Solaris:

```
# showrev
```

For Linux users, this command will produce similar but less detailed results:

```
# uname -a
```

4. Generate a list of your currently running processes:

```
# ps a
```

5. Show the contents of the /proc directory:

```
# ls /proc
```

☑ *Mastery Check*

1. Which command can an admin use to communicate with all currently logged in users at once?

   a. talk

   b. write

   c. wall

   d. email

2. Referring to the following output line, how much swap space is currently used?

```
total: 39488k bytes allocated + 12520k reserved = 52008k used, 1062656k available
```

3. What is the Linux command to create a swap file?

   a. mkswap

   b. swapon

   c. swapoff

   d. mkfile

4. What Linux file system tool is useful in adjusting swap files?

5. On Solaris, the _____ tool can be used, which provides both low-level and operating system configuration information.

☑ Mastery Check

6. Which command discussed in this module would have generated the following line of output?

   `Kernel version: SunOS 5.8 Generic 108529-07 February 2001`

   a. `prtconf`

   b. `showrev`

   c. `showrev -c`

   d. `ls /proc`

7. In the `/proc` directory, what do numbered subdirectories represent?

   a. User IDs

   b. Group IDs

   c. Process IDs

   d. Protocol IDs

8. The `/proc/`_____ directory shows a detailed listing of the defined partition maps on the system.

Module 20

Using DHCP

Critical Skills

20.1 Use the Solaris DHCP Configuration Manager

20.2 Configure DHCP Clients

The Dynamic Host Configuration Protocol (DHCP) is a facility that supports Internet Protocol (IP) allocation and diskless boot capabilities to network client systems. In both small and large organizations, DHCP is one of the best ways to manage the corporate IP address space. This facility is responsible for dynamically assigning addresses to client host systems as they are brought on the network, thus making it much easier to manage connectivity to the corporate network. DHCP can be used to support both local and remote systems that range from dial-up to LAN-based connectivity. When configured, the DHCP server also supports the BootP protocol, which means that client systems can obtain boot information from the server. In certain situations, having clients boot from a server can be both an effective and a cost-effective deployment strategy.

The DHCP service can be divided into two sections: the client and the server. The client portion makes requests to a server for IP address information specific to the local network to which the client is attached and network and/or booting information or data. The client obtains network information by negotiation with the server. For example, the server will determine how long the information can be used on the network, thus placing an expiration date for client access. This is known as a "lease"—the client can only use the information for a fixed period of time. In practice, for generic LAN-based connectivity, the server is configured to support an open-end lease—that is, one that really never expires.

The DHCP client component available on Solaris is known as dhcpagent and is used to make requests from the network. The dhcpagent program has been integrated with the ifconfig command. As you recall, ifconfig is used to set up one or more network interfaces on the local system. Thus, when the system normally boots, the appropriate network information is obtained from a DHCP server (via the ifconfig command) and then the system continues to boot normally.

Because DHCP support is available on a wide variety of systems, any compatible DHCP client can request services from the DHCP server. For example, a Windows system that has been configured to request an IP address from the network can be supported using the Solaris DHCP server.

The server component consists of several different modules: the server process, a configuration file, and the configuration manager. The server process receives DHCP/BootP requests from the network and emits responses back to clients. The server, known as `in.dhcpd` (on Solaris) continuously runs in the background, waiting to service DHCP requests. The DHCP server generally behaves like many of the other network-related processes—it provides command-line arguments that control, for example, both logging and debugging facilities. The server supports two modes of operation: normal DHCP/BootP mode and BootP relay mode. The BootP relay mode is used to provide client connection across one or more subnetworks.

The Solaris DHCP server uses a configuration file called `/var/dhcp/dhcptab`, which contains information about the address space that clients will use when they become active on the network. Before basic DHCP services can be used, this file must be updated to include IP addresses that will be allocated to clients. However, the DHCP configuration need not be defined manually; rather, a configuration manager tool has been provided that can assist the administrator when setting up DHCP services.

A number of applications and tools are used to support DHCP on each of the different operating systems. Table 20-1 lists each of the tools and provides a quick summary.

As you can see from the table, several different tools are available for the management of DHCP services. For example, to show the DHCP client information on the Linux system, the `pump` utility is provided. To view the same type of information on Solaris, use the `ifconfig` command. The tools used to configure and manage DHCP services are described in the following sections.

20

Operating System	DHCP Server	DHCP Service Configuration Application	Tools
Solaris	`in.dhcpd`	`dhcpmgr`	`ifconfig`
HP-UX	`dhcpd`	`sam`	`lanscan`
Linux	`dhcpd`	`none`	`pump`

Table 20-1   DHCP Tools by Operating System

20.1 Use The Solaris DHCP Configuration Manager

The configuration manager can be used to define and control DHCP services for client systems. The configuration manager provides an X-Windows-compatible GUI tool that maintains configuration information for a local and/or NIS DHCP database. The manager can be used to accomplish the following:

- Configure DHCP services

- Configure BootP relay services

- Control DHCP/BootP processes

- Manage DHCP addresses

The DHCP configuration manager provides a wizard-like interface to handle many of the configuration aspects for deploying a DHCP server. If the DHCP facility is not set up when the configuration manager is invoked, it begins the configuration process by guiding you through the steps necessary to set up a functional server. This procedure is presented only when a DHCP server hasn't been configured on this system. If you start the configuration manager after the basic DHCP services are set up, you will see a different window that shows the defined IP address ranges and not the DHCP Configuration Wizard.

Starting the Solaris DHCP Configuration Manager

To invoke the DHCP configuration manager, issue the following command:

```
/usr/sadm/admin/bin/dhcpmgr
```

Since this program supports X-Windows, it can be run either from a system that contains an attached display or from a system that doesn't have a display device, and the display is redirected (using the DISPLAY variable) to another system that does support X-Windows and has an attached display device. When this command is executed before any basic DHCP services have been configured, you should see a window, as shown in Figure 20-1. Otherwise, if the DHCP

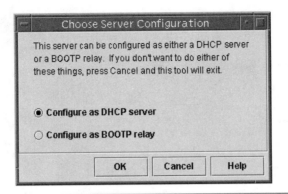

Figure 20-1 Initial DHCP configuration manager window

service has been set up, a different window will appear. See "Configuring DHCP Service for the First Time" for more information about how to provide an initial configuration for DHCP services.

Configuring DHCP Services for the First Time

In Figure 20-1, the window displayed asks how you would like to configure the DHCP server. Two options exist: as a normal DHCP server or as a relay for BootP requests. The BootP option basically means that you can forward BootP requests from one or more networks. For the purposes of understanding the DHCP facility, we want to set up a normal DHCP server. Thus, to configure normal DHCP services, make sure the Configure as DHCP Server item is selected and click the OK button.

Once this has been done, a new window is displayed that replaces the previous one. This window represents the DHCP Configuration Wizard, which will provide a step-by-step process to configure basic DHCP services. This window is labeled the "DHCP Configuration Wizard," and is shown in Figure 20-2.

The Configuration Wizard window is divided into two sections: the list of required steps is on the left, and specific questions that must be answered are on the right. As you can see, a total of eight steps are required to define basic DHCP services. When the wizard goes through each step, that step is highlighted. Thus,

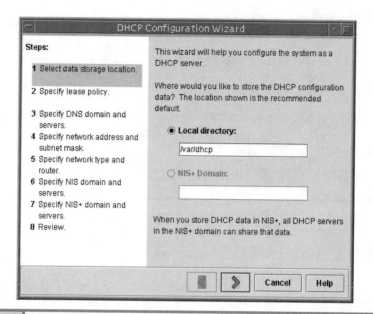

Figure 20-2 DHCP Configuration Wizard window

the first step (selecting the data storage location) is marked with a colored bar. Using the control buttons at the bottom, you can navigate between each of the defined steps. Complete the following to set up the basic DHCP server:

1. Choose the location to store the DHCP configuration data.

2. Determine the DHCP lease policy.

3. Provide the DNS domain servers.

4. Provide basic network address information.

5. Determine network configuration.

6. Provide NIS or NIS+ domain server information.

7. Review the configuration.

Step 1: DHCP Configuration Location

In this step, the wizard asks at which location it should store the DHCP configuration information. If NIS is not running, a local directory is preselected for you. However, if NIS is operational, you can use a NIS location instead. The default is the /var/dhcp directory, and when NIS isn't running, it should be used unless there is some overwhelming reason to change it. If you desire to change the directory location, type the new name in the text box and click the > button to accept this configuration option and proceed to the next step.

─┤**Note** ────────────────────────────────

In the examples provided in this section, it is assumed that NIS is not running and only a local DHCP configuration is necessary.

Step 2: Determine the DHCP Lease Policy

20

At this point, the wizard wants the administrator to determine the length of the address lease for each client that will request an IP address. The lease indicates how long a client may use an IP address once it has been assigned. Once the lease is up, the IP address will become invalid and the client will need to request another IP address.

As an option, the DHCP server can permit a client to renew their existing lease for the allocated IP address. In this case, the client sends a renew notice to the server so that the client may continue to use the existing IP address. Without this option selected, when the client's lease expires, the client will be forced to request another IP address. Permitting clients to renew leases effectively means that they don't have to obtain a new IP address every time the address expires. The only exception to this is when the client boots, it must request a new IP address (or it can request to use its previous assigned IP address).

The lease section is shown in Figure 20-3. The lease value may be expressed in hours, days, or weeks. The default value is one day, which is reasonable when the Renew check box is selected. From a practical standpoint, using a lease of either days or weeks might be the best way to go, but you will need to determine the best configuration as dictated by the requirements of your site. In general, unless you want to maintain fairly tight control over the IP assignment process, the best configuration would be to renew the IP address on a weekly or monthly basis. In Figure 20-3, the lease value has been configured for one week.

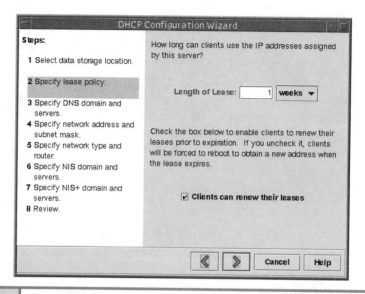

Figure 20-3   Lease Value window

Step 3: Provide the DNS Domain Servers

Next, you must provide DNS information if the DHCP server is going to use DNS services, as shown in Figure 20-4. See Module 14 on DNS for more information about setting up or configuring a domain name server.

As you can see, two different elements are needed to complete this step. First, the DNS domain is required, and one or more DNS server IP addresses are needed. In the example, the DNS domain is called home.com and two DNS servers have been defined: 216.155.202.10 and 216.155.202.11. The DNS name refers to the domain to which the local system belongs. sWhen the Configuration Wizard window is displayed, it includes any DNS information found within the /etc/resolv.conf file.

When adding a DNS server, type the IP address of the server in the appropriate text box and click the ADD button. You must include a valid IP addresses within this field; hostnames are not permitted. If you have added more than one DNS server, you can change the order in which the servers are queried. You can use the ∧ or ∨ buttons to reposition the servers within the list as required.

Click the > button to accept any DNS information entered and move to the next step to continue configuring DHCP services.

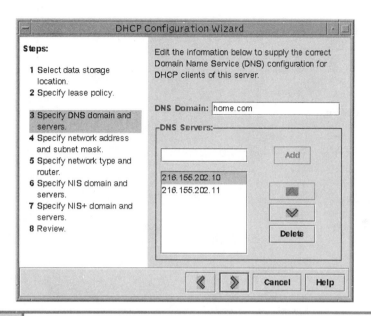

Figure 20-4 Supply DNS information

Step 4: Provide Basic Network Address Information

The next window displayed, as shown in Figure 20-5, is used to specify the IP network and associated subnet mask for the network served by the DHCP server. See Module 10 for additional information on IP networking that includes a description of IP addresses and subnet masks. The network address information is obtained from the defined system network interfaces. This is used to tell the DHCP server which IP network should be used to allocate IP addresses to clients.

Hint

You don't actually need any DNS facilities running to configure or use DHCP services. Without any DNS, the DHCP server would simply use IP addresses when displaying information about DHCP clients. However, it is recommended that you use domain name resolution services because it will make DHCP administration easier.

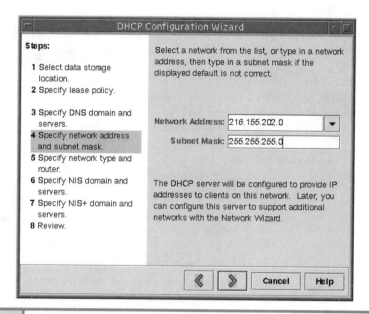

Figure 20-5 Network Address Information window

If the system only has a single network interface, only a single network entry will be displayed in the Network Address selection box. By default, the entry contains the network address of the primary network interface. If multiple IP networks are defined on the system, you can only select one from a list of addresses. Once the basic configuration setup of the DHCP server have been accomplished, additional IP networks may be assigned.

Input the desired subnet mask value within the Subnet Mask text box. By default, the assigned subnet mask is taken from the previously defined network configuration parameters as reported by the `ifconfig` command.

Click the > button to accept the network information shown in the window and move to the next step in the process.

Step 5: Determine Network Configuration

The next step involves selecting the type of network and additional routing parameters that will be used with the DHCP server and for associated DHCP clients, as shown in Figure 20-6. The Network Type box includes either local-area (LAN) or point-to-point selections. The local-area (LAN) selection

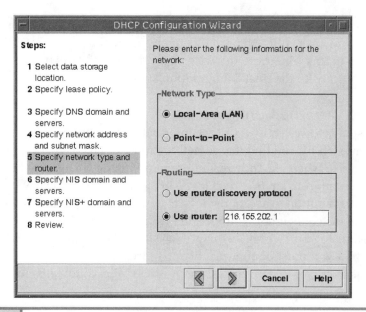

Figure 20-6 | Network Type/Routing Information window

indicates that DHCP will operate under the local data link protocols (such as Ethernet or FDDI).

By default, the LAN network type is selected, and this should be what is used unless you are configuring DHCP to operate within a fixed point-to-point network topology. Next, the window provides the option to specify a default network router to obtain routing information. This information is provided to the client systems when they request DHCP services. If you don't know a default router, then select to use the router discovery process. This way, the clients, when necessary, will discover all local routers. If you have a default router attached to the local system, enter the IP address of the device within the Use Router text box.

Click the > button to accept the network information and proceed to the next step.

Step 6: Provide NIS or NIS+ Domain Server Information

The next two steps involve specifying the NIS or NIS+ domain names and any associated NIS/NIS+ servers. This is very useful for those sites that use NIS,

20

because this information can be supplied to any client when they request DHCP services. If you have either NIS or NIS+ operating within your network, add this information to this window. Otherwise, leave the fields blank. Click the > button to proceed to the final configuration step.

Step 7: Review the Configuration

The final step involves verifying all the information that has been entered from the previous steps. If you find that something must be changed, use the < button to go to the step where the incorrect information can be changed. When the configuration information is correct, click the > button to the review step and click the Finish button to accept the information. Figure 20-7 shows the review step with all the configuration information from the preceding examples.

Next, a dialog box will be displayed, as shown in Figure 20-8, which indicates that you must configure a list of addresses for allocation to clients, and it asks if it should start the Address Wizard for this purpose.

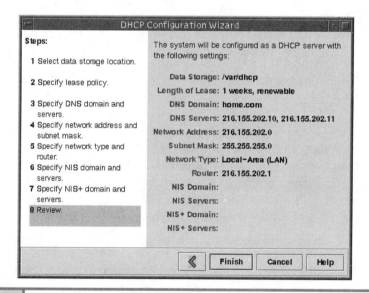

Figure 20-7   The DHCP Configuration Summary window

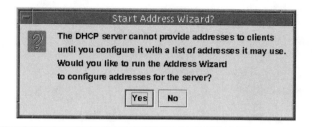

Figure 20-8 Start Address Wizard Dialog window

Answering Yes to the dialog box question causes another window to be displayed. This window represents another setup wizard, which will guide you through the process of adding IP addresses to the DHCP server. See the section "Adding IP Addresses to the DHCP Server" later in this module for a detailed description and explanation of the Address Wizard.

20

1-Minute Drill

● What are the UNIX DHCP server component modules?

● What does the DHCP lease policy define?

Using the Configuration Manager

The DHCP configuration manager is used to administer and configure DHCP services. This section reviews the menus and functions that this application supports. The high-level menus are listed in Table 20-2.

The application contain the following submenus.

File Menu

Contains just a single menu element—Exit. This item is the standard way to close the configuration manager.

● Server process, configuration file, configuration manager
● How long a client's DHCP-obtained IP address is valid before the client must recontact the server for a new address

Menu	Description
File	Contains the Exit menu item; used to quit the configuration manager
Edit	Used to manage the IP address space for DHCP clients
View	Toggles IP address and grid elements
Service	Controls the DHCP server process and configuration
Help	Online help facility.

Table 20-2   Configuration Manager Menu Items

Edit Menu

The Edit menu contains the following items:

Create   Set up a new IP address range for DHCP client systems.
Delete   Remove an existing IP address range.
Duplicate   Make a copy of an existing IP address range.
Properties   Display the properties of an existing IP address range.
Address Wizard   Step-by-step process for IP address range creation.
Release Addresses   Clear the lease of an existing assigned IP address.
Network Wizard   Step-by-step process for creating a new network that can be used with the DHCP server.
Delete Networks   Delete an existing network.

View Menu

The View menu contains the following items:

- **Refresh**   Refreshes the display.

- **Show Addresses**   Displays the IP address of the DHCP clients instead of hostnames.

- **Show Grid**   Displays grid lines for the main DHCP configuration screen. These lines make it easier to view each DHCP client entry.

Service Menu

The Services menu contains the following items:

- **Restart**   Restarts an already existing dhcpd process.

- **Stop**   Shuts down the dhcpd process.

- **Start** Enables the dhcpd process.

- **Disable** Permanently disables the dhcp process from executing.

- **Enable** Reverses the disable function.

- **Modify** Alters some of the DHCP server options.

- **Unconfigure** Removes DHCP server configuration information from the system.

Help Menu

The Help menu contains on-line help for the configuration manager. The help facility uses HTML, which means you will need to have a Web browser installed on the system to view the help files. The submenu items include the following:

- **Overview** Provides an overview of DHCP configuration manager.

- **How To** Provides a topical index to how to accomplish specific tasks with the configuration manager.

- **Index** Provides an index to all of the help sections with links so that the administrator can navigate the entire online book.

- **On Service** Explains what the DHCP or BootP facilities do, and how to use and configure them.

- **On Addresses** Shows how to configure and use IP addresses for DHCP clients.

Adding IP Addresses to the DHCP Server

Before the DHCP server can allocate addresses for DHCP clients, a range of IP addresses must be configured within the server. If you are configuring the DHCP server for the first time, you were prompted to start the Address Wizard or you have selected the Address Wizard from the main Edit menu. After you have started the wizard, you will see a window similar to that shown in Figure 20-9.

As you can see, this wizard will help you configure an address range for DHCP clients; like the previous wizard, the specific steps are on the left while the questions are located on the right-hand side of the window. A total of six steps are necessary to accomplish the IP address configuration, and they are described in the following sections.

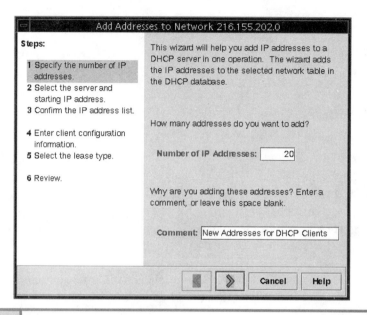

Figure 20-9 Address Wizard window

Step 1: Determine the Number of IP Addresses

Within the Number of IP Addresses text box, you must indicate the total number of addresses you will need to support all the DHCP clients for this IP network. Several factors can affect how many addresses are allocated for DHCP services. For example, are all the clients active during the same period of time, or how many addresses are currently unallocated within the network? That is, if this IP network is used for other purposes and addresses have already been assigned to systems, how many IP addresses are available for DHCP? If the clients represent nomadic users that access the network on an infrequent or ad hoc basis, the total number of IP address may be much lower as compared to users that access the network on a more regular and frequent basis.

Note that the total number of addresses for DHCP must be contiguous within an IP network. That is, they must all be within a specific range of addresses. For example, as shown in Figure 20-9, if you entered 20 within the Number of IP Addresses text box, then you are saying that 20 continuous addresses are available within the network, such as 216.155.202.200 through 216.155.202.219. This is an important point, since you can't specify gaps of ranges within an IP network. Also, notice that the range above (200-219) represents 20 addresses. One might think that this only represents 19 addresses, but in fact, we must count 216.155.202.200 as the first address.

Once the number of addresses has been determined, the configuration manager provides a comment field to help track when changes are made to the configuration. Use this field to record any changes to the ranges of IP addresses that have been configured with the DHCP server.

Selecting the > button will move the wizard to the next step.

Step 2: Select the Starting IP Address

Once the wizard has moved to the next step, a new window is displayed. This window will be similar to what is shown in Figure 21-10. As you can see, several important configuration parameters are required. First, you must make sure that the correct DHCP server is listed within the Managed by Server text field. By default, the hostname of the system, which is running the configuration manager, is added to this text box. Using Figure 20-10 as the example, we see that the system called bedrock is the DHCP server.

20

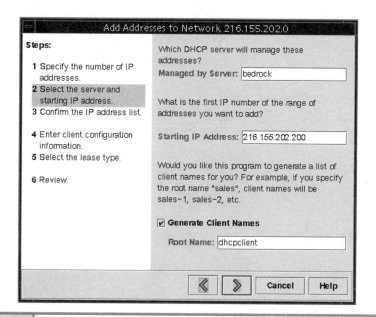

Figure 20-10 Starting IP Address window

Second, the administrator must determine the starting point or first IP address that will be used for DHCP clients. In other words, what is the start of the address range that the DHCP server will be using when allocating addresses to clients? Also, remember that we specified the total number of addresses that will be allocated with the IP address range. Thus, the DHCP server simply determines the IP address range by adding the total number of addresses to the address starting point.

Third, as an option, the configuration manager can automatically assign hostnames to the range of IP addresses for DHCP clients. Select the Generate Client Names check box if you want to enable this option. As you can see, the administrator can configure a prefix string that will be added to the beginning for each hostname. In this example, the Root Name text box contains the string dhcpclient. This tells the DHCP server to add this string to the start of each hostname. The DHCP server will automatically number each of the hosts defined. Thus, if ten systems were specified with the IP address range, then the DHCP server will define the following hostnames:

- dhcpclient-1
- dhcpclient-2
- dhcpclient-3
- dhcpclient-4
- dhcpclient-5
- dhcpclient-6
- dhcpclient-7
- dhcpclient-8
- dhcpclient-9
- dhcpclient-10

Selecting the > button will move the wizard to the next step.

Step 3: Confirm the IP Address List

The wizard now asks the administrator to confirm the list of added IP addresses and corresponding hostnames. Assuming that a total of 20 addresses were defined with the starting IP address of `216.155.202.200` and that the `dhcpclient` string was added to the Root Name text box from the last step, you should see a window similar to that shown in Figure 20-11.

As previously indicated, for each IP address, a hostname was defined. The hostname string name contains the last byte of the IP address so that it is very easy to identify the IP address from the hostname itself. Selecting the > button will accept this configuration and move the wizard to the next step.

Step 4: Define Client Information

The configuration manager supports the concept of a configuration macro, and basically a macro provides the specific parameter information to each DHCP client. The next step using the wizard is shown in Figure 20-12. A default macro name, which represents the network address, is set up automatically.

20

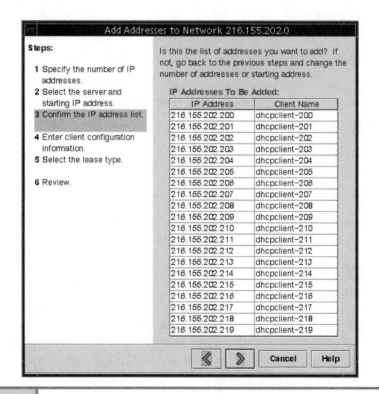

| **Figure 20-11** | The IP address list with associated hostnames |

Within the figure:

Add Addresses to Network 216.155.202.0

Steps:

1 Specify the number of IP addresses.
2 Select the server and starting IP address.
3 Confirm the IP address list.
4 Enter client configuration information.
5 Select the lease type.
6 Review.

Is this the list of addresses you want to add? If not, go back to the previous steps and change the number of addresses or starting address.

IP Addresses To Be Added:

IP Address	Client Name
216.155.202.200	dhcpclient-200
216.155.202.201	dhcpclient-201
216.155.202.202	dhcpclient-202
216.155.202.203	dhcpclient-203
216.155.202.204	dhcpclient-204
216.155.202.205	dhcpclient-205
216.155.202.206	dhcpclient-206
216.155.202.207	dhcpclient-207
216.155.202.208	dhcpclient-208
216.155.202.209	dhcpclient-209
216.155.202.210	dhcpclient-210
216.155.202.211	dhcpclient-211
216.155.202.212	dhcpclient-212
216.155.202.213	dhcpclient-213
216.155.202.214	dhcpclient-214
216.155.202.215	dhcpclient-215
216.155.202.216	dhcpclient-216
216.155.202.217	dhcpclient-217
216.155.202.218	dhcpclient-218
216.155.202.219	dhcpclient-219

Cancel   Help

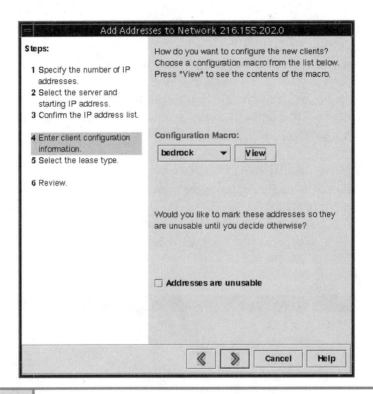

Figure 20-12 DHCP server macro

Examples of a macro include DNS information, lease configuration, and so forth. Click the View item to see the details information contained with the macro. Figure 20-13 shows the default `bedrock` macro. Select the default configuration by selecting the clicking the > button.

Step 5: Select the DHCP Lease Type

You have the option of selecting either a dynamic lease or a permanent (static) lease, as depicted in Figure 20-14. A dynamic lease means that it can be assigned to different clients over a period of time, whereas the static lease is assigned to a single client just once. However, you can alter the lease types after you have configured the DHCP server. The most common type is the dynamic lease.

Click the > button to move to the next and final step in the Add Address Wizard process.

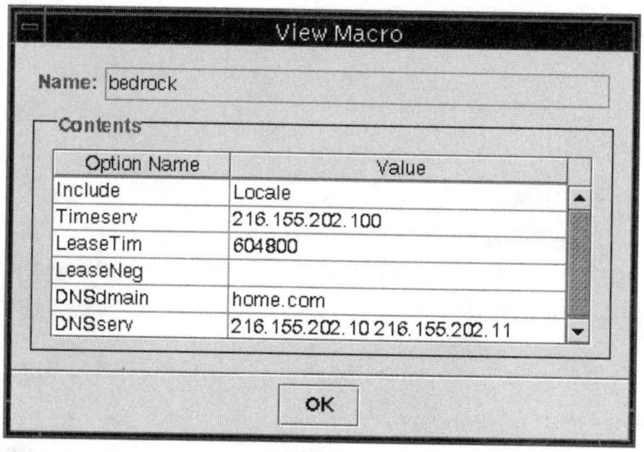

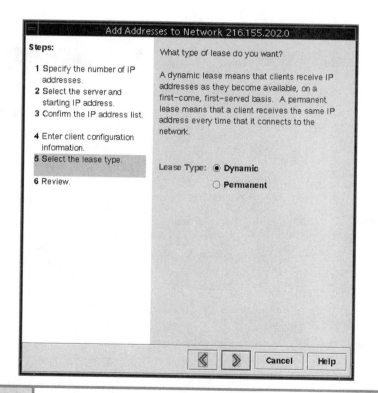

Figure 20-13 Detailed macro information

20

Figure 20-14 Select the appropriate DHCP lease type

Step 6: Review the DHCP Configuration

The final step is to review the DHCP configuration information. A window is displayed that contains all of the configuration details that were specified in the previous steps. The example configuration is shown in Figure 20-15.

Click the Finish button to accept the configuration or use the < button to move back through the process to alter any necessary parameters.

Once the wizard process is complete and the new address range is added, the main configuration window is updated with a new network icon.

Hint

One of the more important things to check is the assignment of IP addresses and hostnames. You can use the window to scroll through the list of IP addresses to make sure the range that was selected is correct.

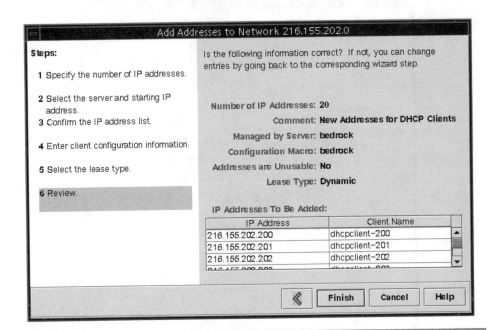

Figure 20-15   Review window

20.2 Configure DHCP Clients

This section reviews the procedures involved with both manually and automatically configuring UNIX systems as DHCP clients. Depending on the operating system, different sets of steps will be necessary.

Manual DHCP Configuration

If you would like to manually configure DHCP on UNIX, you must use the appropriate DHCP network tools. For instance, on Solaris, you must use the ifconfig tool to configure an interface that uses DHCP. On Linux, you would use the dhcpcd command, and on HP-UX, you would use the dhcpclient command.

To manually configure DHCP on Solaris, execute the ifconfig with the interface name followed by the dhcp keyword. Thus, the command

20

```
ifconfig hem0 dhcp
```

will manually configure the hme0 interface (100-Mbps Ethernet interface on most Sparc systems).

On Linux, use the dhcpcd command:

```
dhcpcd eth0
```

Hint

The Linux dhcpcd command will only function when the interface is being set up for the first time or when the dhcpcd process is not running. Normally, the system starts this process automatically when the system detects an interface that has been configured to use DHCP.

The HP-UX system works the same way, but the command to use is dhcpclient. The same rule applies to this tool as to the dhcpcd command on Linux when attempting to run the command manually.

Set Up Automatic and Permanent DHCP Configuration

Configuring DHCP client services on UNIX to be both automatic and permanent (that is, it will persist across system reboots) generally is a straightforward and simple process. On the Solaris system, if the machine has already been installed on the network, the procedure is quite easy— simply create a special file within the /etc directory. The filename is important—the format is dhcp.*interface*, where interface is the name of the UNIX network interface which DHCP services should be configured. For example, on Solaris, the first 100-Mbps Ethernet interface might be eri0. Thus, the command

```
touch /etc/dhcp.eri0
```

will create an empty file called dhcp.eri0. When the system is rebooted, the existence of this file will tell the system to issue DHCP requests to the network for network configuration information.

When the system boots, you should see the following message on the console:

```
starting DHCP on primary interface eri0
```

For HP-UX, modify the value of the keyword DHCP_ENABLE that is contained within the /etc/rc.config.d/netconf file. Assigning the value of 1 to this keyword enables DHCP on the associated network interface. The sample output of this file is shown here:

```
HOSTNAME=mb-auto-1
OPERATING_SYSTEM=HP-UX
LOOPBACK_ADDRESS=127.0.0.1
INTERFACE_NAME[0]=lan0
IP_ADDRESS[0]=216.155.202.171
SUBNET_MASK[0]=
BROADCAST_ADDRESS[0]=216.155.202.255
INTERFACE_STATE[0]=up
DHCP_ENABLE[0]=0   ◄─────────  Set to "r" to enable DHCP client
```

As you can see, the variables are self-explanatory based on the individual name. For example, the HOSTNAME variable represents the name of the host.

On Linux, modify the value of the keyword BOOTPROTO that is contained within the /etc/sysconfig/network-scripts/ifcfg-eth0 file. This file, ifcfg-eth0, corresponds to the first Ethernet interface on the system. Your system may have multiple interfaces, in which case you will see more than one of these files. Select the appropriate file when configuring DHCP client services. If the interface was previously configured with an IP address, you must change the keyword from static to dhcp. If the keyword isn't present in the file, simply add it with the correct keyword of dhcp. The sample output shows the correct entry in the ifcfg-eth0 file:

```
DEVICE=eth0
BOOTPROTO=dhcp
ONBOOT=yes
TYPE=Ethernet
PEERDNS=no
```

When the system reboots, it will attempt to obtain DHCP configuration for the eth0 interface. If you want to stop using DHCP, change the BOOTPROTO keyword to have the value of static and add the following additional keywords if they are not present in the file:

```
IPADDR=216.155.202.163
IPGATEWAY=216.155.202.129
NETMASK=255.255.255.0
```

Assign the appropriate keyword values that match your network environment.

Obtain DHCP Agent Status Information

Once the interface has been configured to use DHCP, the administrator can view the status of the interface using the ifconfig command. For example, to view the status on Solaris, use the following:

This interface is not configured to use DHCP.

-a option returns results for all network interfaces

```
# ifconfig -a dhcp status
ifconfig: lo0: interface is not under DHCP control
Interface  State           Sent  Recv  Declined  Flags
eri0       BOUND              2     1          0  [PRIMARY]
(Began, Expires, Renew) = (12/11/2001 22:47, 12/18/2001 22:47, 12/15/2001
10:47)
ifconfig: eri1: interface is not under DHCP control
```

The eri0 interface is configured to use DHCP and is the primary network interface.

another network interface not using DHCP

On Linux, the `pump` command is used to obtain status and configuration information about the interface that is using DHCP. Thus, the command

```
pump -s
```

when executed, will shown all the information for each interface that is configured to use DHCP. The sample `pump` output might look like this:

```
Device eth0
        IP: 216.155.202.200
        Netmask: 255.255.255.0
        Broadcast: 216.155.202.255
        Network: 216.155.202.0
        Boot server 216.155.202.100
        Next server 0.0.0.0
        Gateway: 216.155.202.1
        Hostname: dhcpclient-200
        Domain: home.com
        Nameservers: 216.155.202.10 216.155.202.11
        Renewal time: Fri Jan 18 01:39:23 2002
        Expiration time: Fri Jan 18 03:09:23 2002
```

In this example, all the relevant DHCP information is obtained for `eth0` interface and, naturally, the IP address, network, and lease information will be different depending on which network the DHCP server is running on.

On the Windows family of operating systems, the `ipconfig` command can be used just like the UNIX `ifconfig` command, which is discussed next.

1-Minute Drill

● What type of DHCP lease assigns an IP address to different clients over a period of time?

● In Linux, how does the `dhcpcd` process normally start?

Configuration of DHCP Clients

This section will help you configure client DHCP services on other platforms. More specifically, Linux and Windows operating systems will be covered. Like

---

● Dynamic
● The system starts this process automatically if an interface is configured to use DHCP.

other UNIX operating systems, DHCP is supported on Microsoft's family of operating systems. In particular, Windows 98, Windows Me, Windows 2000, and Windows XP are all supported. Although these operating systems provide different features and run on a large number of computer systems, the DHCP support is generally uniform. To configure a Windows 2000 system to support DHCP, perform the following steps.

Hint

The assumption in these steps is that you have already installed a NIC and that basic networking services are already operational.

Step 1: Access the Network and Dial-up Connections Panel

Using the Start menu, select the Network and Dial-up Connections item from the Setting submenu. When done, a new window will be displayed that contains at least one network icon and a Make New Connection icon. A LAN connection known as Local Area Connection 5 has been defined. This window is used to add new networking connections or display configuration information for one or more existing network interfaces.

20

Step 2: Display the Status of the LAN Connection

Double-click the network icon appropriate for your system. When done, a new window is displayed. This window shows basic network status and performance information and can be used to navigate to more detailed network information.

Step 3: Display the Properties of the LAN Connection

Next, select the Properties button on the Local Area Connection window. Once this has been done, a new window is displayed. This window provides information about the higher-level protocols and services that are bound to the network interface. The 3com3cs74 TXFast EthernetPC card is the LAN interface that is used. Note that three different services are configured for this card: Microsoft Networks Client software, file and printer sharing software, and TCP/IP.

Step 4: Display the Properties of the TCP/IP

Highlight the Internet Protocol (TCP/IP) item and then click the Properties button. When this is done, the Internet Protocol (TCP/IP) Properties window is displayed.

Click the Obtain an IP Address Automatically selection (if it isn't already checked) and then click the OK button. This instructs Windows to request an IP address for the DHCP server using the DHCP protocol.

Next, select the OK button and close the LAN Properties window. Then, close the LAN Status window by clicking the Close button.

You should reboot the system for this networking change to take effect, and when the system reboots it will attempt to obtain network information from a DHCP server.

Viewing Network Information on Windows

The Windows family of systems provides the means to display network configuration information using a command-line tool called `ipconfig`. This utility provides two basic services: to show network configuration information and to exercise limited control over the behavior of the DHCP client. Depending on the version of Windows you are using, the `ipconfig` options will be slightly different. However, the basic options are supported on most of the versions of Windows. This tool can show both static and dynamic (such as from a DHCP server) networking parameters for all defined interfaces on the system. This command is basically equivalent to the UNIX `ifconfig` utility, but it provides only a small number of services as compared to the UNIX version. To invoke this tool, open a command prompt window and type the `ipconfig` command.

The `ipconfig` command was invoked with the `/help` option, which displays a list of the available command-line options that are supported. This command provides a small number of command-line arguments, as described in Table 20-3.

Option	Meaning
/?	Displays a list of command-line options.
/help	Displays a list of command-line options.
/all	Displays all the configuration information available.
/release	Releases the IP address for the specified network interface.
/renew	Obtains (renews) a new expiration date for the assigned IP address.
/Batch	Writes the output to a file.
/renew_all	Renews all interfaces that are configured with DHCP.
/release_all	Releases each IP address for all interfaces configured with DHCP.

Table 20-3 ipconfig command-line options

View DHCP Information

To view network configuration for each defined interface on the system, such as IP addresses, DHCP information, or generic networking parameters, use the `/all` option. For example, issuing the command

```
C:\WINDOWS>ipconfig /all
```

displays output similar to that shown next.

Although the second Ethernet adapter is configured to use DHCP, the missing IP address and lease information indicates this dial-up adapter is not currently connected to the network and therefore has not obtained an address through DHCP lease information.

20

```
C:\WINDOWS>ipconfig /all
Windows IP Configuration
        Host Name . . . . . . . . . : SOCRATES.home.com
        DNS Servers . . . . . . . . : 216.155.202.10
                                      216.155.202.11
        Node Type . . . . . . . . . : Broadcast
        NetBIOS Scope ID. . . . . . :
        IP Routing Enabled. . . . . : No
        WINS Proxy Enabled. . . . . : No
        NetBIOS Resolution Uses DNS : No

0 Ethernet adapter :
        Description . . . . . . . . : Linksys LNE100TX Fast EtheE100TX v4)
NDIS5 Driver
        Physical Address. . . . . . : 00-20-78-0E-77-5E
        DHCP Enabled. . . . . . . . : Yes
        IP Address. . . . . . . . . : 216.155.202.202
        Subnet Mask . . . . . . . . : 255.255.255.0
        Default Gateway . . . . . . : 216.155.202.1
        DHCP Server . . . . . . . . : 216.155.202.100          Uses DHCP
        Primary WINS Server . . . . :
        Secondary WINS Server . . . :
        Lease Obtained. . . . . . . : 12 23 01 12:15:38 AM
        Lease Expires . . . . . . . : 12 30 01 12:15:38 AM

1 Ethernet adapter :
        Description . . . . . . . . : PPP Adapter.
        Physical Address. . . . . . : 44-45-53-54-00-00
        DHCP Enabled. . . . . . . . : Yes
        IP Address. . . . . . . . . : 0.0.0.0
        Subnet Mask . . . . . . . . : 0.0.0.0
        Default Gateway . . . . . . :                          Doesn't use
        DHCP Server . . . . . . . . : 255.255.255.255          DHCP
        Primary WINS Server . . . . :
        Secondary WINS Server . . . :
        Lease Obtained. . . . . . . :
        Lease Expires . . . . . . . :
```

In the example output, three sections are displayed: `Windows IP Configuration`, `0 Ethernet adapter`, and `1 Ethernet adapter`. The first section lists generic network information related to the system. For instance, the system name and DNS servers are shown, which are `socrates.home.com`, `216.155.202.10`, and `216.155.202.11`, respectively. The next two sections show specific configuration information related to each of the defined network interfaces on the system. This includes

- Description
- Physical address
- DHCP flag
- IP address
- Subnet mask
- Default gateway
- Lease obtained date
- Lease expiration date

Description   The description string includes the type of interface hardware that has been installed on the system. In this case, the `ipconfig` command identifies a Linksys LNE100TX Fast EtheE100TX as the type of card.

Physical Address   This shows the physical data link protocol address associated with the network interface hardware. In this example, the type of hardware supports the Ethernet data link protocol and has the address of `00-20-78-0E-77-5E`.

DHCP Flag   This flag indicates if the network interface has been configured to use DHCP. If so, then DHCP should be configured to Yes, and IP lease information should also be listed.

IP Address   If DHCP has been configured on the interface, the IP address has been assigned dynamically from a DHCP server. Otherwise, the IP address has been assigned statically using the Network Control Panel icon. The IP address is used to communicate with the local network.

Subnet Mask   If DHCP has been configured on the interface, the subnet mask has been assigned dynamically from a DHCP server. Otherwise, it has been assigned statically using the Network Control Panel icon. The subnet mask is used to determine how to interpret the IP address for the local network.

Default Gateway   The default gateway is used to permit the local system to communicate with other nodes on remote networks. If DHCP has been configured on the interface, generally the default gateway has been assigned dynamically from a DHCP server. Otherwise, it has been assigned statically using the Network Control Panel icon.

Lease Obtained Date   When DHCP is used, the Lease Obtained field indicates when the network configuration for this interface was obtained from the DHCP server. In the earlier example, the 12 23 02 12:15:38 AM string is read as December 23, 2002 at 12:15:38 A.M.

20

Lease Expiration Date   When DHCP is used, the Lease Expires field indicates when the network configuration for this interface expires; that is, when the configuration information will no longer be valid and the DHCP client must request newer configuration information from the DHCP server.

The other two fields, Primary WINS Server and Secondary WINS Server, are used to support Microsoft-specific networking services and protocols.

Moving a Workstation Between Networks

In an environment where users move to different parts of the network, it is very common for DHCP to be deployed across the entire network enterprise. Thus, if a user moves from one building to another (or even one floor to another), DHCP services can be used to provide connectivity—regardless of physical location for mobile users. However, if, for example, a workstation has been attached to different parts of the network when DHCP is used, it is important to reconfigure the network interface when a workstation is moved around.

For example, consider the diagram shown in Figure 20-16 that shows two networks and one workstation. Both networks have DHCP services enabled; Network A uses the IP network of 216.155.202, while Network B uses the IP network of 216.155.203. When the workstation was attached to Network A, it obtained the address of 216.155.202.100. Over some period of time, the user moves the workstation to Network B with rebooting the system. Unfortunately, without any network reconfiguration, the workstation won't be

Network A
216.155.202

Network B
216.155.203

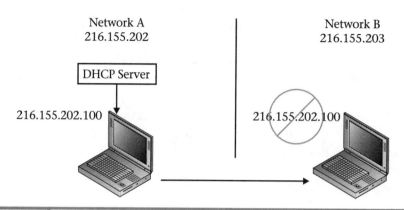

Figure 20-16 DHCP network with moved workstation

able to communicate on Network B because Network B uses a different network address and the workstation is still using the addresses it obtained from Network A.

To resolve this problem, issue the `ipconfig` with the `/release` option and then execute the `ipconfig`, again with the `/renew` option. This tells the DHCP client to release (or let go of) the existing DHCP configuration and then to request a new IP address and associated configuration from the local DHCP server. Thus,

```
C:\WINDOWS>ipconfig /release 0
```

will drop or delete the existing DHCP configuration (that is, the IP address of `216.155.202.100` and so forth) from the first network interface, which is expressed with zero. When using the `/release` option, `ipconfig` must be given which interface to release. When this command is executed, it should display the interfaces with empty values:

```
Windows IP Configuration

0 Ethernet adapter :

        IP Address. . . . . . . . . : 0.0.0.0
        Subnet Mask . . . . . . . . : 0.0.0.0
        Default Gateway . . . . . . :
```

```
1 Ethernet adapter :

        IP Address. . . . . . . . : 0.0.0.0
        Subnet Mask . . . . . . . : 0.0.0.0
```

―Hint―

Sometimes, despite running the `ipconfig /release`, the DHCP configuration isn't always released right away, and therefore it may be necessary to run this command more than once to ensure that this step is complete.

Once the IP address and associated information has been released, we can now request a new IP address from the local DHCP server by using the `/renew` option. When using `/renew`, the network interface must be supplied. Thus, the command

20

```
C:\WINDOWS>ipconfig /renew 0
```

indicates that `ipconfig` should attempt to obtain up-to-date DHCP configuration information for the first interface on the system. When executed, this command would show output similar to this:

```
Windows IP Configuration
0 Ethernet adapter :

        IP Address. . . . . . . . : 216.155.203.100
        Subnet Mask . . . . . . . : 255.255.255.0
        Default Gateway . . . . . : 216.155.203.1

1 Ethernet adapter :

        IP Address. . . . . . . . : 0.0.0.0
        Subnet Mask . . . . . . . : 0.0.0.0
        Default Gateway . . . . . :
```

The "release/renew" steps are depicted in Figure 20-17, and when the `ipconfig` command is executed with the `/renew` option, it displays the new DHCP configuration obtained from the DHCP server. In this example, the new IP address will permit the mobile workstation to communicate with all nodes on Network B because it now contains the correct address.

Network B
216.155.203

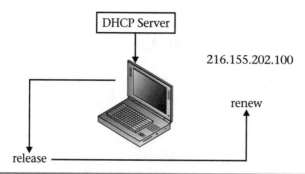

release

216.155.202.100

renew

Figure 20-17 The DHCP release/renew steps

 # Mastery Check

1. True/False: A Windows system cannot get an IP address from a UNIX-based DHCP server.

2. What is the default directory for Solaris DHCP configuration information?

   a. /etc/resolv.conf

   b. /var/dhcp

   c. /etc/dhcp

   d. /etc/dhcpd.conf

3. The _____ indicates how long a client may use an IP address once it has been assigned by a DHCP server.

4. True/False: When adding IP addresses for a DHCP server to assign, you can use any available valid addresses on your network.

☑ *Mastery Check*

5. A _____ DHCP lease is assigned to a single client just once.

6. By default, what Linux file contains DHCP configuration information?

    a. `/etc/resolv.conf`

    b. `/var/dhcp`

    c. `/etc/dhcp`

    d. `/etc/dhcpd.conf`

7. What is the proper tool for manual DHCP client configuration on each of these platforms: Solaris? Linux? HP-UX?

8. On a Solaris client, what is the command to configure DHCP permanently, so it persists when the system reboots, assuming the interface to configure it for is named `ei0`?

9. On a Windows 2000 client, what is the TCP/IP option to use DHCP to obtain an IP address?

    a. Obtain an IP address automatically

    b. Configure DHCP

    c. `ipconfig`

    d. Use the following IP address

10. On a Windows 2000 client, what is the command to view DHCP and IP information?

    a. Obtain an IP address automatically

    b. Configure DHCP

    c. `ipconfig`

    d. Use the following IP address

20

Module 21

Using rdist

Critical Skills

The rdist tool provides a software distribution facility for a cluster of UNIX systems. In particular, it ensures that files and/or directories are synchronized based on a configuration file stored on the software distribution server. The tool pushes new files when one or more file elements, such as file access time, have been changed on the master copy. Maintaining up-to-date files across a number of different systems is a challenge for the system administrator. Why is this type of synchronization important? Consider, for example, a cluster of systems that all use DNS. To configure DNS client services, a correct /etc/resolv.conf file must be placed on every system. Now, suppose that you have to make periodic changes to one or more entries within this file. Without some sort of software distribution mechanism, you would have to manually copy the updated file to each of the target systems. It is simply not efficient to maintain a set of files using a manual approach based on the number of systems deployed at many sites. For example, to manually copy files when they are modified is both time-consuming and error prone. Certainly, a manual approach is possible when the number of systems are quite small. However, when a larger number of systems are involved, things become much harder and more complex. Consider, for instance, having to update a file on a bunch of systems on a regular basis, not just one time. Why not automate the task and make life easy, versus having to do this particular function over and over?

Hint
Due to the incompatibilities of this tool with both Linux and HP-UX, only the Solaris version has been covered.

The rdist tool supports a number of command-line options. However, the most important ones are described and listed in Table 21-1.

Command Option	Meaning
-b	Do a binary comparison of the target files rather than comparing both the size and date of the source files.
-D	Turn on verbose debugging output.
-h	Process symbolic link so that the target file is copied rather than the link itself.
-n	Echo the rdist commands without actually doing any work. This is used for debugging purposes.
-q	Does not display any of the files being processed; quiet mode.

Table 21-1 rdist Command-Line Options

Command Option	Meaning
-R	Removes unnecessary files on the target system, which don't match entries on the local system. This is used to maintain the exact directory structure from the master to each target system.
-V	Verification mode; checks to see if all files are updated on the target systems and any discrepancies are displayed. However, no files are updated on the target systems, nor is any notification sent.
-y	Does not update remote files on the target systems that are younger than the files located on the server system. This is known as younger mode.
-d macroname=value	Defines a macro with a specific value. This causes the macroname to be overridden with a new definition value, which is contained within the distribution file.
-f distfile	Specifies the distribution file to be processed. If no distribution file is specified on the command line, the tool looks into the current directory for a distribution file called distfile.

21

Table 21-1 rdist Command-Line Options (*continued*)

21.1 Create an rdist Distribution File for Synchronizing Files

The rdist command supports a configuration file that can be used to automate the software distribution mechanism. The rdist configuration file is a self-contained description of the hosts, files, and specific directives for keeping files up-to-date across a number of target systems. The command directives are keyword strings and associated values, which then can be used like macros or shell variables. A working sample distribution file has been included here:

```
HOSTS = ( dino fred )
FILES = ( /etc/hosts
          /etc/resolv.conf )
(${FILES}) -> (${HOSTS})
        install -R ;
```

In this example, we have defined two string variables—HOSTS and FILES—and associated values. The HOSTS variable contains a list of target remote hosts that should be updated with the list of files contained within the FILES variable. In this case, the target hosts are dino and fred. The list of files defined with the FILES variable copied to the remote hosts are /etc/hosts and. /etc/resolv.conf. Naturally, these hosts must be official node names that are contained within /etc/hosts, NIS, or DNS. Also, the files must exist on the local system, which is the system where the rdist command will be executed.

The way rdist variables are accessed by enclosing the variable name within brackets and adding the dollar sign in front of the name, thus ${FILES} or ${HOSTS} are both valid. Additional parentheses, such as (${FILES}) are needed around variables when they are used with certain rdist directives, as shown in the above example.

We use the rdist string -> to signify that we would like to copy the contents of the FILES variable to the target machines contained with the HOSTS variable. The install keyword string indicates that the files should be installed on the remote hosts. To invoke the above configuration, assume that we have saved this information to a text file called network-dist and use the rdist command as shown here:

```
# rdist -f network-dist
updating host dino
updating: /etc/hosts
updating: /etc/resolv.conf
updating host fred
updating: /etc/hosts
updating: /etc/resolv.conf
```

The -f option informs rdist to read the accompanying configuration file from the command line. By default, rdist will search the local directory for a file called distfile and, if found, will attempt to process this file for software distribution directives. Thus, if we rename the network-dist file to distfile and run the rdist command again without any arguments, it will accomplish the same work as shown in the above example. As you can see from the output, both hosts are listed and the associated files were updated on each host. If we were to execute the command again, we would find different output:

```
# rdist -f network-dist-3
updating host dino
updating host barney
```

The reason for this is that rdist automatically checks to see if the local files have changed with respect to the remote copies. If no change has been made to the local files, and the command is run again, the result of the `rdist` command differs from the first `rdist` example because it hasn't updated the remote files. Instead, it simply displays that each host has been updated, but in actuality the rdist tool found that it didn't really need to sync up the files because they didn't change.

How does rdist determine if a file has changes? That is a very good question! By default, it uses two methods—first, if the file size has been altered since the last copy, and second, if the modification time of the file has changed with respect to the last copy.

21.2 Debug an rdist Configuration

If we are having trouble getting a particular rdist configuration working, we have two ways to debug the problem. First, we can use the −n option that shows the steps rdist will take when supplied a configuration file. Second, we can use the −D option to display a verbose listing of debugging output during execution of the `rdist` command.

If we are interested in only displaying which files would be updated on a given target versus actually doing the software syncing, we can use the −n option. This option just outputs the files that would be updated versus actually physically copying these files over. Thus,

```
# rdist -n -f network-dist-5
updating host barney
install -R /etc/hosts /etc/hosts
install -R /etc/resolv.conf /etc/resolv.conf
updating host fred
install -R /etc/hosts /etc/hosts
install -R /etc/resolv.conf /etc/resolv.conf
```

From this example, you can see that both systems (`barney` and `fred`) would be updated with both `/etc/hosts` and `/etc/resolv.conf` files. The −D option shows much more information about the steps rdist follows when doing work. Unfortunately, some of the displayed messages can be rather cryptic, which make them hard to interpret. For example, the `rdist` command from the previous example is run with the `debug` command-line option. This

612 | UNIX System Administration: A Beginner's Guide

command-line option is most useful in debugging rdist when more advanced or complex directives or options are used.

```
bash-2.03# rdist -D -f network-dist-7 | cat -n
     1  lookup(HOSTS, 1, 33860)
     2  lookup(FILES, 1, 338a0)
     3  expand(338c0, 3)
     4  list = ( ${FILES} )
     5  lookup(FILES, 0, 0)
     6  expanded list = ( /etc/hosts /etc/resolv.conf )
     7  expand(338d0, 7)
     8  list = ( ${HOSTS} )
     9  lookup(HOSTS, 0, 0)
    10  expanded list = ( dino barney )
    11  insert:  files = ( /etc/hosts /etc/resolv.conf )
insert:  hosts = ( dino barney )
    13  insert:  cmds NULL
    14  docmds:  cmds c_type ARROW, c_name dino, c_label NULL, c_files (
/etc/hosts /etc/resolv.conf )
    15  sc_type INSTALL, sc_options 16<REMOVE>, sc_name NULL, sc_args ( )
    16  c_type ARROW, c_name barney, c_label NULL, c_files ( /etc/hosts
/etc/resolv.conf )
    17  sc_type INSTALL, sc_options 16<REMOVE>, sc_name NULL, sc_args ( )
    18  doarrow(338e0, dino, 350d0)
    19  makeconn(dino)
    20  updating host dino
    21  port = 514, luser = root, ruser = root
    22  buf = /usr/ucb/rdist -Server
    23  install -R /etc/hosts /etc/hosts
    24  target = /etc/hosts, rname = hosts
```

In this example, the rdist command is run and the output is sent to the cat command using the -n option. Recall that this option displays the associated line number within the output, which makes it easier to read. As you can see, the output is quite verbose and has been truncated to only a portion of lines that were actually displayed. However, the output can be used to get a general idea of how the rdist tool is parsing and handling the configuration file.

21.3 Investigate rdist Commands

As previously mentioned, rdist supports a number of directives that control how the installation of remote files is done and helps determine whether other related tasks should be done as well. All of the supported rdist command directives are listed in Table 21-2.

Directive	Meaning
install [options]	Copy any out-of-date files and/or directories to the target systems.
notify address	Send email to the specified users.
except filename	Exclude a file from being updated. This file is supplied with the filename argument.
except_pat pattern	Exclude one or more files from being updated that match a specific regular expression listed in pattern.
special [commandgrep]	Invoke a shell command on the remote target machine when one or more files have been successfully copied.

Table 21-2 **rdist** Command Directives

We have seen the install directive at work in previous examples. However, this rdist command supports a few options that correspond to the regular rdist command-line options—namely, the –b, -h, -i, -R, -v, -w, and –y options, which are listed in Table 21-1 above. One of the more useful options, –R, provides the ability for rdist to maintain truly identical copies of directory structures from the local system to the remote target systems. Consider the following example configuration:

```
HOSTS = ( dino barney )
FILES = ( /stream/bin
          /stream/etc
          /stream/movies)
(${FILES}) -> (${HOSTS})
      install -R ;
```

In this case, we are syncing three different directories under the /stream directory and when we run rdist—these three directories (and their contents) will be copied to the remote systems dino and barney. Let's display the contents of the /stream/movies directory on the system called dino:

```
# rsh dino ls -al /stream/movies
total 196604
drwxr-xr-x   2 root     root          512 Nov  3 16:16 .
drwxr-xr-x   5 root     other         512 Nov  3 16:16 ..
-rw-r--r--   1 root     root      6662846 Oct 11  2000 matrix-1.mov
-rw-r--r--   1 root     root     62020733 Oct 11  2000 powers.mov
-rw-r--r--   1 root     root        91878 Oct 30  2000 rtspam.mov
-rw-r--r--   1 root     root        91878 Oct 12  2000 sample.mov
```

21

```
-rw-r--r--  1 root     root      5893937 Oct 12  2000 swtrailer-1.mov
-rw-r--r--  1 root     root      5863261 Oct 12  2000 swtrailer-2.mov
-rw-r--r--  1 root     root     19929586 Oct 12  2000 swtrailer-3.mov
#
```

Let's now assume that we have removed some of the files stored within the /stream/moves directory on the local system and we would like to resynchronize the other target systems. When we rerun the rdist command, we get the following:

```
# rdist -f directory-dist
updating host dino
removed /stream/movies/swtrailer-1.mov
removed /stream/movies/swtrailer-2.mov
removed /stream/movies/swtrailer-3.mov
updating host barney
removed /stream/movies/swtrailer-1.mov
removed /stream/movies/swtrailer-2.mov
removed /stream/movies/swtrailer-3.mov
```

As you can see, rdist reported that these files were removed from the remote systems as expected. Sure enough, if we again display the contents of the /stream/movies directory on one of the target systems, we get

```
# rsh barney ls -al /stream/movies
total 134620
drwxr-xr-x  2 root     root          512 Nov  4 11:37 .
drwxr-xr-x  5 root     other         512 Nov  3 16:13 ..
-rw-r--r--  1 root     root      6662846 Oct 11  2000 matrix-1.mov
-rw-r--r--  1 root     root     62020733 Oct 11  2000 powers.mov
-rw-r--r--  1 root     root        91878 Oct 30  2000 rtspam.mov
-rw-r--r--  1 root     root        91878 Oct 12  2000 sample.mov
```

Task Notifications

You can use the notify directive to send email when one or more tasks are completed. Email can be sent when a specific task is complete or a group of tasks have been done. For instance, using the example above, we can add the following directive to the end of the rdist configuration file:

```
notify root@pebbles ;
```

This instructs `rdist` to send email to the `root` user on the host `pebbles`. When we resynchronized the `/stream/movies` directory for the `dino` host, the following email was sent:

```
From root Mon Nov 5 17:04:37 2001
Date: Mon, 5 Nov 2001 17:04:37 -0800 (PST)
From: rdist (Remote distribution program)
To: root@pebbles.home.com
Subject: files updated by rdist from pebbles.home.com to dino

removed /stream/movies/swtrailer-1.mov
removed /stream/movies/swtrailer-2.mov
removed /stream/movies/swtrailer-3.mov
```

The output clearly shows what the `rdist` command has accomplished; it shows that it removed three movies files from the remote target called `dino`. Also, a duplicate message was sent for the other host `barney`. Thus, rdist is fairly verbose about what tasks it reports when sending email.

If you wanted to send to several users, you can simply add the required number of `notify` directives, such as

```
        notify root@bedrock ;
        notify anitat@bedrock ;
        notify stevem@pebbles ;
```

However, if you find that a larger number of users might be interested in receiving rdist-specific messages, it might be easier to use a mail alias. For instance, we might create a new alias called `dist-list`. In this case, we update the `/etc/mail/aliases` file with the following entry:

```
dist-list:root@bedrock,anitat@bedrock,stevem@pebbles
```

Once done, we can update the rdist configuration file with notify `dist-list@mail-host`, where mail-host is the name of the mail server.

If a `notify` directive doesn't contain a host portion of an email address, rdist uses the target system as the destination host to send the mail. Thus,

```
    HOSTS = ( peaches cream )
    FILES = ( /src )
    (${FILES}) -> (${HOSTS})
```

21

```
install -R ;
notify root ;
notify dist-list ;
```

will send mail to the accounts of `root` and `dist-list` on both systems called `peaches` and `cream`.

1-Minute Drill

● Why is using rdist preferable to manually copying files when many systems are involved?

● What is the point of the `notify` directive?

Excluding Files

The `rdist` command is great for copying entire directories to remote systems. However, suppose you want to copy most of the files within a directory, but not all files? One approach would be to include every file you wanted. However, this might be both time-consuming and hard to maintain going forward because if files are added and/or deleted on a regular basis, this will be hard to track. Also, consider if the directory contains a larger number of files. We need a better solution, and fortunately rdist provides one! The best way to address this type of problem is to simply exclude the files you don't want copied to the target systems. For example, consider the following:

```
HOSTS = (peaches cream)
FILES = ( /src/package          ◄────  Directories to synchronize
          /src/bin )
(${FILES}) -> (${HOSTS})
      except /src/package/a.out ;
      install -R ;
      notify root@pebbles ;
```

Excluded file within synchronized directory

● rdist saves time and reduces the possibility of error when more than a few files or systems are involved. The time savings are multiplied if the systems need to be synchronized repeatedly, such as a regularly scheduled nightly or weekly synchronization.
● To inform users or administrators when rdist makes changes on their systems so they aren't surprised by the file changes.

On the previous page, two directories (`/src/packages` and `/src/bin`) are being synchronized on target systems `peaches` and `cream`. However, the `/src/package/a.out` file is exclude from the list of files that are copied to both systems. If we find that a larger number of files must be excluded from a particular directory, we can define a variable similar to the `HOSTS` or `FILES` objects. Thus,

```
EXCLUDE_FILES = (/src/package/a.out
                 /src/package/libc.ar
                 /usr/package/libc_test.ar
                 /usr/package/message.o
                 /usr/package/message.as)
```

Here, the variable `EXCLUDE_FILES` is defined with the files that should not be copied to any target systems. We can use this variable with the `except` rdist directive:

```
except (${EXCLUDE_FILES})  ;
```

You can also exclude files that match a particular pattern using the `except_pat` command directive. This command supports matching on shell-type regular expressions. However, the characters "\" and "$" must be escaped if they are going to be used in the `rdist` configuration file. Typical examples include `except_pat "*.h"` and `except_pat ".??*"`, which will not copy any files that have an `.h` extension and no files that begin with leading dot (`.`) followed by a number of characters (which is usually the case with initialization files).

Invoking Commands

Sometimes it might be necessary to invoke a specific UNIX command when a particular file or a group of files has been updated on a remote system. Consider an example where you synchronize a configuration file that a process requires, and once the file has been updated the process must be restarted in order to use the new configuration file. Several UNIX system programs use this model; you must inform or kill a system process before it will pick up any changes made to its configuration file. To expand on this, note the following rdist configuration file:

```
HOSTS = ( dino wilma )
FILES = ( /etc/inet/inetd.conf )
```

```
(${FILES}) -> (${HOSTS})
      install -R ;
      notify root@pebbles ;
      special "/usr/bin/pkill -HUP inetd" ;
```

This configuration will push the `/etc/inet/inetd.conf` configuration file to both `dino` and `wilma`. Once done, it will execute the `pkill` command on both systems using the `special rdist` directive. This `special` command takes a single command argument and executes it on all target systems. The UNIX `pkill` command will send a signal to the `inetd` process, which causes this process to reread its configuration. Thus, any changes to the newly pushed `/etc/inet/inetd.conf` file will take effect immediately. As you can see, the rdist tool makes it very easy to execute a specific function as part of the overall file distribution mechanism.

21.4 Explore an rdist Example

To further explain how rdist might be used in a real world and even perhaps in a product-like environment, a more elaborate example has been provided. Naturally, this configuration example file represents one possible way of addressing the requirements that a typical UNIX shop might have. Some of the requirements for this example include

● Sync a different set of files to different systems

● Provide notification when files change and when synchronization is complete

To address these requirements, the following rdist configuration is supplied:

```
1      SERVERS = ( dino pebbles barney )  ◄
2      WORKSTATIONS = ( pebbles1 pebbles2 pebbles3 pebbles4 )
3      NETWORK_FILES = (
4                        /etc/foo
5                        /etc/hosts
6                        /etc/resolv.conf
7                        /etc/defaultrouter
8                        /etc/nsswitch.conf
9                        /etc/inetd.conf
10                       /etc/netmasks
11                       /etc/networks
```

Defining two different sets of systems for different synchronization requirements

```
12                              /etc/inet/ntp.conf
13                              /etc/inet/ntp.server
14                              /etc/snmp
15                      )
16      GENERAL_FILES = (
17                              /bar
18                              /etc/passwd
19                              /etc/group
20                              /etc/shadow
21                              /etc/aliases
22                              /etc/profile
23                              /etc/projects
24                              /etc/syslog.conf
25                      )
26      SECURITY_FILES = (
27                              /me
28                              /etc/ftpusers
29                              /etc/default/login
30                              /etc/hosts.equiv
31                              /.rhosts
32                      )
33
34      MEDIA_FILES   = (
35                              /streams/mov
36                              /streams/asf
37
38                      )
39      APPS          = (
40                              /packages/vnc
41                              /packages/ssh
42                              /packages/mrgt
43                      )
44
45      (${NETWORK_FILES}) -> (${SERVERS})
46          install -R ;
47          notify root@pebbles ;
48          special "/usr/bin/pkill -HUP xinetd" ;
49      (${GENERAL_FILES}) -> (${SERVERS})
50          install -R ;
51          notify root@pebbles ;
52      (${MEDIA_FILES})    -> (${WORKSTATIONS})
53          install -R ;
54          notify root@pebbles ;
55      ${SECURITY_FILES} :: /dist/timestamp
56          notify dist-list@pebbles ;
```

21

Defining one of several sets of files for the different synchronization requirements

Sending a notification for each synchronization

Synchronizing the different sets of files to different sets of systems

One clear requirement for most environments is to copy a set of files for a given class, type, or functional system on the network. For example, let's say you want to copy certain security-related files to only key file servers, or you may want to maintain a specific system configuration for just Web servers. To accomplish this with rdist, it is simply a matter of creating one or more variables to hold the files for each category. In the example above, the following file classifications are defined: NETWORK_FILES, GENERAL_FILES, SECURITY_ FILES, MEDIA_FILES, and APP_FILES. Each of these groupings is defined and contains a collection of associated files, as shown in lines 3–43.

Next, we need to define one or more different types of target systems, and in the example we have both servers and workstations—rdist variables SERVERS and WORKSTATIONS, respectively—which are defined on lines 1–2. Naturally, the breakdown of systems can be any arbitrary classification that you can imagine. The point here is to define the classification that most suits your particular environment and that you feel most comfortable with.

Once the systems and files are defined, we need to determine the exact requirements for the copy component and also how the notification will be handled. Based on the way rdist works, we must have redundant sections for each file list definition. In other words, each copy action directive (->) must have its own install and notify commands. The notify portion is optional, but the install isn't. If you want to sync the files, you must have this command.

Further, rdist supports the ability to detect when files have changed based on a particular milestone or baseline. This is used, for example, to send notification when files have been updated since a given time. Thus, in the example, whenever any security-related files (defined within the SECURITY_FILES variable) have been updated after the date stamp of the /dist/timestamp file, notification is sent to dist-list@pebble.

Project 21-1

This project provides a template for you to use to create your own rdist configuration file to control distribution for several different system types.

Step-by-Step

Refer to the following code listing for all the steps in this project. The line numbers are for reference only. Do not include them in your configuration file. Please note that some numbers are intentionally skipped in this line numbering.

```
  1          SYSTEMTYPE1 = ( )
  2          SYSTEMTYPE2 = ( )
  3          FILEGROUP1 = (
  4
 10                               )
 11          FILEGROUP2 = (
 12
 20                               )
 21          FILEGROUP3 = (
 22
 30                               )
 31          EXCLUDEFILES1   = (
 32
 40                          )
 41          (${FILEGROUP1}) -> (${SYSTEMTYPE1})
 42                  except (${EXCLUDEFILES1})   ;
 43                  install -R ;
 44                  notify ;
 51          (${FILEGROUP2}) -> (${SYSTEMTYPE2})
 52                  except (${EXCLUDEFILES2})   ;
 53                  install -R ;
 54                  notify ;
 61          (${FILEGROUP3}) -> (${SYSTEMTYPE1})
 62                  except (${EXCLUDEFILES3})   ;
 63                  install -R ;
 64                  notify ;
```

21

1. On line 1, enter the names of all the systems to include in the first synchronization category between the parentheses. If you want, change the name systemtype1 to a more meaningful name for this group.

2. Repeat step 1 on line 2 for the second group of systems.

3. If you need to define more than two system types, add additional lines like 1 and 2 with the additional group names and system names.

4. Beginning on line 4, add a directory of files to be synchronized for SYSTEMTYPE1. Add as many additional lines as needed between lines 4 and 10. If you want, change the FILEGROUP1 name on line 3 to a more meaningful name.

5. Repeat step 4 to define additional synchronization directory groupings on lines 12, and 22, renaming the groups on line 11 and 21 if desired and adding as many lines after lines 12 and 22 as needed for each group.

6. If you need additional file groupings, add additional sections modeled after steps 4 and 5.

7. If you need to exclude files from the directories in any of the groups, add the first set of files, using a filename or pattern matching on line 32. Add additional lines after line 32 for any additional exclusions for this grouping and rename line 31 to something more meaningful if needed.

8. If needed, add and name additional exclusion sets modeled after step 7.

9. On lines 41, 51, and 61, change the names of the file groups and system names to match the files you want synchronized to each group.

10. If you have exclusions to make, change the name of the exclusion groups on lines 42, 52, and 62 to match the set of files you defined to exclude for that group. If you don't have any files to exclude for a particular synchronization, you can delete that line.

11. On lines 43, 53, and 63, leave the -R option on if you want extra files in the target directories removed. Remove this -R option if you don't want extra files deleted.

12. On lines 44, 54, and 64, specify the user account (or distribution list) to send a notification to for each synchronization.

☑ *Mastery Check*

1. What is the command to send an email that rdist has made an update to a system?

   A. `install`

   B. `notify`

   C. `host`

   D. `file`

Please refer to the following rdist configuration file example for questions 2-5.

```
HOSTS = ( dino barney )
FILES = ( /stream/bin
          /stream/etc
          /stream/movies)
(${FILES}) -> (${HOSTS})
        install -R ;
```

2. What systems will this configuration file synchronize files to?

3. What directories will be synchronized on the target systems?

4. On the target systems, what will happen to files in the synchronization directories that aren't in the synchronization directories in the local system?

5. Who will email be sent to for each system when a synchronization is executed?

6. What is the rdist directive to exclude specific files in a synchronization directory from being synchronized?

7. What is the command to execute a system command within an rdist configuration file?

   A. `install`

   B. `command`

   C. `execute`

   D. `special`

21

☑ *Mastery Check*

8. By default, what does rdist compare to determine if a file on a target system has changed and needs to be synchronized?

   A. File size and modification time

   B. Binary content

   C. Modification time and binary contents

   D. Owner and permissions

9. What does the -h command-line option for the `rdist` command copy?

   A. Process symbolic link so that the target file is copied rather than the link itself.

   B. Copy the symbolic link rather than the target file.

   C. Copy all files modified by the currently logged on user.

   D. Copy only files matching the specified pattern, in this case beginning with "h".

10. What rdist command-line option checks to see if all files are updated on the target systems and displays any discrepancies, but doesn't update any files on the target systems or send any notification?

Appendix A

Answers to Mastery Checks

Module 1: Introduction to UNIX

1. Physical hardware, operating system, and applications

2. **A.** Kernel

3. **B.** Proprietary software

4. System Library

5. **D.** Maintains system capacities

6. System administrator

Module 2: Basic UNIX Commands

1. **D.** `ps`

2. `cat -b`

3. `date` `100415302002`

4. **C.** `hostname`

5. `find/-atime+365`

6. File type is directory. Permissions are read, write, and executable for owner, read and executable for group, and only executable for others.

7. **A.** Administrator

8. The ? designates that no terminal was involved when a process started.

9. `uname -r`

Module 3: Using System Administration Tools

1. False

2. /home/gwsmith

3. Modify user

4. Params tab in the User Information window

5. Group definitions button

6. On the Action menu, select the Remove item

7. True

8. Command Interpreter

9. **B.** Archive the Account's Data

10. `/etc/passwrd`

11. `/etc/group`

Module 4: Software Package Management Tools

1. `pkginfo -c system`

2. root

3. **A, C, D**

4. This would delete the XFree86 package from your system if it is installed

5. **A.** `pkgadd -d /cdrom/s8_software_companion/components/ i386/Packages SFWgimp`

6. **B.** `swinstall -i` (**A.** swinstall is also correct because the interactive mode is the default mode for swinstall)

Module 5: Maintaining UNIX Users

1. **B.** `root`

2. **D.** `sh`

3. Groups

4. **B.** 45

5. `passwd -f wilma`

6. `/etc/default/passwd`

7. `usermod -L wilma`

8. `passwd -s` *yourusername*

9. C. KpF4j7. (**A** is a bad choice because it doesn't contain any numbers or special characters. **B** is a bad choice because it is too similar to the current password. **D** is a bad choice because it is based on the username.)

Module 6: File Systems, Disks, and Tools

1. file system

2. C. i-node table

3. disk partition

4. drive letter a, partition 9

5. `prtvtoc`

6. A. mount

7. B. newfs

8. Single user mode

9. C. mount

10. False

Module 7: System Security

1. A. `nmap`

2. `nmap -sU -sT -o proberes`

3. sometimes

4. A. `nmap -sT 192.168.1.*`

5. privileged

6. C. configure the firewall

7. SSH

8. B. `ssh barney`

9. `ssh-keygen`

10. security policy

Module 8: Backup and Restore

1. **A.** Image

2. Incremental

3. **A.** `dump`

4. **C.** `restore`

5. **B.** `dd`

6. First step creates a new file system, second step checks the file system, and third step mounts the file system.

7. `/dev/st0`

Module 9: System Operations

1. **B.** single user mode

2. multi-user mode

3. **A.** init

4. **A.** respawn

5. multi-user mode

6. **C.** `reboot`

7. **B.** `/etc`

8. **A.** `init 0`

Module 10: The TCP/IP Suite

1. Open Standard Interconnect

2. **C.** Interface

3. **A.** Application

4. Internet layer

5. False. Some TCP/IP layers map to more than one OSI layer.

6. Domain Name System

7. **C.** DHCP

8. Host-to-host layer

9. `/etc/services`

10. False. The flow provided by the Internet layer is described as "unreliable."

11. Class C

12. Subnetting

13. `ifconfig`

14. 255.255.255.192 will work providing 62 addresses, and the next smallest subnet, 255.255.255.224, only provides 30 addresses.

15. `ping`

16. **B.** ARP

Module 11: Basic Network Tools

1. Address Resolution Protocol table or ARP cache

2. **C.** `netstat`

3. **D.** `ping`

4. **A.** The system is reachable.

5. **D.** Adding the bruegel system to the ARP table

6. `ifconfig ppp0 down`

7. **A.** Ethernet

8. **C.** Active

9. `netstat -a -n`

10. **B.** `netstat -a -t -u`

11. `ping -R`

Module 12: Advanced Network Tools

1. `tcpdump -q -i ppp0 -c 15`

2. True

3. `traceroute`

4. **B.** `tcpdump -r dump-data`

5. **C.** `ethertype`

6. `tcpdump host not fred`

7. protocol

8. traceroute `barney`

9. traceroute `-m 20 www.whitehouse.gov`

10. **A.** `display`

11. Broadcast

12. False. The only restriction is that it must support IP.

Module 13: Overview of SNMP

1. Universal

2. Application

3. **C.** Trap

4. **B.** Robust security model

5. version field, community field, SNMP protocol data unit (PDU) field

6. nodes

7. **C.** read-only

8. GetRequest

9. GetNextRequest

10. **A**: ii; **B**: iii; **C**: iv; **D**: i

11. **A.** Description; **B.** MTU; **D.** Physical address

12. trap

13. **B.** Community name

14. trap

15. GetBulkRequest

16. NoCreation

Module 14: Using Domain Name System

1. Hierarchical

2. False. Because the companies have different domains, DNS will not have conflicts.

3. Host Resolution

4. Domain: edu; organization: indiana; subdomain: athletics; host: www

5. `nslookup`

6. `Server 192.168.1.215`

7. `host` and `dig`

8. `/etc/resolv.conf`

9. `/etc/nsswitch.conf`

Module 15: Using NIS

1. False. The `ypmake` command doesn't actually exist. Updating the NIS maps on the NIS master is done by running make in the `/var/yp` directory.

2. `yppasswd`

3. `.pag`

4. `.dir`

5. `ypwhich`

6. **A.** `# ypinit -s fred`

7. **D.** `#ypinit -c`

8. `ypwhich`

9. `ypinit -s`

10. `ypset`

Module 16: SNMP System Management Tools

1. **B.** Supplies a list of directories for the command to search for MIB files.

2. `snmpdelta`

3. **D.** `ping`

4. `snmpnetstat`

5. **A.** Reset a user password

6. **A.** `snapstatus host community`

7. traps

8. **D.** `-q`

9. True

10. snmpbulkwalk

11. False. `snmpnetstat` also works with printers, network devices, and any other device that supports the MIB-II standard.

Module 17: Using Network File System

1. nfsd 4

2. lockd

3. False

4. **A.** /etc/dfs/dfstab

5. nfsstat

6. **C.** /etc/fstab

7. 3943

8. 0%

9. bedrock

10. /mnt/bedrock/docs

11. Soft

Module 18: File Transfer Protocol

1. anonymous

2. dir [j-m]*

3. **C.** put

4. hash

5. B. Deny access to that user

6. `/etc/ftpaccess`

7. Turns on logging of all FTP activity

8. auth

Module 19: Important System Administration Tasks/Information

1. C. `wall`

2. 52,008KB

3. A. `mkswap`

4. `fdisk`

5. `prtconf`

6. B. `showrev`

7. C. process IDs

8. `partitions`

Module 20: Using DHCP

1. False

2. B. `/var/dhcp`

3. Lease

4. False. The IP addresses must be contiguous, no skips or gaps.

5. Static

6. D. `/etc/dhcpd.conf`

7. Solaris: `ifconfig`; **Linux:** `dhcpcd`; **HP-UX:** `dhcpclient`

8. `touch /etc/dhcp.ei0`

9. A. Obtain an IP address automatically

10. C. `ipconfig`

Module 21: Using rdist

1. B. `notify`

2. `dino, barney`

3. `/stream/bin, /stream/etc, /stream/movies`

4. Extra files will be removed from the target synchronization directories.

5. No one. No `notify` command is specified.

6. `except`

7. D. `special`

8. A. file size and modification time

9. A. Process symbolic link so that the target file is copied rather than the link itself.

10. `-v`

A

Appendix B

Tools at a Glance

This section contains a quick summary of the tools reviewed and discussed within this book.

Name	Description	Module
admintool	Solaris administration tool.	3
arp	Monitors and controls ARP cache.	11
cat	Show the content of file.	2
control-panel	Linux administration tool.	3
date	Show system date and time.	2
dd	Image backup tool.	8
dhcpmgr	Solaris GUI tool for managing DHCP server.	20
dig	Query DNS server for information.	14
dump	Performs backups of a file system.	8
exportfs	Make a file system available over the network.	17
fdisk	Linux disk partition tool.	6
find	Search for a specific file.	2
format	Disk partition tool on Solaris.	6
fsck	File system check program.	6
ftp	Client File transfer protocol program.	18
grep	Search a file for specified pattern.	2
groupadd	Add a new group to the system.	5
groupdel	Delete an existing group from the system.	5
groupmod	Make changes to an existing group.	5
grpck	Consistence check for the /etc/group file.	5
halt	Halt the system.	9
host	Look up DNS host information.	14
hostname	Display name of system.	2
landiag	Show network diagnostic information on HP-UX.	12
lanscan	Show network information on HP-UX system.	11
ifconfig	Interface configuration.	11
init	Control the master system program.	9
logins	Show user on a Solaris system.	5
ls	List files in a directory.	2
netstat	Display network connections.	12
nfsstat	Show NFS stats.	17
nmap	Network port scanner.	7

Table B-1 Tools Found in this Book

Name	Description	Module
nslookup	Look up DNS entry.	14
more	Show the content of file.	2
mount	Make a file system available.	6
mkfs	Make a new file system.	6
newfs	Simple command to make a new file system.	6
passwd	Change a user password.	5
ping	Determine network node reachability.	11
pkgadd	Add a package on Solaris.	4
pkgrm	Remove a package on Solaris.	4
pkginfo	Query a Solaris package.	4
prtconf	Display configuration information on Solaris system.	19
prtvtoc	Show disk partition information on Solaris.	6
ps	Show status of processes.	2
pump	Show DHCP information on Linux system.	20
pwck	Consistency check for the /etc/passwd file.	5
rdist	Automatic distribution of directories/files.	21
reboot	Restart the system.	9
restore	Retrieve a backup from a dump archive.	8
rpm	Red Hat package manager.	4
sam	HP-UX administration tool.	3
scp	Secure copy command.	7
share	Make a file system available over the network.	17
showmount	Show which clients have mounted NFS file systems.	17
showrev	Show version information for Solaris command.	19
snmpbulkwalk	Obtains a MIB object with SNMP bulk request.	16
snmpconf	Automated SNMP configurations.	16
snmpdelta	Formats SNMP data.	16
snmpget	Regular SNMP retrieval.	16
snmpgetnext	Retrieves multiple SNMP objects in order.	16
snmpnetstat	Retrieves network statistics from SNMP entity.	16
snmpset	Alters SNMP configuration information.	16
snmpstatus	Retrieves important SNMP data.	16
snmptable	Retrieves SNMP table objects.	16
snmptest	Tests SNMP connectivity.	16
snmptranslate	Converts MIB objects into more meaningful information.	16
snmptrap	Sends an SNMP trap message.	16

B

Table B-1   Tools Found in this Book (*continued*)

Name	Description	Module
snmptrapd	Receipt of SNMP traps from network.	16
snmpwalk	Retrieves either a group or entire MIB tree of objects.	16
ssh	Secure remote shell.	7
shutdown	Place the system to single-user mode.	9
strings	Show strings within a file.	2
swap	Control swap space on Solaris/HPUX systems.	19
swapon	Add swap space on the system.	19
swapoff	Remove swap space from the system.	19
swinstall	Add an HP-UX package.	4
swlist	Show HP-UX package information.	4
swremove	Remove an HP-UX package.	4
sudo	Execute privileged commands.	7
talk	Communicate with a user on the system.	19
tar	General-purpose file archiving tool.	8
tcpdump	Show network packets.	12
traceroute	Show network path between two nodes.	12
tripwire	Detect and report file system change.	7
umount	Remove access to a file system.	6
uname	Show system-related information.	2
useradd	Add a new user to the system.	5
userdel	Delete an existing user from the system.	5
usermod	Modify an existing user.	5
vipw	Edit the /etc/passwd file using the Vi editor	5
volcopy	Image backup tool for Solaris.	8
who	Show current users on the system.	2
ypbind	Force NIS client to bind to a specific server.	15
ypcat	Show contents of NIS map.	15
yppasswd	Change password field of NIS passwd file.	15
ypmatch	Show the values of a key from a NIS server.	15
ypmake	Update one or more NIS maps.	15
yppoll	Show information about a NIS map.	15
yppush	Push out updates to NIS servers.	15
ypxfr	Transfer a NIS map.	15
ypwhich	Show to which NIS server a client is bound.	15
unshare	Stop sharing a file system over the network.	17

Table B-1 Tools Found in this Book (*continued*)

Appendix C

Overview of MIB-II

Discover MIB-II

This section provides a short overview of SNMP MIB-II. Since MIB-II is a standard, the MIB objects are available from a wide variety of sources, including Sun, Linux Red Hat and many others such as 3Com and Cisco. In fact, any device that claims to support SNMP is required to support MIB-II. Important information about a particular device or group of devices can be obtained by querying specific MIB-II objects. The objects contained within MIB-II provide both system configuration and network performance information.

The SNMP standards define a collection of Management Information Base (MIB) objects that each SNMP agent supports. The first set of objects was known as MIB-I and was documented in RFC 1156. Over time, these objects were expanded and the collection of objects became known as MIB-II, described in RFC 1213. The MIB-II objects provide generic information about the state of the networking aspect of the device. This MIB is divided into a collection of groups, described in Table C-1.

Group Name	Description
system	Provides overall information about the device or system on which the agent is running.
interfaces	Contains information about the operating network interfaces contained within the system.
at	Address translation table for Internet IP addresses to data link addresses. Note that this is a deprecated group.
ip	Contains statistical information about the Internet Protocol (IP) of the device.
icmp	Contains statistical information about the Internet Control Message Protocol (ICMP) of the device.
tcp	Contains statistical information about the Transmission Control Protocol (TCP) of the device.
udp	Contains statistical information about the User Datagram Protocol (UDP) of the device.
egp	Contains statistical information about the Exterior Gateway Protocol (EGP) of the device.
dot3	Provides information regarding the transmission and access protocols for each network interface.
snmp	Contains statistical information about the Simple Network Management Protocol (SNMP) of the device.

Table C-1   MIB-II Object Groups

The collection of MIB-II groups can also be displayed graphically. The `mib-2` group is shown as a tree structure with group members branching off to the right. The associated number or index for each object identifies the location within the tree hierarchy. Each of the associated `mib-2` groups described in this appendix have additional subgroups or objects beneath them and are displayed in the tree view format. The use of circles next to the object represents a subgroup (where additional subgroups or individual objects may be defined), while the square represents individual discrete objects. This makes it easy to distinguish a collection of objects from individual objects.

System Group

The `system` group consists of objects that provide generic information about the device or system on which the agent is running. The `sysServices`, `sysUpTime`, and `sysOR` prefixed objects require additional explanation.

The `sysServices` object represents a 7-bit code that corresponds to the value of the combined services the device provides. Each bit within the code is associated with one of the layers of the OSI model, and if the device offers a service on a particular layer, the bit for that layer is set. For example, consider a device that provides routing functions. The associated `sysServices` value for this device is 72. The value of `sysServices` is the sum of the bit values, where the value of any particular bit is 2 raised to the power L–1 (where L is the layer).

Thus, for a UNIX system that is a layer 4 and 7 device, we get

$$2^{4-1} + 2^{7-1} = 72$$

For a network switch device that is a layer 1 and 2 device, we get

$$2^{1-1} + 2^{2-1} = 3$$

We include layer 4 in this equation because an application server (such as a UNIX system) provides services on both layer 7 and layer 4.

Hint

Definitions for layers 5 and 6 do not currently exist.

Functional layers used to determine `sysServices` are listed in Table C-2.

C

Layer Number	Device Functionality
1	Physical: A device that operates on this layer is known as a network repeater.
2	Data link and/or subnetwork layer: A device that operates on this layer includes a network bridge or switch.
3	Internet/network: A device that operates on this layer is a gateway or router.
4	End-to-end services, such as an IP host.
7	Application services, such as mail relays, DNS server, and so forth.

Table C-2   SysServices Layer Definitions

The sysUpTime object indicates the amount of time that has transpired since the network management agent was last started. This doesn't necessarily mean that the device itself has been operating since that time. Take, for example, an agent running on top of an operating system. The agent can be restarted independently of the system, and therefore may not represent the true amount of time the system has been in operation. However, with some devices, the agent can't be started or stopped independent of the system. In this case, this object agent should be more accurate.

The system group also contains a few objects related to SNMPv2 devices acting in an agent role. These objects have names that begin with the prefix sysOR and are supported with SNMPv2 (or later) agents. The objects control the dynamic configuration of agent resources. Because these objects were introduced with the SNMPv2 standards, SNMPv1 agents don't support them.

The system group contains the following set of objects:

Object Name: sysDescr
OID: system.1
Object Type: Display String [255]
Access Mode: read-only
Description: A description of the device or entity, such as the type of device, hardware characteristics, operating system information, and so forth

Object Name: sysObjectID
OID: system.2
Object Type: Object Identifier
Access Mode: read-only
Description: The authoritative identification of the vendor of the device

Object Name: sysUpTime
OID: system.3
Object Type: TimeTick
Access Mode: read-only
Description: The amount of time since the network management portion
                 of the system (agent) was last reinitialized

Object Name: sysContact
OID: system.4
Object Type: Display String [255]
Access Mode: read-write
Description: Information noting the contact person and/or other
                 organization that provides support for this device

Object Name: sysName
OID: system.5
Object Type: Display String [255]
Access Mode: read-write
Description: The name of the device; may be the official hostname or
                 another administratively assigned name

Object Name: sysLocation
OID: system.6
Object Type: Display String [255]
Access Mode: read-write
Description: The physical location where the device has been installed

Object Name: sysServices
OID: system.7
Object Type: Integer
Access Mode: read-only
Description: The services this device provides

C

Object Name: sysOrLastChange
OID: system.8
Object Type: TimeStamp
Access Mode: read-only
Description: The value of the sysUpTime object at the time of the most recent change made in any instance of the sysORID object

Object Name: sysORTable
OID: system.9
Object Type: Sequence of SysOREntry
Access Mode: read-only
Description: A table of dynamically configurable object resources within an SNMPv2 system acting in an agent role

Object Name: sysOREntry
OID: SysORTable.1
Object Type: Sequence
Access Mode: read-only
Description: Information on a specific configurable object

Object Name: sysORIndex
OID: sysOREntry.1
Object Type: Object Identifier
Access Mode: read-only
Description: Used as an index into the sysORTable

Object Name: sysORID
OID: sysOREntry.2
Object Type: Display String [255]
Access Mode: read-only
Description: The OID of this entry, analogous to the sysObjectID object

Object Name: sysORDescr
OID: sysOREntry.3
Object Type: Display String [255]
Access Mode: read-only
Description: A description of the object resource, analogous to the sysDescr object

Object Name: sysORUpTime
OID: sysOREntry.4
Object Type: TimeStamp
Access Mode: read-only
Description: Contains the value of the sysUpTime object at the time
                this instance (row) was last updated or instantiated

When the `system` group from a Linux system is queried, the following
objects with their associated values are returned:

```
system.sysDescr.0 = Linux didymus 2.4.7-10 #1 Thu Sep 6 17:27:27 EDT 2001 i686
system.sysObjectID.0 = OID: enterprises.ucdavis.ucdSnmpAgent.linux
system.sysUpTime.0 = Timeticks: (107689) 0:17:56.89
system.sysContact.0 = Steve Maxwell (sjmaxwell@worldnet.att.net)
system.sysservices.0 = 72
system.sysLocation.0 = Graphics Lab
```

In this example, the `sysDescr` object includes information about the
system on which the agent is running. The string provides the same basic
information that is obtained from the UNIX `uname` command:

```
uname -a
Linux didymus 2.4.7-10 #1 Thu Sep 6 17:27:27 EDT 2001 i686 unknown
```

The `sysObject` object contains an OID of the Linux branch that identifies
the agent. The `sysContact` shows that the agent has been running for
approximately 17 minutes and 56 seconds. The `sysContact`, `sysName`, and
`sysLocation` objects contain specific information about the owner (Steve
Maxwell), name (`didymus`), and location (`Graphics Lab`) of the device.
Finally, the `sysServices` object shows that the device provides layer 4 and
layer 7 services.

Interfaces Group

The `interfaces` group provides both configuration and statistical information
regarding the network interfaces installed within the device. As discussed in
Module 13, this group has an `ifNumber` object that contains the total number
of network interfaces installed on the system, regardless of the operating state
of any particular interface. The other object, `ifTable`, is a table that contains
a row for each interface. The table is indexed by the `ifIndex` object and

C

---

contains a value between 1 and the value of the `ifNumber` object. The `ifIndex` number can address each column or interface directly. The `ifTable` contains 22 objects that provide the following:

- Type, capacity, and other interface characteristics
- Operational information
- Performance and statistical information

Querying the interfaces table against a Linux system displays output similar to the following:

Maximum speed for each interface

Two interfaces defined on the system

```
interfaces.ifNumber.0 = 2
interfaces.ifTable.ifEntry.ifIndex.1 = 1
interfaces.ifTable.ifEntry.ifIndex.2 = 2
interfaces.ifTable.ifEntry.ifDescr.1 = lo0
interfaces.ifTable.ifEntry.ifDescr.2 = hme0
interfaces.ifTable.ifEntry.ifType.1 = softwareLoopback(24)
interfaces.ifTable.ifEntry.ifType.2 = ethernet-csmacd(6)
interfaces.ifTable.ifEntry.ifMtu.1 = 3924
interfaces.ifTable.ifEntry.ifMtu.2 = 1500
interfaces.ifTable.ifEntry.ifSpeed.1 = Gauge: 10000000
interfaces.ifTable.ifEntry.ifSpeed.2 = Gauge: 10000000
interfaces.ifTable.ifEntry.ifPhysAddress.1 = ""
interfaces.ifTable.ifEntry.ifPhysAddress.2 =  Hex: 0 10 5A 28 5D 7C
interfaces.ifTable.ifEntry.ifAdminStatus.1 = up(1)
interfaces.ifTable.ifEntry.ifAdminStatus.2 = up(1)
interfaces.ifTable.ifEntry.ifOperStatus.1 = up(1)
interfaces.ifTable.ifEntry.ifOperStatus.2 = up(1)
interfaces.ifTable.ifEntry.ifLastChange.1 = Timeticks: (0) 0:00:00.00
interfaces.ifTable.ifEntry.ifLastChange.2 = Timeticks: (0) 0:00:00.00
interfaces.ifTable.ifEntry.ifInOctets.1 = 373912
interfaces.ifTable.ifEntry.ifInOctets.2 = 50204
interfaces.ifTable.ifEntry.ifInUcastPkts.1 = 1218
interfaces.ifTable.ifEntry.ifInUcastPkts.2 = 163
interfaces.ifTable.ifEntry.ifInNUcastPkts.1 = 0
interfaces.ifTable.ifEntry.ifInNUcastPkts.2 = 0
interfaces.ifTable.ifEntry.ifInDiscards.1 = 0
interfaces.ifTable.ifEntry.ifInDiscards.2 = 0
interfaces.ifTable.ifEntry.ifInErrors.1 = 0
interfaces.ifTable.ifEntry.ifInErrors.2 = 0
interfaces.ifTable.ifEntry.ifInUnknownProtos.1 = 0
interfaces.ifTable.ifEntry.ifInUnknownProtos.2 = 0
```

Maximum data unit size for each interface

Administrative and operational status of each interface

```
interfaces.ifTable.ifEntry.ifOutOctets.1 = 381304
interfaces.ifTable.ifEntry.ifOutOctets.2 = 174020
interfaces.ifTable.ifEntry.ifOutUcastPkts.1 = 1242
interfaces.ifTable.ifEntry.ifOutUcastPkts.2 = 565
interfaces.ifTable.ifEntry.ifOutNUcastPkts.1 = 0
interfaces.ifTable.ifEntry.ifOutNUcastPkts.2 = 0
interfaces.ifTable.ifEntry.ifOutDiscards.1 = 0
interfaces.ifTable.ifEntry.ifOutDiscards.2 = 0
interfaces.ifTable.ifEntry.ifOutErrors.1 = 0
interfaces.ifTable.ifEntry.ifOutErrors.2 = 0
interfaces.ifTable.ifEntry.ifOutQLen.1 = Gauge: 0
interfaces.ifTable.ifEntry.ifOutQLen.2 = Gauge: 0
interfaces.ifTable.ifEntry.ifSpecific.1 = OID: .ccitt.nullOID
interfaces.ifTable.ifEntry.ifSpecific.2 = OID: .ccitt.nullOID
```

Notice that the ifNumber object equals 2 because a total of two interfaces are defined on the system. As a result, the ifIndex.1 and ifIndex.2 objects are set to 1 and 2, respectively, so that they can be used to index each interface separately. The ifDescr object contains the name of the interface as it is known by the agent running within the device. For instance, using the output above, the first Ethernet interface is known as eth0. As a result, the ifDescr object will contain this interface name, with each character converted to hexadecimal ("eth0" Hex: 65 74 68 30). Thus the hexadecimal value of eth0 is 65 74 68 30. The interface names provided by the agent are the same strings displayed when using the ifconfig or netstat commands.

The ifType object records the type of the network interface using a single integer identifier. The number can be mapped to a keyword string that gives more descriptive information regarding the actual interface used. A large number of network interface types have been defined by the MIB-II standard. Consult RFC 1213 for a complete list. The ifMtu object, or the maximum transfer unit (MTU), identifies the maximum size of the protocol data unit (PDU) or frame that is allowed for the interface. Standard Ethernet is 1500, while the software loopback is much higher at 3924. Different systems may implement the MTU for the software loopback with various values as deemed appropriate for each system. The ifSpeed object shows the maximum capacity of the interface. In the example, both interfaces contain the same speed of 10000000. This value represents the theoretical performance of an Ethernet LAN that is 10 Mbps. Other interfaces will show either higher or lower capacities, depending on the interface type. Here is a case in point: A serial interface that supports PPP contains an ifSpeed of 9600, which represents 9,600 bits per second that can be supported, given the hardware characteristics of a serial RS-232 interface.

C

The `ifPhysAddress` object identifies the data link protocol address (where appropriate) for the interface. The `eth0` interface has an `ifPhysAddress` of `00 10 5A 28 5D 7C`, while the `ifPhysAddress` contains a null string value (""). The reason for this is that the software loopback doesn't use any hardware, and no data link address is needed or required. The address contained within the `ifPhysAddress` is used for low-level network communications between systems. Every time a packet is emitted from this interface, this address is used as the source of the packet.

The `ifAdminStatus` and `ifOperStatus` objects show the administrative status and operational status of the interface. The network administrator uses the administrative status to control the interface. This object provides the ability to control when the interface is marked as up or down. Also, a third state, testing, can be set. The `up` state means that packets are permitted to flow across the interface, while the `down` state implies that no packets are to be received or sent from this interface. This is regardless of the state of the physical connection to the interface. In other words, a network interface may be connected to an operating network, but if it is marked down, no network traffic will be read by the interface. The `testing` state enables internal interface diagnostics to validate the correct operation of the interface. The `ifOperStatus` object shows the current status of the interface, which is one of the defined states represented by the `ifAdminStatus` object. This object obtains the state of a particular interface.

The access of the `ifAdminStatus` object is read-write; all of the other objects in the interface group can't be modified by a network manager because they have read-only access. The reason for this is quite natural and straightforward. It is reasonable that counters and descriptive information about an interface should not be changed, because it is important to maintain interface type information to avoid networking configuration problems and because it provides accurate performance metrics.

Hint

The `ifSpecific` objects contain the value of `ccitt.nullOID`, which represents a valid but null OID string.

The `interfaces` group contains the following set of objects:

Object Name: `ifNumber`
OID: interfaces.1
Object Type: Integer
Access Mode: read-only
Description: The total number of network interfaces contained within the local system

Object Name: `ifTable`
OID: interfaces.2
Object Type: Sequence of ifEntry
Access Mode: not accessible
Description: A list or row of the interface entries for this table

Object Name: `ifEntry`
OID: interface.ifTable
Object Type: Sequence
Access Mode: not accessible
Description: A specific interface entry that contains all the objects defined below it

Object Name: `ifIndex`
OID: ifEntry.1
Object Type: Integer
Access Mode: read-only
Description: An MIB reference definition that is specific to a particular media type that is used to access the network interface

Object Name: `ifDescr`
OID: ifEntry.2
Object Type: DisplayString [255]
Access Mode: read-only
Description: A string description of the interface that includes the name of the interface from an operating system standpoint; possible values include `eth0`, `ppp0`, and `lo0`

C

Object Name: `ifType`
OID: ifEntry.3
Object Type: DisplayString [255]
Access Mode: read-only
Description: The type of interface. Table 6-3 lists specific types.

Object Name: `ifEntry.4`
OID:
Object Type: Integer
Access Mode: read-only
Description: The maximum transmission unit of the interface. This
                 represents the largest frame that can be sent and/or received
                 on the interface.

Object Name: `ifSpeed`
OID: ifEntry.5
Object Type: Gauge
Access Mode: read-only
Description: The data rate (capacity) of the interface

Object Name: `ifPhysAddress`
OID: ifEntry.6
Object Type: PhysAddress
Access Mode: read-only
Description: The data link address of the interface

Object Name: `ifAdminStatus`
OID: ifEntry.7
Object Type: Integer
Access Mode: read-only
Description: The administrative status of the interface, which is one of the
                 defined states listed in the `ifOpeOrStatus` object. The owner
                 of the device can control the interface with this object.

Object Name: `ifOperStatus`
OID: ifEntry.8
Object Type: Integer
Access Mode: read-only
Description: The present operational state of the interface. The defined
                  states include up(1), down(2), and testing(3).

Object Name: `ifLastChange`
OID: ifEntry.9
Object Type: TimeTicks
Access Mode: read-only
Description: The time when the interface was last updated to its present
                  operating state

Object Name: `ifInOctets`
OID: ifEntry.10
Object Type: Counter
Access Mode: read-only
Description: The number of octets (bytes) received on the interface,
                  including any data link framing bytes

Object Name: `ifInUcastPkts`
OID: ifEntry.11
Object Type: Counter
Access Mode: read-only
Description: The number of unicast packets delivered via a higher-level
                  protocol to a subnet

Object Name: `ifInNUcastPkts`
OID: ifEntry.12
Object Type: Counter
Access Mode: read-only
Description: The number of non-unicast packets that were delivered to
                  a higher-level networking protocol

C

Object Name: `ifInDiscards`
OID: ifEntry.13
Object Type: Counter
Access Mode: read-only
Description: The number of inbound packets discarded (despite no
                   errors), and that will not be delivered to a higher-level
                   networking protocol

Object Name: `ifInErrors`
OID: ifEntry.14
Object Type: Counter
Access Mode: read-only
Description: The number of inbound packets with errors that caused them
                   not to be delivered to a higher-level networking protocol

Object Name: `ifInUnknownProtos`
OID: ifEntry.15
Object Type: Counter
Access Mode: read-only
Description: The number of inbound packets discarded due to an
                   unknown or unsupported networking protocol

Object Name: `ifOutOctets`
OID: ifEntry.16
Object Type: Counter
Access Mode: read-only
Description: The number of octets (bytes) transmitted on the interface.
                   This includes any data link framing bytes as well.

Object Name: `ifOutUcastPkts`
OID: ifEntry.17
Object Type: Counter
Access Mode: read-only
Description: The number of packets that higher-level protocols (such as
                   IP) requested be transmitted to a network unicast address.
                   This includes those that were discarded or otherwise not sent.

Object Name:	`ifOutNUcastPkts`
OID:	ifEntry.18
Object Type:	Counter
Access Mode:	read-only
Description:	The number of packets that higher-level protocols (such as IP) requested to be transmitted to a non-unicast address. This also includes packets that were discarded or, for some other reason, not sent.

Object Name:	`ifOutDiscards`
OID:	ifEntry.19
Object Type:	Counter
Access Mode:	read-only
Description:	The number of packets that could not be transmitted due to some reason unrelated to a specific error condition. This could be caused, for example, by the TTL of a packet expiring.

Object Name:	`ifOutErrors`
OID:	ifEntry.20
Object Type:	Counter
Access Mode:	read-only
Description:	The number of packets that could not be transmitted due to errors

Object Name:	`ifOutQLen`
OID:	ifEntry.21
Object Type:	Gauge
Access Mode:	read-only
Description:	The length of the output packet queue on the device

Object Name:	`ifSpecific`
OID:	ifEntry.22
Object Type:	Object Identifier
Access Mode:	read-only
Description:	The MIB reference definition that is specific to the particular media type used to realize the network interface

C

Index

O

INTERNATIONAL CONTACT INFORMATION

AUSTRALIA
McGraw-Hill Book Company Australia Pty. Ltd.
TEL +61-2-9415-9899
FAX +61-2-9415-5687
http://www.mcgraw-hill.com.au
books-it_sydney@mcgraw-hill.com

CANADA
McGraw-Hill Ryerson Ltd.
TEL +905-430-5000
FAX +905-430-5020
http://www.mcgrawhill.ca

GREECE, MIDDLE EAST,
NORTHERN AFRICA
McGraw-Hill Hellas
TEL +30-1-656-0990-3-4
FAX +30-1-654-5525

MEXICO (Also serving Latin America)
McGraw-Hill Interamericana Editores S.A. de C.V.
TEL +525-117-1583
FAX +525-117-1589
http://www.mcgraw-hill.com.mx
fernando_castellanos@mcgraw-hill.com

SINGAPORE (Serving Asia)
McGraw-Hill Book Company
TEL +65-863-1580
FAX +65-862-3354
http://www.mcgraw-hill.com.sg
mghasia@mcgraw-hill.com

SOUTH AFRICA
McGraw-Hill South Africa
TEL +27-11-622-7512
FAX +27-11-622-9045
robyn_swanepoel@mcgraw-hill.com

UNITED KINGDOM & EUROPE
(Excluding Southern Europe)
McGraw-Hill Education Europe
TEL +44-1-628-502500
FAX +44-1-628-770224
http://www.mcgraw-hill.co.uk
computing_neurope@mcgraw-hill.com

ALL OTHER INQUIRIES Contact:
Osborne/McGraw-Hill
TEL +1-510-549-6600
FAX +1-510-883-7600
http://www.osborne.com
omg_international@mcgraw-hill.com